Between Providence and Choice Biography

Classic Theology and Contemporary Issues

Series editor:
Gijsbert van den Brink (VU Amsterdam)

Volume I

Cornelis van der Knijff

Between Providence and Choice Biography

An Account of Divine Guidance from
a Reformed Perspective

Summum

This publication is made possible by the generous support of de Gereformeerde Bond, Fonds Legaat 'Ad Pias Causas', Stichting Aanpakken and Stichting Het Scholten-Cordes Fonds.

Cover design: Brainstorm
Typesetting: Gewoon Geertje

ISSN 2666-2434
ISBN 9789492701053

Copyright © Summum Academic Publications, Kampen, The Netherlands.
www.summumacademic.com

All rights reserved. No part of this publication may be reproduced, translated, stored in a retrieval system, or transmitted in any form by any means, electronic, mechanical, photocopying, recording or otherwise, without prior written permission from the publisher.

Table of Contents

Acknowledgements	1

Chapter 1: Introduction   5
1.1 Guidance in Christian Spirituality   5
    1.1.1   'Guidance' is everywhere…   5
    1.1.2   The need for guidance   7
    1.1.3   Contextualizing the theme   9
    1.1.4   Divine guidance between choice biography and providentialism   10
1.2 Guidance in Academic Theology   11
    1.2.1   Introduction   11
    1.2.2   Guidance as direct object of investigation   12
    1.2.3   Guidance in systematic theology   14
    1.2.4   Guidance and vocation   20
    1.2.5   Historical studies   22
    1.2.6   Other disciplines   24
1.3 Methodological Remarks   26
    1.3.1   Necessity and relevance of the current study   26
    1.3.2   On working from a Reformed perspective   27
    1.3.3   Starting with contemporary evangelicalism   32
    1.3.4   Choice of conversation partners   33
    1.3.5   Research question   34
1.4 Outline of the argument of the dissertation   35

Chapter 2: A Typology of Divine Guidance in Contemporary Evangelicalism   37
2.1 Introduction   37
2.2 Body of Literature and Methodological Approach   37
    2.2.1   Introduction   37
    2.2.2   Body of literature   37
    2.2.3   Selection of books for analysis   38
    2.2.4   Methodological approach   40
    2.2.5   Evangelical literature on guidance before 1980   41
    2.2.6   Historical and socio-cultural backgrounds   45
    2.2.7   Key biblical material and terminology of the discussion   47

2.3	Analysis of evangelical literature 1980-1989		49
	2.3.1	Introduction	49
	2.3.2	Hosier	49
	2.3.3	Friesen	50
	2.3.4	Ashcraft	52
	2.3.5	Shepson	54
	2.3.6	Ferguson	55
	2.3.7	Ogilvie	57
	2.3.8	Sproul	58
	2.3.9	Willard	60
	2.3.10	Cleave	62
	2.3.11	Stanley	64
	2.3.12	LaHaye	65
	2.3.13	Observations	67
2.4	Analysis of evangelical literature 1990-1999		68
	2.4.1	Introduction	68
	2.4.2	Blackaby and King	68
	2.4.3	Bockmühl	70
	2.4.4	Morris	72
	2.4.5	Robinson	73
	2.4.6	Sanders	75
	2.4.7	Jensen and Payne	76
	2.4.8	Pritchard	78
	2.4.9	Waltke	80
	2.4.10	Masters	81
	2.4.11	Kincaid	83
	2.4.12	Smith	85
	2.4.13	Hayford	86
	2.4.14	Adams	88
	2.4.15	Petty	89
	2.4.16	Swindoll	91
	2.4.17	Elliff	93
	2.4.18	Observations	95
2.5	Analysis of evangelical literature 2000-2010		95
	2.5.1	Introduction	95
	2.5.2	McDowell and Johnson	96
	2.5.3	Sittser	97
	2.5.4	Rasnake	99
	2.5.5	Jeffress	100
	2.5.6	Carter	102
	2.5.7	Swavely	104

	2.5.8	*Meadors*	106
	2.5.9	*Lake*	107
	2.5.10	*Benner*	109
	2.5.11	*Packer and Nystrom*	111
	2.5.12	*DeYoung*	113
	2.5.13	*Huffman*	115
	2.5.14	*Observations*	116
2.6	A Typology of Guidance		117
	2.6.1	*Introduction*	117
	2.6.2	*Existing typologies*	117
	2.6.3	*Evaluation of current typologies of guidance*	119
	2.6.4	*A new typology of guidance as conceived in contemporary evangelicalism*	119
	2.6.5	*Guidance through information*	120
	2.6.6	*Guidance through intimation*	121
	2.6.7	*Guidance through transformation*	123
	2.6.8	*Merits and limations of the proposed typology*	124
2.7	Implications for Remainder of Project		125
	2.7.1	*Introduction*	125
	2.7.2	*Formal features of the body of literature*	125
	2.7.3	*Argumentation*	126
	2.7.4	*Theological issues*	128

Chapter 3: John Calvin on Divine Guidance — **131**

3.1	Introduction		131
3.2	Calvin on Divine Providence		132
	3.2.1	*Introduction*	132
	3.2.2	*Calvin on divine providence: some preliminary remarks*	132
	3.2.3	*Universal and special providence*	134
	3.2.4	*Spheres of divine providence*	137
	3.2.5	*Providence and the will of God*	140
	3.2.6	*Providence and causality*	142
	3.2.7	*The praxis of providence: between believing and perceiving*	143
	3.2.8	*Conclusion*	146
3.3	Calvin on Vocation and Calling		146
	3.3.1	*Introduction*	146
	3.3.2	*The foundation of vocation in Calvin's theology*	147
	3.3.3	*Calvin's use of vocation terminology*	148
	3.3.4	*The civic use of vocation terminology*	149
	3.3.5	*The discernment of vocations*	153

3.3.6 Concerns in emphasizing vocation 155
3.3.7 Implications for Calvin's view on guidance 156
3.4 Calvin on the Spirit as Guide 157
3.4.1 Introduction 157
3.4.2 The common background: Calvin against the Libertines 158
3.4.3 Two critical treatments: Krusche and Bockmühl 159
3.4.4 More is to be said: Milner, Kelly, and Hesselink 163
3.4.5 Calvin's commentary on Acts 167
3.4.6 Calvin's use of instinctus 173
3.4.7 Conclusion 181
3.5 Guidance in Calvin's Personal Life 181
3.5.1 Introduction 181
3.5.2 Important decisions in Calvin's early years 182
3.5.3 Called to Geneva? On 'providential accidents' 183
3.5.4 Banished from Geneva: "I know assuredly that our Lord will guide me" 185
3.5.5 "I am horrified at the mere mention of a recall" - On returning to Geneva 187
3.5.6 Correspondence with mr. and mrs. De Falais 190
3.5.7 Concluding general observations 192
3.6 Conclusion 193

Chapter 4: Jonathan Edwards on Divine Guidance **197**
4.1 Introduction 197
4.2 Edwards on Divine Providence 198
4.2.1 Introduction 198
4.2.2 Edwards on divine providence: two main metaphors 199
4.2.3 The universe created out of nothing every moment 203
4.2.4 Providence and the secret will of God 205
4.2.5 Human perspective and the will of God 207
4.2.6 The praxis of providence 209
4.2.7 Conclusion 211
4.3 Edwards on Vocation 212
4.3.1 Introduction 212
4.3.2 Traces of vocation thought in Edwards's writings 212
4.3.3 Vocation to the ministry as a telling example 214
4.3.4 Conclusion 215
4.4 Edwards on the Guidance of the Spirit 216
4.4.1 Introduction 216
4.4.2 On impressions, texts, and the leading of the Spirit 216
4.4.3 Being led by the Spirit 220

		4.4.4	'A spiritual and distinguishing taste'	222

      4.4.4   'A spiritual and distinguishing taste'   222
      4.4.5   The concept of beauty in relation to guidance   224
      4.4.6   The indwelling of the Spirit   227
      4.4.7   Conclusion   230
 4.5 Edwards on Virtues and Character Formation   230
      4.5.1   Introduction   230
      4.5.2   Virtues, grace, and justification   231
      4.5.3   The Nature of True Virtue   232
      4.5.4   Habits, dispositions, and character formation   234
      4.5.5   Maintenance of and growth in virtues   235
      4.5.6   Conclusion   237
 4.6 Guidance in Edwards's Personal Life   237
      4.6.1   Introduction   237
      4.6.2   Guidance in Edwards's life: general remarks   238
      4.6.3   Pastor at Bolton, tutor at Yale, pastor at Northampton   240
      4.6.4   From Northampton to Stockbridge   241
      4.6.5   From Stockbridge to Princeton   242
      4.6.6   Conclusion   244
 4.7 Conclusion   244

Chapter 5: Intermediate Conclusion and Transition   247
 5.1 Introduction   247
 5.2 Models of Guidance: Information, Intimation, or Transformation?   247
 5.3 Learning from Calvin and Edwards   248
 5.4 A Reformed Approach to Guidance   250
 5.5 Areas for Further Development   254

Chapter 6: Towards a Reformed Account of Divine Guidance   257
 6.1 Introduction   257
 6.2 Vocation as a Key Concept for a Reformed Account of Guidance   257
      6.2.1   Introduction   257
      6.2.2   The classic Reformed account of vocation   258
      6.2.3   Vocation as a disputed concept   260
      6.2.4   On the value of maintaining the concept of vocation   263
      6.2.5   Essentials of a concept of vocation   265
      6.2.6   Implications for guidance   269
 6.3 Wisdom as an integral part of guidance   270
      6.3.1   Introduction   271
      6.3.2   'Wisdom' in Friesen's wisdom view of guidance   272

	6.3.3	*Phronesis or prudence as starting point*	273
	6.3.4	*The distinctive nature of Christian wisdom*	277
	6.3.5	*Wisdom in the theo-dramatic accounts of Wells and Vanhoozer*	280
	6.3.6	*Concluding reflections*	285
6.4	Discerning the Will and the Way		286
	6.4.1	*Introduction*	287
	6.4.2	*Dietrich Bonhoeffer on discerning the will of God*	287
	6.4.3	*James Gustafson on general and Christian discernment*	295
	6.4.4	*Oliver O'Donovan on finding one's path*	298
	6.4.5	*Discernment beyond evangelical misunderstandings*	300
6.5	'Be Transformed': On Guidance, Character, and Transformation		302
	6.5.1	*Introduction*	302
	6.5.2	*Romans 12:1-2 and the transformation of the mind*	303
	6.5.3	*On the object of transformation*	307
	6.5.4	*The transformation of our desires*	310
	6.5.5	*Imagination and guidance*	313
	6.5.6	*But what about sin?*	316
6.6	Community and Guidance		318
	6.6.1	*Introduction*	318
	6.6.2	*The Christian community as a place of (trans)formation*	319
	6.6.3	*Community as place of inspiration and challenge*	321
	6.6.4	*Community as a place of advice and accountability*	323
	6.6.5	*The special role of the 'friend'*	324
6.7	Guidance and the Holy Spirit		326
	6.7.1	*Introduction*	326
	6.7.2	*A deist account of guidance?*	327
	6.7.3	*The Spirit, the ordinary, and the extraordinary*	329
	6.7.4	*The indwelling of the Spirit*	330
	6.7.5	*On speaking about 'guidance'*	332
	6.7.6	*Living in the Spirit*	333
Conclusion			337
Bibliography			345
Name Index			371

Acknowledgements

A deep paradox lies at the heart of all writing, and especially at the heart of writing a dissertation: no undertaking can at times feel so lonely, that at the same time depends so radically on various kinds of community. At the end of this journey, I want to express my profound gratitude to a number of people without whom this book would not have seen the light of day.

In this project, I have been guided from the very first day by my supervisor, Gijsbert van den Brink. Although the original PhD position came a little early during my masters, he encouraged me to apply nonetheless and has been a trusted guide ever since. His reading of my texts was always very precise, his questions insightful, and his trust encouraging. Although he was closely involved in the entire process, he gave me full space to develop my own argument. I also want to thank my co-supervisor, Mark Elliott, for our discussions in Amsterdam and St. Andrews, and for the many helpful comments and suggestions in the margins of my texts.

A special word of thanks must go to the 'Gereformeerde Bond' (Reformed League) in the Protestant Church of the Netherlands (PKN) for funding several PhD positions, including mine. Without their support, I would not have been able to conduct this research. I hope it will in one way or another contribute to the academic study of Reformed theology in the Netherlands. I thank drs. P.J. Vergunst and dr. M. van Campen, and in them the 'Commissie Theologie', for their support and involvement. I also thank the Gereformeerde Bond, together with the fund 'Ad Pias Causas', Stichting Aanpakken, and Stichting Het Scholten-Cordes Fonds for making the publication of my research possible through their generous contributions.

Within the PThU community, I have benefitted from interactions with many colleagues, especially within the *Beliefs* department. The *Dogmatics* seminar, in changing formations, has been an ideal setting to learn from each other's work. I hope parts of my texts show that I listened to and learnt from Rinse Reeling Brouwer, Jan Hoek, Klaas-Willem de Jong, Wim Moehn, Jan Muis, Martine Oldhoff, Arjan Plaisier, Edward van 't Slot, Erik Willemsen, Maarten Wisse, and Gerard van Zanden. I look back with gratitude to our discussions. A special word of thanks also to Eleonora Hof, with whom I shared the office almost daily during the first years of my research. Our discussions, but also the way she introduced me to the PThU and NOSTER have been of great help to me. Without the many pleasurable hours spent unplanned in the office of Dominique de Boer, this book could have been so much better, but my time at the PThU most certainly not. Furthermore, the librarians of the PThU have done an outstanding job in tracing and collecting the innumerable books I requested.

Outside the walls of the PThU, I have found a stimulating academic environment in the activities of NOSTER, especially in the 'Research Seminar on Dogmatics, Ethics and Philosophy of Religion'. I have benefited greatly from the learned 'mentors' of this seminar, first Marcel Sarot and Stephan van Erp and later on Peter-Ben Smit and Rick Benjamins. Many thanks also to the other long-time participants, Christiane Alpers, Eleonora Hof, Anton ten Klooster, Marianne Kuipers-Sedee, Jos Moons, and Sjoerd Mulder. I have always enjoyed our fruitful discussions. I would also like to thank those scholars who at some point during the process have provided feedback on some part of my research, either in a NOSTER setting or elsewhere: Henk van den Belt, Sarah Coakley, Karen Kilby, Kirsteen Kim, Cornelis van der Kooi, and Bert-Jan Lietaert Peerbolte.

Outside the walls of the university, I want to thank my church congregation, the Maranathakerk in Rotterdam, for providing me with a spiritual home, and especially the members of the church council, with whom I shared both burdens and blessings for several years. It has proven very beneficial to me not only to study theology in an academic setting but also to bear a shared responsibility for an actual congregation. Furthermore, I want to thank two great groups of friends for their companionship. Geerten, Teunis, and Wilco have been those kinds of friends in the back of my head when writing section 6.6.5, and it has been a blessing to have such friends. Chris(tiaan), Hendrik-Jan, Johan, Martijn, Ralph, and Thijs have been one of the strangest forms of 'Gezindte' one could imagine, but I still look forward to our meetings with the same anticipation I once had for the cycling holidays during our secondary school years.

Finally, I want to thank my family. Many thanks to my parents, Arie en Jannie van der Knijff, for raising me in a Christian family, stimulating me to think about my faith, and supporting me throughout this research project. Many thanks also to my parents-in-law, Hans and Corrie Hakbijl, not the least for all those moments in which you took care of the kids, enabling Esther and me to work, study, and concentrate. I also want to express my gratitude to my brothers and sisters (in-law) for their support and interest over the past years. Marianne, Reint and Laura, Henrieke, Jorina, Bernhard and Ariette, Arjen and Tanja, Job and Aline, thank you all.

Most of all, I am grateful to my wife Esther, and to our children Hannah and Nathan. I know of no better way to instantly forget a disappointing day at the office than having two children vying for your attention the moment you arrive home. Esther, you have been a source of support, joy, and love throughout the project, by stimulating me, believing in me even if I didn't, and drawing my attention to all the other (and often more important) parts of life when I tended to become too involved in my writing. The best way of telling you how grateful I am is by telling you I can't tell you how grateful I am.

CHAPTER 1:

Introduction

1.1 Guidance in Christian Spirituality

1.1.1 'Guidance' is everywhere...
"I had rather see coming toward me a whole regiment with drawn swords, than one lone Calvinist convinced that he is doing the will of God." These words, attributed to an anonymous seventeenth-century English writer,[1] will likely meet with two opposite responses: On the one hand recognition by those who have themselves experienced situations in which someone was so convinced to be guided by God that no further discussion was possible. But on the other hand a sense of bewilderment on the part of those who think the guidance of God is a crucial aspect of Christian spirituality and who are sincerely trying to discern God's will in their lives. For what could be more important and fitting than to know and do the will of God, even when opposed by a whole regiment with drawn swords?

That a sense of being guided by God is indeed a crucial element of much of contemporary Christian spirituality can be easily shown: a quick online search will lead to millions of sermons, youth messages, blogs, and forum discussions on the question 'How do I find the will of God?' Later on, we will see that many popular books have been published over the last 50 years on the same question. The pervasiveness of the topic of divine guidance is most clear from its ubiquity in the medium that probably provides the best insight in the spirituality of contemporary Christians: their hymns and songs. The metaphor of God as guide and the prayer for insight into God's will or way is a key element in many of these songs.[2] Sometimes God's guidance is invoked in the sense of his 'providential guidance' to which the singer submits, but in many instances clearly something more concrete is meant.[3]

---

[1] Quoted by Nicholas Wolterstorff, *Until Justice and Peace Embrace* (Grand Rapids: Eerdmans, 1983), 9.
[2] For example, the thematic song selector of CCLI (Christian Copyright Licensing International) lists 2300 songs under the theme of guidance, compared to, among others, 736 on atonement and 2087 on the cross. See https://songselect.ccli.com/search/themes (visited 19-12-2017).
[3] See Klaus Bockmühl, *Gesetz und Geist: Eine kritische Würdigung des Erbes protestantischer Ethik* (Giessen: Brunnen Verlag, 1987), 473–81 on 'Führung durch den Heiligen Geist' in a

As an example, William Williams's famous hymn *Guide me, O Thou great Jehovah* is a pilgrim's prayer for guidance.[4] In its second stanza, Williams (1717-1791) uses Exodus imagery that intensifies this plea and makes it more explicit:

Let the fire and cloudy pillar
Lead me all my journey through.

Pleading for guidance with the image of the fire and clouds from Exodus, one is praying for a form of divine guidance in which concrete and discernible signs and directions are expected. The same combination of exodus imagery and a prayer for divine guidance is found in the hymn *Lead, kindly Light,* based upon Henry Newman's poem 'The Pillar of Cloud'. In it, Newman prays for guidance for the next step:

Lead, Kindly Light, amidst th'encircling gloom,
Lead Thou me on!
The night is dark, and I am far from home,
Lead Thou me on!
Keep Thou my feet; I do not ask to see
The distant scene; one step enough for me.

In the stanzas that follow, Newman confesses that once he 'loved to choose and see my path,' because pride ruled his will. Now, however, he submits to God's guidance.

Underlying both pleas for guidance is a deep sense of personal fallibility and sinfulness, an acknowledgment of the limited and often misdirected human perspective. This is even more clear in Horatius Bonar's *Thy way, not mine, O Lord.*

Thy Way, not mine, O Lord,
However dark it be;

---

section on 'Die Hauptthemen der Ethik des Gesangbuchs.' Well-known hymns that primarily convey providential guidance and submission are a.o. Crosby's *All the way my Savior leads me,* Neumark's *If Thou but Suffer God to Guide Thee,* and Ter Steegen's *Let Him Lead Thee Blindfold Onward.*

4 Williams originally wrote the hymn in Welsh in 1745. After the first stanza was translated into English by a Rev. Peter Williams in 1771, William Williams published his own English translation in Lady Huntingdon's Collection in 1772. For more background information, see e.g. Louis F. Benson, *Studies Of Familiar Hymns: Second Series* (Philadelphia: The Westminster Press, 1923), 68–79.

*Lead me by thine own hand
Choose out the path for me.*

Trusting that God's way is always better than one's own, the hymn expresses a deep distrust of one's own choices and preferences:

*I dare not choose my lot;
I would not if I might:
Choose Thou for me, my God,
So shall I walk aright.*

The path prayed for includes the choice of friends, health, poverty, and wealth (stanza 5). The final stanza once again brings all elements together: A refusal of personal choice, both in great and small things, and a passionate plea for God to be guide, wisdom, and strength:

*Not mine, not mine the choice,
In things both great and small;
Be Thou my guide, my strength,
My wisdom and my all.*[5]

Though all three hymns mentioned are older, they have been translated in many languages and are still sung across the world; clearly, this plea for guidance resonates with Christians throughout the ages and across the earth, including many present-day Christians.[6]

1.1.2 The need for guidance
When believers sing about or pray for God to be their guide, what are they asking for? What are the situations that incite them to such prayers? In the final chapter of his book *Finding and Seeking*, in which he focuses on the concept of discernment, Oliver O'Donovan carefully characterizes these precise situations. Having discussed the role of *deliberation* in moral decision-making in the preceding chapter, he concludes that not all has been said. Even when all relevant factors are carefully weighed in deliberation, there are situations that are 'indifferent' yet full of meaning: "Weighty decisions that do not fall under any moral law – what work

---

[5] A hymn with a very similar content in Dutch is Van der Waals's *Wat de toekomst brengen moge.*
[6] Many more examples could have been given, but these suffice to introduce the topic. As the song selector of the CCLI suggests, in contemporary Christian songs the topic is at least as prominent as in the older ones.

should I pursue? should I marry? where should I make a home? – may be pregnant with the greatest good or harm to myself and others."[7] What we face in such situations is "a deficit of moral normativity" that as rational beings we cannot simply resolve by "tossing a coin."[8] Hence, seeking for reasons that allow us to move beyond arbitrariness in major decisions is a common human endeavour. For O'Donovan, the deficit we experience arises both from our position as fallible agents in time and from the limitation of the moral law. For the law, although it can tell us what to do, cannot tell us what to do *next*.[9] It is precisely in this context, this "moment of dangerous opportunity,"[10] that we begin to look for "a sequential ordering or direction in the complex of circumstances, objective and subjective, which comprise our narrative situation."[11] Referring to the biblical metaphor of the 'path,' O'Donovan shows how it is in such situations that those who believe in a personal God start to think in terms of divine guidance and begin to pray for God to be their guide.[12]

With the help of this clarification by O'Donovan, we can now sketch a number of important aspects of the 'conceptual field' of divine guidance as we approach it in the current study. The situations in which believers approach God for guidance are characterized by: a) the need to make important decisions with a considerable biographical impact;[13] b) a variety of good options;[14] c) a certain amount of freedom to choose between

---

7   Oliver O'Donovan, *Finding and Seeking*, Ethics as Theology 2 (Grand Rapids: Eerdmans, 2014), 214. Cf. Edward P. Hahnenberg, *Awakening Vocation: A Theology of Christian Call* (Collegeville: Liturgical Press, 2010), 128: "We can all think of examples of people we know for whom a poor choice among 'goods' in the realm of career or marriage was far more detrimental than that more isolated choice for evil the church condemns as sin." The examples O'Donovan provides are, as often in discussions of guidance, typically decisions of young adults. Recently, there has been more attention for vocation and guidance as issues across the lifespan. See esp. Kathleen A. Cahalan and Bonnie J. Miller-McLemore, eds., *Calling All Years Good: Christian Vocation throughout Life's Seasons* (Grand Rapids: Eerdmans, 2017).
8   O'Donovan, *Finding and Seeking*, 214. Although a hard distinction between moral and nonmoral situations is both impossible and undesirable, in what follows we focus on those situations O'Donovan describes as 'morally underdetermined'.
9   O'Donovan, 215.
10 O'Donovan, 222.
11 O'Donovan, 216.
12 O'Donovan, 221–22. For a further discussion of O'Donovan's perspective see sections 6.2.5 and 6.4.4.
13 Hence, the Spirit's leading or enlightening in the explanation of Scripture or in making theological decisions is not in focus.
14 With 'good options' we point at what O'Donovan labeled 'a deficit of moral normativity.' Sometimes, this type of decisions is described as 'nonmoral decisions.' As this does presuppose a non-realistic neat distinction between moral and nonmoral decisions we do prefer not to use this distinction. Cf. the rejection of quandary ethics in the final chapter.

these options; d) an accompanying sense of bewilderment because no clear criteria are available upon which one's decision can be based.

1.1.3 Contextualizing the theme

Given the preceding description of the situations in which believers start to pray for guidance, one might object to devoting a theological study to the topic of guidance. For is the question in itself not a very individualistic, modern, Western, middle and upper class question? Is not the grim reality for most people throughout history and around the world that there are not many good options and that usually there is no freedom to choose? Are not most people through their circumstances destined to be more concerned with surviving than with good living?[15]

There is no need to deny the instinct behind these critical questions and it should be admitted that the question of guidance is indeed rather modern, mostly Western, and especially prominent in the higher social classes: as we will see later on, the amount of attention given to the topic of guidance has grown enormously since the second half of the 19th century, and this rise is obviously tied in a myriad of ways to major cultural and sociological changes that have taken place over the course of the last two centuries. In light of the processes of industrialization, globalization, and the enormous increase in possibilities for both geographical and social mobility, it can come as no surprise that the number of important decisions and the pace in which they appear have increased enormously. The paradox of choice as such is a modern phenomenon:[16] with the growth of our set of options, the number of important decisions to be taken and the accompanying responsibility have dramatically increased. Given this background, it is only reasonable to assume that there is an increased awareness among western Christians for the need of guidance.

Still, even when the perceived need for guidance can be explained from our specific historical situation, one could argue that the search for concrete divine guidance in important decisions is a form of 'religious coping' with the otherwise bewildering ocean of unlimited possibilities and the corresponding anxiety. While this cannot be excluded on the individual level, and while (as we will see) some views of divine guidance might bring with them a tendency towards the avoidance of responsibility

---

15 Cf. Paul van Tongeren, *Leven is een kunst: Over morele ervaring, deugdethiek en levenskunst*, 5th ed. (Zoetermeer: Klement Pelckmans, 2013), 17.
16 On this paradox, see esp. the extensive treatment of Barry Schwartz, *The Paradox of Choice: Why More Is Less* (New York: Harper Collins, 2004). The German equivalent 'die Qual der Wahl' and the Dutch 'keuzestress' point even more strongly to the downsides of endless choice people experience.

for one's decisions, this study is driven by the conviction that the question of guidance as a genuine *theological* question must be taken seriously.[17]

Given the fact that theology can in part be understood as the self-reflection of the church on its speaking about God, one could even argue that thinking through the question of guidance as a theological question is an urgent task in the light of its pervasiveness in contemporary Christian spirituality. In that case, the question whether attention should be devoted to a specifically modern, Western, middle class problem must be reversed: Since this is our given context, in which we are called to do the work of theology, we cannot forego to try to answer the question that comes to us more intense than ever before: What does it mean, in a society characterized by almost endless possibilities, to confess that Jesus is Lord, also of my life and time? As such, this study is an exercise in contextual theology.

1.1.4 Divine guidance between choice biography and providentialism
Although the introduction to divine guidance given in the preceding sections is sketchy in nature and needs to be sharpened, it helps us to delineate the topic under investigation and set the boundaries for the account of guidance we will develop throughout this book.

These boundaries exist in the form of two extreme views on the nature and character of life amidst an ocean of possibilities. On the one hand, for a Christian account of human life the notion of choice biography does not account sufficiently for the understanding that life is to be lived *coram deo*.[18] In focusing on the individual as an autonomous subject who manages the own course of life based upon personal convictions and preferences, the ongoing structuring (constraining) role of traditions and institutions is underemphasized, whereas the possibility of divine involvement in the course of human lives is even excluded a priori.[19] Although it cannot be denied that the individual is one of the authors of her own life, Christian theology must continually question whether the individual is the only and even the primary author of her life.

---

17 Cf. Hahnenberg, *Awakening Vocation*, 127: "Unless we are willing to rule out all claims to a divine call we have to attend theologically to its possibility."
18 Although, as Frits de Lange has pointed out, there are some affinities between Protestant theology and central notions in modern anthropology. See his "Becoming One Self: A Critical Retrieval of 'Choice Biography,'" *Journal of Reformed Theology* 1, no. 3 (2007): 272–93.
19 The concept of 'choice biography' is commonly attributed to Ulrich Beck and his *Risk Society: Towards a New Modernity*, trans. Mark Ritter (London: Sage, 1992). The concept itself is, however, not to be found in that book. Beck is often criticized by other sociologists for his overemphasis on agency and his underestimation of structural constraints. For a helpful overview and a generous re-reading of Beck, see Dan Woodman, "The Mysterious Case of the Pervasive Choice Biography: Ulrich Beck, Structure/Agency, and the Middling State of Theory in the Sociology of Youth," *Journal of Youth Studies* 12, no. 3 (2009): 243–56.

On the other hand, in what follows we need to steer clear of the opposite extreme: providentialism. In a providentialist approach, the widely shared Christian belief in divine providence is solidified into a worldview in which God's finger can be detected in many occurrences, and especially the more inexplicable ones.[20] In such a worldview, God is pictured as "an assiduous, energetic deity who constantly intervened in human affairs,"[21] history is seen as "the canvas on which the Lord etches his purposes and intentions,"[22] and particular providences are God's preferred way to communicate with the elect.[23] Such an approach to divine providence tends to undervalue God's involvement in *ordinary* processes, neglects the fact that the Biblical material that gave rise to the doctrine of providence often expresses faith in God's caring hand in situations that seem to contradict that faith, and risk to reduce God's activity to particular episodes we do not (at present) understand.

When we propose a theological interpretation of the experience of many believers of being somehow led by the Spirit, we must both avoid accounts in which the individual is the sole agent and author of his or her life, and accounts in which everything that happens can be interpreted in a very straightforward manner as 'the finger of God.' In what follows, we will set out to face that challenge, and we will do so from a Reformed perspective. How exactly we will approach this challenge will be explained in more detail in section 1.3, but in the next section we will first explore what research has already been done in this area.

1.2 Guidance in Academic Theology

1.2.1 Introduction
In this section we will sketch the current state of research on divine guidance. In contrast to the pervasiveness of the theme in popular Christian

---

20 Although the term providentialism is commonly used, especially in historical studies, a clear definition and a discussion of the differences between faith in divine providence and providentialism seems to be lacking.
21 Alexandra Walsham, *Providence in Early Modern England* (Oxford: Oxford University Press, 1999), 2.
22 Walsham, 2.
23 Walsham, 15. In her study, Walsham shows how such providentialism was not restricted to the Puritans in Early Modern England, but was a pervasive phenomenon at the time. See esp. p. 2-3: "Providentialism was not a marginal feature of the religious culture of early modern England, but part of the mainstream, a cluster of presuppositions which enjoyed near universal acceptance. It was a set of ideological spectacles through which individuals of all social levels and from all positions on the confessional spectrum were apt to view their universe, an invisible prism which helped them to focus the refractory meanings of both petty and perplexing events."

literature, its treatment in academic studies is scarce. We will start with an overview of studies that have guidance as their direct object of investigation (§1.2.2), followed by a discussion of guidance as a topic in surveys of Christian dogmatics or studies on specific doctrinal loci (§1.2.3). Next, we turn to literature on *vocation* that thematically moves close to our research interests (§1.2.4), to a discussion of guidance in historical studies (§1.2.5), and finally we point to a number of other disciplines in which issues related to guidance are discussed (§1.2.6).

1.2.2 Guidance as direct object of investigation
In light of the enormous amount of attention given to guidance among Christians, it is remarkable that only a few scholarly monographs about guidance have appeared. One such monograph is Garry Friesen's dissertation *God's Will as it Relates to Decision Making*, which entails a biblical critique of what Friesen calls the 'traditional view' and proposes an alternative view. Unfortunately, besides exegesis of a number of important biblical passages it lacks a substantive theological discussion of the topics involved.[24] Since Friesen's dissertation was reworked into an accessible book and as such played a major role in the evangelical discussion on guidance, it will be discussed in more detail in chapter 2.

In his *Led by the Spirit* (1996) Stephen E. Parker discusses divine guidance from the perspective of Pentecostal theology. While claims to direct guidance from the Spirit are a central part of Pentecostal spirituality, Parker states that "understanding and evaluating such claims has been problematic for Pentecostals and non-Pentecostals alike."[25] Observing a lack of theological reflection, in his book Parker sets out to "construct a 'practical theology' of Pentecostal discernment and decision making."[26] Parker is concerned that, through its focus on historical and exegetical issues, Pentecostalism is mainly in dialogue with fundamentalist Evangelicals. Therefore, in his own argument he gives a prominent place to Paul Tillich's theology "because he takes 'spirit movements' seriously."[27] Parker combines an ethnographic study of a local Pentecostal congregation, a psychological analysis of what happens when guidance is experienced,

---

24 Garry Friesen, "God's Will as It Relates to Decision Making" (PhD diss., Dallas Theological Seminary, 1978). Stephen D. Kovach, "Toward a Theology of Guidance: A Multi-Faceted Approach Emphasizing Scripture as Both Foundation and Pattern in Discerning the Will of God" (PhD diss., Trinity Evangelical Divinity School, 1999), 30 mentions Friesen's dissertation as "the only academic theological treatment."
25 Stephen E. Parker, *Led by the Spirit: Toward a Practical Theology of Pentecostal Discernment and Decision Making* (Sheffield: Sheffield Academic Press, 1996), 9.
26 Parker, 12.
27 Parker, 53.

and an analysis of Tillich's theology to propose a 'model for ideal Pentecostal discernment' that integrates the Pentecostal emphasis on holistic ways of knowing.[28] For our purposes, Parker's book too easily presupposes the existence of guidance without arguing for it. He is more concerned with the process of discernment than with the nature of guidance.

Stephen Kovach's dissertation *Toward a Theology of Guidance* (1999) comes closest to what we intend to do in the present study. As the subtitle suggests, Kovach offers 'a multi-faceted approach to emphasizing Scripture as both foundation and pattern in discerning the will of God,' trying to offer a robust theological framework for dealing with guidance.[29] In order to do so, after his introduction of the topic he offers an exegesis of 'selected church era passages' (biblical material from the period after Pentecost) that are related to guidance and the will of God (Ch.2). Furthermore, he argues that God uses the text of Scripture "in a subjective, personally transformative way" to guide individuals.[30] This subjective use of Scripture is described as a form of "subordinate revelation."[31] Finally, using Alston's work on mystical perception, Kovach develops what he calls "an epistemological framework for hearing the voice of God."[32] When combined, these elements form a defense of the statement that "God occasionally guides the Christian in relation to his larger Kingdom purposes," a view he dubs the 'directional view' on guidance.[33]

Although Kovach's work is driven by the same motive as mine, viz. to offer a theological framework for dealing with guidance, his approach suffers from a number of problems. First, Kovach sees no need to discuss and analyze the popular literature on divine guidance and only provides "a sampling of books written by significant evangelical authors in the last thirty years."[34] As a result, his rendition of the major views on guidance, while performing a key function in his argument, is superficial, imprecise, and at times skewed.[35] Second, Kovach wants to interact with historical theology but does so in a sporadic and imprecise way.[36] Third, after

---

28 Parker, 175.
29 Kovach, "Toward a Theology of Guidance," 31.
30 Kovach, 180.
31 Kovach, 210.
32 See the subtitle of chapter 5. Kovach bases his thought on William P. Alston, *Perceiving God: The Epistemology of Religious Experience* (Ithaca: Cornell University Press, 1991).
33 Kovach, "Toward a Theology of Guidance," iii.
34 Kovach, 2, nt. 4.
35 Especially Friesen's 'wisdom view' is presented in a rather biased way. Furthermore, the 'directional view' Kovach takes as his point of departure includes the views of authors like Blackaby, Bockmühl, Smith, Willard, and Waltke, who, as we will see in the next chapter, have radically different and even colliding views on guidance.
36 For example, in his short treatment of Calvin, while acknowledging that caution is needed in affirming a change in Calvin's thought on guidance, Kovach devotes a lot of attention to

having proposed the relation of Word and Spirit as one between objective meaning and subjective application (beyond Scripture's objective meaning), Kovach is too eager to interpret various narratives from Acts in this mold without careful exegesis.[37] Finally, and most importantly, Kovach argues that God *occasionally* guides believers in direct ways, but his entire argument focuses on the possibility and importance of this occasional form of guidance. Whereas he obviously agrees that these instances are extraordinary, no attention is devoted to what would be the 'ordinary' way in which God guides. In the present study, these are exactly the problems we try to overcome.

1.2.3 Guidance in systematic theology
Underneath the questions of guidance and vocation lies a thicket of theological assumptions and decisions.[38] In this light it is somewhat remarkable that the topic itself is almost absent in surveys of systematic theology, although one could argue that it is more at home in treatments of theological anthropology or spirituality. The topic is, for example, not treated in the systematic theologies of Herman Bavinck, Louis Berkhof, Wolfhart Pannenberg, Robert Jenson, Norman Geisler, and Van den Brink and Van der Kooi.

Guidance is mentioned in passing in the works of Emil Brunner and Paul Tillich. In a chapter on "The Christian in the World," Brunner asserts that "every living member of the Ekklesia will perceive every day the summons and the guidance of his Lord." As many decisions cannot be covered by a moral law, "the Christian is dependent on, and must seek for, the leadings of the Spirit, which are never predictable."[39] For Brunner, a fuller treatment of this topic belongs to the task of ethics. Paul Tillich mentions 'personal guidance' in his discussion of divine providence when focusing on 'individual providence.' Without clarifying what this guidance entails, he writes: "In Christianity providence is an element in the

---

strands in Calvin's thought that would possibly allow for more direct forms of divine guidance without discussing more critical sections, see esp. 50-52.
37 See esp. Kovach, "Toward a Theology of Guidance," 202.
38 Hahnenberg, *Awakening Vocation*, xi-xii, speaking of vocation, mentions the following issues: "the relationship of the divine will to human freedom, the nature of providence and predestination, the workings of grace and the limits of spiritual experience" and adds that these questions tap "into our deepest assumptions about God, ourselves, church, and moral commitments."
39 See Emil Brunner, *Dogmatics, Vol. III: The Christian Doctrine of the Church, Faith, and the Consummation*, trans. David Cairns and T.H.L. Parker (Cambridge: The Lutterworth Press, 1962), 321. For Brunner, seeking guidance is done in a "life of prayer," part of which means to "be quiet before God and hear His voice, which has something new, original, and, for the unbeliever, perhaps strange to say about every concrete problem of life."

person to person relationship between God and man; it carries the warmth of belief in loving protection and personal guidance."[40]

Three major systematic theologies devote more attention to the issues of guidance and decision-making. Karl Barth deals with the individual course of life and God's involvement in it in a number of places, but most explicitly in his discussion of *Beruf* in KD III/4.[41] In that context, Barth argues that God has "eine besondere Absicht" with every individual, which can also be called his will or plan. According to Barth, God makes his will known "imperativisch, in seinen besonderen Gebot."[42] Barth's unique contribution in his discussion of vocation is found in his insistence on the beneficence of the limitations God has set for our lives. Especially in an age of seemingly endless possibilities, limitations come as a kind of grace. According to Barth, God gives us genuine freedom within the limitations provided through age, our unique historical position, our personal aptitude, and our office.[43] Within these limitations, humans are free to choose, but their choices are always incorporated in divine providence.[44]

G.C. Berkouwer discusses guidance in his treatment of 'providence and history.' Having discussed the universal character of providence before, Berkouwer asks whether this blinds us to the particular. Does a focus on general providence "allow for distinctions within God's providence over all things, for *special* leading in particular circumstances?"[45] If general providence is a matter of God's *hand* in history, doesn't a hand consist of individual *fingers*, so that general providence should be split up as it were in various particular acts? In this way, although the main focus of his chapter is on history, Berkouwer also zooms in on the individual level: "Does this mean that the simple faith which witnesses to God's

---

40 Paul Tillich, *Systematic Theology, Vol. I* (Chicago: University of Chicago Press, 1951), 268.
41 See Karl Barth, *Kirchliche Dogmatik III/4* (Zürich: EVZ Verlag, 1951), 683–744. Note the distinction Barth makes between *Beruf* and *Berufung*. For a more detailed discussion of Barth's contribution, see section 6.2.
42 KD III/4, 683. Cf. 693: "imperativische Bekanntmachung des Willens Gottes".
43 As Barth has rightly shown, against a pervasive modernist myth vocation is more a closing down than an opening up.
44 KD III/4, 727: "Die Wahrheit ist, dass das menschliche Wählen in seiner ganzen Selbständigkeit und Verantwortlichkeit im Raum und Rahmen des göttlichen Wählens, Planens und Bestimmens stattfindet, dass seine Entscheidungen als solche in den Beschluss und in das Geschehen des Willens Gottes einbezogen sind."
45 G.C. Berkouwer, *The Providence of God*, trans. Lewis B. Smedes, Studies in Dogmatics (Grand Rapids: Eerdmans, 1952), 161. Berkouwer takes a very critical stance in this chapter, which must be understood against the background of his references to 1933 and Nazi-Germany.

leading in one's own life is illusory?"⁴⁶ Can we know nothing of God's involvement in our own life, family, and work than "that they all fall within the circle of God's mysterious almighty rule?"⁴⁷ Berkouwer's answer to these questions contains four elements. In the first place, he points at a number of dangers in interpreting specific circumstances as revelatory.⁴⁸ Such interpretations tend to focus on "unique and striking" events, are subjective and arbitrary, incite people to "seek only the special intervention of the finger of God instead of living with confidence in the hand of God which governs *all* things", and hence fragmentize divine providence.⁴⁹ In the second place, Berkouwer points out what is at stake behind these dangers: people move "outside the sphere of faith into the area of observation," where the facts begin to speak for themselves.⁵⁰ What lacks here is a sense of awe before the hiddenness of God. Third, Berkouwer shows how such interpretations of history lack a norm and are based upon some form of "religious intuition or divination."⁵¹ Finally, Berkouwer underscores that proper theological thinking on God's guidance should make clear that "God's leading directs all things with a view to the coming of His kingdom and not to our individual lives."⁵² All close links between leading and prosperity should be rejected.

Another explicit discussion of guidance is found in Hendrikus Berkhof's *Christian Faith*. In §46, under the header of "Guidance and Security," Berkhof shows how people, when they enter in a relationship with God, come to believe that "there is Someone who cares for and guides" them.⁵³ For Berkhof, this is a special and distinct form of divine providence, around which many misconceptions exist.⁵⁴ On the one hand, in

---

46 Berkouwer, 175.
47 Berkouwer, 178. Here, the Dutch original is sharper than the English translation. "Kunnen we niets 'weten' van Gods zeer *reële* hand, Zijn vinger hier en nu, in eigen leven, in gezin en arbeid dan slechts dit éne, dat álles krachtens Zijn absolute macht binnen de cirkel van Zijn regering valt?" See G.C. Berkouwer, *De Voorzienigheid Gods*, Dogmatische Studiën (Kampen: J.H. Kok, 1950), 218.
48 For Berkouwer, this is essentially what happens in seeking concrete instances of guidance: "A fragment of history [is] in effect canonized as a new revelation" (162).
49 See Berkouwer, *Providence*, 162.
50 Compare this with our earlier distinction between faith in divine providence and providentialism, §1.1.4.
51 Berkouwer, *Providence*, 171. See also 172: "Where fragments of history are not interpreted by God Himself, we are not permitted to explain them out of their entire context as though their meaning were intuitively and, hence, irrationally perspicuous to us." And later, on p. 178: "there can be no place for intuition alongside of faith and apart from the word of revelation."
52 Berkouwer, 181.
53 Hendrikus Berkhof, *Christian Faith: An Introduction to the Study of the Faith (Revised)*, trans. Sierd Woudstra (Grand Rapids: Eerdmans, 1986), 450.
54 Although general providence and guidance for Berkhof are closely related, he consciously separates their treatment because "they are ... faith statements with a different origin and

some circles guidance plays a central role (later on he explicitly mentions "European Pietism and Anglo-Saxon evangelical, revival and Pentecostal movements", 452) but unfortunately this often tends to views in which God is there to satisfy personal wishes and where guidance can be unproblematically shown in the actual course of events. On the other hand, and as a reaction to the former attitude, there are many people who "no longer dare to link God with what happens to them personally."[55] For Berkhof, the core of a proper belief in guidance is knowing that in all that happens "we are securely in the hand of God."[56] In the covenant-relationship established through faith, "God becomes the goal of man, ... who now learns to submit his thoughts and plans to those of God."[57] Such a belief in guidance must always remain a matter of faith, not sight.[58] Given the many references to God's personal care for believers in the Bible, the 'exuberance' in hymnology, and the pervasiveness of guidance in some Christian traditions, Berkhof deplores the reticence of systematic theology to discuss this topic.[59]

Besides these protestant voices, guidance receives more attention from theologians from the catholic, and especially the Ignatian, tradition. Here, Karl Rahner's *Das Dynamische in der Kirche* (1958) stands out.[60] In this book, Rahner asks whether there is place for a "sittlich verpflichtenden, existentiellen Anruf, für einen Imperativ?"[61] Taking Ignatius's *Exercises* as an important source, Rahner discusses questions like "What happens when the will of God is found? What does it consist of? What

---

character." As Berkhof helpfully explains: "The belief in God's general guidance of the world stems (directly) from the belief in his saving operations in history and the belief in creation connected with it. But the belief in the personal union *with* and guidance *by* God is the other side of the covenant relationship into which the believer enters through justification. That belief, having its own origin and character, requires its own theological reflection."

55 Berkhof, *Christian Faith*, 450.
56 Berkhof, 451.
57 Berkhof, 450.
58 Berkhof, 451. He adds that, though we sometimes ("It can happen...") have the impression that "we seem to detect something of God's purposes with us," it often turns out that we are mistaken: "The interpretation falls away, but the faith remains."
59 Berkhof mentions Ritschl, Althaus, and Barth as positive exceptions, but at least in the cases of Ritschl and Althaus this seems to be so because they treat God's personal care for believers apart from their discussion of general providence, not because they discuss the issue of guidance. Berkhof's sense of regret that guidance is not discussed in systematic theology is amplified by his suggestion that "it is likely that precisely the silence in the study of the faith has contributed to the excesses which apart from it arose in the churches since the end of the 17th century" (453).
60 Karl Rahner, *Das Dynamische in der Kirche* (Freiburg: Herder, 1958).
61 Rahner, 20. Rahner deplores that "die Geschichte der Lehre von dieser individuellen Führung des Heiligen Geistes und der Individualmoral noch so gut wie ganz zu schreiben ist," 11. This verdict has not changed since the publication of his book.

exactly is being found?"⁶² Distinguishing between principles and imperatives, Rahner defends the possibility and importance of *"individuelle Willenskundgabe Gottes"*⁶³ in a way that tries to avoid "cheap mysticism or enthusiasm."⁶⁴

As could be expected, the topic of guidance receives more than average attention in systematic theologies from an evangelical perspective. Recent examples are found in the surveys of Michael Horton and John Frame.⁶⁵ Horton mentions guidance in his discussion of providence and the traditional distinction between God's hidden and revealed will. On the one hand, he is convinced that "God has decreed all that comes to pass," but on the other hand he explicitly states that "we lack any promise that we can access this information [contained in the divine decree, CvdK]."⁶⁶ For Horton, many struggles over guidance come from a misunderstanding of texts like Romans 12:1-2.⁶⁷ John Frame discusses guidance both in the context of providence and in his treatment of the divine will. Asking whether through his providence God offers guidance, Frame denies that providence is revelatory in itself but argues that "providence supplies the 'situation' to which the Word of Scripture must be applied."⁶⁸ Further on, in his discussion of the distinction between the decretive and preceptive aspects of the divine will, Frame treats the question of 'God's will for my life.'⁶⁹ He argues that the divine will is not to be thought of as the "only possible course of action" in our decisions, but that, on the other hand, the reality of God's guidance in making specific decisions should not be negated. Frame points to Scripture, wisdom, and vocation as an alternative to the mainstream evangelical interpretation of guidance.⁷⁰

---

62 Rahner, 80: "Was geschieht, wenn der Wille Gottes gefunden wird? Worin besteht er? Was wird gefunden?"
63 Rahner, 84.
64 'Billige Mystizismus' and 'Schwärmerei', 91.
65 Michael Horton, *The Christian Faith: A Systematic Theology for Pilgrims on the Way* (Grand Rapids: Zondervan, 2011); John M. Frame, *Systematic Theology: An Introduction to Christian Belief* (Phillipsburg: P&R Publishing, 2013). Frame's *Systematic Theology* is an abridged version of his 4-volume 'Theology of Lordship'. Horton and Frame belong to the conservative Reformed wing of evangelicalism.
66 Horton labels attempts to access God's hidden will as "characteristic of superstition rather than of Christian piety," *The Christian Faith*, 363.
67 "Many believers struggle to discern God's secret will in daily decisions because they confuse it with his 'perfect will' in this passage." Horton, 363.
68 Frame, *Systematic Theology*, 180.
69 Frame, 353–56. As we will see later on, in treatments of divine providence a distinction is often made between the will of God referring to his decree (decretive will) and the will of God as it is expressed in his commandments (preceptive will).
70 On p. 355, Frame summarizes his view as follows: "It is thus that God guides his people: through Spirit-given wisdom, based on Scripture, wisdom that enables us to understand

More positive accounts of guidance are found in the theologies of Wayne Grudem and Millard Erickson, who both discuss guidance under the header of *prophecy*. Grudem discusses biblical instances of the Spirit's guidance in his chapter on the work of the Holy Spirit,[71] but the question of contemporary occurrences of guidance under the topic of prophecy in his chapter on the gifts of the Spirit.[72] Likewise, Erickson briefly discusses guidance in a chapter on 'Recent Issues regarding the Holy Spirit' in relation to the question of prophecy.[73] Both lack a thorough theological analysis and mainly defend the possibility of supernatural guidance vis-a-vis strictly cessationist views.

Finally, in a number of instances the topic of guidance is discussed in separate treatments of *providence*. Paul Helm treats guidance in a chapter of his *The Providence of God* (1993), where he discusses two related questions: "First, how do Christians *recognize* divine providence in their lives? ... Does it ever become visible? Secondly, how can Christians align themselves with divine providence in the future so as to be in harmony with the divine purpose?"[74] In answer to the first question, Helm distinguishes between providence as a descriptive term and providence as a normative or evaluative term.[75] Arguing that "as human beings we do not have sufficient data to make definitive judgments on the significance of the events in our lives,"[76] Helm warns against the "temptation" to get a definitive view by "tapping into providence."[77] Instead, trusting in divine providence we are to face the fact that "there are decisions to be made which

---

what is at stake in our choices and to evaluate those circumstances in a godly way. Through such guidance God reveals to us our vocation, to invoke a good Reformation term." And later (p. 355), on the relation between decree, Word, and wisdom: "God guides us through his decrees, his written Word, and Spirit-given wisdom: (1) By his decrees, he opens doors and closes them, giving us some opportunities and withholding others; but those circumstances of our lives do not in themselves tell us how to behave. (2) By Scripture, he tells us what he wants us to do, showing us how to respond to these circumstances. (3) By Spirit-given wisdom, God enables us to apply Scripture to circumstances."

71 Wayne Grudem, *Systematic Theology: An Introduction to Biblical Doctrine* (Nottingham: Inter-Varsity Press, 1994), 642–44.
72 Grudem, 1040–42.
73 Millard J. Erickson, *Christian Theology*, Third Edition (Grand Rapids: Baker Academic, 2013), 806–11.
74 Paul Helm, *The Providence of God*, Contours of Christian Theology (Downers Grove: Inter-Varsity Press, 1993), 122.
75 Helm, 122. With providence as an evaluative term, Helm points at the way people tend to interpret specific events as 'providential.' Such events are characterized by "an element of unexpectedness or unreservedness or disproportion about the events, and the outcome of the events is believed to be a benefit of some kind to the person concerned" (124).
76 Helm, 128. Cf. his statement that "recognizing divine providence is a difficult and tentative business."
77 Helm, 130. He holds that there is no basis for thinking we might receive some intimation from God on the future (129).

are often complex and personal, where the command of God may offer general guidance but nothing like the detail that is required."[78] John Sanders picks up the theme of guidance at the end of his plea for a risk-view of providence.[79] For Sanders, a no-risk view of providence necessarily entails a view on guidance in which God has a detailed blueprint for every individual's life.[80] For him, "it remains inappropriate for proponents of the no-risk model to ask whether we are following God's guidance, for we cannot but follow it."[81] Only in a risk-view of providence, in which God has a general goal with our lives but no specific routes, real guidance is possible. Making decisions in line with what we know of God, "together we decide the actual course of my life."[82]

In summary, we see that most major systematic theologies do not treat the topic of guidance at all or only in a very marginal way (Brunner, Tillich). Among those who devote more attention to it, Berkouwer is most critical, Berkhof is open but brief, and only Barth and Rahner try to develop fresh accounts of guidance. Among the evangelical theologies, once again some reject popular views on guidance (Horton, Frame), while others treat it in passing under the header of prophecy and the gifts of the Spirit (Grudem, Erickson). In general we could say that the enormous interest in guidance among lay believers is not reflected in the systematic theologies of the last century.

1.2.4 Guidance and vocation
The most direct link between the topic of guidance and other theological work is found in recent attempts to reassess the notion of vocation. Four recent studies especially stand out for their close relationship to our project.

Gordon Preece's *The Viability of the Vocation Tradition* (1998),[83] based upon his PhD dissertation supervised by Miroslav Volf, takes up Volf's challenge by arguing for an account of vocation that is neither exclusively protological (Luther) nor pneumatological or eschatological (Volf) but Trinitarian in its basis. Using the work of Wingren, Barth, and Moltmann

---

78 Helm, 135. "Part of the agony of such decision-making is that often there does not seem to be any outcome that is obviously the correct and divinely commanded one."
79 John E. Sanders, *The God Who Risks: A Theology of Divine Providence* (Downers Grove: InterVarsity Press, 1998), 275–78.
80 Sanders criticizes Friesen on this point, see p. 275, nt. 119.
81 Sanders, 276.
82 Sanders, 277.
83 Gordon R. Preece, *The Viability of the Vocation Tradition in Trinitarian, Credal, and Reformed Perspective: The Threefold Call* (Lewiston: Edwin Mellen, 1998). Volf had previously argued that in order to be viable, vocation must be construed in pneumatological and eschatological terms, not protological.

respectively, Preece argues that vocation must be grounded in the first, second, and third articles of the confession.

Like Preece, Douglas J. Schuurman tries to "develop a contemporary articulation of the classic Protestant doctrine of vocation" in his *Vocation: Discerning our Callings in Life* (2004).[84] Schuurman clearly writes against the background of the evangelical reflection on guidance we will investigate in chapter 2, treating especially a blueprint approach as a distortion of the Reformed idea of vocation. He attempts to retrieve key features of the Protestant doctrine of vocation, considers the uses and abuses that can be made of the concept, and applies it to 'decisions and the moral life.' Schuurman's book is academic in nature but practically oriented. His book comes closest to our own project, but whereas Schuurman's focus is practical we focus on the theological questions implied in the ideas of guidance and vocation.

Michael R. Wassenaar's 2009 dissertation *Four Types of Calling* is different in that its main objective is to describe the dominant approaches to vocation, without trying to formulate a theological proposal of his own.[85] All four types are "rooted in Scripture and Christian tradition, and defensible from a Christian perspective."[86] Taking a wide perspective on vocation ('anything to which God calls a particular person or group,' p. 13), Wassenaar discusses each type using the work of a prominent theologian: vocation as divine command (Kierkegaard), vocation through the natural order (Brunner), vocation as self-actualization (Scheler), and vocation as election, the call to belong to a chosen community (Barth). In the final chapter, Wassenaar discusses three strategies through which the types might be integrated into a more comprehensive theory of vocation.

Finally, Edward P. Hahnenberg's *Awakening Vocation: A Theology of Christian Call* (2010) is a recent account of vocation from a Roman Catholic perspective. Hahnenberg welcomes the widening of vocation in *Vatican II*, but asserts that that is only a starting point, in that most implications for vocation have yet to be thought through.[87] To do so, Hahnenberg

---

84 Douglas J. Schuurman, *Vocation: Discerning Our Callings in Life* (Grand Rapids: Eerdmans, 2004), xi.
85 Michael R. Wassenaar, "Four Types of Calling: The Ethics of Vocation in Kierkegaard, Brunner, Scheler and Barth" (PhD diss., Yale University, 2009).
86 Wassenaar, 6.
87 Hahnenberg, *Awakening Vocation*, xi. In the Vatican II dogmatic constitution of the church the category of calling / vocation is no longer restricted to the priesthood or religious life but applied to all Christians. See esp. *Lumen Gentium*, V.40: "Thus it is evident to everyone, that all the faithful of Christ of whatever rank or status, are called to the fullness of the Christian life and to the perfection of charity; by this holiness as such a more human manner of living is promoted in this earthly society. In order that the faithful may reach this perfection, they must use their strength accordingly as they have received it, as a gift from

first provides a brief history of developments in the doctrine of vocation and then develops his own account in conversation primarily with Ignatius, Barth, and Rahner. Interestingly, the questions Hahnenberg addresses as raised by the teaching of Vatican II are easily recognized as central questions in evangelical thought on guidance: "Does God have a specific plan for each of us, or is it more like general guidelines for all of us? ... When I face difficult decisions, how am I to know what God wants me to do?" and, in accordance with a leading concern behind this book's project, "Is that even the right way of framing the question?" (xi).

Clearly, the concepts of guidance and vocation are closely intertwined, and these authors will be included as discussion partners throughout the present book, especially in §6.2.

1.2.5 Historical studies

No historiography of the way Christians received and interpreted divine guidance exists. Yet in historical studies, three related phenomena have received some attention: the concept and history of enthusiasm, Christian approaches to divination, and the way guidance was conceived and searched for in the puritan tradition or more broadly in early modern England. Ronald Knox's extensive *Enthusiasm* provides a broad sketch of the history of enthusiasm, in which enthusiasts are characterized among other things by an 'ultrasupernaturalism'[88] that leads them "to be more attentive to the guidance (directly felt, they would tell you) of the Holy Spirit."[89] Knox focuses on the seventeenth and eighteenth centuries, as do many other studies of enthusiasm.[90] That divine guidance is indeed at the heart of what defines enthusiasm can be readily seen from Archibald Campbell's definition:

Christ. They must follow in His footsteps and conform themselves to His image *seeking the will of the Father in all things*. They must devote themselves with all their being to the glory of God and the service of their neighbor" [emphasis CvdK].

[88] Ronald A. Knox, *Enthusiasm: A Chapter in the History of Religion, with Special Reference to the XVII and XVIII Centuries* (Oxford: Oxford University Press, 1950), 2. Knox gives no clear and concise definition of enthusiasm. According to Michael Heyd, this is correct, because it is a "misguided historical exercise to search for a clear definition of enthusiasm," *Be Sober and Reasonable: The Critique of Enthusiasm in the Seventeenth and Early Eighteenth Centuries* (Leiden: Brill, 2000), 5. Heyd himself describes enthusiasm as a "label by which to designate individuals or groups who allegedly claimed to have direct divine inspiration, whether millenarians, radical sectarians or various prophesiers, as well as alchemists, 'empirics' and some contemplative philosophers" (2).

[89] Knox, *Enthusiasm*, 1. Cf. 3: "A direct indication of the Divine will is communicated to him at every turn."

[90] See for the most pertinent ones Heyd, *Sober and Reasonable*; Lionel Laborie, *Enlightening Enthusiasm: Prophecy and Religious Experience in Early Eighteenth-Century England* (Manchester: Manchester University Press, 2015); Helen Boyles, *Romanticism and Methodism: The Problem of Religious Enthusiasm* (London: Routledge, 2017).

An Enthusiast is one, who in the course of his devotion, keeps not within the compass of reason, but having given up himself to the power and influence of an over-heated fancy, is *mechanically* wrought up into such extraordinary heats and fervours, thet he verily believes he is immediately under the benign emanations of Heaven, and has divine revelations made to him…[91]

Throughout the ages people have tried to divine the will of their gods. In the Christian tradition one method especially stands out: *sortes biblicae* or bibliomancy. In this practice, Bible verses are selected randomly and interpreted as divine directions in specific situations. Van der Horst has shown how this practice occurred already in the time of the Maccabees and continued throughout the Christian tradition, albeit in modified forms.[92] Van Lieburg complements this picture by giving examples from the later ages,[93] stating that this practice found fertile ground in Protestantism as a result of some of its emphases: the Bible as the sole norm of faith, the importance of personal Bible reading, and the strong faith in divine providence.[94] This final remark is important in the present context: practicing bibliomancy is only an option if the practitioner beliefs that there is a divine will to be discovered.

A prominent place is given to divination in Keith Thomas's *Religion and the Decline of Magic*. Thomas shows how prayer as a means of divination,[95] sortilege (bibliomancy), and casting lots were common practices until at least the seventeenth century.[96] Walsham likewise shows how the divine will was sought in domestic decision-making and personal crises, arguing that "Calvinist theology not merely accommodated but arguably even enhanced aspects of pre-Reformation practice and belief."[97]

---

[91] Archibald Campbell, *A Discourse Proving That the Apostles Were No Enthusiasts: Wherein the Nature and Influence of Religious Enthusiasm Are Impartially Explain'd* (London: A. Millar, 1730), 4.

[92] P.W. van der Horst, *Sortes: het gebruik van heilige boeken als lotsorakels in de oudheid*, Mededelingen van de Afdeling Letterkunde, Nieuwe Reeks, 62(3) (Amsterdam: Koninklijke Nederlandse Akademie van Wetenschappen, 1999).

[93] Fred van Lieburg, "De bijbel als orakelboek: Bibliomantie in de protestantse traditie," in *Materieel Christendom: Religie en materiële cultuur in West-Europa*, ed. Arie L. Molendijk (Hilversum: Uitgeverij Verloren, 2003), 81–105.

[94] Van Lieburg, 105.

[95] Keith Thomas, *Religion and the Decline of Magic: Studies in Popular Beliefs in Sixteenth and Seventeenth Century England* (London: Weidenfeld and Nicolson, 1971), 117: "Many diaries and autobiographies of the period show how devout men were able by praying to focus their minds upon a problem, and so to hit upon a solution." Thomas lists examples like cures for sicknesses, solutions to mathematical problems, leaving an unsatisfactory wife, deciding where to live, etc.

[96] Thomas, 113–20.

[97] Walsham, *Providence in Early Modern England*, 168.

With regard to research focusing on guidance and the will of God in early modern England, we have already seen how Walsham argued that providentialism was a widely shared perspective, not just restricted to the Puritans. In that context, she also showed how "providence played a key role in domestic decision-making, in household divinity, and in the private management of crisis and calamity."[98] For the Puritan tradition, this is shown in more detail by Barbara Donagan, who provides a lot of interesting material on puritan practices with regard to decision-making: "seeking to perceive God's will was the essence of the decision-making process for the conscientious Puritan."[99] Discerning the divine will was tried through two venues that needed to be brought into a delicate balance: on the one hand through the activities of prayer, conference, casuistry and "the inspection of providential evidence," on the other hand through seeking inner peace and certainty.[100]

1.2.6 Other disciplines

Topics related to the question of guidance are also discussed within a number of other fields. In biblical studies there has been some interesting research into the meaning of discernment in the New Testament.[101] Most relevant to our investigation is Munzinger's *Discerning the Spirits*. From the first page onwards Munzinger connects the concept of discernment with the topic of guidance, asking: "How does the Spirit guide each believer personally?"[102]

Next, questions related to guidance and personal nonmoral decisions are sometimes treated in Christian ethics, as we saw before in O'Donovan. Jochem Douma, for example, treats them under the rubric of *adiaphora*. He argues that adiaphora as a neutral zone do not exist, as the entire Christian life is under the lordship of Christ. However, there is an

---

98 Walsham, 19.
99 Barbara Donagan, "Godly Choice: Puritan Decision-Making in Seventeenth-Century England," *The Harvard Theological Review* 76, no. 3 (1983): 307. Once again, Donagan stresses that "many of the methods and criteria of decision-making were peculiar neither to Puritans nor to the seventeenth-century" (310), and "acceptance of an overriding divine Providence which guided all events in the world, and then issued in particular providences directed to individual persons and happenings, was a traditional Christian doctrine" (319).
100 Donagan, 332. In the next chapter we will see a very similar approach from the side of contemporary evangelicalism.
101 Mainly through studies of the words *diakrinô, diakrisis, dokimazô*.
102 André Munzinger, *Discerning the Spirits: Theological and Ethical Hermeneutics in Paul* (Cambridge: Cambridge University Press, 2007), 3. Munzinger clearly relates discernment and questions of guidance, but his focus is on discernment more broadly. He tries to answer the twin questions "What requires discernment?" and "How should and can discernment function?" (18).

"immensely wide terrain in which the Christian may make his own decisions in the maturity bestowed upon him by Christ."[103] Douma mentions the examples of marriage and career and stresses Christian liberty in those areas.[104]

Helmut Thielicke addresses guidance in his *Theologische Ethik* in a number of places, especially in two sections on 'das Problem der Geistesleitung' and the concept of 'Beruf'.[105] With regard to *Geistesleitung*, Thielicke opposes views that regard it as "supranaturaler Einflüsterung"[106] and instead employs the idea of improvisation. For Thielicke, believing in divine guidance does not reduce "das Wagnis der Entscheidung."[107] In his discussion of vocation, Thielicke focuses on cultural differences between the time of the Reformation and our time and the challenges these differences pose to the concept of vocation. Nonetheless, he attempts to uphold the concept.

From the perspective of practical theology, some work has been done under the notion of discipleship studies. Where these focus on notions of wisdom, improvisation, and transformation we will interact with them in the final chapter.

One could think of many non-theological disciplines that study themes that are vaguely related to the topic of divine guidance. Most concrete are sociological discussions related to choice biography, authorship of life, and the structure versus agency debate. From the field of psychology, there might be many interesting venues,[108] but divine guidance as such is

---

103 J. Douma, *Responsible Conduct: Principles of Christian Ethics*, trans. Nelson D. Kloosterman (Phillipsburg: P&R Publishing, 2003), 169. Douma prefers to speak of *diapheronta*, discerning 'that what is excellent' (Phil. 1:9-10) instead of focusing on what is indifferent, 173.
104 Cf. Douma, 166: "It is clear that when a person is making even very important decisions in life, he cannot appeal to a special revelation from God, but may and can discern the proper path in freedom."
105 For 'Problem der Geistesleitung' see Helmuth Thielicke, *Theologische Ethik II. Band: Entfaltung. 1. Teil: Mensch und Welt*, 4. unveränderte Auflage (Tübingen: Mohr Siebeck, 1973), par. 1079-1163. For 'Beruf' see Helmuth Thielicke, *Theologische Ethik, III. Band: Entfaltung, 3. Teil: Ethik der Gesellschaft, des Rechtes, der Sexualität und der Kunst*, 2. verbesserte Auflage (Tübingen: Mohr Siebeck, 1968), par. 486-546.
106 Thielicke, *TE II/1*, par. 1094.
107 Thielicke, *TE II/1*, par. 795. Cf. par. 905: "Der Blick auf das Weltregiment Gottes enthebt mich folglich nicht der eigenen Entscheidung, ermöglicht mir nicht das laissez-faire und erspart mir somit auch nicht die Konfliksituation."
108 E.g., there might be an interesting link between some interpretations of divine guidance and the phenomenon of Post-Decisional Dissonance Reduction, see for PDDR e.g. Eddie Harmon-Jones and Cindy Harmon-Jones, "Testing the Action-Based Model of Cognitive Dissonance: The Effect of Action Orientation on Postdecisional Attitudes," *Personality and Social Psychology Bulletin* 28, no. 6 (2002): 711–23.

only thematized in the field of transpersonal psychology.[109] Insights from those disciplines will not receive separate treatment in this study.

1.3 Methodological Remarks

1.3.1 Necessity and relevance of the current study
In the preceding sections we have seen how many contemporary believers are looking for some kind of divine guidance amidst the overwhelming amount of decisions that is to be taken. Yet a balanced and integrated attempt to wrestle with this question as a *theological* and not only a practical question is still lacking, at least from a Reformed perspective. Where it is discussed in systematic theology, this is done only in passing under the rubric of another locus.

Given that the paradox of choice is a problem of our specific time and place, thinking through decision-making and divine guidance is an urgent theological task, which we will undertake in this book. It can be understood both as a form of reflection on the experiences of many believers and a theological interpretation and in part a critique of them. As such, we set ourselves to the following tasks:

1. To gain an understanding of the spectrum of views on divine guidance;
2. To delineate which theological questions are relevant to the topic of guidance;
3. To bring the modern question of guidance and decision-making into interaction with voices from the tradition;
4. To provide a thick description of guidance that is theologically informed, in conversation with relevant current issues in academic theology, and that in the end can also provide a framework for answering the very practical question from which the topic evolved in the

---

109 Transpersonal psychology can be defined as "an approach to psychology that 1) studies phenomena beyond the ego as context for 2) an integrative/holistic psychology; this provides a framework for 3) understanding and cultivating human transformation", Glenn Hartelius, Mariana Caplan, and Mary Anne Rardin, "Transpersonal Psychology: Defining the Past, Divining the Future," *The Humanistic Psychologist* 35, no. 2 (2007): 145. See e.g. Mark Allan Kaplan, *The Experience of Divine Guidance: A Qualitative Study of the Human Endeavor to Seek, Receive, and Follow Guidance from a Perceived Divine Source* (Pacific Grove: Original Gravity, 2007); A.S. Alschuler, "Inner Teachers and Transcendent Education," in *Cultivating Consciousness: Enhancing Human Potential, Wellness, and Healing* (Westport: Praeger Publishers, 1993), 181–93; A. Hastings, *With the Tongues of Man and Angels: A Study of Channeling* (San Francisco: Holt, Rinehart and Winston, 1990); M.B. Liester, "Inner Voices: Distinguishing Transcendent and Pathological Characteristics," *Journal of Transpersonal Psychology* 28, no. 1 (1996): 1–30; J. Klimo, *Channeling: Investigations on Receiving Information from Paranormal Sources* (Berkeley: North Atlantic Books, 1998).

first place: What does it mean, in a society characterized by endless possibilities, to confess that Jesus is Lord, also of my life and time? How these aims will be pursued and integrated will be discussed in the remainder of this section.

1.3.2 On working from a Reformed perspective

In pursuing the above aims, in this book I explicitly try to think through the topic of guidance from a Reformed perspective. In order to be able to formulate a constructive proposal on thinking about guidance from such a Reformed perspective, some kind of instrument or guideline is needed to assess which approach to guidance is most coherent with the overall contours of Reformed theology. For this reason, in this section I will elaborate on my approach to Reformed theology.

Defining the nature of Reformed theology and the Reformed tradition is notoriously difficult, and many who call themselves Reformed have difficulty explaining why they are so and what it means to be Reformed.[110] For this difficulty many reasons can be given: unlike in Lutheranism, there is no clearly delineated Reformed *corpus doctrinae*;[111] an overarching ecclesial structure is absent; many interrelated Reformed traditions have developed from the beginning of the Reformation onwards;[112] and for many Reformed Christians the question of their Reformed identity is a second order question, because they want to be first of all identified as Christians.[113] Eberhard Busch has argued that what could be seen as the "confessional weakness" of the Reformed tradition is at the same time the source of its strength and richness.[114] Busch detects three theological

---

110 Cf. Marco Hofheinz and Matthias Zeindler, *Reformierte Theologie weltweit: zwölf Profile aus dem 20. Jahrhundert* (Zürich: Theologischer Verlag Zürich, 2013), 9–10.
111 Arthur C. Cochrane, *Reformed Confessions of the Sixteenth Century* (London: SCM Press, 1966), 15, as cited by: I. John Hesselink, *On Being Reformed: Distinctive Characteristics and Common Misunderstandings* (Ann Arbor: Servant Books, 1983), 11.
112 Hofheinz and Zeindler, *Reformierte Theologie weltweit*, 14 describe Reformed theology as a pluraletantum.
113 John H. Leith, *An Introduction to the Reformed Tradition: A Way of Being the Christian Community* (Atlanta: John Knox Press, 1977), 23; Hendrik M. Vroom, "On Being 'Reformed,'" in *Reformed and Ecumenical: On Being Reformed in Ecumenical Encounters*, by Christine Lineman-Perrin, Hendrik M. Vroom, and Michael Weinrich (Amsterdam: Rodopi, 2000), 155; Eberhard Busch, "Reformed Strength in Its Denominational Weakness," in *Reformed Theology: Identity and Ecumenicity*, by Wallace M. Alston Jr. and Michael Welker (Grand Rapids: Eerdmans, 2003), 26. According to George Stroup, Karel Blei explicitly argues that one should not be concerned with the question of Reformed identity, see George W. Stroup, "Reformed Identity in an Ecumenical World," in *Reformed Theology: Identity and Ecumenicity*, by Wallace M. Alston Jr. and Michael Welker (Grand Rapids: Eerdmans, 2003), 257.
114 Busch, "Reformed Strength," 22. For Busch, "it belongs to the structure of the Reformed tradition itself to question its confessional identity" (20).

reasons for the relative freedom with which the Reformed approach their confessions: "the unconditional subordination of the confession to Scripture," the wish of the Reformed believers to confess the faith of the one church instead of their own 'Reformed faith,' and the acknowledgement that any confession is a confession of a pilgrim people.[115]

Yet this difficulty of formulating the nature of Reformed theology and the broad scope of the Reformed tradition does not mean that there are no distinctive contours at all.[116] On the contrary, the fact that Busch can point out these theological reasons suggests that they are somehow embedded in a distinctively Reformed way of doing theology. Indeed, there is a typically Reformed approach to theology, but it is not evident in a straightforward way, and any reductionist formulation of its nature is precluded. In what follows, we will discuss two recent proposals, one by Stroup and one by Van den Brink and Smits, before delineating the implications for our project.

In an insightful article, George Stroup has described five common ways of interpreting the particular Reformed identity. The first approach describes the Reformed identity "by means of polity and church structure."[117] In the second approach, the nature of Reformed theology is described by a list of essential tenets, and in some cases this list consists of one central principle. Thus, Klooster lists the scriptural principle as the unique distinguishing feature of Reformed theology and Osterhaven the "sense of the presence of God and consecration of all of life to him."[118] A closely related but more subtle approach is the third one mentioned by Stroup: Reformed theology is characterized by a number of 'themes' and 'emphases' that function more like symbols and metaphors than like doctrines and propositions. Thus, the reality of multiple interpretations of a common theme within a single tradition is acknowledged.[119] The fourth

---

115 Busch, "Reformed Strength," 22. It could be added that this freedom is of course quite relative, given the fact that there is much more ambivalence towards confessions or doctrinal declarations alongside Scripture in for example the Baptist and Pentecostal traditions.
116 Cf. David Willis and Michael Welker, *Toward the Future of Reformed Theology: Tasks, Topics, Traditions* (Grand Rapids: Eerdmans, 1999), x.
117 Stroup, "Reformed Identity," 259. This approach seems to be used mainly at the organizational level. Stroup gives the example of the application form for the World Alliance of Reformed Churches, in which most of the questions concentrate on polity issues and none on theological or confessional questions.
118 Fred H. Klooster, "The Uniqueness of Reformed Theology: A Preliminary Attempt at Description," *Calvin Theological Journal* 14 (1979): 39; M. Eugene Osterhaven, *The Spirit of the Reformed Tradition* (Grand Rapids: Eerdmans, 1971), 8.
119 The language of themes or emphases is found in, for example, Leith and Hesselink, but functions in a less 'elastic' form than hinted at by Stroup. See as an example of the approach Stroup describes Eberhard Busch, who writes about "gemeinsame und bestendige Grund-

approach Stroup describes is the one in which the Reformed identity is approached more as an (intellectual) *habit* than as primarily a doctrinal issue. Here, the obvious example is Brian Gerrish's proposal of a "Reformed habit of mind."[120] In his article, Gerrish described the Reformed habit of mind in five points: deferent to the past; critical, especially of the own tradition; open to wisdom from outside; profoundly practical; and following the maxim of *ecclesia reformata semper reformanda*.[121] The final approach Stroup describes is the use of a cultural-linguistic model to describe the Reformed identity, where the Wittgensteinian concepts of grammar, family resemblances, and forms of life perform a crucial role.[122]

For Stroup, all of the models introduced have their drawbacks, but in his opinion a combination of the themes and emphases model, the habitus model, and the cultural-linguistic model could provide an adequate description of the Reformed identity:

> In an increasingly diverse and pluralistic world, Reformed identity is best understood in terms of a combination of the last three proposals – that is, certain general theological themes and emphases; the *habitus* or disposition, practices, and character of a community; and a cultural-linguistic model that focuses on the relation between the language and life of a church.[123]

---

haltungen, Einsichten und Interessen," *Reformiert: Profil einer Konfession* (Zürich: TVZ, 2007), 9.

120 See Brian A. Gerrish, "Tradition in the Modern World: The Reformed Habit of Mind," in *Toward the Future of Reformed Theology: Tasks, Topics, Traditions*, ed. David Willis and Michael Welker (Grand Rapids: Eerdmans, 1999), 3–20. For a sharp critique of accounts of the 'Reformed identity' that reduce it to 'Grundhaltungen' or 'habits of mind', see Bruce L. McCormack, "The End of Reformed Theology? The Voice of Karl Barth in the Doctrinal Chaos of the Present," in *Reformed Theology: Identity and Ecumenicity*, ed. Wallace M. Alston Jr. and Michael Welker (Grand Rapids: Eerdmans, 2003), 46–64. For McCormack, what lacks in contemporary Reformed theology is a sense of ecclesial authority and the fidelity to creeds that was crucial to the 'doctors of the church' of earlier generations.

121 Gerrish, "Habit of Mind," 13ff. McCormack, 48, n.8, responds that these habits "cannot be divorced from serious attention to doctrinal distinctives without a serious reduction of his list."

122 Stroup, "Reformed Identity," 264, points to Dietrich Ritschl and George Lindbeck as examples.

123 Stroup, 258. Note that Stroup describes the nature of the Reformed *identity*, and not the nature of Reformed *theology* per se. For Michael Allen, this is the main reason not to use Stroup's proposal in his account of Reformed *theology*, see R. Michael Allen, *Reformed Theology* (London: T&T Clark, 2010), 2. In our opinion, the distinction indeed makes some of Stroup's categories less relevant for thinking about the nature of Reformed *theology*, yet it is a very un-Reformed move to place too much of a gap between Reformed theology and Reformed identity.

In a recent article Gijsbert van den Brink and Johan Smits propose an account of Reformed theology that comes close to the combination of elements Stroup searches for.[124] To do so, they make use of a concept coined by philosopher of science Bas van Fraassen in describing Reformed theology as a *stance*. Van Fraassen describes a stance (in his case the 'empiricist stance') as follows:

> A philosophical position can consist in a stance (attitude, commitment, approach, a cluster of such – possibly including some propositional attitudes such as beliefs as well). Such a stance can of course be expressed, and may involve or presuppose some beliefs as well, but cannot simply be equated with having beliefs or making assertions about what there is.[125]

In their development of what it would mean for Reformed theology to be described as a stance, the authors use the concept of stance to describe "a set of mutually related commitments, maxims, inclinations and concerns"[126] and use the maxim *ecclesia reformata quia semper reformanda secundum verbum Dei* as "the bottomline of the Reformed stance."[127] From this maxim a number of Reformed emphases and concerns are identified: *sola Scriptura* and *tota Scriptura*, the importance of the Old Testament, the concept of covenant, infant baptism, a strong theocentric bend, the ontological distinction between Creator and creation, *duplex gratia* and the *tertius usus legis,* and a correlated emphasis on pneumatology. In describing those emphases, the authors stress the coherence of the Reformed stance and the interrelatedness of most of the emphases, without making any of them compulsory. In this way, a picture of Reformed theology is painted that does not present it as a checklist of core beliefs

---

[124] Although interestingly, Van den Brink and Smits do not mention the article of Stroup and refer to the *habitus* proposal of Gerrish only in a footnote, while both approaches have strong affinities with their own position. It seems McCormack's critique of those positions was taken very seriously by them as shown in their insistence on the *catholicity* of Reformed theology, see Gijsbert van den Brink and Johan Smits, "The Reformed Stance," *Journal of Reformed Theology* 9, no. 4 (2015): 337 (and passim).

[125] Bas C. van Fraassen, *The Empirical Stance* (New Haven: Yale University Press, 2002), 47–48.

[126] Van den Brink and Smits, "The Reformed Stance," 340.

[127] Van den Brink and Smits, 341. There has been considerable debate on the question whether this maxim is a modern invention or has premodern roots. Although the exact formulation may be later than often suggested, there is ample historical evidence that its content goes back to at least the early 17th century. See e.g. Fred van Lieburg, "Dynamics of Dutch Calvinism: Early Modern Programs for Further Reformation," in *Calvinism and the Making of the European Mind*, ed. Gijsbert van den Brink and Harro Höpfl (Leiden: Brill, 2014), 43–46; Theodor Mahlmann, "'Ecclesia semper reformanda': Eine historische Aufarbeitung. Neue Bearbeitung," in *Hermeneutica Sacra: Studien zur Auslegung der Heiligen Schrift im 16. und 17. Jahrhundert*, ed. Torbjörn Johansson, Robert Kolb, and Johann Anselm Steiger (Berlin: De Gruyter, 2010), 381–442.

but as a "conglomerate of doctrinal foci, attitudes, commitments et cetera"[128] while at the same time Reformed theology is not reduced to a logically closed system.

Perhaps the main strength of this approach is that it presents the Reformed tradition and its theology as a dynamic configuration that is to be seen as a specific instantiation of the *catholica doctrina*, "intensifying notions and views that are also to be found in most other ecclesial traditions."[129] Although in this way a non-reductionist and compelling account of the nature of Reformed theology can be given, it does not solve our methodological question. For this nuanced approach precludes a checklist not only for identifying a particular theologian as Reformed or not, but also for evaluating in a straightforward way which approach to a specific topic is most useful from a Reformed perspective. Thus, following the nuanced account of Reformed theology formulated by the use of the concept of *stance*, a nuanced approach to the question of which view on guidance fits best within the broader contours of Reformed theology is needed. Therefore, in this thesis a strictly analytic approach cannot be followed; instead, we first need to listen carefully to some major voices of the Reformed tradition to distinguish their commitments, emphases, and concerns in relation to guidance. When it comes to an evaluation, especially in the final chapters of this book, these emphases and concerns will be brought in and the focus will be mainly on the coherence of a view with the broader contours of Reformed theology.

Finally, the catholic intention underneath Reformed theology results in a firm methodological openness to voices of other traditions, especially when trying to engage in constructive theology. Thus, in order to propose an account of guidance from a Reformed perspective, not all conversation partners need to be strictly Reformed. Working constructively from a specific Reformed perspective can only be done from the twin convictions that

---

128 Van den Brink and Smits, "The Reformed Stance," 340.
129 Van den Brink and Smits, 346. Cf. Vroom, "On Being 'Reformed,'" 162, who describes a tradition as a "web, a dynamic configuration, in which the relative weight of insights changes somewhat all the time, depending on the context." "It is not isolated doctrines in themselves that are typical for a confessional family, but their configuration, their order and 'hierarchy'. This implies that the question of Reformed identity cannot possible be answered by enumerating some beliefs ... but by spelling out the priorities of Reformed theology"(163). Vroom commends to picture traditions as rivers, "going through different landscapes and trying to find ways through hills and fields," because this picture allows for differences within the same tradition.

being Reformed is more a task than an accomplishment[130] and that the *semper reformanda* is at its deepest level a prayer for the continuing enlightenment by the Holy Spirit in reading Scripture.[131]

1.3.3 Starting with contemporary evangelicalism
Yet, while we aim for a Reformed perspective on divine guidance, a different starting point is chosen. In order to get insight into contemporary views on and approaches of such guidance in chapter 2 we will focus on evangelical discussions of guidance. Although no neat distinction between Reformed and evangelical theology is possible, and many would identify as both Reformed and evangelical, it is in the evangelical context that much of the recent debate on guidance that we will analyze in chapter 2 has taken place.

Finding a precise definition of evangelicalism, like of Reformed theology, is notoriously difficult. In the literature on evangelicalism, David Bebbington's description ("Bebbington's Quadrilateral") of evangelicalism is employed almost universally.[132] In his *Evangelicalism in Modern Britain* (1989), Bebbington captured evangelicalism in four characteristics: conversionism, activism, biblicism, and crucicentrism. However, as Timothy Larsen has pointed out, the definition has important practical limitations for using it in scholarly studies. His main critique is that Bebbington's definition lacks the contextual information that is necessary to use it to indentify a specific Christian tradition. It is so general, that "an argument could be made that St. Francis of Assisi was an evangelical."[133]

Larsen himself sets out to formulate a "definition that is intended to locate an actual, self-identified 'evangelical' Christian community in existence," and since this is exactly what we need for our purposes, in what follows we will work with the following approach to evangelicalism:

An evangelical is:
1. an orthodox Protestant
2. who stands in the tradition of the global Christian networks arising

---

130 Cf. Hesselink, *On Being Reformed*, 8.
131 Cf. Martien E. Brinkman, "De toekomst van de Gereformeerde theologie," *Theologia Reformata* 41, no. 3 (1998): 144.
132 See e.g. the remarks of Mark A. Noll, *American Evangelical Christianity: An Introduction* (Oxford: Blackwell, 2001), 185; Derek Tidball, *Who Are the Evangelicals? Tracing the Roots of the Modern Movements* (London: Marshall Pickering, 1994), 14. For Bebbington's original formulation, see David W. Bebbington, *Evangelicalism in Modern Britain: A History from the 1730s to the 1980s* (London: Unwin Hyman, 1989), 2-17.
133 Timothy Larsen, "Defining and Locating Evangelicalism," in *The Cambridge Companion to Evangelical Theology*, ed. Timothy Larsen and Daniel J. Treier (Cambridge: Cambridge University Press, 2007), 2.

     from the eigtheenth-century revival movements associated with John Wesley and George Whitefield;
3. who has a preeminent place for the Bible in her or his Christian life as the divinely inspired, final authority in matters of faith and practice;
4. who stresses reconciliation with God through the atoning work of Jesus Christ on the cross;
5. and who stresses the work of the Holy Spirit in the life of an individual to bring about conversion and an ongoing life of fellowship with God and service to God and others, including the duty of all believers to participate in the task of proclaiming the gospel to all people.[134]

This definition, that includes the characteristics mentioned by Bebbington but provides them with some much-needed context, enables us to select the contemporary authors for our analysis in the next chapter.

1.3.4 Choice of conversation partners

Now that the concepts of Reformed theology and evangelicalism have been delineated, we are in the position to explain who will be our main conversation partners throughout this book, what functions they serve, and how we approach their writings.

In our investigation of contemporary evangelical authors in chapter 2, the main aim is to procure an overview of the main approaches to divine guidance. Hence, the authors discussed in that chapter will be studied exclusively for their views on guidance and only a minimal amount of background will be provided. Their function in the overall argument is to delineate the field and provide insight into the theological issues at stake underneath their positions on guidance.

The most important decision is made in the way I decided to interact with the Reformed tradition. As a complete historical overview of positions on guidance is both impossible within the aims of this book and would lead to brief and shallow treatments of most theologians involved, we chose to study two main Reformed voices more in depth and use their thinking, and especially their theological emphases and concerns, as important reference points for the constructive proposal that will be formulated in the final chapter. For this purpose, I decided to investigate the writings of John Calvin and Jonathan Edwards. For several reasons these authors were considered most suitable in helping to meet the aims of this book. In the first place, they are considered not only as key Reformed theologians, but are also highly regarded in most of contempary evangelicalism. Second, they

---

[134] Larsen, 1. See his chapter for a further elaboration of this definition.

have developed their thought in different times and theological contexts, enabling us to compare their views and extract the core ideas. Third, in their respective contexts, both theologians devoted a lot of attention to the work of the Holy Spirit and had to relate themselves to enthusiast movements in a way that was both appreciative and critical. As such, they are considered as our primary conversation partners throughout this book and their views on questions related to guidance are studied in depth through an analysis of their writings in chapters 3 and 4. Clearly, more theologians could have been chosen for equally valid reasons. In a number of places we point to interesting insights from other theologians, but extended interaction with their thought on the possibility and nature of guidance is not possible within this volume.

After our interaction with contemporary evangelicalism and both Calvin and Edwards, in chapter 5 we will provide the contours of a Reformed approach to divine guidance and the key concepts of such an approach. This proposal will be further developed in the final chapter. As we elaborate on the key concepts in interaction with contemporary theology, our interlocutors will not be selected *a priori* based upon their theological convictions, but based upon the question whether their views on the concepts we discuss proves helpful for our own constructive proposal. Hence, our interaction with a number of theologians in the final chapter will necessarily be more tentative and eclectic than our investigation of the writings of Calvin and Edwards. Here, the catholic intention of Reformed theology as I approach it will be shown in the way we try to learn from theologians across the theological spectrum.

1.3.5 Research question
In light of the aims formulated before and our considerations on the nature of Reformed theology, evangelicalism, and the appropriate conversation partners to meet our goals, in this study we set out to answer the following main question:

> *How can the contemporary evangelical focus on the notion of divine guidance be incorporated in a Reformed theological account of the Christian life as informed by the writings of John Calvin and Jonathan Edwards?*

In order to answer this complex question, we need to answer the following sub-questions:

(1) Which different approaches to divine guidance can be found in contemporary evangelical literature?

(2) What theological emphases and concerns can be found in John Calvin's writings that influence his views on divine guidance?
(3) What theological emphases and concerns can be found in Jonathan Edwards's writings that influence his views on divine guidance?
(4) Given the views found in answer to (1) and the concerns and emphases found in answer to (2) and (3), which view on divine guidance would be most coherent within the overall contours of Reformed theology?
(5) What areas need to be further developed in order to formulate a robust contemporary account of divine guidance from a Reformed perspective?

Questions 1, 2, and 3 will be discussed in Chapters 2, 3, and 4 respectively. The preliminary conclusion sought after in question 4 will be presented in the *intermediate conclusion* of chapter 5, while chapter 6 is devoted to answering question 5, and with it, the main research question. Given the nature of the topic and our argumentation this final chapter will have the nature of a theological proposal based upon coherence with the concerns and emphases underlying Reformed theology.

1.4 Outline of the argument of the dissertation
In the preceding sections, I have introduced the topic and aims of this book, the relevant research that has already been done, and the methodological choices made. Before turning to the research itself, in this section a brief outline will be given of what follows in the next chapters.

In chapter 2 we will start with the first element of this research project, an analysis of the approaches to divine guidance in contemporary evangelicalism. In evangelical literature, we find an extensive discussion of the nature and means of divine guidance that displays a number of divergent perspectives. Based upon a careful reading of popular books published between 1980 and 2010, a typology of guidance is introduced that consists of three models: (1) guidance is conceived primarily as an act of God in which he provides *information* that enables the believer to find 'the will of God'; (2) guidance takes place through believers having an *intimate* relationship with God that enables them to become increasingly attuned to the inner voice of the Spirit and the *intimations* given in the heart; (3) God does not guide believers by pointing them to a concrete decision that equals 'the will of God,' but transforms them in such a way that they receive wisdom to make good decisions.

In chapters 3 and 4, we turn to the writings of Calvin and Edwards armed with the theological questions derived from the various views of guidance. As a result, in these chapters we focus on issues related to divine providence, the concept of vocation, the inner guidance of the Holy Spirit, and, in the case of Edwards, of virtue and transformation. With regard to providence, we investigate their views on providence in general with a focus on the place of human beings in divine providence, the distinction between the various aspects of God's will, and the practical consequences in daily life of believing in divine providence. With regard to vocation our focus will be on the questions what vocations are and how vocations are to be discerned according to Calvin and Edwards. In discussing the guidance of the Spirit we move to the more explicit discussions of guidance in the works of both authors. Both chapters are concluded with an account of how both Calvin and Edwards reflected on questions of guidance with regard to their personal biography.

In the brief fifth chapter, we will combine the main elements of on the one hand chapter 2 with its typology of guidance, and on the other hand the chapters on Calvin and Edwards in order to formulate an intermediate conclusion. There, it will be argued that the logical starting point for a Reformed approach of guidance is the view that conceives of guidance primarily as taking place through transformation that results in wisdom. In a series of theses the basics of this approach are sketched. These theses also point to concepts crucial to a Reformed account of guidance.

Finally, in the sixth chapter, the theses and their key concepts will be developed into a more extensive account of guidance. Here, the concepts of vocation, wisdom, discernment, transformation, the role of the Christian community, and the involvement of the Holy Spirit will be discussed in interaction with a number of different conversation partners.

CHAPTER 2:
A Typology of Divine Guidance in Contemporary Evangelicalism

2.1 Introduction

As explained in the previous chapter, a logical starting point for an investigation of divine guidance is the discussion on such guidance in contemporary evangelicalism and the insight into the various positions such an analysis yields. Therefore, in this chapter we will analyze the body of popular evangelical literature on divine guidance and the will of God as a starting point for our argument in the next chapters.

We start with an introduction of the literature we investigate and the method with which we approach it (§2.2), followed by a detailed analysis of the books on guidance published between 1980 and 2010 (§2.3-2.5). Based upon this analysis, we will propose a typology of models of guidance encountered in contemporary evangelicalism (§2.6), and consider the implications for our proceedings in the next chapters (§2.7).

2.2 Body of Literature and Methodological Approach

2.2.1 Introduction

In this section, the body of literature under analysis will be introduced (2.2.2), and I will explain the criteria for selecting the exact books to be analyzed (2.2.3). Furthermore, I will discuss which questions will be asked of the books included in our analysis (2.2.4). Following upon that, we will briefly look into evangelical literature on guidance published before 1980 (2.2.5) and the historical and socio-cultural background behind the emergence of the topic (2.2.6). This section will be closed by a number of remarks on biblical material and specific terminology that is needed to understand the literature discussed in the coming sections (2.2.7).

2.2.2 Body of literature

In the introductory chapter it was shown that there is an enormous amount of interest in divine guidance within Christian spirituality. This is especially true for the evangelical world. In 1968, Joseph Bayly wrote:

> If there is a serious concern among Christian students today, it is for guidance. Holiness may have been the passion of another generation's Christian young men and women. Or soul winning. Or evangelizing the world. But not today. Today the theme is getting to know the will of God.[1]

Bayly is not alone in noting this, for remarks of the same kind can be found in many of the books on guidance and the will of God.[2] One could even argue that a focus on guidance functions as one of the distinctive marks of contemporary evangelicalism.[3]

That it is indeed a prominent and ongoing concern is shown especially in the number of books devoted to the questions of divine guidance and 'finding' the will of God. Douglas Huffman provides an extensive bibliography of almost 100 books written with divine guidance as their main topic[4] and, as shown in the literature discussed later in this chapter, his list could have been considerably extended.[5] Most of the books on the topic have been published since the beginning of the 20th century.

2.2.3 Selection of books for analysis
Because of the enormous amount of books available, the following restrictions are used in selecting the books for our analysis. In the first place, we only discuss books that were written originally in English. Given the (evangelical) context in which most of the discussion takes place, this is not a major restriction and will presumably not influence the outcomes of the research in a profound way.[6] Secondly, the focus is on contributions

---

1 Joseph Bayly, *Essays on Guidance* (Chicago: Inter-Varsity Press, 1968), preface.
2 See e.g. Morris Ashcraft, *The Will of God* (Nashville: Broadman Press, 1980), 11; Charles W. Shepson, *How to Know God's Will: Divine Direction for the Road Map of Life* (Beaverlodge: Horizon House, 1981), 16; Haddon W. Robinson, *Decision-Making by the Book: How to Choose Wisely in an Age of Options* (Grand Rapids: Discovery House, 1991), 12. Many other authors make similar remarks in the first pages of their books.
3 Cf. Maarten Wisse in his description of evangelical Christianity in his *Zo zou je kunnen geloven* (Franeker: Van Wijnen, 2013), 60–61.
4 Douglas S. Huffman, ed., *How Then Should We Choose? Three Views on God's Will and Decision Making* (Grand Rapids: Kregel Publications, 2009), 251–56. Huffman's categorized bibliography is an invaluable source for the study of the discussion, but it has two important drawbacks. The first is that it is far from complete (see e.g. the next note), the second and perhaps more important one is that Huffman is inconsistent in his choice of the various editions of books. That is, some are listed in their first edition, others in later editions. In this way, no clear picture of the development of the discussion over time can be established.
5 A brief comparison of Huffman's bibliography with section 2.4 shows that for example the books of Sanders (§2.4.6), Jensen and Payne (§2.4.7), Masters (§2.4.10), Hayford (§2.4.13), Adams (§2.4.14) and Elliff (§2.4.17) are absent from his list.
6 E.g., only a handful of books on the topic were written in Dutch, but quite a few of the English books have been translated into Dutch. See e.g. Packer (*De belofte van de Herder*), Waltke (*Gods wil ontdekken*) and Willard (*God verstaan*). The same seems to apply to for example the German, in which a few original German books exist, but here again most

from evangelical authors. Given the way we approach evangelicalism (§1.3.3), the literature on for example Ignatian spirituality and discernment will not be discussed separately, although it will feature in the analysis of some writers influenced by it.[7] Literature from an expressedly charismatic background is also beyond the scope of our research, for there the modus of divine guidance takes a different shape.[8] In the third place, we decided to analyze only the books that have divine guidance, the will of God, and Christian decision-making as their main topic. Thus, separate articles or book chapters will be referred to when appropriate, but will not get independent discussion.

From the resulting selection of books those published between 1980 and 2010 will be investigated and discussed in detail. As we will see, in 1980 the book by Friesen and Maxson, *Decision Making and the Will of God,* was published. As the first book that positioned itself explicitly over against what the authors called the "traditional view,"[9] it started a discussion that still continues. Huffman describes the effect of the book as causing "a significant stir among evangelicals"[10] and the editor of *Eternity* wrote of a 'War over wisdom'.[11] The year 2010 is chosen as the *terminus ad quem* not only for practical reasons, but also because of the publication of another important book in 2009. Edited by Douglas Huffman, the book

---

books are translations from the English, e.g. Friesen (*Hilfe, ich muss mich entscheiden...*), Petty (*Mein Leben - Sein Plan*) and Blackaby, Blackaby and King (*Gott erfahren*). Examples of books written originally in Dutch are amongst others J.J. Grandia, *Levensleiding: hoe God het leven leidt* (Kampen: De Groot Goudriaan, 1998); Pieter van Kampen, *Door Zijn hand: Gods leiding in ons leven* (Kampen: Kok Voorhoeve, 1993); Wim Markus, *Multiple Choice? Over Gods leiding en jouw leven* (Zoetermeer: Jes! / Boekencentrum, 2014). For German books, see e.g. Thomas Schirrmacher, *Wie erkenne ich den Willen Gottes: Führungsmystik auf dem Prüfstand* (Hamburg: Reformatorischer Verlag Beese, 2001); Eberhard Mühlan, *Führung durch den Heiligen Geist: Warum wir sie brauchen; Wie wir sie erleben* (Erzhausen: Leuchter Edition GmbH, 2004).

7 Examples of books advocating the Ignatian approach are Thomas Dubay, *Authenticity: A Biblical Theology of Discernment* (San Francisco: Ignatius Press, 1977); John J. English, *Spiritual Freedom: From an Experience of the Ignatian Exercises to the Art of Spiritual Guidance* (Chicago: Loyola University Press, 1995); Pierre Wolff, *Discernment: The Art of Choosing Well. Based on Ignatian Spirituality* (Liguori: Liguori Publications, 2003).

8 The most important difference is that in charismatic accounts of guidance the entire process is much more immediate and (as a result) the message needs less discernment. See for example Jack Deere, *Surprised by the Voice of God: How God Speaks Today through Prophecies, Dreams, and Visions* (Grand Rapids: Zondervan, 1996). However, in Pentecostal circles awareness is also rising for the problematic aspects of the uncritical acceptance of claims to divine guidance. See for an interesting attempt to point in the right direction Parker, *Led by the Spirit*.

9 Garry Friesen and J. Robin Maxson, *Decision Making and the Will of God* (Colorado Springs: Multnomah Publishers, 1980), 13.

10 Huffman, *How Then Should We Choose?*, 12.

11 See 'The War over Wisdom: What is God's Way for Finding God's Will', *Eternity,* June 1986, 37-38, as referenced by Kovach, "Toward a Theology of Guidance," 29, note 99.

How Then Should We Choose? contains the first explicit discussion of the topic between proponents of the distinct views that evolved since 1980.

The books that meet all these conditions will be discussed in the following sections, where each section will cover a decade. For the period 1980-89 eleven books will be discussed, for 1990-99 sixteen books, and for the period 2000-2010 twelve books. The books will be discussed in chronological order so as to provide an overview of the development of the discussion. Given the nature of the books, the authors involved, and the range of publishers interested in this type of literature, absolute exhaustiveness cannot be guaranteed; however, we believe to present a fairly complete representation that is accurate enough to draw conclusions from.[12]

2.2.4 Methodological approach
In order to analyze the contents of the selected literature in a systematic way, the following questions will guide us in our reading and discussion of the books. In answering those, a detailed picture of the literature will emerge that focuses on the relevant aspects of the literature.

Author
1. What is the (theological, professional, ecclesial) background of the author and does this background play an explicit role in the book?

---

[12] For various reasons the following types of books have been excluded from the analysis:
Workbooks that only ask questions from the readers and do not give (enough) content of their own to extract a sufficiently elaborated view. Examples of this kind of book would be Warren Myers and Ruth Myers, *Discovering God's Will: A Study and Meditation on How to Experience God's Good Plan for You* (Colorado Springs: NavPress, 1980); and Donald Baker, *Decisions, Seeking God's Guidance: 10 Studies for Individuals or Groups* (Downers Grove: InterVarsity Press, 2001).
Short books that consist more of a list of Bible texts than of distinct content. Example: Mark Water, *Knowing God's Will Made Easier* (Peabody: Hendrickson, 1998).
Books that cover a wide terrain of (psychological) issues under the header of 'the will of God'. Examples are the books of Ben Campbell Johnson, notably Ben Campbell Johnson, *To Will God's Will: Beginning the Journey* (Louisville: Westminster John Knox Press, 1987); Ben Campbell Johnson, *To Pray God's Will: Continuing the Journey* (Louisville: Westminster John Knox Press, 1987); Ben Campbell Johnson, *Discerning God's Will* (Louisville: Westminster John Knox Press, 1990).
Books that present general advice and wisdom to young believers, e.g. James C. Dobson, *Life on the Edge: The Next Generation's Guide to a Meaningful Future* (Carol Stream: Tyndale, 1995).
Books that deal with the issues of calling and vocation in a way that is not explicitly focused on guidance and the will of God. Here examples would be Os Guinness, *The Call: Finding and Fulfilling the Central Purpose of Your Life* (Nashville: W Publishing Group, 1998); Christine Sine and Tom Sine, *Living on Purpose: Finding God's Best for Your Life* (Grand Rapids: Baker Books, 2002).

The Will of God
2. Does the author define what he/she means by 'the will of God' or does he/she take the meaning for granted?
3. Does the author believe that there is a specific will of God that believers can/need to find out?
4. If so, how important is it for believers to 'find' this will of God?
5. Is the author only concerned about the individual and the will of God or is the question placed within a more comprehensive theological framework? If so, how?

Praxis
6. What decision-making practices does the author prescribe and how are those related to the view on the will of God?
7. Following the prescribed practices, is absolute certainty possible and necessary?

Argument
8. Does the author show that she/he is aware of other views on the topic of divine guidance and the will of God?
9. Which Biblical texts are pivotal for the author's argument?
10. Does the author engage with (a) theological tradition? If so, which tradition and what is its function in the argument?
11. To what extent does the author use doctrinal concepts (e.g. providence)?

Contribution
12. Does the author add unique insights or contributions to the discussion?

Using these questions, the books will be discussed in three separate chapters according to their initial publication date. This will be done in chronological order. In the presentation of the various books, we will largely follow the categories used above, first introducing the book and its author(s), followed by a discussion of its view on the will of God. After that, the prescribed praxis, the argumentation, and the specific contribution of the book to the debate will be examined. However, before we turn to this analysis, a few introductory questions with regard to the literature up to 1980 will be addressed.

2.2.5 Evangelical literature on guidance before 1980
The current flood of books and other materials on 'finding the will of

God' started to appear in the last quarter of the 19th century. As stated by Douglas Huffman, it was "after George Müller (1805-1898) that the 'how-to' approaches began to multiply."[13] Müller, evangelist and director of a famous orphanage in Bristol, wrote what indeed seems to be one of the first lists of steps in finding the will of God under the title "How I Ascertain the Will of God".

1. I seek at the beginning to get my heart into such a state that it has no will of its own in regard to a given matter. Nine-tenths of the trouble with people is just here. Nine-tenths of the difficulties are overcome when our hearts are ready to do the Lord's will, whatever it may be. When one is truly in this state, it is usually but a little way to the knowledge of what His will is.
2. Having done this, I do not leave the result to feeling or simple impression. If I do so, I make myself liable to great delusions.
3. I seek the will of the Spirit of God through, or in connection with, the Word of God. The Spirit and the Word must be combined. If I look to the Spirit alone without the Word I lay myself open to great delusions also. If the Holy Ghost guides us at all, He will do it according to the Scriptures and never contrary to them.
4. Next I take into account providential circumstances. These often plainly indicate God's will in connection with His Word and Spirit.
5. I ask God in prayer to reveal His will to me aright.
6. Thus, through prayer to God, the study of the Word, and reflection, I come to deliberate judgment according to the best of my ability and knowledge, and if my mind is thus at peace, and continues so after two or three more petitions, I proceed accordingly.
    In trivial matters, and in transactions involving most important issues, I have found this method always effective.[14]

Müller's list presumably had a major influence because of the remarkable story of his life and work.[15] It already contains many of the basic elements

---

13 Huffman, *How Then Should We Choose?*, 22.
14 A.E.C. Brooks, *Answers to Prayer from George Müller's Narratives* (Chicago: Moody Press, 1897), 6.
15 Known especially from his autobiography, George F. Müller, *Autobiography of George Müller, or, A Million and a Half in Answer to Prayer* (London: Pickering & Inglis, 1905). The most recent full edition is George F. Müller, *Autobiography of George Müller: A Million and a Half in Answer to Prayer*, Reprint Edition (Denton: Westminster Literature Resources, 2003). The biography most used is Arthur T. Pierson, *George Müller of Bristol and His Witness to a Prayer-Hearing God* (Grand Rapids: Kregel Publications, 1999). Originally published as "Authorized Memoir" (Old Tappa: Fleming H. Revell, 1899).

of what would grow into a broadly accepted view: The surrender of the own will (step 1), the importance of prayer and Bible reading (steps 5 and 3, respectively), the idea that God speaks plainly through circumstances (4), and the decisive function of inner peace (6). It is telling that Müller uses the word 'method' and underlines its applicability in both trivial matters and important issues.

The first books on the issue appear around the turn of the century by authors that are closely related to the Keswick or Higher Life Movement. Examples are *The Secret of Guidance* by Frederick B. Meyer and *Thy Will be Done* by Andrew Murray.[16] In this sense it seems justified that Garry Friesen points to the Keswick Movement as one of the main sources of the 'traditional view' on guidance, although he does not give any proof of it.[17] Those early books are written in the same spirit as the list of steps Müller provided. Meyer for example tries to give "practical directions in order to be led into the mind of God" (4). The key of his view is that "God's impressions within and His word without are always corroborated by His Providence around, and we should quietly wait until these three focus into one point" (7). And again: circumstances are to us "an infallible indication of God's will when they concur with the inward promptings of the Spirit and with the Word of God" (8). Those three – the Word, the inward prompting, and outward circumstances – are "God's three witnesses" (7). Andrew Murray, a South-African revivalist, is less focused on the method of discerning the will of God. However, in his 30 meditations on texts about the will of God (*Thy Will be Done*) the underlying spirituality is present on every page. For example, he writes that "the one thing needful for a Christian is that he live in the will of God" (preface), that this is "the very essence of true religion" (Ch.13) and that "the believer who would truly live to the will of God in all things, will deeply feel the need of a divine guidance, leading him day by day in the path and the steps of our Lord Jesus" (Ch.28).[18]

---

16 F.B. Meyer, *The Secret of Guidance* (Chicago: Fleming H. Revell, 1896); Andrew Murray, *Thy Will Be Done* (Chicago: Fleming H. Revell, 1900).
17 Garry Friesen, "Walking in Wisdom: The Wisdom View," in *How Then Should We Choose: Three Views on God's Will and Decision Making* (Grand Rapids: Kregel Publications, 2009), 105. "What I call the traditional view of guidance was an integral part of the theological culture of the Keswick Movement, which was very influential in England and America. As Keswick-trained missionaries spread across the globe, this view of guidance became part of the evangelical tradition through their teaching."
18 Although Murray is the better-known theologian of the two, it seems that Meyer's practical methodological remarks about finding the will of God have had a bigger impact on the discussions on the will of God and divine guidance than the work of Murray. Meyer is cited in numerous later books on the subject, see e.g. Robert Jeffress, *Hearing the Master's Voice: The Comfort and Confidence of Knowing God's Will* (Colorado Springs: WaterBrook Press, 2001), 3; Lloyd John Ogilvie, *Discovering God's Will in Your Life* (Eugene: Harvest House

After those first books not much new books on the subject were published in the first quarter of the 20th century.[19] However, the interest in divine guidance and finding the will of God seems to have grown in the period up to World War II under the influence of the growing charismatic movement.[20] It is only after the end of World War II that the number of books on divine guidance suddenly begins to multiply.[21] In 1952, the four spiritual laws of the Campus Crusade for Christ were formulated, with the first law stating "God loves you and has a wonderful plan for your life."[22] The following period, from 1960 until 1980, is especially rich in contributions, with an average of more than one book per year.[23] Although some critical books appear in this period[24] the general picture is still the one provided already by Müller and Meyer: if we perform certain

---

Publishers, 1982), 69; Dallas Willard, *Hearing God: Developing a Conversational Relationship with God* (Downers Grove: InterVarsity Press, 1999), 14. Views similar to those of Müller, Meyer, and Murray can be found in the writings of their contemporaries and allies G. Campbell Morgan and R.A. Torrey. See esp. the epilogue to G. Campbell Morgan, *God's Perfect Will* (London: Morgan and Scott, 1901); and ch. 15 of R.A. Torrey, *How to Succeed in the Christian Life* (New York: Fleming H. Revell, 1906).

19 An example of a book published in this period is Henry B. Wright, *The Will of God and a Man's Life Work* (New York: Association Press, 1909).

20 Se e.g. James I. Packer and Carolyn Nystrom, *Guard Us, Guide Us: Divine Leading in Life's Decisions* (Grand Rapids: Baker Books, 2008), 14–15.

21 Examples include S. Maxwell Coder, *God's Will for Your Life* (Chicago: Moody Press, 1946); G. H. Lang, *Divine Guidance: Its Reality, Methods, Conditions* (Rushden: Stanley Hunt, 1947); Christian G. Weiss, *The Perfect Will of God* (Lincoln: Good News Broadcasting Association, 1950); Alan Redpath, *Getting to Know the Will of God* (Downers Grove: Inter-Varsity Press, 1954). It is difficult to establish in how far this was the result of an increased interest in the topic of guidance and in how far of the general rise in book publications.

22 See the site of Cru, the former Campus Crusade for Christ: http://www.crustore.org/fourlawseng.htm (accessed 11-09-2014). The pamphlet containing those laws was distributed more than 2.5 billion times in total until 2013. The other three 'laws' focus on sin and the need of a personal faith in Jesus Christ in order to share in this divine plan.

23 For the period 1960-1970, examples are Fred H. Wight, *The Secret of Divine Guidance* (Los Angeles: Cowman, 1960); Marion H. Nelson, *How to Know God's Will* (Chicago: Moody Press, 1963); T. B. Maston, *God's Will and Your Life* (Nashville: Broadman Press, 1964); Newman R. McLarry, *His Good and Perfect Will* (Nashville: Broadman Press, 1965); J. Sidlow Baxter, *Does God Still Guide? Or, More Fully, What Are the Essentials of Guidance and Growth in the Christian Life?* (London: Marshall, Morgan & Scott, 1968); Bayly, *Essays on Guidance*. The years 1970-1980 are especially full of contributions, with 1976 and 1977 (both 5 books) as peaks. Examples are Elisabeth Elliot, *God's Guidance: Finding His Will for Your Life* (Grand Rapids: Revell, 1973); Kenneth E. Hagin, *How You Can Know the Will of God* (Tulsa: Kenneth Hagin Evangelistic Association, 1974); George Sweeting, *How to Discover the Will of God* (Chicago: Moody Press, 1975); J. Grant Howard, *Knowing God's Will and Doing It* (Grand Rapids: Zondervan, 1976); Charles G. Coleman, *Divine Guidance: That Voice Behind You* (Neptune: Loizeaux Brothers, 1977).

24 See e.g. John MacArthur, *Found: God's Will. Find the Direction and Purpose God Wants for Your Life* (Colorado Springs: David C. Cook, 1977); Oliver R. Barclay, *Guidance: What the Bible Says about Knowing God's Will* (Downers Grove: Inter-Varsity Press, 1978).

steps and pay close attention to the combination of 'signs' from God, we will eventually succeed in finding the will of God.

We will see in the following sections how this picture has changed since 1980, but for now we pause to reflect on one additional question: Why is it that so many people are obsessed with this question of decision-making and the will of God? Is this unique for our time, and if so, why?

2.2.6 Historical and socio-cultural backgrounds

Is this focus on divine guidance among contemporary evangelicals unique? A number of authors do indeed argue so and use this as a means to criticize the widespread blueprint-approach to guidance.[25] Although we cannot deny that there are at least unique elements to it, however, the overview of the previous chapter (esp. §1.2.5) points out that religion and forms of divination are almost inseparable. Research into the history of enthusiasm, divination, and puritanism in early modern England are just the most prominent examples of this pattern. What those examples make clear is that thinking in terms of a specific and knowable divine will is by no means an unusual historical phenomenon. Yet, two features of the contemporary discussion stand out as being more or less new.

First, the contemporary focus on following a certain method to 'find' the will of God seems distinctive. In many cases the heuristic question ('How do I find God's will?') is answered in an almost algorithmic fashion. This approach stands in contrast to the more reticent approach in which a strong belief in God's guidance was often complemented by the acceptance of mystery with regard to the method of his guidance.[26] Second, the idea of finding the will of God is now also widely propagated by members of the clergy. Whereas in former times many pastors and theologians opposed the idea or at least had an ambivalent attitude towards it,[27] nowadays pastors and church leaders are the authors of books recommending the various practices.[28]

Although the rise in interest for the idea of divine guidance and decision making is obviously tied in a myriad of ways to major historical, cultural

---

25 Packer and Nystrom, *Guard Us, Guide Us*, 14; Friesen, "Walking in Wisdom," 105; James C. Petty, *Step by Step: Divine Guidance for Ordinary Christians* (Phillipsburg: P&R Publishing, 1999), 29.
26 Think e.g. of the famous puritan hymn by William Cowper, *God moves in a mysterious way*...
27 See the remarks on this topic in Walsham, *Providence in Early Modern England*, 179–80.
28 As we will see later on, many of the books we analyze in this chapter are written by pastors or seminary professors.

and sociological changes that have taken place over the last two centuries (see also §1.1.3), this aspect is largely neglected in the popular literature on the theme. Only James Petty devotes some pages to this aspect of the topic, whereas other authors only mention theological reasons or movements.[29] Petty sees a relationship between the upcoming industrialization of Western society and the emphasis on making choices according to the will of God. He shows how the number of important decisions and the pace in which they appear have increased with the number of options available to many people today.[30] He combines this general idea of industrialization with the related issues of changes in the world of work, distribution of income, and views on morality, to conclude that if ever there was a time in which people yearned for guidance, it is our time.

We agree with Petty that no single generation throughout the history of humanity has had so many different options for each of life's major and minor choices as our generation. Technology, globalization, and mass media have not only contributed to *information* on all possible options, but also to their *availability*. This enormous growth in options from the 19th century onwards as a result of the industrialization has had a huge impact on consumer behavior, resulting in a continual quest for the newest, best, and most special products. That this development does have a serious downside can be seen in the terminology that is introduced for this specific problem: for example the English 'paradox of choice',[31] the German 'Qual der Wahl', and the Dutch 'keuzestress'.[32] With the growth of our set of possibilities, the number of decisions and the accompanying responsibility has also dramatically increased. It is only reasonable to assume that this has led to an increased awareness among Christians for the need of guidance in making important decisions.

A second, closely related phenomenon influencing the focus on guidance is modern individualism. One of the results of this process is the idea that our life in some way must 'count', that in order to have a good and meaningful life we must do our best to 'get out what is in it', and that this is an individual process in which we do not follow the mass. This emphasis has a tendency to increase the weight of every single decision to be made. The process of individualization has also decreased the influence

---

29 Petty, *Step by Step*, 19-24.
30 Petty, *Step by Step*, 20-21.
31 See e.g. Barry Schwartz, *The Paradox of Choice: Why More is Less* (New York: Harper Collins, 2004) for an extensive treatment of this phenomenon.
32 One is also reminded of Sartre's frequent remark that human beings are "condemned to be free." See e.g. Jean-Paul Sartre, *Being and Nothingness: A Phenomenological Essay on Ontology*, trans. Hazel E. Barnes (New York: Washington Square Press, 1992), 439.

of traditions, frames of thought, and collective lifestyles on our decision-making processes.[33]

Although these, and other, developments must not be used to downplay the importance of the question of divine guidance, they can at least be used to explain the growth in interest the question has received over the past decades.

2.2.7 Key biblical material and terminology of the discussion
In order to be able to present our analysis of the books in the next section as concisely as possible, here the most commonly used Biblical material and the key terminology featuring in the literature will be introduced.

In the contributions on the will of God, a number of biblical texts frequently reoccur. Four groups of texts stand out.[34] First, the narrative of Acts is used more than any other part of the Bible. From it, the episode from Acts 16 in which Paul and his companions 'were denied by the Spirit' to go into some areas, and subsequently were guided towards Macedonia through a dream, is the most important. Also prominent are Paul's accounts of his conversion and especially his question "What shall I do, Lord?" (22:10).

Second, references to the words 'the will of God' from the New Testament letters are foundational for the discussion about divine guidance. Here, not only the letter openings, in which especially Paul often refers to himself as apostle 'according to the will of God', but also some other texts occur frequently. These include especially Rom. 12:1-2, Eph. 5:17, Col. 1:9 and 4:12. Hebr. 10:36 is also used occasionally.

Third, a number of Old Testament texts contain a promise of guidance. Examples of texts of this kind that are frequently used in the discussion are Ps. 32:8, Ps. 48:14, Prov. 3:5-6 and Prov. 16:9. Some other texts that are less clear but are used to make a similar point are Isa. 30:20-21 and Jer. 29:11.

Fourth, some New Testaments texts on being led by the Spirit are frequently used. Primarily those include Rom. 8:14 and Gal. 5:18, but John 16:12-14 is also regularly cited.

A number of other (independent) texts that are used to add further support to the various views, or are debated in the discussion, include

---
33 Ulrich Beck, *Risk Society: Towards a New Modernity*, trans. Mark Ritter (London: Sage, 1992) has worked out this point since the first publication from his book in 1986 in German.
34 The most complete discussion of the Biblical material is presented by Garry Friesen, *Decision Making and the Will of God*, especially chapters 3, 4, and 7.

Col. 3:15 and Phil. 4:7 on the peace of Christ and the peace of God, and John 10:27, where Jesus states that 'His sheep hear his voice'.

Besides, the narrative parts of the Old Testament play a major, and in some cases even decisive, role. Frequent examples referred to are the stories of Abraham, Moses, Gideon, and David. On the other hand, some passages that could be expected to play an important role in the debate are remarkably absent or at least under-represented. Most notably, these are the struggle of Jesus in the garden of Gethsemane (e.g. Mt. 26:36-46), the third petition of the Lord's prayer, and the *conditio Jacobi* from James 4:13-15.

Evangelical writing on the will of God and divine guidance is characterized by a jargon that is specific for this type of literature. Seven important examples will be briefly introduced.

Fleecing: a term based upon the story of Gideon from Judges 6, points to the practice of setting 'tests' for God that enable him to confirm a certain course of action. This practice is rejected almost unanimously, although there are some exceptions.

The 'center' of God's will: Many authors write about the will of God in spatial terms, that is, as something to be 'in' or 'out'. As a result of this spatial focus, several authors further specify the ultimate aim of the Christian life as living in 'the center' of God's will. What exactly is meant by those words is never specified.

Nudges: One of the most frequent ways the Spirit is said to be involved in the process of guidance is by giving 'nudges': unspecified inner stimuli to act in a certain way.

The still small voice of God: this phrase, based upon the story of Elijah in 1 Kings 19 (especially verse 12), describes the inner voice of God in the believer that the believer learns to recognize by living in close fellowship with God.

Sortes: This term refers to what many authors describe as 'Bible picking': the practice of randomly opening the Bible and see which text God 'gives' the believer. Most authors reject the practice.

'Plan B': A number of authors believe that God's will can be 'missed'. If this happens with regard to a major life issue, the believer will end up in God's 'plan B', meaning that the ultimate plan of God is unattainable and the believer must make the best of the given situation.

Open and closed doors: Paul occasionally writes about doors opened for him by God (e.g. 1 Cor. 16:9). In the literature on divine guidance open and closed doors are presented as one of the main ways God guides: By providing unexpected opportunities ('open doors') or by restricting the options where necessary, thus 'closing doors'.

2.3 Analysis of Evangelical Literature 1980-1989

2.3.1 Introduction
In this section the evangelical literature on the will of God, divine guidance, and decision-making that was published between 1980 and 1989 will be discussed according to the themes introduced in the previous chapter (see esp. §2.2.4). Eleven authors and their books will be discussed in sections 2.3.2-2.3.12. The section will be closed by an evaluative section (§2.3.13), in which we will make some preliminary observations about the developments within this period.

2.3.2 Hosier
Hosier, Helen K. *How to Know When God Speaks*. Irvine: Harvest House Publishers, 1980.[35]

Author - Hosier (1928), a free-lance writer who authored more than fifty books, has written a number of introductory biographies of well-known Christians and furthermore has mostly written on practical issues.

Will of God - Hosier is disappointed with the loose ways believers often speak about God's messages to them, leading some to doubt God's speech entirely (11). Therefore, she sets out to answer the question 'How do we know it is God who is speaking?' Given this specific concern, the underlying question whether God still speaks and guides into his will is not discussed at all, but rather presupposed. The idea of a 'will of God' is never defined, but the many examples in the book indicate that Hosier thinks of a detailed plan of God that he actively communicates to believers. No blueprint should be expected, but "God's plan for you is like a scroll which reveals His will bit by bit as the scroll is unrolled" (107). Yet, it is clear that the scroll is already fully written. No attempt is made to see individual lives within a bigger story or perspective.

Praxis - Hosier's focus is largely on the praxis of hearing God. She is a prototype of the view prominent since George Müller. That is, she starts with the Bible (24) and prayer and at the end of her book emphasizes those two again (172), but also lists numerous other ways God speaks, concluding that "God has his ways of getting our attention" (88). Those

---

[35] In this and the following sections we will refer to the relevant page number of the book under discussion between brackets in the text.

other means include circumstances (24), dreams and visions (25), counsel of other Christians (46), and the use of our mind (72). Hosier never gives a list of steps to be applied, but prominence throughout the book goes to the inner 'nudges' of the Spirit and to peace in the heart: "As people become spiritualized more and more ... the guidance becomes inner. The inner nature is tuned to listen to God, to hear the divine whisper within" (18). Hosier warns that "disregarding inner nudges can be costly" (95) and that if there is no peace in making a decision, God is warning (69). Closely related to the need for inner peace is the admonition to wait on the Lord until such peace arrives (135).

Argument - The book does not contain a well-structured argument. Many points are repeated in several chapters and as a result of the many stories included in the book it has a fragmentary and anecdotal character. Hosier nowhere explicitly places herself within a discussion and only uses other authors to support her own points. Besides a number of quotes from Matthew Henry and one from Augustine the theological tradition plays no role in the book. The Biblical places that are pivotal are the well-known verses from Acts, the Psalms, Romans and Isaiah 30:21 (see §2.2.7).

Contribution – Hosier has asked a number of Christian leaders to share their stories and these are referred to throughout the book. This way, the book gives insight into the widespread acceptance of her approach to guidance.

2.3.3 Friesen
Garry Friesen and J. Robin Maxson, *Decision Making and the Will of God*, Colorado Springs: Multnomah Books, 1980.[36]

Author - The publication of *Decision Making and the Will of God* caused a stir in the evangelical world. Friesen was a teacher at Multnomah Bible College (Portland, Oregon) since 1976. In 2013 he moved to Kigali, Rwanda, to teach at Africa College of Theology. He is mainly known for this book. Friesen is ordained to preach in North American Baptist churches.

---

36 For this section we used to 25th anniversary edition of 2004, Garry Friesen and J. Robin Maxson, *Decision Making and the Will of God: 25th Anniversary Edition* (Colorado Springs: Multnomah Books, 2004). We will refer to this book as the book of Friesen from now on, although officially J. Robin Maxson is listed as co-author. The book is written in first person and based on the research done by Friesen. In the literature it is consistently referred to as the book of Friesen.

The Will of God - Friesen's book consists of four parts. In the first two parts he outlines and criticizes what he calls the 'traditional view'. In the third part he explains his alternative, which he calls the wisdom view, and in the final part he applies this wisdom view to some real-life examples and decisions.

His view on the will of God as something fixed that believers can expect to be revealed to them by God is clear: "Many believers are wasting a great deal of time and energy searching for *something that does not exist*" (41, emphasis CvdK). That 'something' is what Friesen calls 'the dot': that point within the field of decisions that are morally allowed that God has picked for a specific individual (29). Friesen's entire book is written to criticize the idea that "for each of our decisions, God has an ideal plan that He will make known to the attentive believer" (28). The alternative that Friesen proposes is summarized in four basic statements (14-15):

1. Where God commands, we must obey.
2. Where there is no command, God gives us freedom (and responsibility) to choose.
3. Where there is no command, God gives us wisdom to choose.
4. When we have chosen what is moral and wise, we must trust the sovereign God to work all the details together for good.

In his own words, this is "fundamentally different from the traditional view" (79). Key elements are the emphasis on the coexistence of multiple good options and the freedom and responsibility that result from that situation.

Praxis – One could expect that such a major change in perspective results in entirely different practices. It is, however, not the *kind* of practices that changes, but their *function*. The focus is no longer on isolated decision-making moments, but on the way the believer grows through them, for "God is more concerned about who we are than what we do" (285). Thus, Bible reading and study still have a major function, as does prayer, but their function is building the character of the believers and (in)forming their worldview, not giving specific directions. Furthermore, proper planning processes gain more emphasis, for "God's sovereign determination of all things in no way diminishes the need or importance of wise planning" (203). Circumstances like the so-called "open doors" are no plain indicators of the divine will, but are themselves in need of careful evaluation (213).

The key of Friesen's view is the role he assigns to wisdom. According to Friesen, "the pursuit of wisdom in decision making permeates the entire Bible" (160). Thus, many of the practices that were endorsed in the 'traditional view' as indicators of the will of God are now transformed into sources of wisdom. In this context, Friesen mentions for example prayer, Scripture, careful research of all relevant information, counselors, and experience as ways to acquire Christian wisdom (180-182).

Argument - The book of Friesen, and especially the parts in which he criticizes the traditional view, are based on the exegesis of frequently used biblical texts. After discussing many of those texts, Friesen concludes that "careful exegesis of the relevant passages fails to support the basic premise of the traditional view" (75). For his own position, he uses a combination of biblical material and common sense. For example, he states that "the nature of effective law making requires that where there is no command, there is an assumed area of freedom" (144). In his choice of the biblical material, he stresses that the texts that are often used in defense of the traditional view are special occasions (think e.g. of Acts 16), whereas the people involved (e.g. Paul) do normally explain their decision-making processes in different terms. A key example for Friesen is the way Paul repeatedly explains his priorities and plans for the future, for example in Romans 1 and 15 (225-230). Whereas Friesen focuses on exegesis of Biblical material, arguments from systematic theology or tradition are absent from his book.

Contribution - Friesen's book was influential partly because it gave a critical response to the standard ('traditional') view. Some of his concerns were raised before, but never in such a systematic and thorough way. His book is still the most extensive treatment of guidance.

2.3.4 Ashcraft
Morris Ashcraft, *The Will of God*, Nashville: Broadman Press, 1980.

Author - Morris Ashcraft (1922-2011) was professor of Christian Theology at Southern Baptist Theological Seminary, Louisville (5 years), Mid-Western Baptist Theological Seminary, Kansas City (22 years) and dean and professor at SouthEastern Baptist Theological Seminary, Wake Forest (7 years) before he resigned in 1989 in reaction to the conservative policy of the Baptist seminaries following debates over biblical inerrancy. Ashcraft has written several books, of which his *The Will of God* is relevant for our research. In this book, Ashcraft states that most existing books are practically oriented but "do not deal adequately with the biblical and theological materials" (9). Being a professor of theology, he himself sets out to do so, but in language understandable for lay people (9).

Will of God - Ashcraft does not explicitly define the concept of the will of God, but in his book several elements stand out. In the first place, Ashcraft remarks that speaking about the will of God "is a very personal way of speaking about providence" (109). It includes questions of personal salvation, vocation, but also suffering and adversity (12). Second, Ashcraft states that "the will of God is his purpose for us within the rest of his creation" (65). Third, he repeatedly emphasizes the very personal nature of this purpose of God (e.g. 103) in order to guard against any idea of fate (23). Relatedly, the reader is warned not to think in terms of a finished, detailed plan or blueprint (65). The biblical material on the will of God is too complex to be captured in such basic images. Ashcraft strongly emphasizes the importance of the topic: "To know and do the will of God is human existence at its highest level" (12). When we see that the will of God was the whence, whither, what, who, and why of Jesus' life (35), it must be of supreme importance for us.

Ashcraft places the topic in a more comprehensive theological framework by defining it in terms of providence and placing it in the context of the entire creation. He does so most explicitly in his discussion of Eph. 3:8-11, where he reads about God's "comprehensive purpose ... for all creation and all ages" (100). His conclusion: "So when you and I consider God's will for our lives, we need to look briefly at this plan of God for the ages and note how our small lives fit into what God is doing throughout history" (108).

Praxis - When it comes to the praxis, Ashcraft explains that, given his view on the will of God, he cannot present a set of rules that could be applied (132), but instead will give a number of guidelines. His most important point is that we learn the will of God only *en route* (76), "under the yoke, alongside others, with the burden" (72). His focus throughout is on the Christian life as a life of discipleship (79), and not only on the singular moments of decision-making. The guidelines he lists for living such a life in which God's will can be found are "Know your beliefs" (134), "Know your Bible" (135) and "Prayer and worship" (136), complemented by "Converse with the church" (137)[37] and "Know your world" (138).

---

37 Here he means the church of all ages and points explicitly to the importance of engaging with older sources, mentioning Augustine, Luther and Calvin explicitly (137). In this light, it seems strange that this tradition does not play a major role in Ashcraft's own argument.

Ashcraft emphasizes the freedom we have in many matters (48) and the importance of ordinary human planning and principles (52).

For Ashcraft, absolute certainty is impossible. "We have to make decisions in life in light of the information we have" (141) and "when we say we know the will of God, we mean that we recognize God's purpose for our lives to a degree adequate for us to live for him" (73).

Argument - Although Ashcraft is apparently aware of many other books on the topic, they nowhere receive attention in his book. Although there is a brief chapter on providence in his book where the views of some historical theologians are sketched, the role of the theological tradition in his book is minor, especially in light of his critique of others in his introduction. Key place in his argument goes to the Biblical material, and distinct from most authors, Ashcraft gives extended explanations of key texts, like the third petition of the Lord's prayer, Jesus' anguish in Gethsemane, the opening verses of Paul's letters (44), Romans 8:28, and Romans 12:1-2. Furthermore, the Ephesian passages on God's cosmic plan with the world play a major role.

Contribution – Ashcraft's contribution is found in his systematic treatment of the topic, his discussions about how the human will relates to the will of God in light of Jesus' cry that not his will, but the Fathers must be done (Mt 26:39), and in his emphasis that God's way is only learnt on the way, as a pilgrim.

2.3.5 Shepson
Charles W. Shepson, *How to Know God's Will: Divine Direction for the Road Map of Life,* Beaverlodge: Horizon House, 1981.

Author - Charles W. Shepson is an American pastor, author, and conference speaker. Shepson served in different ministries for over fifty years and is known as the founder of Fairhaven Ministries, an interdenominational retreat center for pastors and missionaries. Shepson has written several books, most of them on practical pastoral themes.

The Will of God - Shepson's perspective on the will of God is already clear from his preface: "God has enriched my life immeasurably through the clear communication of His will for me. I sincerely belief that He *enjoys* communicating clearly with His own" (7). This last claim is the leading one throughout his entire book. According to Shepson, a longing for concrete divine guidance is a basic instinct of born again persons (16). The will of

God is perfect in the sense that it covers everything, even minor details (like missing a bus, 16). One of the reasons for longing to know the will of God is that it "would add a dimension of purposefulness and meaning to our lives that we could never achieve by ourselves" (20). Shepson's focus throughout is on the individual life, but he does remark that the Christian life is "spent primarily for God, and secondarily for others, and lastly for yourself" (113).

Praxis - Shepson repeatedly emphasizes the variety of ways in which God speaks (34). The frequent ones he mentions are closed doors (34) and open doors (55), remarkable revelations (36), difficult experiences (38), specific instructions (41), sanctified reason (45), and counsel of Godly people (48). Two elements stand out. In the first place, in his argument and examples Shepson frequently points to the importance of devotional Bible reading and the way God applies texts to the individual life (50): "Don't miss the thrill of hearing the voice of God to your own soul because you are afraid of subjectivity" (51). Shepson speaks about a "devotional dialogue" (84). In the second place, Shepson emphasizes the importance of inner peace: "When your final decision is made, there should be a substantial measure of inner peace that accompanies it, or it might be well for you to reevaluate that decision" (57, see also 141).

Logically, in his "checklist of specific steps that can be taken" (101) much attention is given to reading, studying, and memorizing Scripture. In this way, God delights to reveal his will, so we need not speak about 'seeking' it (24).

Argument - Shepson's argument consists of a combination of the standard biblical material and examples from his own life and the lives of others. There is no explicit attention for Christian tradition or well-known theological concepts. When Shepson advocates the importance of inner peace in the decision-making process he briefly mentions that this is a debated issue, but he does not elaborate on this (56).

Contribution - The book of Shepson is a good representation of the traditional view and as such does not contribute many new things.

2.3.6 Ferguson
Sinclair B. Ferguson, *Discovering God's Will*, Carlisle: Banner of Truth, 1982.

Author - Sinclair B. Ferguson (1948) is a Scottish Reformed theologian, professor of Systematic Theology at Redeemer Seminary, Dallas, and visiting professor at Westminster Theological Seminary, Philadelphia. He served as a minister in the Church of Scotland from 1971-2005 and in the First Presbyterian Church of Columbia, South Carolina, from 2005-2013. Ferguson is a council member of the Alliance of Confessing Evangelicals and has published a number of pastoral and theological books.

The Will of God - Although Ferguson opens his book with the statement that it is difficult to imagine a Christian who does not believe that God is the Guide of his or her life (9), it is hard to say what exactly is his view on the will of God. On the one hand, he speaks about "the special, personal will of God for our lives" (51), about living "in the will of God" (54) and about the question "what is the will of God in this particular, unique situation in which I find myself?" (64). All this suggests that Ferguson sees the will of God as something fixed, detailed, and knowable. On the other hand Ferguson stresses "matters of indifference" (18) and states that "at the end of the day, *we* will have to decide what the will of God is" (78). That is, we will have to make the decisions.

Ferguson puts the question of the individual life in a wider perspective by referring to the destiny of the Christian life: God, his glory, and his presence (16, 20). Furthermore, he repeatedly speaks of the Christian life as a life of pilgrimage, focused on the future, not on our everyday decisions (17).

Praxis - Guiding principle in the practices Ferguson prescribes is that the Biblical idea of guidance may not result in feelings of perplexity and uncertainty, as he thinks often happens (9). In line with the Westminster Shorter Catechism, he states that the Word of God is the only rule for our life (27): "There is much mysterious about the way God guides us. But we are not called by God to make the mysterious, the unusual, the inexplicable the rule of our lives, but his Word" (32). Scripture provides us with commandments, principles, and illustrations to guide us in living our own lives (29).

On the more specific level, Ferguson emphasizes the importance of carefully thinking through situations in light of biblical truth: "Guidance is the way in which God leads us as we think through the implications of his truth, and seek to find application of it in our lives" (61). Furthermore, Ferguson argues that when a decision is lawful, beneficial, not enslaving, consistent with Christ's lordship, helpful to others, and consistent with biblical examples (66-72) it cannot be out of the will of God. In that sense uncertainty is not necessary. This does not mean that the decision-making process is not long and arduous (11), but that is the way God molds us into wise persons. In any case, we must "turn aside from instant methods" (111).

Although his language about the will of God suggests that Ferguson aligns with the traditional approach, the practices he describes depart from it in that he stresses the importance of ordinary processes of decision-making to arrive at wise choices.

Argument - Ferguson clearly develops his view as a response to others, but he never explicitly mentions them. His discussion of several biblical texts and the superficial way in which they are often used to support a view on the will of God is quite critical. Ferguson's own view rests heavily on the Reformed maxim of *Sola Scriptura,* on which he cites the Westminster Shorter Catechism (27). Furthermore, Ferguson uses material from amongst others Calvin (29) and John Newton (32). His book is clearly aimed at lay people and is devoid of technical theological terms.

Contribution - Ferguson's contribution is mainly found in his emphasis on the Christian life as a pilgrimage, in which the present life is not the ultimate goal, the journey is not easy, and the focus is on the 'way' as a way of life and not on the individual steps.

2.3.7 Ogilvie
Lloyd John Ogilvie, *Discovering God's Will in Your Life,* Eugene: Harvest House Publishers, 1982.

Author - Lloyd John Ogilvie (1930) pastored the First Presbyterian Church of Hollywood from 1972-1995, but is better known as the Chaplain of the US Senate from 1995-2003. Ogilvie hosted a television ministry for several years and has written over 50 books.

The Will of God - According to Ogilvie, there is no more important subject for Christians than knowing and doing the will of God: "We all want to be sure we are in the will of God and to receive guidance for our daily choices and decisions" (5). However, he is also clear from the outset that "the will of God is not a mysterious set of sealed orders we search for and receive if we happen to hit on the right formula. Rather, the will of God is a relationship with Him in which He discloses His purpose, power and plan for our lives – and in that order" (10). Hence, the practical 'steps' that can be taken are only introduced at the end of the book.

Ogilvie emphasizes that thinking about the will of God must not be done with fear, but with thankfulness, because it is something "in which we are privileged to live" (22). Ultimately, God's will is that we know, love, and glorify Him and grow into an intimate relationship with Him (22). At the deepest level, Christ himself is God's will for us (38). However, when it comes to the more specific decisions that are to be made, Ogilvie is clear that God also reveals a private, personal, individual plan (149): "Our gracious and loving God has a personal plan for each of us, our own way of living out His essential will that we know, love, glorify and serve Him" (150). This is not argued for, but simply assumed.

Praxis - The concrete praxis of "finding" the will of God is only explained in the final chapter of the book. However, throughout the book references are made to this practical part. For example, Ogilvie warns the reader early in his book that guidance must never become more important than the Guide himself (22), and that thus our primary focus should be on our relationship with God. As a result, an important criterion in decision-making is whether any choice brings us closer to Him (29). Furthermore, following Romans 12:1-2, we must dedicate ourselves completely to God, be not conformed to the world, and renew our minds (90-93).

When Ogilvie finally comes to the five 'steps' for or 'friends' in knowing the will of God, those are largely in accord with the advice found in most books. The five friends are the Bible (151), prayer as communication with God (161), our own thoughts, feelings, and talents (164), a small band of prayer partners (171), and commitment of the decision to God, waiting for His peace as confirmation (172). Ogilvie assures the reader that in this way "we can be sure of His will in our lives" (146). This can be strengthened by particular circumstances or other means, but their function is to support the choice, and they can never stand alone.

Argument - Ogilvie assures the reader that he carefully studied all the relevant Scriptural texts and "dozens of history's greatest thinkers on the subject" (6). Throughout his book, the well-known biblical texts on the will of God are discussed and in some places other authors are cited, but not at key points of his argument. No reference to any discussion is made and theological terminology is rare.

Contribution – Ogilvie does add no substantially new insights to the discussion.

2.3.8 Sproul
R.C. Sproul, *God's Will and the Christian,* Lake Mary: Reformation Trust, 1984.

Author - Robert C. Sproul (1939-2017) was Professor of Systematic Theology and Apologetics at Reformed Theological Seminary, Orlando and Senior Minister of Saint Andrew's Chapel, Sanford, Florida. He was the founder and chairman of Ligonier Ministries, an international discipleship organization that produces theological resources for lay people. Sproul has written over 80 books, mostly on philosophy, (systematic) theology, and apologetics.

Will of God - Sproul does not reject the way the phrase 'the will of God' is often used, and sometimes even speaks about "being in the center of God's will" himself (e.g. 59), but in his book he is mainly concerned with the preceptive will of God, instead of his decretive will: "One of the great tragedies of contemporary Christendom is the preoccupation of so many Christians with the secret decretive will of God to the exclusion and neglect of the preceptive will" (17). Too many Christians search for something hidden instead of following the principles already revealed. According to Sproul, the discussion about the will of God does not sufficiently take into account that "the biblical meaning of the will of God is a very complicated manner" (13) and that "to approach it simplistically is to invite disaster" (13). Sproul tries to show that the different Greek words for 'will' have very specific nuances and are used in various ways in different contexts.

While being somewhat critical, Sproul underlines the importance of submission to the will of God in words that sound very traditional: "The Christian pursues God, looking for his marching orders, seeking to know what course of action is pleasing to Him. This search for the will of God is a holy quest" (11). He also calls it a "desperately important matter for every Christian" (32).

Sproul does not explicitly point to a context beyond the individual, but in emphasizing the preceptive will of God and the importance of righteousness he implicitly does so. Furthermore, in several places he refers to the importance of the Kingdom of God (e.g. 58).

Praxis - Sproul's writing on the praxis of decision-making focuses heavily on the areas of vocation and marriage. Most of his practical advice is contained in the chapter about work. Four questions are crucial, according to Sproul: 1. What can I do? 2. What do I like to do? 3. What should I like to be able to do? 4. What should I do? (61). The order of the questions reveals a lot about Sproul's position. In his answers to these questions, it is clear that for Sproul common sense and practical wisdom are of major importance: "The most practical advice I can give is for you to do what your motivated ability pattern indicates you can do with a high degree of motivation" (65). Gifts and motivation are crucial. No call like for example Moses received is to be expected (70). In urging the reader to follow personal motivation, Sproul presupposes that a Christian has a renewed mind and lives a life of prayer and Bible reading.

Sproul occasionally speaks about God's inward call (71), the guidance of the Spirit (74), and the promised peace of God (74), but these function within the parameters sketched above.

Argument - Sproul's argument differs from many of the other contributions, in that he does not give proof texts for every point he makes. Instead, he provides some important exegetical remarks on the different words for 'will' used in the Bible. As important parts of his argument he discusses works from Augustine and Jonathan Edwards, mainly on divine sovereignty and human freedom. Although Sproul is aware that other views on guidance exist, he nowhere explicitly enters into debate with other authors.

Contribution – More than other authors Sproul places the topic of guidance in the field of the human will and its freedom. Furthermore, his stress on the complexity of the Biblical material is important.

2.3.9 Willard
Dallas Willard, *In Search of Guidance: Developing a Conversational Relationship with God*, Ventura: Regal Books, 1984.[38]

Author - Dallas A. Willard (1935-2013) was professor of philosophy at the University of Southern California from 1965 until his death in 2013. His main interest was in the phenomenology of Edmund Husserl. In the evangelical world, Willard is best known for his writings on spiritual disciplines, spiritual formation, and living with God.[39]

The Will of God - Throughout his book Willard makes clear that his main concern is not with the moments of decision-making, but with the entire Christian life-style: "God has created us for intimate friendship with Himself" (x). According to Willard, the Biblical ideal is "a hand-in-hand, conversational walk with God" (xii).

Given this perspective, the will of God for us is leading a certain kind

---

[38] References are to the renamed 1999 edition, *Hearing God*.
[39] See e.g. Dallas Willard, *The Spirit of the Disciplines: Understanding How God Changes Lives* (San Francisco: Harper & Row, 1988); and *The Divine Conspiracy: Rediscovering Our Hidden Life in God* (San Francisco: Harper & Row, 1998).

of life, more than making the right decisions (xi). Hence, "extreme preoccupation with knowing the will of God 'for me' may only indicate, contrary to what is often thought, an overconcern with myself, not a Christ-like interest in the well-being of others or the glory of God" (14). Accordingly, Willard warns against seeing God as a 'cosmic boss', 'foreman' or 'taskmaster' (20).

On the other hand, Willard does not dismiss the idea of direct divine involvement and guidance, for "in the last analysis nothing is more central to the practical life of the Christian than confidence in God's individual dealings with each person on a one-to-one basis" (9). He states, "I believe we cannot, as disciples of Jesus Christ, abandon faith in the availability of God's personal and intelligible guidance for our minds and lives" (13). This guidance is, however, nowhere referred to as the revealing of God's fixed will, but "leaves a lot of room for initiative on our part" (xi).

Praxis - When it comes to receiving guidance the key is what Willard calls a 'conversational relationship' with God. Behind this terminology lies his conviction that the experiences of Adam and Eve, Enoch, and Moses "are not meant to be exceptional at all" (4). Thus, hearing God should neither be uncommon nor difficult and requires no "mechanical formulas" (x).

Although Willard acknowledges that God can speak in a variety of ways (e.g. 94) he points to the Bible as the primary objective way of speaking and to the "still small voice" as the primary subjective way of God's speaking (91). With regard to the use of the Bible, Willard remarks that it must be read in a realistic manner (22, over against a dogmatic reading) and the reader must use his "God-given imagination" (23). However, Willard is clear that we need guidance "*within* the principles of the Bible, but *beyond* the details of what it explicitly says" (47).

Fundamental to his entire book is his focus on the 'still small voice' of God. According to Willard, it "has a vastly greater role than anything else" (78) and he links it to the 'candle of the Lord' mentioned in Prov. 20:27 (91). This voice of God is recognizable by its quality, spirit, and content (168). Especially the quality is crucial, for the voice of God leaves "a certain weight or impact of the impression ... on our consciousness" (169).

Willard hesitates to give practical advice, but on the presupposition that guidance only makes sense in the context of a personal relationship with God, he lays down "something close to a formula for *living with God's guiding voice*" (206). Crucial is alertness and attentiveness to what happens in our life, mind, and heart (207): "We must purposefully, humbly and intelligently cultivate the ability to listen and see what is happening in our own souls, and to recognize therein the movements of God" (208). In the end, when God doesn't speak, it can happen that the individual has to act on what seems best, but Willard assures that this will only rarely be necessary (209).

Argument - In one place in his book (45-50) Willard discusses several different views on guidance. Those views include the message-a-minute view, in which every decision to be made is accompanied by a message from God. He also opposes Friesen's 'Bible deism' (99), the view he describes as 'it is all in the Bible' (46). Finally, Willard opposes the idea that whatever happens is the will of God, which comes too close to the ancient idea of fate.

With regard to Biblical material, Willard takes his point of departure in the narrative parts of Scripture and the experiences of (especially Old Testament) believers with God. As a result of his focus on the still small voice of God, 1 Kings 19 does have a special place in his argument. Willard uses more theological sources than most authors do, but these mostly are individual citations and not extended discussions.

Contribution - With his explicit defense of the crucial place of inner experience ('the still small voice of God') as a reliable source of knowledge of the will of God, Willard gives more depth to an element that is implicitly present in the books of many authors.

2.3.10 Cleave
Derek Cleave, *How To Know God's Will,* Darlington: Evangelical Press, 1985.

Author - Cleave is an evangelist from Bristol who has worked with the National Young Life Campaign, the Movement for World Evangelization, and with Christian Ministries, an organization he co-founded with Peter Andersen and John Blanchard. Cleave has written several books, mainly on home evangelization. His interest in the topic of divine guidance comes from the experience he has of working with young people, although he does not consider himself an expert (9).

Will of God - Cleave is clear in his conviction that "the most important thing in anyone's life is to know the will of God and to follow it" (13). He even calls it "the deciding factor" when it comes to the quality of our relationship with God (13). Cleave does not explicitly define what he means by the will of God, but points to the difference between the secret and the revealed will of God (16). As the secret will of God is hidden from us, what he discusses concerns the revealed will of God, but for Cleave this revealed will clearly includes a part that has yet to be revealed. Implicitly, it is clear that Cleave speaks about an individual life-plan for each believer when using the words "the will of God". In his book, Cleave is mainly concerned with God's plan for the individual life.

Praxis - Because "individual circumstances are different and God calls people in various ways and to a multiplicity of tasks" (67) we need guidance in situations that go beyond the guidelines provided in the Bible. Cleave proposes "a procedure that can be followed in endeavoring to find out just what God wants us to do in this situation" (68). It is important that for Cleave this procedure is not a formula but rather a number of proven means (72). The procedure consists of three parts. First, in preparation, it is important always to watch our spiritual condition and attitude towards God (68-72). Second, the procedure itself consists of five proven means: 1. Dealing with hindrances, especially sin. 2. Ask God in prayer to reveal his will and guard you from wrong decisions. 3. We must *seek* his will by the Spirit through the Word. 4. We must take into account providential circumstances. 5. We must listen to wise counsel of mature Christian friends (72-73). The third stage of the procedure is to have patience, because God does not give instantaneous answers. Besides this procedure, Cleave warns against expecting shortcuts, a detailed blueprint, intense feelings, or clear signs (75). He does nowhere explicitly state that following his procedure will result in absolute certainty in making decisions, but throughout the tone is positive in this respect. Although patience can be required, ultimately we will know what God expects us to do.

Argument - Cleave's argument is mainly based on Biblical texts; remarkably, in light of his view, he makes no use of those narrative sections in which persons were led by God. Some 'standard texts' play a major role (e.g. Romans 8:14 and 12:1-2, Psalms 25 and 32, and Proverbs 3:5-6). Cleave briefly discusses the third petition of the Lord's Prayer (29) and Christ's prayer that not his will be done, but the will of his Father (35-36).

Throughout the book, no references are made to other books on the topic or other existing views. Furthermore, besides a single citation from Luther (53), no theological sources are used or cited. Common theological terms are absent, except for the imprecise distinction between the secret and revealed will of God.

Contribution – Cleave does not add distinctive new insights to the discussion.

2.3.11 Stanley
Charles F. Stanley, *How to Listen to God,* Nashville: Oliver Nelson Books, 1985.

Author - Charles F. Stanley (1932), senior minister of First Baptist Church in Atlanta, Georgia since 1971, is the founder of 'In Touch Ministries', former president of the Southern Baptist Convention, and author of over 30 books.

The Will of God - Stanley's main concern is whether and how God speaks, but it is clear from the outset that this speaking of God is all about guidance, directions, and decisions: "We need his definite and deliberate direction for our lives, as did Joshua, Moses, Jacob or Noah" (9). Stanley even states that this kind of speaking is a divine responsibility: "Since He wants us to make right choices, He is still responsible for providing accurate data" (9, note especially the word *data*).

Although Stanley does not write on "the will of God" the concept is fundamental for his entire book. This is especially clear in remarks like "God does speak to us personally about our families, our businesses, our finances, our hurts, our frustrations, our fears" (128) and his warnings that when we do not listen carefully we end up "out of the will of God" (72) and "miss His very best" (146). God "is out to give us specific guidance and help us move into His wonderful plans and purposes for our lives" (48).

Those warnings underline the importance of listening for the divine will. Indeed, "one of the most valuable lessons we can ever learn is how to listen to God" (8), for nothing is more urgent, necessary, and rewarding.

Praxis - Although there were many ways God spoke in biblical times, Stanley distinguishes "four principal methods of revealing Himself to the contemporary believer" (13): the Bible, the Holy Spirit, other people, and circumstances. Besides, "God has His ways of getting our undivided attention" (31), like a restless spirit, disappointments, and tragedies. In short, "we must learn to look for the presence of God in every circumstance of life" (40).

By mentioning the Bible and the Spirit as the two most important ways of divine guidance, Stanley attributes a major role to meditation, calling it "a daily priority for believers" (93). Through meditation, "God will often lead us to an incident in Scripture, a passage or even a single verse that will relate to what concerns us" (14). In that process, the Spirit communicates the divine will in the mind of the believer, who hears God in his "inner being" (16). Following John 10:27 ('my sheep hear my voice'), Stanley asserts that "the natural walk of Spirit-filled, committed believers is such that when God speaks, we can identify His voice" (50).

Besides this basic practice of meditation, Stanley gives some additional guidelines. For example, he states that Gods call can be expected to clash with what we think the natural, reasonable course of action (52, with reference to Gen. 22), to clash with our fleshly nature (52), and to challenge our faith (53). Furthermore, he points to the importance of inner peace (61) and warns that the absence of it can be a divine warning (146). Finally, Stanley describes a listening attitude and several hindrances to hearing God.

Argument - The arguments in Stanley's book are mainly based on personal and biblical examples. No discussion with other authors takes place and no references to theologians, theological traditions, or technical theological terminology are made.

Contribution - Stanley's contribution is mainly found in his chapter on 'the listening attitude', in which he stresses topics like expectancy (80), patience (82), openness (87), and gratefulness (90).

2.3.12 LaHaye
Tim F. LaHaye, *Finding the Will of God in a Crazy, Mixed-up World*, Grand Rapids: Zondervan, 1989.

Author - Tim LaHaye (1926-2016) was pastor of Shadow Mountain Community Church for 25 years and founder of the Institute for Creation Research. LaHaye has attracted attention by his controversial views on homosexuality and global conspiracies, but is best known for his *Left Behind* series in which he presents a story around his dispensational premillenialist views. LaHaye has been frequently listed as one of the most influential evangelicals of the last quarter of the 20th century.

The Will of God - For LaHaye, the question whether God has a plan for the life of individual believers is beyond debate: "And the best part of all is that your heavenly Father has a will for your life" (17), a will that is "his tailor-made plan just for you" (44). Not only does God have such a plan, but "He also wants to reveal that plan to us" (44). However, "God shrouds

His will so that we must seek Him continually on a personal basis" (46). The examples LaHaye uses throughout his book show that the will of God he speaks about is a very detailed plan for each individual life.

In a chapter based on Rom. 12:1-2 LaHaye distinguishes between three levels of the will of God: the perfect, the acceptable, and the good will of God (53). Many Christians do God's good will, others his acceptable will, "but all too few fulfill God's supreme desire, which requires that we start early in our Christian life and walk in consistent obedience to Him *most* of our life to complete His perfect will for our lives" (54). On the other hand, LaHaye is very clear about the danger of "going out of God's will" (20), his own "one real fear in this world" (114).

The book of LaHaye is only concerned with God's will for the individual believer. Besides a remark that our life "must count for God and His Kingdom" (20) a wider perspective is entirely absent.

Praxis - The main focus of the book of LaHaye is on the practice of finding the will of God. He sets out to "illustrate biblical techniques that can help you to make the difficult decisions that will mold the course of your life" (8) and is secure that "by the time you finish this book, you, too, will be equipped to make right decisions about finding God's will for your life" (21).

The core of this equipment is what LaHaye calls the "66-volume road map" full of guidelines, principles, and examples (71). Listening to the Bible is one of the most important prerequisites to finding the will of God. Besides this road map, God "also gives us signs that further guide us and confirm His direction for our lives" (85). These signs provide more specific directions than the Bible does. LaHaye lists eight road signs: the ability to surrender, prayer, the indwelling of the Holy Spirit with his "still small voice" (93), circumstances, peace in your heart, the own desires, godly advice, and common sense (86-111). Key for LaHaye is keeping all road signs in mind: "When the road signs begin to line up in a straight line, we know we're properly approaching the 'runway' to God's will. It's a matter of coordination" (112).

Finally, LaHaye warns the believer not to be too quick, but to "give God ample time to intercept us in case our decision is not His will" (116). In order to gain more confidence the use of a fleece, a specific request for a divine sign, can be appropriate (127-128).

Argument - LaHaye is one of the first authors to mention explicitly that a new view has emerged that is opposite to his own view, and clearly means Friesen when he writes: "Recently a somewhat controversial book emerged, suggesting, in essence, that God doesn't have an individual or specific will for each Christian; the book suggests that once you've responded to the moral or universal will of God, you then can use your own judgment and proceed as you wish" (45-46). LaHaye strongly warns against what he calls "this new fad" (44), for "it's only a matter of time before we begin to function independently from God" (46).

In his own argument, the 'standard' selection of texts appears to be fundamental: Romans 12:1-2, Proverbs 3:5-6, the narratives of Acts, and the Pauline references to the will of God. No explicit references to theological loci or traditions are made in the book.

Contribution - The specific contribution of LaHaye can be found in his exegesis of Romans 12:1-2 and the different levels of the will of God. Furthermore, he writes a chapter on the influence of character on decision-making and describes the circumstances in which a proper use of fleeces can be made, a practice that is discouraged by most authors.

2.3.13 Observations
Given our review of the books on the will of God and divine guidance from the period 1980-1989, a few observations can be made. A fuller analysis will be presented in sections 2.6 and 2.7.

1. Many authors write from a position of dissatisfaction with what they see as the current state of thought and speech about the topic of divine guidance. Their dissatisfaction is however based on different aspects: the looseness of speech (Hosier), the lack of theological robustness (Ashcraft), or even a complete denial of the validity of the "traditional view" (Friesen). Yet, in expressing this all authors seem to presuppose a type of thought about guidance that seems to be to a large measure identical, and is described as widespread.
2. Although the appearance of Friesen's book is stated to cause a major stir in the evangelical world, this is not reflected in the *books* on the topic published in the decade after its publication. Only LaHaye explicitly refers to some dangerous 'new fad' that appeared recently and strongly opposes it. In this light, no real 'discussion' takes place within the books. Even when authors disagree with others, names are often not mentioned explicitly.
3. As a result, many contributions suffer from imprecision, a strange fact given that most authors are highly educated pastors or seminary professors. Especially those who deplore the lack of theological depth could have been expected to contribute more preciseness in this regard.

4. A number of distinct positions can be delineated yet precise classification of the books is difficult. Hosier, Shepson, Cleave, Stanley, and LaHaye see God's will as a plan for individual lives that believers can expect to be revealed to them. Friesen, Ferguson, and Sproul stress wisdom, whereas Ashcraft, Ogilvie, and Willard focus on intimacy of relationship with God and on his inner voice.
5. With respect to the practices prescribed it strikes that authors advocating different views to a large extent prescribe the same practices, but add different weights to them. Thus, in one view something can count as fresh divine revelation that is presented in another view as a source for wisdom or a means of bonding with God. For example, all authors agree on the importance of prayer, but ascribe quite divergent functions to it with respect to guidance.
6. With regard to the arguments used, most authors discuss a recurring set of biblical texts, whereas especially tradition is largely absent as an important source for theologizing.
7. Most authors add only new examples and some subtle nuances to the discussion, while few fresh arguments are introduced. Only Friesen can be said to really add a major contribution to the topic that is clearly supported by a lot of research.

2.4 Analysis of Evangelical Literature 1990-1999

2.4.1 Introduction
In this chapter the popular evangelical books on the topics 'the will of God' and 'divine guidance' that were published in the period 1990-1999 will be introduced, discussed, and analyzed.

2.4.2 Blackaby and King
Henry T. Blackaby and Claude V. King, *Experiencing God: Knowing and Doing the Will of God,* Nashville: LifeWay Press, 1990.[40]

Authors - *Experiencing God* is one of the most influential books on guidance, as it is translated into more than 45 languages and has been sold worldwide over seven million times. Henry Blackaby is founder and former president of Blackaby Ministries International, he pastored churches in California and Canada, and served as president of the Canadian Bap-

---
[40] We use the revised edition of 2008, published by B&H Publishing Group. In this version, Richard Blackaby first appears as co-author. The book is written basically in first person with Henry Blackaby as main author. See http://www.blackaby.net/expgod/ (accessed Oct. 6, 2014) for the translations and sales numbers.

tist Theological College and the Canadian Southern Baptist Conference. He is the author of several books. His son Richard Blackaby is the current president of Blackaby Ministries International, pastor, and former president of the Canadian Southern Baptist Seminary. Besides co-authoring with his father he has published several books himself. Claude King is the 'Discipleship Specialist' for LifeWay Christian Resources, Nashville.

Will of God - The book starts out with the assertion that "within the heart of every Christian is an innate desire to know God and to do his will" (2). Because of God's love, omniscience, and omnipotence, his will is best (21), his directions are right (25), and he enables believers to accomplish his will (27). Thus, the view of God's will is directly based on the underlying view of God. As a result of this particular view of God, no doubt about the existence of an individual divine plan seems possible (33), and the reader is assured that "God does not want you to miss out on what He has intended for you from eternity" (80). Given the examples used in the book, the authors believe that the will of God for each individual life covers everything, from major decisions to minor daily choices. This is confirmed by the statement that "God's assignments come on a daily basis" (35). In those 'assignments', "God always provides enough specific directions so you can do what He wants you to do at the moment" (150).

In the book, the will of God is related to the Kingdom of God (162) and as such not a primary goal in itself. The authors emphasize the importance of living in a close relationship with God over the finding and doing of his will, although the two are intimately connected (33).

Praxis - The core of the book is centred around the "seven realities of experiencing God" (51). Those seven realities are formulated as follows (54-61):
1. God is always at work around you.
2. God pursues a continuing relationship with you that is real and personal.
3. God invites you to become involved with Him in His work.
4. God speaks by the Holy Spirit through the Bible, prayer, circumstances and the church to reveal Himself, His purposes and His ways.
5. God's invitation for you to work with Him always leads you to a crisis of belief that requires faith and action.
6. You must make major adjustments in your life to join God in what He is doing.
7. You come to know God by experience as you obey Him and He accomplishes His work through you.

Key statements are that "God is always at work around you" (54) and "God invites you to become involved with Him in His work" (56). Thus, the will of God for the individual believer is closely tied to the mission of God. In order to see where and how God is working, believers must be attentive and accustomed to hearing God, for "if a Christian doesn't know when God is speaking, that person is in trouble at the core of his or her Christian life" (134).

This knowing of God's voice is "not a matter of honing a method or discovering a formula," but instead it comes from living in an "intimate love relationship" with God (139). In his grace, "God intended for the Holy Spirit to be extremely active in the believers lives, communicating His will and purposes for them" (138). The Spirit does so through the Bible (167), prayer, circumstances, and through the church: "When what God says through the Bible, prayer, circumstances, and the church line up to say the same thing, you can proceed with confidence to follow God's directions" (205).

Argument - The argument of the book is mainly based on examples from the authors' lives. At every crucial point a narrative is included introducing a situation in which God provided clear direction. Those narratives are supported by references to biblical material, in which Old Testament narratives (especially the story of Moses and the burning bush) play a major role. The authors explicitly disagree with Friesen's wisdom view (34), but no further references to this discussion or any theological background are made.

Contribution - In emphasizing the missio Dei as the ultimate starting point for thinking about divine guidance and the will of God the authors contribute an important theological idea.

2.4.3 Bockmühl
Klaus Bockmühl, *Listening to the God Who Speaks: Reflections on God's Guidance and the Lives of God's People,* Colorado Springs: Helmers and Howard, 1990.

Author - Klaus Bockmühl (1931-1989), a German theologian, was professor of Systematic Theology at Regent College, Vancouver from 1977 until his death in 1989. Bockmühl was a member of the theological committee of the World Evangelical Alliance for several years. His works focus on a range of topics, from Marxism via social ethics to the practice of discipleship. In his scholarly work, Bockmühl also discussed the question of guidance, most explicitly so in his *Gesetz und Geist*.[41] In the foreword, James M. Houston calls his book on guidance, which was published shortly after his death, "very much his last will and testimony to the church" (ix).

The Will of God - As the title of the book indicates, Bockmühl's focus is mainly on divine communication. The key statement of the book reads: "When people listen, God speaks" (8). No clear view on the will of God is developed, but through various statements in the book Bockmühls shows that Gods direction for his people is based on a divine plan (36). Furthermore, "the instructions of the Spirit are mostly of a practical nature, they ... address certain individuals in certain situations" (82). It seems that Bockmühl's view on divine communication is based on the assumption of a will of God for each individual Christian.

Praxis - Bockmühl uses Augustinian language when he refers to the Holy Spirit as the *doctor internus* (63), who communicates with us "in the innermost soul" (147). With the Reformation and against the spiritualists, Bockmühl sees the need for certain tests of this kind of divine guidance. He mentions various kinds of tests in his book, like the *regula fidei* (98), love for God and the neighbor (98), and a Kingdom focus instead of a self-centered focus (149). However, over against Reformation theology, which completely excluded any guidance of God outside Scripture out of fear for extremes (13), he gives guidance an important place. A reduction of the work of the Spirit to speaking exclusively through Scripture does no justice, according to Bockmühl, to the example of Christ as the "Great Listener" (48-50) and to the entire message of the book of Acts and the Pauline and Johannine letters (80). In order to hear this inner guidance, there is need for immediacy in our relationship with God (54) and for developing a "listening heart" (154).

Argument - Central to Bockmühl's argument is a chapter on "Living Testimonies: Luminaries in Church History", where he shows that, especially in pre-Reformation theology, there was a legitimate place for direct guidance by the Spirit: "Listening to the God who speaks has been of central importance in the lives of some of the greatest figures in Christian history" (103). In this chapter, he describes the experiences of Augustine, Bernard of Clairvaux, Francis of Assisi, but also people from the late Middle Ages, like Thomas à Kempis and Johannes Tauler.

---

41 Klaus Bockmühl, *Gesetz und Geist: Eine kritische Würdigung des Erbes protestantischer Ethik* (Giessen: Brunnen Verlag, 1987).

This emphasis on church history is complemented by material from the Psalms, from Acts, from the Gospel of John, and from the Apostolic Letters. The book of Acts, for example, shows "Paul's movements under the direction of the Holy Spirit" (75), and we see that Paul receives "divine instruction at almost every corner of his Christian life" (75).

Contribution - An important contribution of Bockmühl to the discussion is the way he uses material from church history to support his view. No author before him has done this so extensively.

2.4.4 Morris

Danny E. Morris, *Yearning to Know God's Will: A Workbook for Discerning God's Guidance for Your Life* (Grand Rapids: Zondervan, 1991).

Author - Danny E. Morris, a United Methodist pastor, is one of the leading figures behind The Upper Room, a Tennessee-based ministry focusing on spiritual growth. Morris founded the Academy for Spiritual Formation, and started a United Methodist monastery. Besides this book, he coauthored the related *Discerning God's Will Together*, with Charles M. Olsen.[42] *Yearning to Know God's Will* is structured as an eight-week workbook with guidelines for daily reading and weekly discussion.

The Will of God - The focus of the book is on the discernment of the will of God. Morris is convinced that God has a detailed and specific will for each decision individuals or groups make: "You can know God's will for your life! You can know whether a particular thing you have decided to do (or not to do) is God's will!" (31). As a result, spiritual discernment is defined in terms of the will of God: "Spiritual discernment is a capacity to see our lives clearly in the light of God's will" (27), and this capacity, as Morris adds, is "potentially available to all of us" because "God wants *everyone* to know God's will" (9).

Morris lists three key convictions on the will of God (106): "1. God's will ... is so essential that we must do whatever it takes to know it. 2. God's will is not so multifaceted or diffused or cloudlike that it cannot be discerned. 3. God's will is revealed in our seeking, for God wants us to know and act upon the divine will far more than we are prone to do."

---

42 Danny E. Morris and Charles M. Olsen, *Discerning God's Will Together: A Spiritual Practice for the Church* (Nashville: Upper Room Books, 1997).

Praxis - Key for Morris's discernment praxis is the conviction that God does not pose riddles to us: "God does not play games with us as though the divine will were hidden and only God knows what it is" (29). The problem is not that God communicates too little (75), but that we do not know how to hear His voice.

The actual decision-making process consists of two phases. In the first phase, "reasoning time" (51), the ordinary steps of a decision-making process must be taken: information gathering, consultation, consideration, and decision. Only when a preliminary decision is made the second stage of discernment is necessary: "Spiritual discernment questions are always yes or no questions, never choices among alternatives" (44).

In the actual process of discernment, the two best helps Morris prescribes are the Ignatian method, in which either consolation or desolation will become dominant (42), and the Quaker Committee of Clearness (45). Underlying both methods is the idea of the "still small voice of God", which Morris introduces early in his book (10). Ultimately, this kind of "non-intellectual perception" (57) or "spiritual intuition" (56) is of primary importance. In order to be conscious of the little nudges, feelings, and hunches (57) God gives, we must "open and utilize all the ports of entry that are available to God" (75): our mind, emotion, imagination, memory, and will (70).

Argument - Morris's book is based on Biblical narratives (see e.g. 10-14) and on his personal experience. No particular theological tradition stands out, although at key places he seems to be mainly influenced by Roman Catholic theology and especially Ignatian spirituality.

Contribution - The major point Morris adds to the discussion is his idea that discernment always has to do with situations in which only two options are left: yes or no. Discernment is only necessary when a provisional choice has been made. Furthermore, Morris makes a case for a practice of corporate discernment in which churches and ministries abandon worldly methods like voting and start making decisions based on spiritual consensus (106).

2.4.5 Robinson
Haddon W. Robinson, *Decision-Making by the Book: How to Choose Wisely in an Age of Options,* Grand Rapids: Discovery House, 1991.

Author - Haddon W. Robinson (1932-2017) was distinguished professor at Gordon-Conwell Theological Seminary, with an expertise on expository preaching and homiletics. He is former president of Denver Seminary (Baptist) and former president of the Evangelical Theological Society. He has written a number of books, mostly on preaching.

The Will of God - Robinson is clear in his rejection of an individual will of God for believers that they can expect him to communicate: "God works out His sovereign will through all men and women. He has revealed to us His moral will. But He doesn't necessarily reveal His specific, individual will to us" (24). The entire question "How do I find the will of God?" is not a Biblical question (39, see also 61).

Robinson distinguishes between God's sovereign, moral, and individual will, rejecting the existence of the last (22-24). He links thinking in terms of the will of God for individual lives to ancient practices of divination (e.g. 15) and explicitly says that "many modern followers of Christ do seek guidance in ways dangerously close to divination" (18). Instead of asking for the will of God to be revealed, we should ask how to make good decisions, for that is the way "to become the kind of people God wants us to be" (54), with the ultimate goal that God may be glorified (43).

Praxis - Given his view on the will of God, Robinson points believers to the Bible, for "Christians have guidance. It's unambiguous and direct. It's from God, it's for us, and it's found in His Word" (32). The Bible functions as a compass, giving a direction, not as a detailed map (61). The reader is assured that "if we apply the characteristics of God's sovereign and moral will to every decision we make, we will be well on the road to glorifying Him and living a fuller, happier life" (45) with "a great deal of freedom" (49). Submission to God's sovereign and moral will must be accompanied by a motivation of love towards God and the people around us (83), by a knowledge of our strengths and weaknesses (93), and by carefully analyzing the options and circumstances, that do not function as divine messages, but as the "boundaries of our decisions" (110).

In the process of making major decisions, godly counsel can help, but "we are responsible for weighing the counsel and for making the choices" (130). Direct words from God can occur (134), but in the New Testament those are restricted to ministry decisions (136).

Argument - Robinson opposes a view held by "many modern followers of Christ" (18), but nowhere mentions other authors or explicitly discusses their books. Most Bible references in his book are used to show that these texts do not support the view for which they are often used. His own argument is based on warnings against divination (e.g. Deut. 18) and on the ethical teachings of the New Testament, especially Romans 12 (Ch.7). No references are made to dogmatic concepts or the theological tradition.

Contribution - Robinson's contribution can be found in his recommendation to make use of the results of (secular) decision-making studies (Ch.12). He shows some of the implications of those studies himself.

2.4.6 Sanders

J. Oswald Sanders, *Every Life Is a Plan of God: Discovering His Will for Your Life* (Grand Rapids: Discovery House, 1992).

Author - J. Oswald Sanders (1902-1992) served for Overseas Missionary Fellowship from 1946 to 1969, from 1954 onwards in the function of general director. He is the author of more than 30 books on the Christian life and Christian leadership. Sanders writes on the issue of guidance from his experiences in a major missionary organization.

Will of God - Sanders is clear on the existence of a specific will of God for individual believers: "We are each the expression of a unique divine idea, and our purpose in life should be to cooperate with our Father in the outworking of that idea" (12). Later on he adds: "Not everyone believes that God has an individual will and plan for each life, but that is what the Bible seems to teach" (40). Furthermore, "the concept has met with wide acceptance among evangelical Christians the world around" (11). Although Sanders give no formal definition of this divine will, it is clear throughout the book that it involves all the major parameters of the believer's live.

For Sanders, the will of God is definitely something that is to be sought (15). The important question everyone has to answer is "What is God's will and plan for my life?" (133). However, as Sanders makes clear, "the whole guidance process is calculated to increase our knowledge of God himself, not only of His will" (13). Sanders is well aware that a number of "myths" (29) surrounds the issue, which he hopes to evade.

Praxis - Characteristic for Sanders' prescribed praxis is an openness to special experiences, accompanied by the frequent warning to "be wary of any guidance that belittles or overestimates the use of the intellect" (52) and that "all subjective guidance should be crosschecked by more objective standards" (123).

Basic elements in the search for guidance are the Bible, which he calls a "compendium of principles, precepts, prohibitions and promises" (76), and "submissive, expectant prayer" (51). With regard to the use of the Bible, Sanders states that "God delegates to us the responsibility of using our sanctified intelligence to work out the best application of the biblical principles to our own situation" (78). Besides the Bible and prayer, Sanders mentions the role of "wise and godly counsel" (99), of "circumstances as confirmations" (104), and of our desires (106). To this last element he adds the remark that "God *generally* guides along the lines of the natural gifts and abilities with which He has endowed us" (107).

Sanders mentions a number of points with important consequences for the decision-making process. In the first place, he emphasizes the indwelling of the Spirit – "our permanent indwelling Guest" (82) – who will transform us in such a way that "our decisions will be the product of a Spirit-illumined and guided mind" (89). Second, Sanders states that divine guidance is directed primarily to the mind and will, not to the emotions (134). Thirdly, he stresses that no extra special guidance is needed for foreign missions (139), as is often thought.

Finally, coming down to the practical moment of the actual decision, Sanders writes: "I would make the best judgment I could in the light of the facts, believing that the Lord had answered my prayer for guidance" (151). That is: do everything possible to make a wise and informed decision, but in the end put your trust in God and his providence.

Argument - Sanders' argument for the existence of a specific divine will is mainly based on the well-known texts from for example Acts and Proverbs. This biblical material is supported by examples and experiences from the world of missionary organizations. This gives the book an openness to various experiences of guidance, combined with a clear eye for the potential dangers of some of these, resulting in a sober and common sense approach. Tradition and theological conceptuality are largely absent.

Contribution - Citing Leslie T. Lyall, Sanders gives an interesting definition of callings that integrates the subjective side of it, the temporal aspect, and the way it becomes a question of obedience: "A call is a conviction that steadily deepens when faced with the facts of the case, so that sooner or later it becomes a matter of obedience or disobedience" (142).

2.4.7 Jensen and Payne
Phillip D. Jensen and Tony Payne, *The Last Word on Guidance* (London: Matthias Press, 1991).[43]

---

[43] The book was republished in 1997 as *Guidance and the Voice of God* (Sydney: Matthias Media, 1997). Page references are to the 1997 edition.

Authors - Phillip Jensen is a cleric in the Anglican Diocese of Sydney and dean of St. Andrew's Cathedral, founder of the Australian publishing house Matthias Media and involved in numerous Australian ministries. Tony Payne is the publishing director of Matthias Media and editor of the magazine *The Briefing*.

The Will of God - The authors start with the recognition that "decision-making is one of the constant burdens of our existence" and that therefore it is logical that Christians are interested in guidance (13). However, God's guidance seems for many people more a complicating than a comforting factor (15). Over against this uncertainty, they pose that "God does promise to guide us and ... this is meant to reassure us and remove anxiety" (15).

According to the authors, any speech about the will of God must be embedded in God's wider plan: "The God of the Bible is the Lord of history, who draws up a plan and then pursues it to completion. God guides according to a plan" (25). This divine plan will be executed because of God's sovereignty and therefore "it is impossible to be 'outside the will of God' as some people use that phrase" (36). A further implication is that no distinction between God's general and God's special plan must be made (99) and this is exactly what the authors see as the problem of the "traditional approach" (98). Instead, in the view of Jensen and Payne God's will is something already known, something they are able to "outline" (16). His will is for believers "to be under Christ" (31), to inherit what He has provided for his followers (32). God's will is that believers become more and more like Jesus (34) and do good works (36).

Praxis - Key to the praxis resulting from this view on the will of God are the assertions that "God's will is not something hidden that has to be unearthed" (113) and that "God's guidance is more like a compass than a map" (112). Most of God's guidance belongs to the category of "behind the scenes"-guidance (75). And although the authors assert that God can guide in many and various ways, we are not promised that he will do so (79). Based on Hebrews 1:1, they state that "God speaks to us today by his Son through his Spirit in the Scriptures" (77), indicating that many believers wrongly expect forms of guidance beyond the Bible, an idea that is "virtually taken for granted" (90).

Instead, "the biblical idea of wisdom" (102) is key to their view, and this wisdom must be applied to different "categories of decisions" (105): matters of righteousness, matters of good judgement, and matters of triviality. If anything is not a matter of right and wrong, ultimately we cannot make a wrong decision (109), only a more or a less wise decision.

Argument - Jensen and Payne do not use church history or systematic theology in their argument, but abound in references to Scriptural material. Their main material is not the list of texts on "the will of God" found in many other books, but a series of grand statements about God's purposes, mainly from the Pauline letters (e.g. Rom. 8; Eph. 1 and 2). Furthermore, as said before, Hebrews 1:1 is a key text in their view on divine revelation.

Contribution - Compared to other books that propose a wisdom approach to divine guidance Jensen and Payne do not add any real new points or arguments.

2.4.8 Pritchard
Ray Pritchard, *The Road Best Traveled: Knowing God's Will for Your Life*, Wheaton: Crossway Books, 1995.[44]

Author - Ray Pritchard is founder and president of Keep Believing Ministries, a ministry focused on evangelism and encouragement. His book on guidance is based upon a series of sermons on guidance. Pritchard was pastor of churches in Los Angeles, Dallas, and Chicago for over 26 years and is the author of more than 25 books.

Will of God - Pritchard is critical of a lot of the writing on the will of God and speaks about "much misinformation", "bad teaching" and "faulty theology" (38), especially in the more mechanical ideas on finding the will of God. However, his key conviction is "that you *can* discover God's will for your life. More than that, I am fully persuaded that if you want to do God's will, you will do it" (13, emphasis in original). God does have a blueprint for every individual life, but Pritchard assures that we are not promised to get a copy (40). Throughout his book, Pritchard shows that much thinking about God's guidance is overconcerned with specific decisions, when "knowing God's will is really all about knowing God" (18). Pritchard emphasizes the relational aspect of the will of God and states that the will of God is not a location (32). In other words, knowing the will of God "is a journey, not a destination" (37). As a result, "God is much less concerned with what you do than with what kind of person you are" (101).

---

44 Reprinted as *Discovering God's Will for Your Life* (Wheaton: Crossway Books, 2004). Page references are to the 2004 edition.

Praxis - Translating his view on the will of God into the practice of life, Pritchard opposes four myths (38): The idea that God wants believers to know the future (39), the idea that God wants believers "to have 100 percent certainty" before making a decision (42), the idea that God's highest goal is the happiness of believers (46), and the idea that God deliberately makes his will hard to find (49). Over against the last point, Pritchard states that God does not play some version of "cosmic hide-and-seek" (19), but that "God wants you to know his will more than you want to know it, and therefore he takes personal responsibility to see that you discover it" (19).

Pritchard repeatedly emphasizes that "God's guidance is revealed to us one step at a time" (24) and comes in various forms. Although he admires people "who seem to have a direct connection with the Lord" (28) he is clear that this is not what can be normally expected. Often it just means taking the next step, without certainty and without knowing the result.

In two separate chapters Pritchard discusses the use of "fleeces", which he rejects, and the place of dreams, visions and supernatural signs. He acknowledges the possibility of supernatural signs, but stresses the need to "test" them (84-86).

In general, Pritchard's advice comes down to the following aspects: "Build your life on the Word of God" (87), "stay in touch with the Holy Spirit" (87), involve God in every important decision you make (Ch.5.), and be guidable, soft, bendable (108). For those who live in such a way, guidance will certainly come, through ordinary decision-making processes (99% of the time, 109), through changing circumstances (113), sometimes through supernatural events (115) and often through "wise counsel joined with common sense" (116). In the end, he advises to "make the best decision you can and leave the results with God" (123).

Argument - Pritchard's argument is based on a combination of personal experiences and discussion of a number of key biblical passages. In various places, Pritchard draws lessons from the story of the cloud and the pillar, from Proverbs 3:5-6, and from Acts 16. No references to other theologians or theological concepts play an important role in his argument.

Contribution - Pritchard demonstrates how the will of God is often presented in spatial categories (being 'in' the will of God, the 'center' of God's will etc.) and opposes this way of thinking and speaking.

2.4.9 Waltke
Bruce K. Waltke, *Finding the Will of God: A Pagan Notion?* (Grand Rapids: Eerdmans, 1995).[45]

Author - Bruce K. Waltke (1930) is a Reformed evangelical Old Testament scholar, professor at Knox Theological Seminary, Ft. Lauderdale. Waltke has been professor of Old Testament at several of the major evangelical seminaries in the United States and served as a committee member for a number of Bible translations. He is the author of multiple books, most of them scholarly works on the Old Testament.

Will of God - As the subtitle of the book suggests, Waltke is critical of speaking about 'finding' the will of God. From the outset of the book he makes clear that the words 'the will of God' are "tough to define" (8). He shows how several meanings coexist within the Bible, one of them being related to specific choices to be made. However, "it should be noted that this specific term is never used after the Holy Spirit came upon the church at Pentecost" (10). Waltke does believe that a divine plan exists, but "simply because God has a plan does not mean that He necessarily has any intention of sharing it with you" (15). According to Waltke, "we ought to stamp out of our vocabulary the nonbiblical and misleading expression 'finding God's will'" (169).

Praxis - A major part of Waltke's book consists of a critique of methods and practices that resemble pagan divination methods: "To rely on some manner of divination, rather than on the character of God and an individual's relationship to Him, is a shortcut" (42). Thus, instead of a method to find the will of God, Waltke proposes a program to grow into the kind of maturity God wants believers to have (62). In his Scripture-focused program, the transformative reading of the Bible is the primary part (59). Studying the Bible will result in a heart for God, and "the heart that loves God completely can be trusted to have godly desires" (92). Furthermore, Waltke stresses the importance of the Christian community and godly counsel, the necessity to make wise use of the opportunities that come to us, and the priority of making use of the normal decision-making capabilities given to us. Only at the end of his book he points out that every believer must be open to the possibility of supernatural divine intervention.

---

[45] In 2016 a revised and updated edition of the book appeared under the same title with Eerdmans.

Argument - As a result of his Old Testament expertise, key to Waltke's argument is his interpretation of Biblical material and additional material from the Umwelt of the Old Testament. Furthermore, his focus on salvation history, seen for example in his emphasis on the change occurring at Pentecost, plays an important role.

In the few places where Waltke refers to other sources, he clearly shows his Reformed background in citing for example the Scots Confession and Calvin (e.g. 178-179). In general, however, Waltke's use of technical theological terminology is limited.

Contribution - New elements are Waltke's explicit comparison with ancient pagan practices and the informed exegesis of Old Testament material.

2.4.10 Masters
Peter Masters, *Steps for Guidance in the Journey of Life* (London: Wakeman Trust, 1995).[46]

Author - Peter Masters is pastor of the Metropolitan Tabernacle in London since 1970, editor of the magazine 'Sword and Trowel', and dean of the London Reformed Baptist Seminary. Masters is the author of more than 25 books.

Will of God - Masters' book is written as a reaction against what he calls a 'new view', launched in 1980 by Friesen and Maxson (8). According to Masters, there is an "increasing tide of opinion ... against 'specific' personal guidance" (9), whereas before 1980 (and throughout church history) "the need to seek God's guidance in all the major decisions of life was firmly fixed in the minds of those who followed Christ" (7). Masters uses strong words to warn against the dangers he sees in this new view (e.g. "grave error" (8), "utterly destructive" (8), "has already gravely damaged the dedication and commitment of many Christians" (10)). He fears that Christians adopting this new view will end up "at the mercy of our personal inclinations and desires" and "will more easily sheer away from hard callings and irksome situations", leading to a comfortable kind of Christianity (10).

Masters defends the "precious and fundamental principle – that God has a *specific* plan and purpose for the life of his children, and that they should seek his direction in all the great issues of life" (7). The 'great

---

[46] Page references are to the 2008 reprint.

issues' are specified as "all decisions relating to life's overall pathway or direction" (15). Masters describes the plan of God as his "blueprint" (29) and repeatedly stresses the beauty of the idea: it is "one of the greatest blessings of salvation, and a vital spur to true and living godliness" (28), an "overwhelming honour and privilege" (31).

Masters never defines what exactly the will of the Lord is. That this is problematic becomes clear in his defence against the idea of 'missing' God's will. He first asks: "Is it possible to fall into an inferior course of action which thwarts God's will for us?" (12) and then answers: "Of course not, because there is a sense in which the believer is *never* out of the will of God." He adds: "If we fail to seek the guidance of the Lord properly, and follow instead some whim of our own, then the 'wrong' outcome *is* the will of God". Clearly this does not solve the problem, but no further explanation is provided.

Praxis - The praxis Masters proposes is based on his conviction that "we will not always have an advance view of where he [God, CvdK] is taking us, but if we seek guidance and submit our way to him, we may be sure that his superintending hand will shape our circumstances and affairs" (26).

Masters presents the "biblical steps" (30) in an extended discussion of psalm 25. The first step consists of prayer and submission: "Submit yourself entirely to God and pray fervently for guidance and protection" (30). Secondly, 'clear the decks', that is, "identify and dispose of all wrong desires, attitudes and motives" (32). Step 3 consists of studying the Scriptures, "an indispensable stage of guidance" (38), and to look for principles and passages "which bear on the case" (38). In the fourth place, pros and cons must be weighed in the "exercise of discernment" (39). Here, "we weigh the issues carefully, praying for the help of God, and as we do so, he graciously sharpens our mind and increases our wisdom, in accordance with his promises" (39). Masters warns against focusing on feelings, because "the faculty of the mind is not to be bypassed" (40). As the fifth step, we look for God's "overruling" (41): "Overrulings are often used by the Lord to lead us into situations for which we would never have considered ourselves suited, and our most careful reasoning might well lead us away from the Lord's intended goal" (42). The process is finished by the sixth step of "being sensitive to any operation of the Spirit of God in our hearts or consciences, either warning of a wrong decision, or assuring us that we are on the path of his bidding" (43). Steps five and six are crucial, but must not be used in isolation of the other steps (44).

Masters warns against the kind of "pietistic speech" in which believers "constantly ascribe all kinds of everyday events to the special and direct intervention of the Lord, as though their lives were filled with minor miracles" (93).

Argument - The book consists of 8 chapters, the first two consisting of Masters's defense of the traditional view and the other six chapters of applications. The first and decisive argument is the example of Christ ("the life of our Saviour is compelling for us", 14), who was focused on doing the will of God. This primary argument is backed up by the discussion of a long list of biblical texts that hint at divine guidance (15-27). The narrative of the book of Acts stands out, for "the entire narrative of Paul's journeys is the record of a ministry under the constant superintendency and direction of the Holy Spirit" (23).

Although he only refers to Richard Baxter it is clear that puritanism is an important benchmark for Masters (e.g. 13, 15).

Contribution - Master's contribution to the discussion is the fact that his book is an explicit and extended defense of the traditional view directed primarily against Friesen.

2.4.11 Kincaid
Ron Kincaid, *Praying for Guidance: How to Discover God's Will* (Downers Grove: InterVarsity Press, 1996).

Author - Ron Kincaid has been pastor of Sunset Presbyterian Church in Portland for over 29 years. After a split in the church he is pastor of the newly founded Portland Community Church since 2011.

The Will of God - Kincaid starts his book with the observations that the topic of guidance is important for many believers (10) and that it is confusing that totally different answers are given within the evangelical community (11). He then describes what he calls the "traditional view" (13-14) and lists five problems he sees with this view (14-19).[47] According to his own alternative, "Scripture instructs us that instead of struggling to find the one and only right choice and God's blueprint for our lives, we should simply seek to make wise choices" (19). Kincaid does not believe the idea of a divine blueprint is biblical, and repeatedly emphasizes the freedom given to us. His conclusion about the entire discussion follows from this point of view: "I cannot help but think that this whole issue of

---

47 As admitted in note 1, p. 177, four of those five problems are inspired by the work of Garry Friesen.

divine guidance, which draws throngs of people to seminars and sells thousands of books, is overrated" (36).

Praxis - The first part of Kincaid's practical advice is in line with his view on the will of God. He describes "seven principles that form the foundation of a more Biblical approach" (22). The primary principle is the need to "seek to understand and obey God's grand design" (22). This grand design, formulated in line with Rom. 8:28-29, comes down to knowing Christ, being conformed to the likeness of Christ, and sharing Christ with others. Anything that is in line with this grand design is the will of God. Other principles include enjoying the freedom God gives us to make wise choices (26), wholehearted commitment (29), the renewing of the mind (30), trusting God to give wisdom (31), simply getting on with living for Christ without anxiety (34), and taking full responsibility (35). Ultimately, everything comes down to this: "In areas where the Bible gives no command, you are free to choose the course of action that best helps you fulfill God's grand design" (32).

Kincaid's position becomes more ambivalent in the third chapter, on 'The Role of the Holy Spirit in Guidance'.[48] In this chapter, he describes ten ways in which the Holy Spirit leads us in making wise choices (38), coming very close to the traditional view he just rejected. The reader is urged to "take time to listen to God", who "speaks through a still small voice" (43). Words like urges and hunches, inward impressions, and gut-level feelings abound in this chapter (44, 51). In this chapter, dreams and visions, feelings, circumstances, and conscience play a major role. At the end of the chapter Kincaid stresses his former view again.

Argument - The argument of the book is mainly based on Kincaid's conviction that most of the biblical references to the will of God are concerned with the moral will of God, not some kind of individual plan (16). His own view is then backed up by exegesis of key Biblical texts and real life examples.

Contribution - Kincaid has no distinct contribution that adds new insights to the discussion.

---

[48] Friesen, who reviewed the book of Kincaid, writes about a confusing "hybrid", and given the contents of the book, this seems to be a fair depiction. See http://gfriesen.net/sections/review_ron_kincaid.php (accessed Oct. 8, 2014).

2.4.12 Smith
Gordon T. Smith, *Listening to God in Times of Choice: The Art of Discerning God's Will*, Downers Grove: InterVarsity Press, 1997.

Author - Gordon T. Smith, president of Ambrose University College and Seminary, Calgary, Alberta, is professor of Systematic and Spiritual Theology, former vice president and dean of Regent College, Vancouver, and author of a number of books. Besides *Listening to God*, his books *Courage and Calling* (1999) and *The Voice of Jesus* (2003) also deal with the issue of discernment, although the link with 'the will of God' is less explicit.[49] Smith writes from a Wesleyan perspective that is strongly influenced by his contacts with Jesuit spirituality.

The Will of God - In his first chapter, Smith makes clear that he is dissatisfied with both the "blueprint school" and the "wisdom school" when it comes to the issue of the will of God (16): "in both cases God is distant from the decision-making process" (16). Over against the blueprint view, he denies that there is a "neat will to discover", over against the wisdom view he stresses that "it is not just a matter of applying principles to life" (20). That being said, Smith does belief "that we can know the mind of God, not merely in a general sense, but in a specific, existential sense for the choices and decisions that shape our lives" (18).

Thus, Smith is convinced of the importance of being "resolved to know and do the will of God" (38) and believes this extends to our individual decisions and choices (14). However, he stresses that "in the biblical narrative the primary concern of each recipient was communion with God, not specific directives from God" (20).

Praxis - The conviction that "when we formulate simplistic rules ... we cut the vital cord of communication between the believer and God" (33) leads Smith to propose the "art of discernment" as an alternative approach that is "essential to Christian maturity" (15). He writes: "Our only hope for sanity is if we can in some measure know that we are able to speak with God, hear the voice of our loving Shepherd amidst competing voices and know that he is guiding us" (15). Discernment functions in the context of "a dialogue, a conversation, a relationship" with God (23).

The kind of discernment Smith proposes focuses strongly on the inner role of the Spirit and the idea that "recognizing the prompting of the

---

[49] Gordon T. Smith, *Courage & Calling: Embracing Your God-given Potential* (Downers Grove: InterVarsity Press, 1999); Gordon T. Smith, *The Voice of Jesus: Discernment, Prayer, and the Witness of the Spirit* (Downers Grove: InterVarsity Press, 2003).

Spirit is essential during this period between Christ's departure and his return" (35). Scripture functions as the "objective standard" for testing subjective impressions (46), but Smith criticizes Calvin for being overly cautious in accepting direct communication of the Spirit (47). In his opinion, a "healthy balance between Calvinist self-suspicion and Wesleyan self-confidence" is needed (65).

Important parts of the discernment process are Ignatius' ideas of consolation and desolation (54), the questioning of "own motives", and the recognition of the "possibility of self-deception" (59). Furthermore, "effective discernment does not negate a rational consideration of our circumstances" (71), but "God may lead us to do something that is humanly speaking inadvisable" (72). The kind of discernment Smith proposes means that "we make our decisions and take responsibility for them" (114) and that "we will not have absolute, unambiguous peace and rational certainty" (65) as is promised by some other methods and techniques.

Argument - In his book, Smith mainly works with a combination of ideas of John Wesley and Ignatius of Loyola, whose *Spiritual Exercises* are fundamental for the book. Compared to other authors, Smith does not refer to biblical material often. With regard to theology and tradition, we saw before that he clearly opposes Calvin and the Reformed tradition in their denial of the possibility of direct communication of the Spirit.

Contribution - Smith' Wesleyan background, combined with his interest in the Ignatian tradition, leads to a view in which points of both traditions are incorporated.

2.4.13 Hayford
Jack W. Hayford, *Pursuing the Will of God: Reflections and Meditations on the Life of Abraham,* Sisters: Multnomah, 1997.

Author - Jack W. Hayford (1934) is the former pastor of The Church on the Way, Van Nuys, California. After his retirement, he served a period as president of the International Church of the Foursquare Gospel (2004-2008).[50] He is also founder and chancellor of The Kings University, based in Los Angeles and Dallas. Hayford is a well-known author of over 50 books and over 500 hymns.

---

50 A denomination founded in 1923 by Aimee Sample MacPherson which has currently over 60.000 congregations in 144 countries. The name refers to the fourfold ministry of Christ in which the church beliefs: Savior, Baptizer (with the Holy Spirit), Healer, and King.

The Will of God - The chapters of the book are based on different episodes from the life of Abraham, the best example of "walking in the Lord's will" (16). The general message gained from the life of Abraham throughout the book is this: "Don't presume to direct your own life on your own terms. Discovering the will of your Creator and Savior – and walking in that will – may not be the most 'secure' way to live, according to the world's standards. But I assure you of this: It will be the most fulfilling thing that could ever happen to you" (9). Hayford stresses that following God's will is the daily responsibility of every believer (11-12).

Waiting for God's daily "instructions" (9) or "directives" (171) is possible, because "[t]he will of God in your life and mine will always be a beautifully progressive revelation. There's a constant unfolding of His way, His will, and His purpose for our lives with the passing of seasons and years" (54). Although Hayford repeatedly assures that the will of God is very personal (e.g. 14), he also points out that our response to God's directives can have major implications for the people around us: "If we resist God's call, it's very likely there are other people who aren't going to be in the will of God either" (23). And later on in the book: "One of the grand reasons we must trust the Lord's timing is because there is so great an interweaving in what He is doing in *our* lives with what He is doing in other lives" (96).

Praxis - As became clear already, Hayford focuses on daily guidance: "Neither you nor I will ever outgrow our need for today's bread, today's guidance, today's instruction" (35). Apparently, this guidance is so clear that Hayford does not need to discuss the question how the will of God can be found. However, two elements stand out. First, Hayford emphasizes the need to wait on God: "Move when He says move… but not until!" (36) and "key to remaining in God's will is simply to wait where the Lord tells you to wait and not to move until the Lord tells you to move" (38).[51] The second element that stands out is Hayford's emphasis on the inner impulses (156) given by the Spirit as the primary means of guidance. Those inner impulses come in the form of God speaking into the heart (87), prompting (87), the whispering of the Spirit (133), but sometimes also a simple "God told us…" (36).

Hayford makes two remarks that are important in correctly assessing his position. He emphasizes that walking in God's will is no guarantee for worldly success, but "may very well wrench you away from that which is

---

51 In this respect, it seems somewhat contradictary when Hayford later states: "But don't fear movement simply because you don't have a specific direction for every issue or step or decision in your life" (167), where he urges not to wait endlessly.

familiar to you" (18) and "God's purpose and will challenges us at an elemental level in our lives" (150). Furthermore, he comforts his readers by assuring that "[a]s long as we are fully committed to His will and purpose for our lives, He will *never* permit us to remain in confusion" (41, emphasis in original).

Argument - Most of Hayford's view is based upon a spiritualizing reading of the Abraham narrative, from which he draws numerous direct lines to the contemporary situation. Reference to other Biblical material happens occasionally, while references to other sources or theological material are entirely absent.

Contribution - Hayford adds important remarks about the interconnectedness of individual lives and the results of that interconnectedness for thinking about the will of God and guidance. Although he does not draw its logical consequences, the observation in itself is important.

2.4.14 Adams
Jay E. Adams, *The Christian's Guide to Guidance: How to Make Biblical Decisions in Everyday Life* (Woodruff: Timeless Texts, 1998).

Author - Jay E. Adams (1929), a Reformed evangelical author who is mainly known as the founder of the Christian Counseling movement and his method of 'nouthetic counseling.' He is the author of over 100 books on a range of (mainly practical) subjects.

The Will of God - According to Adams, both those who always wonder what the will of God is and those who always seem to have divine direction available have a problem (viii), because both in a way distort the biblical teaching: "Much that is wrong has been said and written about the subject. It is time to set forth clearly and cogently what the Bible teaches" (ix).
　　The key conviction of Adams is "the simple fact that you can know God's will" (ix). And knowing this divine will is crucial for Adams: "Since life *is,* essentially, a series of day-by-day decisions that are either made according to God's will or not, few matters are more important to the sincere Christian than learning how to discern the will of God" (56).
　　Adams strongly asserts that "God's will is unequivocally known to be such" and that therefore, 'seeking' the will of God is literally impossible. This is also seen in the fact that he uses the terms 'directive will' and 'revelatory will' interchangeably (27). This directive will always has to do with

either ministry or righteous living, and on other decisions no specific guidance is to be expected (29).

Praxis - Adams is convinced that all instances of special revelation have come to an end since revelation in Scripture was completed (25). As a result of this stance, he is very critical of many of the forms of guidance proposed in other books (e.g. 32). His own position is a strong version of a practical sola Scriptura: "So, the conclusion of the matter is that if you want to know God's will, if you desire guidance that will enable you to make righteous decisions, then you have a place to turn to – the Bible" (63). No other form of guidance is to be expected.

Adams deduces two main decision-making principles from Scripture. The first is the 'Holding Principle' from Rom. 14:5: Only act if you are fully convinced in your own mind that something is right to do (66). The second is what Adams calls the 'Expediency Principle' (74), based on 1 Cor. 6:12. Here the important consideration is not whether a certain act is lawful, but whether it is helpful, advantageous.

These general principles, combined with the more specific principles found in Scripture, are all that is necessary for the believer. Adams points at two consequences: the first is the immense importance of Bible study and the second the fact that we are expected to make the difficult decisions ourselves (79). Life with God is "an adventure" (81) and many people expect too much certainty or even expect "God to make their decisions for them" (96).

Argument - Key points in the argument of Adams are his conviction that all special revelation has ended and his firm adherence to sola Scriptura. In the one instance where Adams refers to a historical source, it is to the Westminster Confession on the sufficiency of Scripture (95). His argument is mainly backed up by Biblical references, in which, as a result of his view on salvation history, Old Testament narratives play a minor role.

Contribution - Adams contribution to the wisdom view can be seen in his formulation of two important New Testament (or: Pauline) principles, which he calls the holding principle and the expediency principle.

2.4.15 Petty
James C. Petty, *Step by Step: Divine Guidance for Ordinary Christians*, Phillipsburg: P&R Publishing, 1999.

Author - James C. Petty is the former director of development at the Christian Counseling and Education Foundation, Pennsylvania, and former executive director of the Children's Jubilee Fund, Erdenheim, Pennsylvania. Petty is a member of the Presbyterian Church in America (PCA).

Will of God - Petty sets out "to systematically examine what the Bible says about knowing the will of God" (11). He intends to do so in a more theological way than most other books do (12). According to Petty, the biblical phrase 'the will of God' "can mean either the *plan* of God or the *commandments* of God" (56), echoing the traditional theological distinction between the sovereign and the revealed will of God.

God's sovereign plan means "that (1) God does have one specific plan for your life and (2) the events and choices of your life irresistibly and sovereignly work that plan in every detail" (59). Thus it is clear that Petty works with a high view of divine providence, including "all your mistakes, blindnesses and sins" (59). One consequence of this is that it is unthinkable to accept the concept of a 'plan B'.

What Petty rejects in what he calls the "traditional view" (29) is the hidden assumption "that if there is such a plan, God wants us to know it and will reveal it to those who ask" (31). Therefore, the idea of an individual will of God as proposed in much literature "should be rejected" (101).

Praxis - The praxis of divine guidance results from Petty's view on the will of God: "Rather than being treated as servants, subject to a stream of directives, we are offered the very mind and wisdom of Christ" (149). Thus, Petty rejects various "shaky methods" (102, an example is the practice of 'fleecing') and states that "methods of guidance can never go back to the situation before the giving of the Spirit" (153).

Petty's view on how wisdom works out in the life of the believer can be seen in the following quote:

> Each of us must therefore develop a sense of priorities reflecting our gifts, our situation, and our callings, and our goals to glorify God. These are the issues that constitute the real battleground of guidance. This is where we seek to know and do the will of God. As each of us applies the great commandments to our own individual circumstances, our own unique path will emerge. Our calling will develop, and our work and ministry will be embodied. There we will find our path – following Christ's steps, yet taking our own. (92)

Key components of his view are the emphasis on the need to set priorities, the application of Scriptural commands and principles to the specific situation of the individual's life, and the responsibility for one's own choices. He describes two perspectives to look at Christian wisdom: "From God's perspective it is a direct gift, supernaturally given by the Spirit. From our perspective, it is our renewed mind enabled by God to see as Christ sees"(165).

In practice, the application of wisdom to concrete situations involves a number of elements. These elements form no logical sequence, but Petty believes "that these elements need to be part of every search for guidance from God" (192). The elements are total consecration to God, gathering information about the situation, supplication in prayer, consultation with other people, meditation, making a decision, and expectation for the future.

Argument - Key to Petty's argument is his claim that many authors "address the issue in a nontheological way. That is, their books offer no serious study of Scripture, no in-depth interaction with larger theological principles. We are given stories, illustrations, and references to Scripture, but little or no critical theological reflection" (26). Over against this tendency, he holds that "the biblical doctrines of providence, revelation, inspiration, and illumination carry within them the answers our theologically unaware generation needs" (11). One practical problem with the book of Petty is that where he discusses other views, in principle he does not name other authors "for the sake of charity and Christian unity" (13).

Although still not an academic treatment of the subject, Petty's book is characterized by a more careful use and discussion of Scripture and by the use of more precise theological conceptuality. His discussion of divine providence is of major influence on his resulting view on divine guidance. When referring to classic theological statements, Petty almost exclusively points to the Westminster Confession (e.g. 59, 119).

Contribution - Besides offering more robust arguments, Petty adds a unique emphasis to the discussion by pointing to the sociological background of many questions on the will of God. He mentions for example changes in the labor market (21), individualism (23), and the changed "pace of decision making" (20).

2.4.16 Swindoll
Charles R. Swindoll, *The Mystery of God's Will: What Does He Want From Me?*, Nashville: Word Publishing Group, 1999.

Author - Charles R. Swindoll (1934) is founder and senior pastor of Stonebriar Community Church, Frisco, Texas, and host of *Insight for Living*, a worldwide Christian radio program founded in 1979. Swindoll served as president of Dallas Theological Seminary. He presently serves the seminary as its chancellor. Swindoll is affiliated to the Evangelical Free Church of America.

Swindoll has previously published a booklet on the same topic, *God's Will: Biblical Direction for Living*.[52] In this 24-page pamphlet, he emphasized that God wants believers to know and do his will and therefore "is actively engaged in the process of revealing it" (1). He clearly states that "the Bible teaches us that God had a predetermined plan for every life" (7).

Will of God - In the introduction to the book published in 1999, Swindoll writes that he has come to "a new understanding of God's will" (ix), mainly as a result of personal experiences. Three keywords of his book are already mentioned in this introduction: the will of God is often convoluted, surprising and painful (x). Too much writing about guidance gives the impression that it is all "quick, simple, and easy" (xi). Over against these easy answers, Swindoll states that "searching, disturbing questions far outnumber absolute, air-tight answers" (4).

Yet, the topic of the will of God remains "one of the most profound subjects in the Christian life" (4), and Swindoll adds that the number of times he has been asked about the topic is endless (39). Because the subject is "inscrutable" (6), he does not promise to give definite answers in the book.

With regard to the will of God, Swindoll distinguishes between God's decreed will and his permitted will (18). His decretive will is "His sovereign, determined, immutable will" that we can only know for sure after it has happened (18). God's permissive will includes evil, but we can never say that God decreed it (26). Through the examples Swindoll gives it becomes clear that in his opinion God does have a detailed personal will for all believers. He also speaks about "His special plan for your life" (67). However, Swindoll never makes clear how God's decretive will and his "special plan for your life" relate to each other. He does make clear, however, that God's personal plan is "fixed" (100) and "continually unfolding" (99).

Throughout his book, Swindoll emphasizes that there is a tendency to focus exclusively on the *destination* God has planned for individuals, whereas "God's concern is the process that He is taking us through to

---

52 Charles R. Swindoll, *God's Will: Biblical Direction for Living* (Portland: Multnomah Press, 1981).

mature us..." (ix). Thus, we must "not forget that His plan is not designed to make us comfortable; it's designed to make us more like Christ, to conform to His will" (204).

Praxis - Initially, both in his view on the will of God and the resulting praxis Swindoll seems to stay close to his former writings. For example, the "four most significant methods of God's leading" are the precepts and principles of His written Word (44), the inner prompting of the Holy Spirit (46), the counsel of "wise, qualified, trustworthy people" (48), and an inner assurance of peace (49). Most emphasis is given to the inner prompting of the Spirit, both in the direct discussion and in the examples Swindoll gives (e.g. 48). In other places, Swindoll stresses wisdom (even "good old garden-variety common sense", 41) and patience (99). He also makes much of God's use of open and closed doors (Ch.11).

However, the 'new' element in Swindoll's view is the mysteriousness of God's will. Although we must use the methods previously described, Swindoll strongly emphasizes that "surprises are among God's favorite things" (173) and that "we sometimes come to a place where we cannot explain why things turned out as they did" (176). Difficult experiences are not the exception, but the rule in serving God (179): "more often than not, God's will is downright humanly illogical" (204) and we better stop trying to make them logical. In all this it is important to keep in mind that "behind God's surprises are purposes we are not aware of" and "when God surprises us, He supplies sufficient grace to handle the unexpected" (180).

Argument - Swindoll's argument is based on a combination of Biblical material and his personal experience. The biblical material he uses is mainly the same as in most other books. In some instances, he gives a longer treatment of important passages. Swindoll occasionally refers to other authors, amongst whom Henry Blackaby receives positive remarks (e.g. 50). Other theologians or theological concepts do not play major roles in his argument.

Contribution - The contribution of the book of Swindoll is found in its emphasis on the unpredictability of the will of God and the mysteriousness of life.

2.4.17 Elliff
Jim Elliff, *Led by the Spirit: How the Holy Spirit Guides the Believer*, Dundas: Joshua Press, 1999.

Author - Jim Elliff is founder and president of Christian Communicators Worldwide, Parkville, Missouri. Before, he served as a pastor in various churches for 20 years. Currently, Elliff is a major advocate for home congregations. He is the author of several books.

Will of God - Elliff describes how he moved from a traditional view on guidance to a "more rational approach" (5). His concern is not with the idea that God speaks with believers and guides them, but "it is the way he does it that is in question" (5). In Elliff's view, the will of God in the Bible is something to be done, not something to be sought. As a result, he does not say much about the will of God in his book, for according to him there is no relationship between a hidden will of God and the decisions believers have to make.

Elliff focuses on the terminology of 'being led by the Spirit' and strongly asserts that "Paul is maintaining [in Rom. 8, CvdK] that everyone who is a genuine believer is led by the Spirit *in some way*" (9) and therefore the leading of the Spirit does not refer to the special experiences for which the words are often used.

Praxis - Elliff proposes a view in which the Spirit works mainly mediate, not immediate, "within the mind and affections of the person" (12). The concept of the renewed mind plays a major role, fueled by a "living interaction with the Scriptures" (14) and "the Spirit's indwelling" (21). Elliff positions his view between the illuminist (22) and the "cold intellectualist" (23).

In practice, his view comes down to the following statement: "We are to actually think through the given situation, wrestle with the options, weigh them, sift them, ponder the implications and consequences, and we are to do all of this in the light of the truth as we find it in the Scriptures interpreted in context. And we presume, underneath all of this, God is working" (39). This rational approach "is the normal way" (39), while direct communication is not to be ruled out (25). For Elliff, "the man who makes the wise decision, yet always remains open to God's further intervention in whatever way God pleases, is demonstrating normative spiritual guidance" (43).

Argument - The key point Elliff makes is the superficial interpretation of the phrase 'led by the Spirit' that is underlying many contributions to the discussion. Given the constraints of his book he does not present prolonged arguments and is not able to give detailed exegetical treatments of the key texts. Elliff, who is influenced by the writings of George Müller, tries to show that the way Müller is often presented in the literature does no justice to his actual position.

Contribution - The contribution of Elliff is found in his focus on a single phrase that plays an important role in the field of literature.

2.4.18 Observations
Our review of the sixteen books published on the will of God and divine guidance from the period 1990-1999 yields the following observations to be worked out later in this chapter.
1. Compared to the previous decade, a remarkable shift in content occurred. Whereas in the previous period most authors viewed God's will as something concrete believers may expect God to reveal to them, in the period from 1990-1999 eight of the sixteen books focus on wisdom in decision-making (Robinson, Pritchard, Waltke, Kincaid, Jensen and Payne, Adams, Petty, and Elliff). Only three books (Blackaby and King, Masters, and Hayford) advocate the 'traditional' view.
2. All authors discussed in this chapter have (multiple) theological degrees and have served as professors, pastors, or leaders in Christian organizations. Yet, the popular nature in which the topic is discussed, mainly aimed at lay people, results in a body of literature that is generally low in theological conceptuality, lacks argumentative clarity, and does scarcely interact with tradition as an important source.
3. Still no explicit discussion is being developed between most contributors. Although for example Masters is clearly writing against what he sees as the novelty of the wisdom view, most authors do not mention the others they disagree with and are rather vague in pointing out which exact views they are interacting with.
4. Relatively few new insights are added to the discussion. Exceptions are found in Bockmühl, who attributes a lot of attention to tradition; in Waltke with his emphasis on pagan divination in the Umwelt of the Old Testament; and in Hayford who structures his book around the life of a single biblical figure.

2.5 Analysis of Evangelical Literature 2000-2010

2.5.1 Introduction
In this section twelve books on the will of God and divine guidance that were published between 2000 and 2009 will be introduced and analyzed in chronological order. The chapter will end with a number of preliminary observations that will be elaborated upon in the next evaluative sections.

2.5.2 McDowell and Johnson
Josh McDowell and Kevin Johnson, *God's Will, God's Best for Your Life*, Minneapolis: Bethany House, 2000.[53]

Authors - Josh McDowell (1939) is an American apologist, evangelist, and writer of more than 100 books. He has been working for Campus Crusade for Christ all over the world since 1964. His organization is called Josh McDowell Ministry.

Kevin Johnson is pastor of the Emmaus Road Church (ECC), Hopkins, Minnesota since 2010. Johnson is author and co-author of over 50 books. Johnson has backgrounds in both theology and journalism.

Will of God - The purpose of this book is "to show you how you can find God's plan for every area of your life" (31). As suggested by this statement, the authors believe that God has an encompassing and detailed plan for every believer's life. They later state more specifically that "God has a will that encompasses anything that will ever happen in your life" (39), that it is a "moment-by-moment will for your life", for "each activity" and "each second" (57). Thus, "God is tracking you from above the maze – He sees your past, present and future and can tell you exactly how to go" (16).

This belief in an individual divine will for each believer is combined by the strong conviction that "without a doubt, He has a will for your life and *wants you to know it*" (56-7, emphasis CvdK). God does not play hide-and-seek with believers (56). In this light it appears somewhat strange that the authors later speak about "the whole puzzle of God's will" (112) when writing on the praxis of finding the will of God.

Praxis - The core of the praxis McDowell and Johnson prescribe is derived from Psalm 37:4: "If you delight yourself in the Lord, then He will give you the desires of your heart" (19). When living in such a relationship of delight with God, McDowell and Johnson describe "four basic ways to discover God's guidance" (58) or a "four-step strategy for knowing God's will" (58). The four steps include Scripture, prayer, counsel, and circumstances.

Here, Scripture functions as God's universal will, His will for all Christians, which is already revealed (39-40). Friends play an important role in the counseling (e.g. 70). Especially the influence of circumstances is

---

[53] The book is written from the perspective of McDowell, with Johnson functioning as co-author.

stressed: "Reading your circumstances will tell you a lot about God's specific will ..." (112) for "God uses circumstances to direct us" (113). The idea of open and closed doors is crucial, although the authors are aware that often multiple interpretations are possible (114).

The authors emphasize that "God usually leads one step at a time" (149), but add that "God often shows us in amazing detail what to do right now" (150). Two reasons are given why God leads one step at a time: Because we cannot handle more and because we need to stay close to Him (151). Finally, when it comes to situations in which a choice has to be made and no clear guidance has been received, "God is probably saying 'You pick'!" (152).

Argument - The authors do not engage in discussions on guidance and do not refer to other views on the issue. No references to theologians or theological loci are made in the book. The argument instead is based on a number of biblical texts (Jer. 29:11; Ps. 32:8; Rom. 12:1-2 and others) that occur in most books on the topic.

Contribution - In choosing Psalm 37:4 as central point for their book the authors choose an interesting perspective, that is however not further developed in the remainder of the book. Another distinctive feature of the book is that it is centred around specific "needs" of believers and stresses that God has plans to meet those needs (17).

2.5.3 Sittser
Gerald Lawson Sittser, *Discovering God's Will: How to Make Every Decision with Peace and Confidence* (Grand Rapids: Zondervan, 2000).[54]

Author - Gerald Sittser, professor of religion at Whitworth University, Spokane, Washington, is the author of seven books. He treats the topic of the will of God from his personal experience of losing his wife, mother, and daughter in an accident and raising three other children on his own (21). Sittser is member of a presbyterian church.

The Will of God - Sittser's aim is "to provide perspective, not to outline five easy steps to discovering the will of God" (15), because, in life, "we never know how things will turn out" (20). Thus, Sittser disagrees with what he calls the 'conventional approach': "Convention teaches us that the will of

---

54 Page references are to the 2004 edition, *The Will of God as a Way of Life: How to Make Every Decision with Peace and Confidence,* Grand Rapids: Zondervan, 2004.

God consists of a specific pathway we should follow into the future. God knows what this pathway is, and he has laid it out for us to follow. Our responsibility is to discover this pathway – God's plan for our lives" (22). Sittser's problems with this view are that it focuses on "the important decisions, which might not be as important as we think" (23), that "it betrays a false and negative view of God" (25), and that it "betrays a desire to control a future that simply cannot be controlled" (26-7).

Sittser proposes an alternative approach, or an "old model that has been forgotten" (28). A key statement for Sittser's view is that "God does have only one will for our lives – that we seek first his kingdom" (35). Then, "if we seek first God's kingdom and righteousness, which *is* the will of God for our lives, then *whatever choice we make concerning the future becomes the will of God for our lives*" (34-5, emphasis in original). Throughout his book Sittser emphasizes that the will of God has more to do with the present than with the future.

In asserting that "God's will is like several trails leading to the same goal" (100), the question remains what exactly Sittser means when he holds on to the phrase 'the will of God'. In several places, he seems to suggest that our choices make God's will ("We had other options. All of them *could* have been the will of God, but only one *became* the will of God – the one we chose", 104) but later strongly asserts God's sovereignty: "The hidden will of God consists of his sovereign control over the entire universe. *Everything that happens* is the will of God in this second (first: revealed will, 204, CvdK) sense because God rules by his providence over all of history" (205). As a result of this ambiguity, Sittser is never able to fully evade the language of the conventional view, especially in the chapter on calling and career (Ch.12), where he writes about "the right career, the one God has willed for us" (157).

Praxis - Sittser nowhere presents something close to a method or program. His two main emphases are on doing what we already know (God's revealed will, 14, 204), and on being faithful in the little choices we make every day, for they "often have a cumulative effect far exceeding the significance of the big choices we occasionally have to make" (24).

Other key words for his view are "surrender" (37), "freedom" (e.g. 39) and "daily obedience" (85). He repeatedly stresses the importance of a community of believers (49, 101) and warns against giving too much weight to success (102) and against endless worrying (135). The most concrete chapter is on discovering a calling, for which Sittser gives six 'signs': motivation, talent, experience, opportunity, feedback from the community, and joy (175-182).

Argument - Key to the entire argument of the book is Sittser's experience that life is totally unpredictable and that "decision-making is inherently messy" (95). We must not be "presumptuous about the future", for that is of little value (30).

Relatively little use is made of concrete Bible references. The main tradition of influence on Sittser seems to be the mystical tradition, with Sittser repeatedly pointing to lessons to be learned from Ignatius of Loyola, Thomas Merton, Francis de Sales, and Brother Lawrence. They seem especially important for his focus on "surrendering to God in the ordinariness of the present moment" (88).

Contribution - In bringing his personal narrative of suffering and the unpredictability of life Sittser adds a strong emphasis on the ambiguity of life. A distinct emphasis of Sittser is his focus on obedience in minor everyday issues as outweighing the importance of 'finding' the will of God in major decisions.

2.5.4 Rasnake
Eddie Rasnake, *Living God's Will: Reading and Applying God's Signs for Your Life* (Chattanooga: AMG Publishers, 2001).

Author - Eddie Rasnake worked seven years at Campus Crusade for Christ before becoming pastor of Woodland Park Baptist Church, Chattanooga, Tennessee. He is the author of sixteen books.

Will of God - Rasnake does not argue for the existence of a specific will of God, but clearly accepts the idea as a presupposition. He starts out with the assertion that God wants us to know His will even more than we do (xi) and that therefore "the road to God's will is well-marked with signposts to direct us" (xi). In his book, Rasnake promises to offer "practical, usable principles distilled from God's Word and explained on a grassroots level" (xvi) so that the reader will "learn how to hear what He is saying" (xxi).

In Rasnake's view God's will extends to school choice (xx), buying a car (56) and many "smaller decisions" like where to spend a vacation (14). However, he remarks that "God is far more concerned with my character than with my circumstances" (76) and that we must not restrict following the will of God to specific points in our lives, but see it as a lifelong process (124): "you will spend the rest of your Christian life seeking and finding the will of God. If your call is to follow Christ, then we will never outgrow our need to know His will" (30). Rasnake frequently repeats his conviction that "the will of God is not a hidden mystery revealed to the super-spiritual or held only for a special event. It is an integral part of what it means to walk with Christ" (164).

Praxis - Rasnake's prescribed method to 'find' the will of God is a classic example of the traditional view described already by Müller and Meyer. In twelve chapters he provides twelve 'signposts' that lead to the will of God. The twelve signs he mentions are submission to the Lordship of Christ, prayer, the illumination of Scripture, wise counsel, weighing of the pros and cons, providential circumstances, peace, the voice of the Holy Spirit, stewardship, faith, waiting on God, and the sound use of our mind.

The signs have a similar function as they have in other contributions promoting the traditional view. For example, submission is important because "God is not going to show us His will until we first settle in our hearts that we are willing to do whatever He says" (3), prayer is "communicating with God" (18), and "God speaks through our circumstances, and we can save ourselves much anxiety if we learn to listen to what they say" (70).

Rasnake's emphasis on the need for the signs to "lign up" is crucial, because trusting in only one sign does not sufficiently reduce the danger of subjectivism: "we should wait for God to begin lining up signposts so as not to draw a conclusion from only one source" (44). God's peace, given as a confirmation of our decision, functions as "one of the most important" signs (84).

Argument - Rasnake takes the existence of a specific divine will as his point of departure and does not argue for it. No definition or exact statement of his interpretation of this will is given. Throughout the book, key arguments are derived from the well-known Bible texts. Only in a few places other authors are mentioned in support of a point.

Contribution - The book is a prototype for the traditional view and as such does not offer much new material.

2.5.5 Jeffress
Robert Jeffress, *Hearing the Master's Voice: The Comfort and Confidence of Knowing God's Will,* Colorado Springs: WaterBrook Press, 2001.

Author - Robert J. Jeffress (1955) is the pastor of First Baptist Church in Dallas. Besides, Jeffress is host of the daily radio program 'Pathway to

Victory'. Jeffress gained attention in the USA by his controversial statements on homosexuality and American politics.

Will of God - Jeffress starts his book by introducing "three common approaches" and "the reasons they don't work" (1). The three approaches he mentions are the formulaic, the experiential, and the rationalistic approach (12-4). As his own point of view, he states that "God delights in revealing His desires to us" (17) and Jeffress promises that "in the chapters that follow, we'll discover all the means that God uses to make His perfect plans clear to us" (17).

Jeffres distinguishes three possible meanings of the words 'the will of God': God's providential will, his preceptive will, and his personal will (24-7). God's personal will is "God's individual plan for our own lives" (27) and is referred to as "God's personal blueprint" (30), which "includes the smallest details of your life" (178).

Although he carefully distinguishes between God's providential will and his personal will, in the final chapter Jeffress writes about God's sovereignty as his "safety net" (176). By this, he means that "God has a purpose for your life that won't be compromised by your circumstances, your mistakes, or even your rebellion" (177). Jeffress does not make sufficiently clear how the distinction between the providential will and the personal will is maintained.

Praxis - The key aspects of Jeffress' praxis are introduced early in the book and worked out in later chapters. Early on he writes:

> My study of God's Word, coupled with my own experience and that of others I have counseled, has led me to three conclusions about hearing the Master's voice. First, we must desire to hear God's voice. Second, we must recognize that God speaks in a variety of ways. And third, we must realize that God reveals only what we need to know (20).

With regard to the first point Jeffress stresses that "the Bible continually encourages us to seek God's guidance for our life" (23) and that believers must be careful not to become practical atheists (20). The "variety of ways" boils down to Bible reading, prayer, wise counselors, circumstances, and the own desires (32-5).

The Bible gives us the general direction and purposes God has, but it must not be expected "to predict our future, answer all our questions or provide specific direction for every decision we face" (50). Prayer is presented as a dialogue with God (65) in which He shares His direction, peace, and desires (79). Ultimately, prayer is "aligning your will with God's will" (79). In the chapter on circumstances Jeffress mainly introduces the concepts of open and closed doors and gives guidelines for the evaluation of supernatural experiences. With regard to counseling, he describes three types of counselors: people with (some degree of) authority over the believer, experts on specific issues, and fellow believers. Finally, Jeffress shows how the diverse teachings of the Bible on the trustworthiness of feelings have led to different views on their place in guidance. He holds that, although our feelings are corrupted by sin (126), they can be transformed and "serve as a reliable indicator of God's direction in our lives" (128).

The aspects mentioned reappear in the concrete examples (marriage, work) Jeffress discusses. He summarizes them with 5 prescriptions: Know the precepts, rely on prayer, take notice of what is practical, take heed of your preferences, trust in providence (141-8). Finally, Jeffress stresses that no full revelation about the future is to be expected, but step-by-step guidance, for God "will always reveal the next step we need to take" (36).

Argument - Jeffress's argument is based on a combination of Scripture references and his own experience. He explicitly criticizes Friesen and his denial of a personal will of God and gives some arguments why he believes there is such a will (28-9). Several Biblical passages show that God does care about minor details (hairs, the feeding of sparrows), so he must certainly care about human lives.

No interaction with theological sources takes place in the book and except for his use of providence theological concepts are used sparingly.

Contribution - Jeffress does not add real new insights to the discussion.

2.5.6 Carter
Mack King Carter and Jean Alicia Elster, *Interpreting the Will of God: Principles for Unlocking the Mystery*, Valley Forge: Judson Press, 2002.

Author - Mack King Carter (1947-2013) was senior pastor of the African-American megachurch Mount Olive Baptist Church of Fort Lauderdale, Florida. Carter, who held a doctorate from Southern Baptist Theological Seminary, wrote four books and hosted a television ministry besides being a fulltime pastor.

Will of God - According to the opening statement of the book, "one of the greatest challenges facing Christians today is determining the will of God in their lives" (xv). Carter hopes to "provide readers with keys for knowing God's plan for their lives" (xvi). In Carter's view God has a specific plan for each individual life and believers face the task of "unlocking the mystery of the divine will" (1).

Although he does propose a specific divine will, the distinctions Carter uses to describe the will of God are different from others. Referring to a book by Leslie Weatherhead,[55] Carter distinguishes between God's intentional will, his circumstantial will, and his ultimate or final will (16). "God's intentional will describes what God the Father wants from his children" (16), his circumstantial will results from "the interaction of our free will with God's intentional will" (17), and the end result is called God's ultimate will. Because of the human free will God's intention can be temporarily frustrated (16), but ultimately "what God intends will surely come to pass" (19). Carter explicitly mentions this as a position distinct from Calvinism (26). Following his proposal, 'being out of God's will' becomes a possibility in the sense of being out of God's intentional will (25). Throughout his book, Carter applies this framework to all Biblical narratives he treats.

Praxis - Because "each chapter offers a key that allows believers and seekers alike to effectively interpret God's will for their lives" (xv), no clear 'method' can be derived from Carter's book. This is a deliberate choice, for in the conclusion Carter makes clear that he "tried to stay away from trivializing the mystery of God" and from "giving simple answers to difficult questions" (123).

After the opening chapters on the nature and will of God, Carter starts with a chapter on Jesus and the will of God. Jesus' prayer in Gethsemane receives special attention, for "an examination of the garden of Gethsemane is pivotal in any discussion of the will of God" (39), and "Gethsemane tells us that we can discover God's will through prayer" (28). Another strong emphasis of Carter is on the importance of suffering in discovering God's will, for "the cross is the great medium for understanding God's will" (45): "Often, we cannot see God's will for our lives because we always look for God in that which is strong but never in that which is weak" (49).

Important 'keys' Carter discusses are gifts (65), patience (Ch.6), and fasting (97). However, ultimately his focus is on fellowship with God, for "we are able to discern the divine will as we spend time with God" (94). In our relationship with God, the Bible plays an important role, for without it

---

[55] Leslie D. Weatherhead, *The Will of God* (Nashville: Abingdon Press, 1944).

we are "like a rudderless ship" (94). Carter adds that "often, the insights of others can disclose God's will" (105), and common sense is crucial. Here, "common sense is more than intuition or having a hunch. It is about making decisions based upon what we know about God, history, culture, Scripture, and our own experiences" (111). Although not providing a distinct method, all elements of the traditional view are present in Carter's book.

Argument - All keys Carter discusses are derived from Biblical narratives read through the framework of the three distinct wills of God. No reference is made to other authors besides Weatherhead and few technical theological terms are used.

Contribution - The major contribution of Carter to the discussion is his distinct view on the will of God, coupled with his focus on suffering, oppression, and obscurity.

2.5.7 Swavely
David Swavely, *Decisions, Decisions: How (and How Not) To Make Them*, Phillipsburg: P&R Publishing, 2003.

Author - David Swavely is pastor of Faith Church, a Presbyterian church in Malvern, Pennsylvania. Swavely was pastor of several other churches before and is the author of a number of books, including two novels.

Will of God - The aim of the book is to "help you to make decisions that honor the Lord and benefit you, as well as help you to avoid some common errors that can rob you of joy and send you spinning in the wrong direction" (ix).

Swavely devotes a separate chapter to the meanings of the phrase 'the will of God'. In his view, statements like 'trying to find the will of God' "are often based on a misunderstanding of what the Bible means…" (43). He distinguishes between the sovereign and the moral will of God (44) and states that "much of the confusion and frustration experienced by Christians who are 'seeking the will of God' comes from failing to distinguish between the sovereign and moral will" (51). Swavely rejects the concept of a "unique individual plan for my life" that "I've got to find out" because in his view this is not a biblical concept (54-5).

With regard to decision-making the focus should instead be on the moral will of God, for "the guidance we need for our choices does not have to be somehow mined from the mysterious and unknowable plan devised among the Holy Trinity in eternity past" (51, with reference to Deut. 29:29). This does not mean that God's sovereign will is totally irrelevant, but its bearing should be more on our attitude in decision-making than on the manner of decision-making itself (105): "From God's perspective, he knows all our choices ahead of time and actually planned for us to make them. But from our perspective, we do not know his plan until it happens, so it is our responsibility to make our decisions based on the commands and principles revealed in his Word" (53-4).

Praxis - Because he is convinced that "many Christians already have misconceptions" (x) about guidance, Swavely starts his book with a number of ways how *not* to seek guidance. He warns that "you should never make decisions based on selfish motives, superficial methods, special revelation outside the Bible, or supernatural signs" (5). He repeatedly emphasizes the dangers of expecting new revelations and makes a "case for cessation" (19). In his opinion, "many Christians, who would say that they do not believe in new revelation, are essentially seeking new revelation in their decision making" (65).

Swavely furthermore warns against expecting supernatural signs ("a thing of the past" 39), against giving authority to experiences and feelings (63) without carefully evaluating them in light of Scripture (76), and against using circumstances as 'road signs' (80). Finally, he underlines that Biblical prayer is not reciprocal, not a two-way conversation in which God gives direct answers (92-3).

His own prescribed praxis consists of prerequisites, principles, and a chapter on the actual process of decision-making. Swavely lists as prerequisites that "you are the kind of person who is walking in the Spirit, recognizing the sovereignty of God, and praying for wisdom and providence" (99). Four key words describe the main ingredients of the Christian decision making process: Scripture, wisdom, desire, and counsel (121). Here the Bible receives a prominent position in that it "bears on all decisions you make" (121), either directly or indirectly. Wisdom is "a knowledge of Scripture and the ability to apply that knowledge in your life" (115) gained "through the indwelling Holy Spirit illumining your heart" (115). Following Psalm 37:4, Swavely states that "your personal desires play an important role in decision making" (131) and finally "wise counsel helps us to understand Scripture better, it helps us to grow in wisdom, and it helps us to evaluate our desires more accurately" (135).

In the actual process of decision-making Christian freedom plays a major role (144), excluding any notion of 'missing' God's will (144). As an example of the entire process, Swavely points to Paul's remarks about his priorities in Romans 1 and 15, in which all the elements mentioned can be found.

Argument - The book of Swavely consists of two parts, of which the first deals with how not to make decisions and the second with Swavely's own position. Swavely refers to authors he disagrees with, cites several other sources on guidance, and frequently refers to the Westminster Confession (e.g. 45, 84). He works from a Reformed perspective and writes from an explicitly cessationist point of view. Compared to other authors, Swavely employs more theological concepts and interacts with theological debates.

Contribution - Within the literature on the will of God, the book of Swavely stands out in its use of and reference to other sources.

2.5.8 Meadors
Gary T. Meadors, *Decision Making God's Way: A New Model for Knowing God's Will*, Grand Rapids: Baker Books, 2003.

Author - Gary T. Meadors served as Professor of Greek and New Testament at several seminaries, lastly from 1995 to 2011 at Grand Rapids Theological Seminary. He also served as pastor in several Baptist churches.

Will of God - Meadors sets out to present a "unique" model (9), because "my study of the Bible and my observations about life have slowly merged into a model for discerning God's will in the daily decisions confronting us" (9). Early on in the book he sets out the core of his model: "Knowing God's will about the issues of life confronting you is primarily a process of clarifying life's questions and challenges from a biblical worldview and values set" (13). Later on, he poses that "knowing God's will is not a process of receiving immediate information from God about life's issues but one of discerning life's issues on the basis of the revelation that God has already given to us" (201).

It is clear that Meadors does not urge his readers to find the will of God. He does believe that "God certainly does have a will for my life" (91) but states that "there is no need to find it because it has never been lost" (97). He especially challenges two assumptions underlying the "typical presentation": "the idea that God requires us to find his plan for our lives in order to make life decisions" and "that God will perform some kind of revealing act in order to communicate his will for our individual lives" (130). His focus throughout the book is on the revealed will of God.

Praxis - With regard to the praxis, Meadors' focus is on developing a Christian worldview with the corresponding values. Key resource for such a worldview is found in the Bible, "God's sufficient communication to us to know his will" (36). Thus, "we need to learn to think biblically" (45).

For attaining a biblical worldview, it is important to read the Bible in context (76). For Meadors this means taking into account the influence of "redemptive history" (84). Many biblical stories must be understood "as descriptive of special events within redemptive history rather than prescriptive" (113). For example, Acts should be read "as a story, not a manual" (123).

Meadors suggests "four steps to follow in Christian discernment" (136): knowing the Bible, developing a Christian worldview based upon it, identifying the corresponding values, and applying both worldview and values in a decision-making process. This entire process should be accompanied by much prayer (201).

Finally, Meadors asserts that "God expects each of his children to take the responsibility to develop and apply a biblical worldview and values set. This is not an easy task. There are no shortcuts. But when you invest yourself in this kind of growth, and experience the confidence of settled convictions about your decisions, the reward is far greater than the labor" (221).

Argument - Key to Meadors' argument is his idea of redemptive history, which means at least that many biblical examples cannot be applied in a direct way to our situation. Besides, he asserts that the concept of an individual will of God does not fit to the biblical texts that use the phrase "the will of God". He points to the King James translation as an important cause of this misinterpretation of the phrase (116). Theological tradition or individual theologians do not play an explicit role in his argument.

Contribution - Meadors' concepts of worldview and values add content to the often vague use of the notion of 'wisdom'.

2.5.9 Lake
Kyle Lake, *Understanding God's Will: How to Hack the Equation Without Formulas*, Lake Mary: Relevant Books, 2005.

Author - Kyle Lake (1972-2005), who died at the age of 33 following an accident while performing a baptism, was the pastor of University Baptist Church in Waco, Texas. Lake was involved in the Emerging Church movement.

Will of God - Lake sets out to uncover some myths about God's will stating that "[m]any of these mythical illusions have been tossed around for so long that they've scarcely been questioned" (xxi). Lake admits that he has "always been suspicious of cut-and-dry answers" (xix). The primary 'myth' he is writing against is the approach in which God's will is deciphered in a formulaic way: "The very nature of formulas collides head-on with the ways of God, because formulas are about control, predictability, and certainty" (8). Lake is looking for "an alternative that never elevates God's will above God. We need an alternative that leaves us feeling as though we've returned to the heart of scripture and historical Christianity…" (18).

Looking for an alternative does not mean for Lake to give up the belief "that God has intentions for people's individual lives" (9). He continues to speak of a 'specific will of God' "that applies to everyone individually" (131).

Praxis - Lake gives a central place to three metaphors that help us understand God's guidance. He does so because of the acknowledgement that "in trying to understand a topic as vast as "God's will", it will require more than one metaphor" (83).

The three metaphors he discusses are apprenticeship (discipleship), fatherhood, and kingdom. The metaphor of apprenticeship teaches that "the process of discerning God's will must be just one aspect of our apprenticeship, rather than the end goal of life" (28) and shows that it is "out there" (35) where the Christian life is lived. The life of a disciple is characterized by being on mission, not by safety and an easy life. It places "a major emphasis of our lives on the *journey* rather than the particular destination" (83). The metaphor of fatherhood emphasizes the "history of relationship" between God and the believer (94), instead of the individual decisions. Furthermore, it stresses that "we must own our decisions without pawning them off on God or others, or we will never take responsibility for our lives and experience the growth and maturity found in the process of decision-making itself" (94). It shifts the focus from what the believer does to who the believer is and what he or she is becoming. The third metaphor, of the Kingdom, emphasizes that for the sake of the good of the kingdom, the king gives his subjects tasks that fit their gifts.

Throughout his discussion Lake warns against any formulaic influences and repeatedly stresses the need to take responsibility, to live close to God, and to live freely. He explicitly warns against "Lone Ranger decision making" and "emotionally driven, impulsive decision-making" (95). Ultimately, Lake describes "life with God as an adventure … an adventure that will produce a person of character, sacrifice, and faith – all in all, a person like Jesus" (154).

Argument - Lake's book is written in a casual, provocative style from beginning to end and contains no lengthy argument. The key of his argument is built around the three perspectives provided by the different metaphors. No major interaction with other authors and views takes place, although they clearly function as the background against which Lake writes.

Contribution - Lake's way of presenting the Christian life by three biblical metaphors offers a new way of formulating what it means to follow Christ within the parameters of a wisdom approach.

2.5.10 Benner
David G. Benner, *Desiring God's Will: Aligning Our Hearts with the Heart of God* (Downers Grove: InterVarsity Press, 2005).

Author - David G. Benner (1947) is Emeritus Professor of Psychology, former associate fellow at the Center for Studies in Religion and Society at the University of Victoria, British Columbia and author of over 30 books, including the *Baker Encyclopedia of Psychology and Counseling*.[56] His focus throughout his work has been on the intersection of psychology and spirituality.

Will of God - The focus of Benner's book is on how to desire God's will, because in his opinion the topic is often treated the way "New Year's resolutions" (17) are treated, that is, as "things that are not naturally attractive" (18). In choosing this focus, Benner presupposes a divine plan, but refuses to limit our engagement with this divine will "to points of major decisions" (14) and instead speaks about choosing the will of God in the "moment-by-moment flow of ordinary days" (15).

The divine plan Benner speaks about "cannot be separated from God's kingdom. Establishing the divine reign of love on earth is God's big plan. The smaller details of the divine will all fit within this" (39). As shown in the practical examples he gives later on in the book, those "smaller details" contain for example the books Benner must or must not write (112). Yet, we must not "trivialize" God's will (112).

---

[56] David G. Benner and Peter C. Hill, eds., *Baker Encyclopedia of Psychology and Counseling*, 2nd edition (Grand Rapids: Baker Academic, 1999).

Ultimately, for Benner the focus is not on decisions, but "God's will is that you become the person that from eternity you were destined to be – your true self-in-Christ" (103).

Praxis - Benner emphasizes the opposition between the kingdom of the self and the Kingdom of God. In the first, willfulness and willpower reign, in the second the "God-given gift of willingness" (15): "A spirit of willingness invites me to pause and turn to God, simply opening to God for a moment, letting God bring perspective and clarity..." (23). Such willing surrender "occurs only when we live so close to God's heart that the rhythm of our own heartbeat comes to reflect the divine pulse" (15-6).

Thus, intimacy with God is crucial for the discernment process. In order to know God's heart, believers are encouraged to "cultivate an ongoing awareness of the divine presence" (62). The main question is not what God's will is in a specific situation, but "in every circumstance of our life our question should be *Where is God in this?*" (74). Benner adds that we must expect to find God where we least expect to find him and that the bearing of our cross is an important element in the Christian life.

In the process, "prayer is the place of divine transformation" where "our hearts are slowly transformed into the heart of God" (87). With regard to the Bible, the practice of *lectio divina* is encouraged (64). When writing about one of his own decisions, Benner states that "our discernment process has included a number of elements – rational examination of the pros and cons of each option, extensive prayer and conversation about the possibilities, seeking the advice of spiritual friends and directors" (113). However, based on Ignatius' concepts of consolation and desolation (108), the primary place is given to "God's movements in our souls" (113).

Argument - Benner starts his book with the distinctions between willfulness and willingness and the kingdoms of the self and of God. In the chapters that follow he explains how love, desires and crosses all bring us closer to the heart of God.

In his book, remarkably few Bible texts are cited and no biblical narratives play a role. Benner draws heavily from the mystical tradition. Special attention is given to the works of among others Brother Lawrence (62), Simone Weil (66), and Ignatius of Loyola (108). Also, the work of Gordon Smith (see §2.4.11) is cited with approval (68).

Contribution - Benner's distinct contribution can be found in his distinction between willfulness and willingness, between obedience and surrender.

2.5.11 Packer and Nystrom
J.I. Packer and Carolyn Nystrom, *Guard Us, Guide Us: Divine Leading in Life's Decisions,* Grand Rapids: Baker Books, 2008.[57]

Authors - J.I. Packer is Professor of Theology at Regent College, Vancouver, British Columbia, and is frequently mentioned as one of the most influential figures in American evangelicalism. He works from a low church Anglican, Reformed perspective and is the author of numerous books, among which "Knowing God" stands out as an absolute bestseller.[58] Packer had written before on the topic of guidance in Bible study books, in separate chapters of other books, or in daily devotionals.[59]

Carolyn Nystrom is a freelance writer who has authored more than 80 books and frequently co-authors with well-known evangelical leaders.

Will of God - In the prologue of their book Packer and Nystrom note that since the second half of the nineteenth century "the topic of guidance from God has become a focus of ... fear in many Christian hearts" (10), and that clearly some things have gone wrong:

> First, the notion spread that getting and following direct guidance from God, as something above and beyond making commonsense decisions in Christian terms, was a matter of great importance in the Christian life. Second, God's plan for the Christian individual's life came to be thought of like a travel itinerary in which making planned connections is crucial and missing a connection wrecks the plan and spoils the rest of the journey (10).

Yet, while being critical and concerned about the abuse of certain ideas, the topic of guidance in itself is not the problem, for "there are many places in the Bible where guidance is promised to faithful believers" (13). In discussing Psalm 23, the authors describe guidance as "one aspect of his [God's, CvdK] covenant care" (16) and in this way directly reject any idea of "missing the will of God", for "if the sheep strays of the path, the shepherd brings her back again" (29).

---

57 Also published as James I. Packer and Carolyn Nystrom, *God's Will: Finding Guidance for Everyday Decisions* (Grand Rapids: Baker Books, 2008).
58 James I. Packer, *Knowing God* (London: Hodder and Stoughton, 1973).
59 See for examples of respectively a study book, a book with a separate chapter on guidance and a devotional *Decisions: Finding God's Will. Six Studies for Individuals or Groups* (Downers Grove: InterVarsity Press, 1996); *God's Plans for You* (Wheaton: Crossway Books, 2001); *Knowing and Doing the Will of God: Daily Devotions for Every Day of the Year,* ed. LaVonne Neff (Ann Arbor: Servant Books, 1995).

No separate discussion of the possible meaning of the words 'the will of God' is given. The following statement comes closest to a definition: "The will of God is the course of action in each situation that God sees as good, pleasing, and complete; the most truly and fully God-glorifying response to each set of needs and possibilities" (83). What is important to mark is that in stressing the one best course of action and repeatedly emphasizing that the best must be chosen over the merely good Packer and Nystrom suggest that in each situation God's will is restricted to one option. This is further confirmed by the statement that God's will can be found (146), and in their usage of the language of vocation, which suggests that God calls every individual "to a particular walk of life" (181).

Praxis - The book is more about the praxis of divine guidance than about the will of God. It is an attempt to point away from depending on supernatural experiences: "the idea that you would need a special sign from God, ... is superstition too" (11). Good decisions, according to the authors, are ideally made in the following way:

> As we collect and survey all the available facts that are relevant for making a decision; as we search the Scriptures for the relevant principles and parameters of decision and action; as we ask fellow Christians for words of wisdom and advice on the matter in hand; as we come to terms with the limitations and non-negotiable alternatives, working out the likely consequences of each possibility open to us as to make sure we will not unwittingly choose the merely good in place of the best, we should constantly ask God to judge, correct, and direct our thinking – heading us off from deciding badly and granting us the Spirit-wrought reality of his peace in our hearts as we move into what we see to be the wise way into which he is leading us (38).

Thus, all natural decision-making practices are involved in the process, always accompanied by prayer. A few elements stand out. First, the authors emphasize the role of wisdom and discernment (e.g. 34) and they point to the biblical wisdom literature as an important but often neglected source (61). Second, peace is a decisive factor in their process. This peace is defined as "a sense that the quest is ended, the solution has been found, and no more puzzling over the matter is necessary" (236) and is described as "God's ordinary way of confirming" (236). On the contrary, "withholding peace is one of God's ways of signaling that some rethinking is in order and some adjustment needs to be made" (224). Thirdly, the authors write positively about the importance of Christian "casuistry"

(102), a basic skill all believers need (59) that mainly consists of "the art of applicatory thinking" (102).

Although the authors oppose "the fancy that real guidance from God for the making of each day's decisions is a direct ministry of the Holy Spirit in one's heart" (136), they remain quite open to such supernatural revelatory acts of God, for "it is not for us to place restrictions on God that he has not placed on himself!" (16). Hence, the authors speak repeatedly about God using circumstances to nudge believers (36), and about sensitivity to nudges from God (54), particularly given to "those who know him well and are used to recognizing his voice within" (59).

Argument - The book stands out in clarity of argument among the other books. References to Biblical material are always backed up by concrete exegesis and Biblical narratives are read through a salvation-historical perspective in which both the coming of Christ and of the Spirit are seen as turning points (41-2). Although the book does not contain many explicit references, it is clearly written in the Reformed and Puritan traditions with which the authors associate.

Contribution - Especially the chapters on the importance of role models within the Christian community, a separate chapter on the place of wisdom in the Christian life, and a separate discussion of the role of the Holy Spirit in guidance add new insights.

2.5.12 DeYoung
Kevin DeYoung, *Just Do Something: A Liberating Approach to Finding God's Will, or, How to Make a Decision Without Dreams, Visions, Fleeces, Impressions, Open Doors, Random Bible Verses, Casting Lots, Liver Shivers, Writing in the Sky, Etc.* (Chicago: Moody Publishers, 2009).

Author - Kevin DeYoung (1977) is Senior Pastor of Christ Covenant Church, Matthews, North Carolina. He is the author of a number of books.

Will of God - As the subtitle suggests, DeYoung is critical of what he calls the "conventional approach" (41) to the will of God. His goal "is not as much to tell you how to hear God's voice in making decisions as it is to help you hear God telling you to get off the long road to nowhere and finally make a decision…" (12).

DeYoung distinguishes between God's will of decree (17), his will of desire (19), and his will of direction (22). Here, "the will of decree is how things are, the will of desire is how things ought to be" (19). The will of direction refers to "a secret will of direction that He expects us to figure out before we do anything" (22), and according to DeYoung no such thing exists (22). Believing in such a will and searching for it "is bad for your life, harmful for your sanctification, and allows too many Christians to be passive tinkerers who strangely feel more spiritual the less they actually do" (24). Just God's will of decree and his will of desire are enough, for "because we have confidence in God's will of decree, we can radically commit ourselves to His will of desire, without fretting over a hidden will of direction" (39).

Referring to the arguments of Sittser (see §2.5.2), DeYoung lists five problem he sees in the conventional approach: its exclusive focus on non-moral decisions (42), its implications about the nature of God ("sneaky", 43), its preoccupation with the future (44), its undermining of personal responsibility, accountability, and initiative (46), and its subjectivism (50).

Ultimately, "God's will is your growth in Christlikeness" (59) and "your sanctification" (77) and "God tends to use discomfort and trials more often than comfort and ease to make us holy" (77).

Praxis - DeYoung's alternative is based on the Sermon of the Mount: "If you are seeking first the kingdom of God and his righteousness, you will be in God's will, so just go out and do something" (59). Or in other words: "Die to self. Live for Christ. And then do what you want, and go where you want, for God's glory" (59).

Based on the work of Jensen and Payne (see §2.4.6) DeYoung makes five statements on guidance (63-66):

1. God guides us by His invisible providence at all times.
2. God can speak to His people in many different ways, guiding them with their conscious cooperation.
3. In these last days, God has spoken to us by His Son.
4. God continues to speak to us by His Son through His Spirit in the Scriptures.
5. Apart from the Spirit working through Scripture, God does not promise to use any other means to guide us, nor should we expect him to.

DeYoung warns against seeing open doors, fleeces, random Bible verses, and impressions as "certain words from the Lord" (82).

God's way is the way of wisdom and "Biblical wisdom means living a disciplined and prudent life in the fear of the Lord" (87). Based on Proverbs 2, DeYoung mentions Bible reading, listening to sound advice, and praying as the ways to obtain this wisdom (89). God's way "is to speak to us in the Scriptures and transform us by the renewing of our minds" (39). Therefore "God wants us to drink so deeply of the Scriptures that our heads and hearts are transformed so that we love what He loves and hate what He hates" (90).

When such wisdom is our way of life, the actual decision-making process comes down to four steps: searching the Scriptures for relevant principles, get wise counsel, pray, and then make a decision (97-100).

Argument - The book is divided into ten chapters, of which the first four contain DeYoung's critique of the conventional approach and the others his alternative. DeYoung works from a Reformed perspective, although the nature of his book does not allow for much references. He regularly cites Biblical texts, especially when describing his view on the various 'wills' of God.

Contribution - DeYoung has a very critical stance towards American Christianity. He especially attacks the "postponement of growing up" (13) and the obsession "with safety, security, and most of all, with the future" (38). In his conviction, "our preoccupation with the will of God is a Western, middle-class phenomenon of the last fifty years" (30-1).

2.5.13 Huffman
Douglas S. Huffman (ed.), *How Then Should We Choose: Three Views on God's Will and Decision Making*, Grand Rapids: Kregel Publications, 2009.

In 2009 the first multi-view book on divine guidance and the will of God appeared. Contributors are four authors discussed before: Henry and Richard Blackaby represent what is in the book called the specific-will view, Garry Friesen represents the wisdom view, and Gordon Smith represents the relationship view. Huffman provides an introduction and conclusion. Huffman is professor of Biblical and Theological Studies at Biola University, La Mirada, California. He is the author of various books.

In the book, all contributors are given space to present their own view and after each contribution the other authors respond to it as a way of discussion. The contributions written in the book are all completely in line with what the authors wrote elsewhere, so we will not discuss their contributions extensively (see sections 2.4.1, 2.3.2, and 2.4.11 for their respective views). However, the reactions given in the book point to some important areas of ongoing discussion.

In his introduction, Huffman provides some valuable background information to the discussion. He points to the various distinctions in and terms for the will of God used in systematic theology (15-16), gives a brief historical overview in which he points at some theologians in whose work precursors can be found for the contemporary discussion (21-22), and introduces what he sees as three different approaches or even "schools of thought" (23). The discussion sections make clear that Huffman was right in his introduction that a "multitude of theological questions" (14) is involved in the debate. For example, the authors disagree about their interpretation of biblical texts, especially when it comes to the practical value of narrative sections. Furthermore, the question of immediateness and mediateness of God's working plays a key role, as does the tension between objective and subjective 'input'. Closely related to the last point is the recurring question whether the human ratio and emotions can be trusted or must be feared.

Huffman concludes the book with a brief overview in which he states his hope that a center position can be found (243) that combines strengths of the views and evades weaknesses and extremes. Furthermore, he gives some suggestions for further thought. Finally, as referred to before, Huffman gives an extended annotated bibliography of the discussion.

2.5.14 Observations

Before closing the current section some observations can be drawn based upon our review of the material from the period 2000-2009.

1. Of the twelve books discussed in this chapter, once again the majority presents a wisdom approach to divine guidance (Swavely, Meadors, Packer and Nystrom, DeYoung), or at least leans into the direction of such a view (Sittser, Lake). Three books firmly defend a traditional position (McDowell and Johnson; Rasnake; Jeffress), while two books focus more on the believer's relationship with God (Mack King Carter, Benner). The book edited by Huffman does of course not fit into one of the categories.

2. Most authors who propose a wisdom approach start their books admitting that they come from a specific will view and write from their concern that most other believers (still) hold such a position. This emphasizes the fact that in the eyes of insiders the specific will view is the most widespread view among lay people.

3. At the same time, authors who propose a view differing from the 'traditional' view often work from the assumption that they come with something radically new, while in practice they are mostly reinventing the wheel proposed in several other books before. For example, Mea-

dors presents his view as something entirely new and unique, while much of the components of his view can already be found in Friesen, albeit under different terms.
4. As a result of this lack of overview of the field, combined with the popular nature of most of the literature, the book edited by Huffman is the very first book in which proponents of the various view get into real discussion with each other.

2.6 A Typology of Guidance

2.6.1 Introduction
In the previous sections we have analyzed 39 popular books on divine guidance and the will of God with a special focus on their interpretation of the will of God, the prescribed discernment practices, and their argumentation. Throughout this analysis, we have encountered descriptions like 'the traditional view', the 'wisdom view', the 'relationship view', the 'specific-will view' etc. However, a clear and convincing categorization of the existing views on divine guidance seems to be lacking.

In this section I will develop a typology of views on guidance as encountered in the contemporary evangelical literature. In order to do so, we will first discuss existing categories or typologies (§2.6.2), and evaluate them (§2.6.3). Then, I will introduce a typology I think does more justice to the actual body of literature investigated in the previous sections (§2.6.4). The three views included will each be described in sections §2.6.5-2.6.7. Finally, I will point to the merits and limitations of the proposed typology (§2.6.8).[60]

2.6.2 Existing typologies
Until 1980, no typologies of different views on guidance existed at all. This situation changed with the publication of Friesen's *Decision Making and the Will of God* (§2.3.2). As we have seen, Friesen presented an alternative to what he labelled the 'traditional approach', which stands for the view that God has an ideal plan for every individual believer that he makes known to them through a combination of signs. Friesen labeled his own view on guidance the 'wisdom view' and portrayed this wisdom view and the traditional view as the ends of a spectrum on which all views can be placed. According to Friesen, intermediate options take features of both views, often in an inconsistent way. He described the intermediate

---
60 A condensed version of this section has been published as Cornelis van der Knijff, "'Guide Me, O Thou Great Jehovah': A Typology of Divine Guidance in Contemporary Evangelicalism," *European Journal of Theology* 25, no. 2 (2016): 179–88.

positions as 'traditional view with wisdom leanings', 'synthesis of traditional and wisdom views' and 'wisdom view in traditional vocabulary'.[61] A notable strength of Friesen's approach is that it does justice to the ambiguous positions of many books, where authors prescribe for example a wisdom approach in the language typical of the traditional view. However, Friesen's 'spectrum' does insufficient justice to the distinct views (Gordon Smith, Dallas Willard) that he tends to place in the synthesis-category. Still, his categorization was taken over as the main interpretive grid by a number of authors.

An example of someone who generally adopted Friesen's distinction is James Petty. Although in his *Step by Step* he developed three categories, Petty's traditional and wisdom views correspond with Friesen's proposal; he adds a 'traditional charismatic view' to cover the distinctiveness of views that ascribe a crucial role to the direct and verbal communication of God.[62]

Stephen Kovach, in his dissertation *Towards a Theology of Guidance*, once again adopts Friesen's categories. However, instead of the label 'traditional view' he chooses the more informative 'blueprint view'. His description makes clear that the substance of the view remains the same:

> Under the blueprint view, God has a perfect plan, or blueprint, for each person's life. This plan includes who you are to marry, what school you are to attend, what job you are to take, etc. The goal of each believer is to discover God's perfect plan and to discern the one correct choice God has for you in each and every decision.[63]

A more radical adaptation Kovach made was to add a distinct third category, which he introduced as a moderate position between two extremes and labelled the 'directional view'.[64]

The first author to introduce a really distinct third category that was not primarily a 'moderate' version of either of the two poles was Gordon T. Smith. Arguing that according to both the 'blueprint school' and the 'wisdom school' "God is distant from the decision-making process",[65]

---

61 See the appendix of his book, Friesen and Maxson, *Decision Making*, 2004, 424–68. On his website, Friesen adds the category of 'non-evangelical or miscellaneous' and puts for example the work of Campbell Johnson in this category. See http://www.gfriesen.net/sections/book_reviews.php (accessed Sept. 5, 2014).
62 James C. Petty, *Step by Step*, 29–32. In a note Petty adds a fourth category, the 'priestly view', characterized by the decisive role of either church offices or a strong charismatic leader.
63 Kovach, "Toward a Theology of Guidance," 3.
64 See section 1.2.2 for some further remarks on Kovach's book and his categories.
65 Gordon T. Smith, *Listening to God in Times of Choice: The Art of Discerning God's Will* (Downers Grove: InterVarsity Press, 1997), 16.

Smith proposed a view in which an intimate relationship with God and the discipline of discernment are the central aspects. Here, three "schools of thought" are described in which the third is not automatically a synthesis of the other two approaches.

As we have seen (2.5.13), Huffmann adopts this tripartite approach in distinguishing between a specific-will view, a relationship view, and a wisdom view. The discussion sections of his book show that between the three views serious differences exist.

2.6.3 Evaluation of current typologies of guidance
As will be clear from the above description, there are currently basically two different options: One that presents the various approaches on a continuum between a traditional view and a newer wisdom view (Friesen) and one that distinguishes three distinct approaches in the literature that all have their particular features (Smith, Huffman).[66]

What all these categorizations share is impreciseness in the naming of the models. For example, the label 'traditional view' does not convey any information on the content of the model, while the combination of a blueprint or specific-will view and a wisdom view is theologically strange in that the first describes an element of God's 'side' of guidance, while the latter focuses more on the human side. In order to overcome this problem all proposals share, a typology is needed that describes all models from a single, theological perspective.

2.6.4 A new typology of guidance as conceived in contemporary evangelicalism
Based upon the above consideration, in what follows I will propose a new typology of guidance as encountered in the evangelical literature analyzed. This typology is based upon the following considerations: First, our reading of the contributions on guidance between 1980 and 2010 suggests that a tripartite division does most justice to the differences between the various contributions.[67] Second, the different models of divine guidance take their point of departure in the question: What activity does best describe God's involvement as guide in the various models? Taking this approach has the positive side effect of detracting from accounts of

---

66 Thus far, we have adopted the terminology of different *views* that is used in the literature on guidance. In order to be as precise as possible, from now on we will use *view* when discussing the contribution of a particular author, and *model* when we describe a group of authors whose views share common characteristics. The resulting *typology* is the overview of the existing models.
67 If the existence and communication of a specific divine will is taken as the sole criterion for developing a typology, two models could be sufficient. In my opinion, this would do insufficient justice to the variety of views that would have to be pressed into these models.

guidance in which individual believers and their choices are in the centre of the attention.

The above considerations result in the following three models of guidance: 1) Guidance through information; 2) guidance through intimation; and 3) guidance through transformation. In the following sections the theological essentials, praxis, and argumentation of each of these models will be introduced. Furthermore, we will point out which authors from the previous sections can be seen as proponents of which model.

2.6.5 Guidance through information
In the first model, guidance takes the form of information, in which God reveals parts of his plan for the life of the believer.[68] At its core is the conviction that God has a detailed will or plan for the life of every individual believer. Throughout their lives, and especially at crucial junctures, God will provide information or 'road-signs' to show individuals which way has to be taken or which decision to be made. Thus, basic assumptions of this model are that (a) God has a 'plan' for each individual life and (b) He intends to reveal this plan to believers when they seek his guidance.

Within these constraints, differences exist on a number of issues. The more charismatically inclined authors reckon with concrete divine speaking, while others concentrate on different forms of direction, like specific applications from Scripture or peculiar circumstances ('open doors'). Furthermore, some authors focus only on major decisions, while others include minor details.

The *praxis* of perceiving divine guidance consists mainly of paying attention to the various directions God provides. A key idea is that God often speaks 'in stereo': we can know where God guides us when the different signs support and reinforce each other.[69] The forms of divine direction most commonly mentioned are application of biblical material, specific answers to prayer, circumstances ('open and closed doors'), and (unsolicited) advice from fellow believers. Some authors also include the inner voice of the Spirit or the experience of a 'burden.' Often, the inner peace of the Spirit is decisive. Major differences exist on the value of per-

---

68 In a previous version (article EJT) I labeled this model 'guidance through revelation'. I do still think that what happens in this model according to its proponents is undeniably a form of 'fresh' revelation, but a number of authors promoting this view would certainly not consider it to be 'revelation'. Most of them explicitly subordinate the personal directions to God's revelation in Scripture, speaking not of guidance as revelation, but as the specific *application* of what has already been revealed.

69 E.g. Tim F. LaHaye, *Finding the Will of God in a Crazy, Mixed-up World* (Grand Rapids: Zondervan, 1989), 112: "When the road signs begin to line up in a straight line, we know we're properly approaching the 'runway' to God's will. It's a matter of coordination."

sonal desires, gifts, and common sense as features of guidance.[70] Contributions of this model of guidance often propose a set of 'steps' or a 'method' (at times in an almost algorithmic fashion) to 'find' the will of God.[71] The notion of 'finding' God's will is crucial within this model, displaying the presupposition that God has already provided something to find, or will at least do so when convenient.

This model is most often based upon a combination of a deduction of the author's view of God and a straightforward application of biblical narratives, Old and New Testaments alike. The deduction from the author's view of God to a view on guidance takes the following basic form: God is love, hence his will is always best for us. God is all-knowing, so his directions are always right. God's love also ensures that he will not let us miss out on what he intends for us.[72] With regard to the biblical material, especially Old Testament guidance narratives and the book of Acts play a crucial role.

Key representatives: LaHaye, Blackaby, Masters, Stanley, Hayford.

2.6.6 Guidance through intimation

The second model of guidance encountered in the evangelical literature perceives guidance as a form of intimation. Intimation, and the related verb 'to intimate' stress the delicateness and subtlety of the manner in which God guides believers, while they also convey the sense of the intimacy of a personal relationship.[73] Both aspects are of central importance to this model. Proponents of this model usually maintain that God has a distinct will for the individual believer and that he frequently makes this

---

70 So, for example, Blackaby is quite negative about these, whereas LaHaye is remarkably positive about the importance of common sense given the overall contours of his contribution. See Henry T. Blackaby, Richard Blackaby, and Claude V. King, *Experiencing God: Knowing and Doing the Will of God* (Nashville: Broadman & Holman Publishers, 2008), 35; LaHaye, *Finding the Will of God*, 109.
71 For this methodological focus, see for example Derek Cleave, *How to Know God's Will*, 68, who proposes "a procedure that can be followed in endeavouring to find out just what God wants us to do in this situation" and especially LaHaye, *Finding the Will of God*, 8, 21, who illustrates "biblical techniques that can help you to make the difficult decisions that will mold the course of your life" and who secures his readers that "by the time you finish this book, you, too, will be equipped to make right decisions about finding God's will for your life."
72 However, for some authors this is no guarantee that by being disobedient or by paying no attention we cannot actually 'miss' God's best for us. LaHaye, for example, argues that Romans 12:1-2 means three 'levels' of God's will and that by making the wrong decision believers do actually end up on a lower level of God's will. Most authors do not go this far but the consequences of 'missing' God's will often remain obscure.
73 See for these connotations the *Oxford Dictionary of English*, 3d edition, s.vv. "Intimate1"; "Intimate2"; "Intimation". For the background in ancient Latin see the *Oxford Dictionary of English Etymology*, s.v. "Intimate."

will known. However, they do not advocate 'searching' the will of God as an activity that belongs to the essentials of the Christian life but see it as a by-product. Instead, they stress the importance of growing into an intimate relationship with God, which will result in an ever-increasing awareness of the indwelling of the Spirit in the heart of the believer. This way, believers will develop a growing ability to hear God's 'still small voice' within, nudging them in the right direction.

This focus on God's inner voice brings its own dangers with it, and proponents of the model are well aware of these. They acknowledge that the Spirit of God is not the only one who speaks in the human heart, but that other spirits and personal inclinations also strive for attention. Therefore, in their *praxis*, they introduce the ancient concept of *discernment* as a crucial element. Here, discernment is not primarily a skill, certainly not a method, but an active perception of the promptings of the Spirit within.[74] In developing their concept of discernment, some authors draw explicitly on Ignation (Jesuit) spirituality and its concepts of consolation and desolation, inner peace and turmoil, as decisive concepts. Other, more external, forms of divine communication are not excluded, but according to Willard, "the more spectacular is the less mature."[75] For those matured in their discernment, no spectacular acts from God are necessary to convey his guidance. The crucial role for human discernment in this model reflects on the humility with which interpretations must be held. Whereas in the first model most authors encourage believers to try to achieve certainty regarding God's will for their lives, authors of this model are generally aware that discernment is a human activity and that hence its results will always be fallible.

Key *argumentative* features underlying this second model are the idea of God's inner voice (usually with reference to 1 Kings 19), and the focus on the concept of discernment. The concept of discernment is read through the Ignation and Wesleyan traditions. In general, a salvation-historical approach is taken to biblical narratives. As a result, especially Old Testament narratives are not applied as straightforward to the current situation of believers as under the first model. The focus is on the New Testament concept of the *indwelling* of the Spirit and the mainline Protestant tradition is criticized for its neglect of the personal communication of the Spirit.

Key representatives: Willard, Bockmühl, Smith, Benner.

---

74 See e.g. Smith, *Listening to God*, 33, who protests against the focus on method in especially the first type of guidance: "When we formulate simplistic rules ... we cut the vital cord of communication between the believer and God."
75 Willard, *Hearing God*, 103.

2.6.7 Guidance through transformation
The third model of guidance describes God's involvement primarily in terms of *transformation*. This model is closely related to what was described in earlier typologies as the wisdom view. At its base lies the classical theological distinction between the revealed and the hidden will of God. The major consequence drawn from this distinction is that what God thinks necessary to reveal of his will is already revealed in full in Scripture. Although the details of individual lives are included in God's hidden will, there is neither reason nor promise to expect additional divine revelation or communication.[76] This does not mean, however, that God does not guide believers at all. What it does imply is that such divine guidance is less concrete and more process-oriented than portrayed in the other views. Although this is not made explicit in most contributions of this type, this form of guidance becomes an aspect of the sanctification of the believer. In other literature, especially in contributions advocating the first model, this view is regularly accused of being deistic.[77] From the perspective of the present typology, it will be clear that this is a misunderstanding. The main difference between the views is not whether God is actively involved in guidance, but whether his presence is revelatory or transformative.

Practically, this model shifts the main responsibility of the believer from finding the will of God or discerning his voice within to making wise decisions and bearing full responsibility for them. Hence, freedom, responsibility, and wisdom play different roles here than in the other models. The required wisdom and maturity are both gracious gifts of God and the result of certain spiritual disciplines, again in close parallel to Protestant theological accounts of sanctification. Prayer, Bible reading, meditation and study, and the formative influence of the Christian community are crucial. Among the authors who advocate this model of guidance, different stances exist towards forms of direct guidance. Those differences are closely related to the disputes on cessationism within evangelicalism.[78]

---

76 E.g., James Petty, *Step by Step*, 101, states that "what is often called the 'individual will of God' should be seen simply as the application of God's commands and character to the specifics of our lives"; cf. Friesen and Maxson, *Decision Making*, 2004, 41; Robinson, *Decision-Making by the Book*, 24.

77 See e.g. Packer and Nystrom, *Guard Us, Guide Us*, 220. No one would argue that a strong view on sanctification fits well within a deistic account.

78 Jay Adams, for example, is very radical in his rejection of any direct forms of guidance whereas authors like Friesen and DeYoung are more open to them, but stress that they are exceptions instead of the rule. See Jay E. Adams, *The Christian's Guide to Guidance: How to Make Biblical Decisions in Everyday Life* (Woodruff: Timeless Texts, 1998), 25; Friesen and Maxson, *Decision Making*, 2004, 136; Kevin DeYoung, *Just Do Something: A Liberating*

With regard to the *argumentation* supporting this model, it moves most in line with classic theological accounts of divine providence and sanctification. With regard to the biblical material, and especially the narratives, a strong salvation-historical approach is taken with an emphasis on Hebrews 1:2: Jesus is the final Word of God. As a result, the focus is on the New Testament paraenetic teachings and less on the more narrative parts of the Bible. Some authors point to Old Testament wisdom literature as an important but mostly uncultivated source for Christian living.

Key *representatives* of this model of guidance are Friesen, Waltke, Adams, Petty, and DeYoung.

2.6.8 Merits and limations of the proposed typology
Like any typology, the one presented here has both its merits and its limitations. One of its main merits is that it spells out, more than the existing typologies did, that underneath different views on guidance important *theological* issues are at stake. This result is obtained by abstracting from the often practically oriented popular literature with its focus on what the individual believer can or should do to receive or understand divine guidance. Instead, by focusing on God's activity in guidance, and hence on the theological nature of guidance, a deeper understanding of the similarities and differences between the various models has been reached that focuses not exclusively on the interpretation of the will of God or on the prescribed practices, but also on the underlying presuppositions and argumentation. This deepened understanding is needed to lead us to the questions to ask and venues to pursue in the next chapters. It will help us to trace the issues at stake and to highlight the implications of the various positions in their purest form.

That being said, however, we should note that the proposed models cannot do full justice to the intricacies of the many individual positions of the authors, most of which cannot be neatly categorised. It must be kept in mind that a typology like the one presented will always remain a construct, even when based upon a careful analysis of many individual examples. As Richard Niebuhr commented with regard to another theological typology:

> When one returns from the hypothetical scheme to the rich complexity of individual events, it is evident at once that no person or group ever conforms completely to a type. Each historical figure will show characteris-

---

Approach to Finding God's Will, or, How to Make a Decision Without Dreams, Visions, Fleeces, Impressions, Open Doors, Random Bible Verses, Casting Lots, Liver Shivers, Writing in the Sky, Etc. (Chicago: Moody Publishers, 2009), 68.

tics that are more reminiscent of some other family than the one by whose name he has been called, or traits will appear that seem wholly unique and individual.[79]

This limitation of any typology, and hence also the one presented here, means that it is possible to add further categories or subdivide the current models.[80] Yet, for our purposes in this book a concise typology with sharply delineated models that is based upon consistent categories is most helpful.

2.7 Implications for the Remainder of the Project

2.7.1 Introduction
Although the typology developed in the previous section is the most important result of this chapter, in this section we will discuss a number of additional insights resulting from the overview of the evangelical literature on guidance that can aid us in the remainder of this book. First, we will discuss some noteworthy formal features of the literature reviewed (§2.7.2). Then we will make some remarks on the nature of the argumentation within the literature (§2.7.3), and finally, we will turn to a number of theological questions arising out of the literature that will need to be addressed in what follows (§2.7.4). These will function as guiding questions for the research in the next chapters.

2.7.2 Formal features of the body of literature
The body of literature on divine guidance we discussed in this chapter has some noteworthy formal features. These have to do with the authors involved, the concerns from which they write (and what these concerns reveal about the models on guidance), with a shift in the dominant position within the literature, and finally on the contributions from individual authors.

With respect to the authors involved in the discussion on guidance, several things can be noticed. In the first place, they are almost exclusively male (of the 39 books discussed only one has a female author, Helen

---

[79] H. Richard Niebuhr on his famous typology on the relationship between Christianity and culture: *Christ and Culture* (Harper & Row, 1956) 43-44. Yet Niebuhr continues to stress the importance of using types to call to attention "the continuity and significance of the great *motifs* that appear and reappear…" (emphasis original).
[80] In the description of the models we hinted at a number of places where important differences of opionion existed within the group described by the model. One such point would be for example the question of cessationism in the model which describes guidance in terms of transformation.

Hosier).[81] Second, most authors are highly trained teachers or pastors (or both) with theological degrees. Third, most authors identify with a Baptist or Reformed background. Those clearly identifying themselves as Reformed are more likely to favor a transformation model than other authors.

Nearly all authors write not only because they think the topic interesting, but because of a specific concern. Advocates of the information model are dissatisfied with the current state of affairs because of the lack of precision among Christians (Hosier) or because of the bad influences of 'new views' (e.g. LaHaye, Masters). Without exception, advocates of the other two models deplore the general acceptance of the information model, describe how they once held that view themselves, and explicitly target its weaknesses. Even the more recent books present the information model as overwhelmingly dominant (see e.g. the sharpness with which Lake and DeYoung attack it). Although our focus on literature precludes any definite conclusions on the acceptance of the various models among lay people, the concerns of all authors give strong support to the assumption that the information model is by far the most popular model among evangelicals, at least at lay level.

However, at the level of written literature on guidance a clear shift has taken place since 1980. In the decade between 1980 and 1990 most books promoted an information model, whereas in the later decades the weight shifts to the transformation model. Contributions advocating an intimation model are spread evenly over the periods.

This shift does not, however, mean that many new insights are added to the discussion over the course of the years. Reviewing the unique contributions of the different authors will show a lot of small nuances and minor refinements, whereas the general argument remains largely unchanged.

2.7.3 Argumentation

Whereas we did already point at the main argumentative differences between the various models, a number of more general remarks on the argumentation within the body of literature need to be made.

As could be expected, the Bible stands out as the absolute primary source for theologizing, sometimes even the only one. However, many authors use it exclusively in a biblicistic way, without any sign of herme-

---

81 Although it must be said that in the books left out of our research, either because of their contents or because of their date of publication, some female authors contribute to the discussion. See e.g. Elliot, *God's Guidance*; Jane A.G. Kise, *Finding and Following God's Will* (Minneapolis: Bethany House, 2005); Myers and Myers, *Discovering God's Will*; Sine and Sine, *Living on Purpose*.

neutical reflection. As a result, references to and applications from biblical material are often superficial. Where authors show evidence of hermeneutic reflection, it is mostly through the category of salvation history. The near absence of hermeneutical reflection results in the uncritical incorporation of the author's personal assumptions in their books. Especially authors advocating an information model seem to read every biblical occurrence of 'the will of God', irrespective of its context, as referring to a personal plan of God for individual lives.

The hermeneutical weaknesses are amplified by the fact that most authors write their books independently. In the first place, they write mostly independent of each other, as if no other books on guidance exist.[82] Only in a number of instances traces of other authors' thought are detectable. A major drawback of this absence of cooperation is the fact that no clear development is traceable in 30 years of literature on guidance. The same positions and arguments are repeated again and again, featuring new examples and anecdotes, but few new arguments. Not only do the authors write independently of each other, but most of them write independently of any form of theological tradition. More than half of the books do not refer to theological discussions or any theologian besides the author at all. Even a major contribution like that of Friesen is based exclusively on his exegesis of the relevant biblical material, omitting any discussion of historical positions, arguments, or developments. Only a few authors (e.g. Bockmühl) interact with tradition in a considerable way and use it as an important theological source.

While tradition is neglected as a crucial source for theology, (personal) experience functions as a source rivaled only by Scripture. A considerable part of the books analyzed is a collection of personal narratives. Although in itself this is not *a priori* problematic, combined with the lack of hermeneutical reflection and the neglect of tradition it has a considerable impact on the theological robustness of the argumentation.

This lack of argumentative robustness is shown most clearly in the imprecise use of theological concepts. As a result, most authors seem to be unaware how complex the question of guidance is from a theological perspective, and which major questions they implicitly answer in their books. We will point to a number of the theological debates involved in the next section.

---

82 This is one reason why speaking of 'models of guidance' seems more justified than writing of 'schools of thought', as Smith does.

2.7.4 Theological issues
In the previous section it was claimed that the typology of guidance developed in this chapter provides insight into the underlying theological questions. In the present section, I will mention a number of issues that are mostly not discussed explicitly in evangelical accounts of guidance but must be developed in order to arrive at a more robust theology and a more informed spirituality of divine guidance, unraveling what remains a diffuse theological amalgam in the literature under investigation.

Hermeneutics. The discussion on guidance needs to be informed by thorough hermeneutical reflection, with a special focus on the way biblical narratives can be applied to contemporary Christian lives.[83]

Providence. It is remarkable that in a discourse centering around the phrase 'the will of God' so little interaction with the doctrine of providence takes place. Is God's guidance distinct from his (special) providence, or part of it? In the context of the doctrine of divine providence, what does it mean to say that a believer might 'miss' the will of God? How is the idea of personal guidance related to the notion of God's *gubernatio*, his activity of guiding all creation towards its destiny?

Revelation. In order to understand what people mean when speaking of concrete divine guidance, a firm notion of *revelation* is necessary. Is God's guidance a form of ongoing personal revelation? If inner voices or divine 'signs' carry authority, what then is their (theological) status? And how are subjectivity and objectivity related in such an account of revelation?

Indwelling and illumination. It is a challenge to evangelical theology, but also more generally to Western systematic theology, to develop an account of the Spirit's *indwelling* and his ministry of *illumination*. For example, in how far does the presence of the Spirit in the hearts of believers mean that the inclinations of their hearts are to be trusted? Should the focus of discernment be to distinguish what comes out of the own heart from what the Spirit works within? Or is this too interpersonal an account of indwelling? When speaking about illumination, do we focus on the Spirit's enlightening our interpretation of Scripture, the applications drawn from it, or also illuminations apart from Scripture?

Vocation. The differences of opinion on the nature of divine guidance are also reflected in divergent views on the closely related issue of vocation. Given the original background of the protestant interpretation of vocation (vis-à-vis the Catholic hierarchy of the contemplative and the

---

83 Two especially crucial areas in this regard are the use of Old Testament narratives and the (dis)continuities between the book of Acts and the contemporary church.

active life), and the changed socio-cultural background since the time of the Reformation, does it still make sense to speak of vocations?

Sin and sanctification. The major differences of opinion on the value of personal inclinations, gifts, desires, and character suggest that there is no clarity on the connection between the ongoing influence of sin and sanctification in the Christian life. Are the consequences of sin so pervasive that believers need to suspect anything that comes out of their heart throughout their life, or can they trust in the transforming grace of God and hence follow their heart?

Discernment and wisdom. With respect to discernment, differences of opinion exist on the object of such discernment. Traditionally, discernment is most often treated as discernment of the spirits, or in the context of prophecy. The question is how it can be fruitfully applied to the issue of guidance and decision-making. Concerning wisdom, it is insufficiently clear what makes wisdom into genuine *Christian* wisdom. The renewed interest in virtue ethics, and especially the virtue of prudence and the notion of character, might be a promising line of thought to bring in interaction with the discussion of guidance.

Discipleship. Over the last few decades interest in the language of discipleship has grown. In relation to guidance, accounts of discipleship put interesting questions on the table. What does it mean to be a follower of Christ in the 21st century? And how is the idea of the disciple bearing his or her cross after Christ related to the rather succesful picture of the Christian life as portrayed in some accounts of guidance, where success can even function as a sign of God's approval? On the other hand, does the notion of cross-bearing imply, as some authors suggest, that God's will is most likely the more difficult and unattractive of the alternatives? And what notion of guidance is needed to impel believers to a life of sacrifice?

It is to this interesting thicket of crucial theological questions that we turn our attention in the next chapters with the hope to gain more clarity on the nature of divine guidance.

CHAPTER 3:
John Calvin on Divine Guidance

3.1 Introduction
Near the beginning of his *Institutes*, John Calvin (1509-1564) writes:

> For how can the thought of God penetrate your mind without your realizing immediately that, since you are his handiwork, you have been made over and bound to his command by right of creation, that you owe your life to him? – that whatever you undertake, whatever you do, ought to be ascribed to him? If this be so, it now assuredly follows that your life is wickedly corrupt unless it be disposed to his service, seeing that *his will ought for us to be the law by which we live*.[1]

Clearly, for Calvin the will of God is crucial for the entire Christian life. On the basis of creation, without referring to any other act of God, Calvin claims that ultimately we are not ourselves, but God's: God is Lord over all human lives. In another place, writing on Jonah's call to preach in Nineveh, Calvin mentions another reason for obedience besides honoring God as Creator: God's call.

> [F]or the first rule, as to all our actions, is to follow the call of God. Though one may excel in heroic virtues, yet all his virtues are mere fumes, which shine before the eyes of men, except the object be to obey God. The

---

1 John Calvin, *Institutio Christianae Religionis, in Libros Nunc Primum Digesta, Certisque Distincta Capitibus, Ad Aptissimam Methodum: Aucta Etiam Tam Magna Accessione Ut Propemodum Opus Novum Haberi Possit* (Geneva: Robert I. Estienne, 1559), I.2.2 (emphasis CvdK). OS III, 35, 20-26: "Quomodo enim mentem tuam subire queat Dei cogitatio, quin simul extemplo cogites, te, quum figmentum illius sis, eiusdem imperio esse ipso creationis iure addictum et mancipatum? vitam tuam illi deberi? quicquid instituis, quicquid agis, ad illum referri oportere? Id si est, iam profecto sequitur vitam tuam prave corrumpi nisi ad obsequium eius componitur; quando nobis vivendi lex esse debet eius voluntas." For the *Institutes*, we follow the following translation unless mentioned otherwise: John Calvin, *Institutes of the Christian Religion*, ed. John T. McNeill, trans. Henry Beveridge, vol. I & II (Louisville: Westminster John Knox Press, 2006). References to the *Institutes* will appear as follows: *Inst*. X.x.x. For quotes from the original Latin or French I have followed the following procedure: If available, I cite from the *Ioannis Calvini Opera omnia denuo recognita et adnotatione critica instructa notisque illustrata*, ed. B.G. Armstrong et.al. (Geneva: Droz, 1992—) [COR]. For the 1559 *Institutes*, I refer to the *Joannis Calvini Opera selecta*, eds. P. Barth and G. Niesel (Munich: Kaiser, 1926-1936) [OS]. All other original references are taken from the *Joannis Calvini Opera quae supersunt omnia*, eds. G. Baum, E. Cunitz and E. Reuss [Corpus Reformatorum, vol. 29-87] (Braunschweig: Schwetske, 1863-1900) [CO].

call of God then, as I have said, holds the first place as to the conduct of men; and unless we lay this foundation, we do like him who would build a house in the air. Disordered then will be the whole course of our life, except God presides over and guides us, and raises up over us, as it were, his own banners.[2]

For Calvin, the idea of a personal divine call is a weighty reality. Obeying this call is of crucial importance. Whoever chooses one's own ways over God's Lordship and his guidance will have a "disordered" life. If anything is fearful to Calvin, it is the idea of leading a chaotic and disordered life.

It will be clear that important elements we encountered in the previous chapter are already present in the writings of Calvin. In this chapter, we will investigate the following elements. We first turn to Calvin's views on divine providence and the will of God (§3.2). Next, in section 3.3 we will provide an analysis of his use of the concepts of vocation and calling. Section 3.4 will deal with Calvin's thinking on the Spirit as guide. Section 3.5 contains an investigation of Calvin's experiences of and reflections on divine guidance in his personal life. The chapter will end with a conclusion (§3.6).

3.2 Calvin on Divine Providence

3.2.1 Introduction
Our investigation of Calvin's views on divine guidance starts with an analysis of his doctrine of divine providence. To provide some background to our discussion, we start with a few preliminary remarks (§3.2.2). After that, we will consecutively turn to the relation between universal and special providence in Calvin (§3.2.3), the various 'spheres' of divine providence (§3.2.4), the relation between providence and the will of God (§3.2.5), the role of creaturely means in divine providence (§3.2.6), and finally the resulting 'praxis' of providence (§3.2.7).

3.2.2 Calvin on divine providence: some preliminary remarks
Calvin explicitly discusses the topic of divine providence in a number of writings. Most important among these are his commentary on Seneca's

---

2 *Comm. Jonah* 1:3. CO 43, 208: "Nam regula prima omnium nostrarum actionum est, sequi Deum vocantem. Etiam si quis polleat heroicis virtutibus, tamen fumi erunt omnes eius virtutes, quae refulgent coram oculis hominum, nisi propositum sit Deo obedire. Ergo vocatio Dei, quemadmodum dixi, primas tenet in constituenda hominum vita: et nisi fundamentum illud iacimus, perinde facimus, ac si quis vellet domum exstruere in aere. Confusa igitur erit tota vitae nostrae ratio, nisi praesit Deus et nos gubernet et quasi auspicia sua tollat." For Calvin's commentaries, unless otherwise stated we use the translations of the Calvin Translation Society.

De Clementia (1532), various editions of his *Institutes,* and a number of polemical treatises: *Against the Libertines* (1545), *Against Astrology* (1549), *On the Eternal Predestination of God* (1552), and *On the Secret Providence of God* (1558).

Although there is an increasing consensus in the field of Calvin studies that the *Institutes* should not be isolated as the main or primary source for constructing an account of Calvin's theology,[3] it will be used as the point of departure for this section on providence. Given the specific purposes with which we investigate his account of divine providence and given the fact that the 1559 edition of the *Institutes* is the last systematic work dealing with the topic this seems an appropriate choice.[4] In this final edition of his *Institutes of the Christian Religion* Calvin devotes three chapters (I.16-18) to the topic of divine providence, where he treats a number of issues that are crucial for the purposes of our study.

Calvin places his discussion of divine providence in the first book—on the 'Knowledge of God the Creator'—and directly following his discussion of creation. This way, he emphasizes that creation and providence are inseparable doctrines.[5] Its place under the knowledge of God as creator instead of under the knowledge of God as redeemer must, however, not be overemphasized. Meng-Chai Ong has shown how the chapters on providence are full of fatherly language.[6] Furthermore, Calvin's treatment of providence is not restricted to I.16-18, but appears in various contexts throughout his *Institutes.*[7]

---

3 See e.g. Herman J. Selderhuis, *Calvin's Theology of the Psalms* (Grand Rapids: Baker Academic, 2007), 15; and more extensively Richard A. Muller, *The Unaccommodated Calvin: Studies in the Foundation of a Theological Tradition* (Oxford: Oxford University Press, 2000), 101–58.

4 Meng-Chai Ong, "John Calvin on Providence: The Locus Classicus in Context" (PhD diss., King's College, 2003) refers to Institutes I.16-18 as the "locus classicus" of Calvin on providence.

5 In the first edition of the Institutes (1536) providence was discussed under the first article of the Apostles' Creed, while predestination was discussed under the final article. In the editions from 1539-1554, providence and predestination were discussed together in the section on soteriology, while in the final edition Calvin separates them once again. The discussion of predestination remains in the section on soteriology, while the discussion of providence is moved to the first book. Most of the discussions on those placements focus on the importance of the placement of predestination under soteriology, but in my opinion Ong is right in his remark that this is somewhat strange given the fact that it is the treatment of providence that makes an important move in the final edition. See e.g. Ong, 20.

6 See Ong, 53, where he writes on "the decisive role of God's Fatherhood as the paradigm for his exposition of divine providence."

7 In a certain way, Susan E. Schreiner, *The Theater of His Glory: Nature and the Natural Order in the Thought of John Calvin* (Grand Rapids: Baker Academic, 1995) in its entirety is an excellent proof of this.

As especially his treatises show, Calvin's thought on divine providence can only be understood against the historical and theological background of his time. Historically, this means that we should take into account the fact that Calvin was himself an exile, serving a church that existed to a large extent of exiles,[8] and also the vulnerability of human life in Reformation times.[9] This unstable situation explains why, as Forstman rightly indicates, Calvin writes with a tone of "ecstacy" when writing on divine providence.[10] Michael Horton captures this importance of providence for Calvin in describing it as "a lifeline in the chaos of life."[11] Theologically it is important to keep in mind, as Susan Schreiner has argued, that Calvin developed his views on providence in a polemical context where four major groups function as antagonists: the Libertines, the astrologers, the Stoics, and the Epicureans. Any evaluation of for example Calvin's relation to determinism must take into account his position over against stoicism.[12]

Many recent discussions of Calvin's account of providence have focused on the question whether it is sufficiently Christological in nature. Although an interesting discussion, given the focus of our research we will not discuss this issue extensively.[13] For the same reason, unless directly relevant to our project we will not include detailed discussions of developments in Calvin's thought.

3.2.3 Universal and special providence

Calvin adopts the widespread distinction between universal and special providence, but from the outset of chapter sixteen he indicates that his

---

8 See for an emphasis on this aspect the work of Oberman on Calvin as the one who initiated the *Reformation of the Refugees*. E.g. his *De erfenis van Calvijn: Grootheid en grenzen* (Kampen: Kok, 1988); "Initia Calvini: The Matrix of Calvin's Reformation," in *John Calvin and the Reformation of the Refugees*, ed. Peter A. Dykema (Geneva: Librairie Droz, 2009), 89–130; "Europa Afflicta: The Reformation of the Refugees," in *John Calvin and the Reformation of the Refugees*, ed. Peter A. Dykema (Geneva: Librairie Droz, 2009), 177–94.
9 That this aspect plays a major role for Calvin is especially clear from his *Institutes*, I.17.10, where he gives many examples of the "innumerable ... evils that beset human life; innumerable, too, the deaths that threaten it." OS III, 214, 12-13: "Innumera sunt quae vitam humanam *obsident* mala; *quae totidem ostentant mortes*."
10 H. Jackson Forstman, *Word and Spirit: Calvin's Doctrine of Biblical Authority* (Stanford: Stanford University Press, 1962), 98. Cf. Charles Partee, *The Theology of John Calvin* (Louisville: Westminster John Knox Press, 2008), 106n154: the "passionate celebration of God's care for all things."
11 Michael Horton, *Calvin on the Christian Life: Glorifying and Enjoying God Forever* (Wheaton: Crossway Books, 2014), 72.
12 See esp. Schreiner, *The Theater of His Glory*, 16.
13 See for a recent helpful and balanced contribution to this discussion Sung-Sup Kim, *Deus Providebit: Calvin, Schleiermacher, and Barth on the Providence of God* (Minneapolis: Fortress Press, 2014).

focus is on special providence, thereby reaching beyond what in his opinion all "philosophers teach and human minds conceive."[14] Universal and special providence, as Calvin introduces them in I.16.1, refer to the "universal motion" by which God "drives the celestial frame as well as its several parts" on the one hand, and the fact "that he sustains, nourishes, and cares for everything he has made, even to the least sparrow" on the other.[15] Special providence emphasizes that God "exercises especial care over each of his works."[16] The focus on God's special providence for his creation is characteristic for all Calvin's writings on providence. According to Charles Partee this distinction is Calvin's main theological concern with regard to the doctrine of providence[17] and within the distinction special providence is his "basic standpoint."[18] For Partee, this has everything to do with Calvin's methodological preferences: "While Calvin firmly beliefs in God's universal providence, he focuses on special providence because he thinks more in experiential and personal terms than in logically impersonal categories."[19]

Calvin's problem with the way universal or general providence is often treated is the distance that is created between God and the particulars of the created order.[20] He emphasizes that he does not "wholly repudiate what is said concerning universal providence," if only it does not obscure and conceal "that special providence which is so declared by sure and

---

14 *Inst.* I.16.1. OS III, 188, 19: "philosophi docent, et humanae mentes concipiunt."
15 *Inst.* I.16.1. OS III, 188, 4-7: "id universali quadam motione tam orbis machinam quam singulas eius partes agitando; sed singulari quadam providentia unumquodque eorum quae condidit ad minimum usque passerem, sustinendo, fovendo, curando." Universal providence describes the activity of God in and through the natural order and special providence the specific actions of God towards part of his creation.
16 *Inst.* I.16.4. OS III, 194, 12-13: "...quia peculiarem uniuscuiusque ex suis operibus curam gerit."
17 Partee, *The Theology of John Calvin*, 105. Cf. Mark W. Elliott, *Providence Perceived: Divine Action from a Human Point of View* (Berlin: De Gruyter, 2015), 142:" Special providence—that which concerns believers in their Christian lives—takes precedence in Calvin's scheme."
18 Charles Partee, *Calvin and Classical Philosophy* (Leiden: Brill, 1977), 95.
19 Partee, 114.
20 In this section of the Institutes, Calvin continually responds to a group of opponents that is nowhere explicitly defined. Most likely he still has the general group of "philosophers" mentioned in I.16.1 in mind. Various authors have pointed at the important role of both Epicurean and Stoic philosophies as the background of Calvin's discussion of providence. W.J. Torrance Kirby, "Stoic and Epicurean? Calvin's Dialectical Account of Providence in the Institute," *International Journal of Systematic Theology* 5, no. 3 (2003): 321 argues that "Calvin's dialectical account of providence resolves the predicament of the opposition of human freedom and divine sovereignty by embracing within a single view, in their totality, the two radical extremes of pagan theology." Paul Helm, "Calvin, the 'Two Issues,' and the Structure of the Institutes," *Calvin Theological Journal* 42, no. 2 (2007): 341–48 suggests that Calvin's contemporary opponent Pighius might have been behind these classical opponents, at least implicitly. See also Kim, *Deus Providebit*, 64ff.

clear testimonies of Scripture that it is a wonder anyone can have doubts about it."[21]

Calvin's emphasis on special providence brings with it the conviction that God not only has a general goal (*telos*) with his entire creation, but also with each individual creature. Although these cannot be separated too strictly, Calvin takes these subordinate goals seriously.[22] Calvin often speaks of the "appointed end" of creatures, and even includes human plans and intentions, that are "so governed by his providence that they are borne by it straight *to their appointed end*."[23]

Calvin's view on divine providence can be characterized as 'meticulous' providence.[24] For example, he states, "we make God the ruler and governor of *all things*…"[25] In short: nothing whatsoever takes place without God's determination.[26] This does raise the question whether the distinction between general and special providence is "somewhat artificial."[27] As Oliver Crisp states: "If God deliberately decrees all things or events to occur, then all things or events are deliberate acts of God, and it seems that the difference between 'general' and 'specific' act of providence evaporates."[28] Yet, the distinction between general and special providence in Calvin does not point in the first place to different domains of God's involvement or different levels of divine causal Activity, but to different

---

21 *Inst.* I.16.4. OS III, 194, 20-23: "Sed perperam hoc praetextu tegunt et obscurant quidam specialem providentiam, quae adeo certis clarisque scripturae testimoniis asseritur, ut mirum sit potuisse de ea quempiam dubitare."
22 That God's 'plan' with creation at large and with individual creatures are closely related yet distinguishable is seen in Paul Helm's statement that "we stick closer both to the spirit and the letter of Calvin if we think of providence as the fulfilling of God's plan for the entire creation, and particularly for the human race, and of whatever is embraced by that plan," Paul Helm, *John Calvin's Ideas* (Oxford: Oxford University Press, 2004), 95.
23 *Inst.* I.16.8 (emphasis CvdK). OS III, 199, 2-4: "… sed hominum etiam consilia et voluntates gubernari sic asserimus, ut ad destinatum ab ea scopum recta ferantur."
24 Oliver D. Crisp, "Calvin on Creation and Providence," in *John Calvin and Evangelical Theology: Legacy and Prospect*, ed. Sung Wook Chung (Louisville: Westminster John Knox Press, 2009), 58. Crisp adds that Calvin's is a milder form than the one expounded by Zwingli. This difference is mainly the result of a difference in their method. In Zwingli's crucial *Sermon on Providence* (1530) he bases his view on divine providence in a deductive way on God's supremacy, whereas Calvin, over against the 'philosophers,' tries to build his account of providence more explicitly on the biblical texts. For Zwingli's *De Providentia*, see Ulrich Zwingli, *On Providence and Other Essays*, ed. William J. Hinke (Eugene: Wipf & Stock, 1999). See further Paul Helm, "Calvin (and Zwingli) on Divine Providence," *Calvin Theological Journal* 29 (1994): 388–405.
25 *Inst.* I.16.8 (emphasis CvdK). OS III, 198, 26-7: "sed Deum constituimus arbitrum ac moderatorem omnium…"
26 See also *Institutes* I.16.6.
27 Crisp, "Calvin on Creation and Providence," 53.
28 Crisp, 53.

sorts of divine activity.[29] After having shown that special providence for Calvin does include the entire created order, Kim nicely captures the distinction in his summary: "General providence is, then, 'God's particular and immediate governance of the natural order.' Special providence, on the other hand, is the purposeful directing of all creatures – whether natural or human."[30] That the distinction between universal and special providence does not refer to specific domains of providence per se, does not mean that such domains are not included in Calvin's view of providence.

3.2.4 Spheres of divine providence

A second important distinction in Calvin's discussion of providence in the 1559 Institutes, one that is more clearly defined in several other writings, is that between the different spheres of God's providence.[31] Although they are not explicitly mentioned as such, Calvin first states that God's providence concerns the entire created order, including all things (I.16.3). Then, in I.16.6, he focuses on *mankind* as the special object of God's care. Finally, within this care for mankind in general, in I.17.1 Calvin distinguishes the church as a further sphere of God's yet more specific care, his "vigilance in ruling the church, which he deigns to watch more closely."[32] Thus, three spheres of divine providence can be recognized in Calvin: nature, mankind, and the church.

As Meng-Chai Ong suggests, this issue of different spheres of providence is one of the places where structural refinements in Calvin's treatment of providence can be found.[33] To a certain extent this is true, yet it is remarkable that the distinction is much less explicit in the 1559 *Institutes* than in a number of earlier writings.[34] The division between three spheres

---

29 Crisp himself points in this direction, concluding that the distinction "may be of some theologial use," 53.
30 Kim, *Deus Providebit*, 30, citing the Consensus Genevensis, CO 8:348-49.
31 François Wendel, *Calvin: The Origins and Development of His Religious Thought*, trans. Philip Mairet (New York: Harper & Row, 1963), 179 speaks of "aspects." Ford Lewis Battles, *Interpreting John Calvin*, ed. Robert Benedetto (Grand Rapids: Baker Books, 1996), 168 of "concentric circles." See also Kim, *Deus Providebit*, 26-34. It is interesting that Oberman discusses the three spheres in the context of his discussion of Calvin's preference for the words *arcanum* and *secret*, see Heiko A. Oberman, *The Two Reformations: The Journey from the Last Days to the New World*, ed. Donald Weinstein (New Haven: Yale University Press, 2003), 130.
32 *Inst*. I.17.1. OS III, 202, 13-14: "praecipue vero in regenda Ecclesia (quam propiore intuitu dignatur) se excubias agere."
33 Ong, "John Calvin on Providence," 30.
34 In this respect, it appears strange that Ong explicitly mentions *structural* refinements and later on admits "that the final *structure* of Calvin's treatment of providence in the 1559 *Institutes* bears little resemblance to any of those earlier treatments", Ong, 31. Ong's analysis is weakened by the fact that he uses Cole's translation of *The Secret Providence of God*, in

is first introduced in the treatise *Against the Libertines* (1545), where Calvin mentions three manners of God's working ("besongne en trois sortes"): In the order of nature, in mankind, and in the faithful.[35]

The first way God works is described as "a universal operation by which He guides all creatures according to the condition and propriety which He had given each when He made them."[36] Calvin explicitly states that this guidance (*conduict*) is synonymous with the order of nature. Through the second form of God's involvement he causes all creatures "to serve His goodness, righteousness, and judgment according to His present will to help His servants, to punish the wicked, and to test the patience of His faithful, or to chastise them in His fatherly kindness."[37] As Calvin explains, all creation, both animate and inanimate, is involved as instruments for the divine acts, but the object of God's acting is mankind, consisting of both the faithful and the unfaithful.

For the purposes of this study the third category is most important. Here, Calvin writes: "The third form of God's operation consists in the fact that He governs His faithful, *living and reigning* in them by His Holy Spirit."[38] Because the human will has been depraved by sin, nothing but the presence of the Holy Spirit suffices: God "reforms them and changes them from evil into good" and "in abolishing their perversity He guides them by His Spirit into His obedience."[39] Interestingly, whereas in the 1559 *Institutes* the most recognizable categories Calvin uses are order of

---

which a section of Calvin's *The Eternal Predestination of God (1552)* is presented as part of his *Secret Providence (1558)*. This strange inclusion has only recently been mentioned by Paul Helm in his introduction to John Calvin, *The Secret Providence of God*, ed. Paul Helm, trans. Keith Goad (Wheaton: Crossway Books, 2010), 17–18.

35 John Calvin, *Contre la secte phantastique et furieuse des Libertins qui se nomment spirituelz* (Geneva: Jean Girard, 1545). Unless otherwise stated, we use the following translation: John Calvin, *Treatises against the Anabaptists and against the Libertines*, trans. Benjamin Wirt Farley (Grand Rapids: Baker Book House, 1982). COR IV/1, 93: "ie dis que nous avons à considerer que Dieu besongne en trois sortes, quant au gouvernement du monde."

36 Calvin, *Treatises against the Anabaptists and against the Libertines*, 242–43. COR IV/1, 93: "une operation universelle, par laquelle il conduict toutes creatures, selon la condition et proprieté qu'il leur a donnée à chacune en les formant."

37 Calvin, 243–44. COR IV/1, 94: "Il lest faict servir à sa bonté, iustice et iugement, selon qu'il veut maintenant aider ses serviteurs, maintenant punir les meschants, maintenant esprouver la patience de ses fideles ou les chastier paternellement."

38 Calvin, 247 (emphasis CvdK). COR IV/1, 98: "La troisiesme espece de l'operation de Dieu gist et consiste en ce qu'il gouverne ses fideles, vivant et regnant en eux par son sainct esprit." Wendel emphasizes that this third aspect is "practically indistinguishable from the interior witness of the Holy Spirit," *Calvin*, 179. Note the importance of the indwelling of the Spirit in Calvin's treatment of providence. In our next chapter we will see how for Jonathan Edwards the indwelling of the Spirit receives a similar emphasis.

39 Calvin, *Treatises against the Anabaptists and against the Libertines*, 248. COR IV/1, 99: "nostre Seigneur les reforme et les change de mal en bien"; "C'est qu'en abolissant leur perversité, il les conduit par son Esprit en son obeissance."

nature – mankind – church, in 1545 one of the categories was slightly different: order of nature – mankind – the (individual) faithful.

In his *Concerning the Eternal Predestination of God* (1552), Calvin does not discuss three, but four different categories of divine involvement. The first category Calvin describes is again the general government of the world. The second is "the guards God sets for the government and care of particular parts – of such a kind, indeed, that nothing happens but by His will and assent."[40] The third and fourth categories then again are "His particular care of the human race" and lastly the "truly paternal protection with which He guards His church, to which the most present help of God is attached."[41] Thus, different from the 1545 distinction, here the main categories are order of nature – mankind – church, like in the final edition of the *Institutes*. A new category is, however, added, between the order of nature and mankind, which can be seen as a further emphasis on the importance of special providence.[42]

It is clear that Calvin's basic scheme remains basically the same, with its form of order of nature – humankind – church/faithful.[43] For the third category Calvin used the (individual) faithful in 1545, but speaks more generally of the church as a whole in the 1559 Institutes.[44] Whereas the distinction itself is clear, it is less clear how exactly God's activity is different in each of the spheres. Calvin's wording suggests a growing *intensity* of God's involvement, but the implications of this raised intensity in, for example, protecting the church or governing the faithful are unclear. Calvin does not elaborate, but provides us with two clues: On the one hand,

---

40 John Calvin, *Concerning the Eternal Predestination of God*, trans. J.K.S. Reid (Cambridge: James Clarke & Co., 1961), 164. COR III/1, 226, 20-22: "Deinde considerandae sunt in singulis partibus regendis et curandis Dei excubiae, et quidem tales, ut nihil nisi nutu arbitrioque eius eveniat."
41 Calvin, 164. COR III/1, 226, 22-23: "peculiaris generis humani cura"; 26-27: "Ultimo praesidium vere paternum, quo ecclesiam suam tuetur, cui praesentissima Dei ipsius virtus annexa est."
42 Remarkably, and in tension with his own analysis, Kim, *Deus providebit*, 33, argues that Calvin adds the church as an additional circle *in the center*.
43 Yet, against Ong's suggestion, we agree with Wendel, *Calvin*, 179: "In 1545 ... Calvin distinguished three aspects of Providence which he does not seem to have separated with such care afterwards, at least not in the *Institutes*."
44 Josef Bohatec, "Calvins Vorsehungslehre," in *Calvinstudien: Festschrift zum 400. Geburtstage Johann Calvins* (Leipzig: Rudolf Haupt, 1909), 389, already remarked that "die Frage, ob Calvin als Gegenstand der speciallissima cura mehr die ecclesia schlechthin oder die einzelnen Gläubigen in ihr betrachtet." Randall Zachman establishes an intesting connection with Calvin's *De Scandalis* (1550) in stating that from its publication onwards the church "becomes the focal point of Calvin's discussion of providence." He points explicitly at the difference between the 1545 and 1552 publications. See Randall C. Zachman, *Image and Word in the Theology of John Calvin* (Notre Dame: University of Notre Dame Press, 2007), 88.

Calvin qualifies God's special care for the church and its members as *fatherly* care. Secondly, in his treatise against the Libertines, he explains that God lives and reigns in the faithful through his Spirit.[45] One thing is undisputable: wherever Calvin writes on providence its main object is mankind. Although in making distinctions between different spheres of providence Calvin always starts with the universal and moves to the particular, it is the particular which in his eyes is the real object of divine providence.[46]

3.2.5 Providence and the will of God
Like other theologians of his time, for Calvin divine providence and the will of God are so closely intertwined that he uses the terms as synonyms. Quoting Psalm 115 ('God does whatever he wills') Calvin explains God's will in terms of his providence: "governing heaven and earth by his providence, ... so regulates all things that nothing takes place without his deliberation."[47] When discussing the question whether divine providence also extends to human plans, Calvin explicitly links providence to the divine will: "To sum up, since God's will is said to be the cause of all things, I have made his providence the determinative principle for all human plans and works…"[48] As Susan Schreiner states: "Calvin's God exercises his supreme will and determines all events."[49]

For Calvin, these references to the will of God are an important means in arguing that speaking about divine 'permission' of evil and sin does no full justice to the Biblical language. Maintaining that God is involved even in sinful acts through his "secret direction," he rejects the distinction between permitting and doing as used for example by Lombard:[50] "It is more than evident that they babble and talk absurdly who, in place of God's providence, substitute bare permission."[51] Calvin's emphasis on the divine will as the ultimate cause of everything led to the charge that God

---

45 COR IV/1, 98: "vivant et regnant en eux par son sainct esprit." This final point will be our focus in section 3.4.
46 In this light, the choice of some Reformed theologians to start their treatments of providence with *providentia specialissima* is a very Calvinian move. Gijsbert van den Brink and Cornelis van der Kooi, *Christian Dogmatics: An Introduction* (Grand Rapids: Eerdmans, 2017), 235.
47 *Inst.* I.16.3. OS III, 199, 22-24: "sed quia sua providentia coelum et terram gubernans, sic omnia moderator ut nihil nisi eius consilio accidat."
48 *Inst.* I.18.2. OS III, 223, 17-19: "Summa haec sit: quum Dei voluntas dicitur rerum omnium esse causa, providentiam eius statui moderatricem in cunctis hominum consiliis et operibus."
49 Schreiner, *Theater of His Glory*, 30.
50 See Lombard, *Sentences* I.xlv, 11.
51 *Inst* I.18.1. OS III, 221, 19-21: "satis superque liquet nugari eos et ineptire qui in locum providentiae Dei nudam permissionem substituunt…"

causes many things that He forbids at the same time.⁵² In order to defend himself against this, or at least to clarify what his position exactly entails, Calvin repeatedly uses a well-known distinction⁵³ between God's hidden and his revealed will, or in slightly different terms: his *voluntas beneplaciti* and his *voluntas signi*.⁵⁴ God's revealed will is his will as presented in Scripture, while his hidden will refers to the divine decrees and divine providence.

Calvin accompanies this distinction often with a strong assertion that ultimately God's will is one and undivided. In the *Institutes* I.18.3, he states:

> Yet God's will is not therefore at war with itself, nor does it change, nor does it pretend not to will what he wills. But even though his will is one and simple in him, it appears manifold to us because, on account of our mental incapacity, we do not grasp how in diverse ways it wills and does not will something to take place.⁵⁵

Thus, it would be more in line with Calvin's thought to speak about two aspects or appearances of the will of God than about two distinct wills of God.

---

52 *Inst.* I.18.3.
53 Paul Helm describes it as "standard medieval fare" in his introduction to Calvin, *Secret Providence*, 25. Muller describes it as "a distinction well established in the older theological tradition) and points to Hugh of St. Victor, Lombard, Alexander of Hales and Bonaventure as older theologians who used it. Richard A. Muller, *Post-Reformation Reformed Dogmatics, Vol. 3: The Divine Essence and Attributes*, 2nd edition (Grand Rapids: Baker Academic, 2003), 457.
54 See e.g. *Inst.* I.17.2. Although this distinction between different divine wills could look like a very technical philosophical invention, for Calvin, given the Scripture references in I.17.2, it is almost given in the biblical text itself. The distinction presented here is used in a variety of formulations by different theologians and even in Calvin's own writings different wordings can be found. Richard Muller, who presents a comprehensive overview of the various options, writes: "The hidden or 'secret will' (*voluntas arcana*) of God's 'good pleasure' (*voluntas beneplaciti*) can also be identified as 'the will of [God's] decree' (*voluntas decernens aut decreti*) according to which the elect are predestinate; the latter is well called 'the will of commandment' (*voluntas praecepti*) or the 'revealed will' (*voluntas revelata*) of God. Still, there are slight differences in meaning among the several distinctions." See Muller, *PRRD 3*, 457, in the context of his discussion of the divine will on pp. 432-76.
55 *Inst.* I.18.3. OS III, 224, 25-29: "Neque tamen ideo vel secum pugnat, vel mutatur Dei voluntas, vel quod vult se nolle simulat; sed quum una et simplex in ipso sit, nobis multiplex apparet: quia pro mentis nostrae imbecillitate, quomodo idem diverso modo nolit fieri et velit, non capimus." Joseph Pipa summarizes Calvin's position on the divine will as "God's will is one but it appears to be manifold to us on account of our finite understanding," see Joseph A. Pipa Jr., "Creation and Providence (I.14, 16-18)," in *Theological Guide to Calvin's Institutes: Essays and Analysis*, ed. David W. Hall and Peter A. Lillback (Phillipsburg: P&R Publishing, 2008), 148.

An important question arising from the distinction between the different aspects of the will of God is what role they should play in the practical life of faith. Although this topic will be more extensively discussed in §3.2.7, a few things need to be mentioned in this context. First, wherever the question arises Calvin is very clear that only God's revealed will should be the focus of the believer: "From what source do we learn but from his Word? In such fashion we must in our deeds search out God's will which he declares through his Word."[56] Second, as a logical complement, it follows that God's hidden will, the aspect of his will related to providence, should never be a leading factor with regard to Christian decision making. Horton adequately captures Calvin's view: "We wander into a labyrinth if we try to distinguish God's secret will."[57] In order to understand God's will, we must use the means he has provided.

3.2.6 Providence and causality
Since for Calvin God is actively involved in everything that happens and throughout all the different spheres of creation, the question is what form(s) this divine involvement does take. How does Calvin envision the involvement of God and what are the implications for his views on secondary causality?[58]

There is a widespread consensus in Calvin studies that "Calvin was ambivalent about the role of secondary causality."[59] This ambivalence is immediately clear from a statement on God's use of means Calvin makes at the start of *Institutes* I.17.1. He writes that God's providence "is the determinative principle of all things in such a way that sometimes it works through an intermediary, sometimes without an intermediary, sometimes contrary to every intermediary."[60] Calvin feared that overem-

---

56 *Inst.* I.17.5. OS III, 208, 11-12: "Unde autem edocemur, nisi ex eius verbo? Proinde in rebus agendis ea est nobis perspicienda Dei voluntas quam verbo suo declarat."
57 Horton, *Calvin on the Christian Life*, 78.
58 This question is relevant for our overall project as one of the questions at stake in the discussion on guidance is the nature of God's mediated activity.
59 Schreiner, *The Theater of His Glory*, 30. Pieter Potgieter is right in his claim that although "much has been written ... the use of media [has] not [been] investigated in depth." Pieter C. Potgieter, "Providence in Calvin: Calvin's View of God's Use of Means (Media) in His Acts of Providence," in *Calvinus Evangelii Propugnator: Calvin, Champion of the Gospel. Papers from the International Congress on Calvin Research, Seoul, 1998*, ed. David F. Wright, Anthony N.S. Lane, and Jon Balserak (Grand Rapids: Calvin Studies Society, CRC Product Services, 2006), 176.
60 *Inst.* I.17.1. OS III, 202, 9-11: "deinde sic moderatricem esse rerum omnium, ut nunc mediis interpositis operetur, nunc sine mediis, nunc contra omnia media." Zachman shows how from very early in his career secondary causality is a basic feature of Calvin's theology that he starts to modify later on (he esp. mentions *Eternal Predestination*) in the context of his thinking about miracles. Although Calvin stresses God's freedom with respect to the secondary causes, God's use of them still is regarded as the ordinary execution of his providence, Zachman, *Image and Word in the Theology of John Calvin*, 86.

phasizing God's use of means would lead to deistic tendencies in theology and as a result he emphasized God's sovereignty over the created order and his freedom with regard to creaturely means. Ultimately however, Calvin accepts God's use of means and at times gives it a strategic function in his writings.[61] In some of his major treatises, like *Concerning the Eternal Predestination of God* and the *Treatise against the Libertines* the secondary or remote causes play an important role. In his treatise on the *Secret Providence of God,* where Calvin defends himself against a number of misrepresentations of his earlier works, he explicitly emphasizes the importance of secondary causality for his views on divine providence: "I distinguish everywhere between primary and secondary causes and between mediate and proximate causes."[62] The distinction between the various levels of causality plays a crucial role whereever Calvin tries to uphold God's righteousness but at the same time wants to make clear that even human sin is included in God's decree. On the one hand, Calvin frequently used the distinction as an important theological instrument to defend and clarify his views, while on the other hand he can without hesitation assert that God acts against or without creaturely means.

For the purposes of our study it is interesting that wherever secondary causality and the practical Christian life are discussed within the same context, Calvin consequently stresses God's use of creaturely means as his ordinary way of operating. At the same time, in this context there also remains some ambiguity. For example, in the *Institutes* I.17.4, Calvin states that "God's providence does not always meet us in its naked form, but God in a sense clothes it with the means employed."[63] The words 'not always' (*non semper*) raise questions as to whether Calvin thinks that providence can meet us in its naked form and to the frequency with which this might occur. In our next section we will focus on the practical implications of Calvin's views on providence for the issue of divine guidance.

3.2.7 The praxis of providence: between believing and perceiving
What is perhaps most striking to the modern believer in Calvin's treatment of providence is that the doctrine for Calvin is eminently practical. It is so vital and practical a doctrine for him that he states that "ignorance

---

61 That not all early Reformers accepted secondary causality is again seen in the writings of Zwingli, who practically denies such causality. Based upon his *a priori* reasoning from God's supremacy in his *De Providentia*, there is little room to take secondary causality as seriously as Calvin does. See e.g. Helm, *Calvin's Ideas*, 121.
62 Calvin, *Secret Providence*, 101. CO 9, 306: "Primam causam vel remotam a mediis et propinquis ubique distinguo."
63 *Inst.* I.17.4. OS III, 207, 34-36: "Ideo ante admonui, providentiam Dei non semper nudam occurrere, sed prout adhibitis mediis eam Deus quodammodo vestit."

of providence is the ultimate of all miseries; the highest blessedness lies in the knowledge of it."[64] One of the most important results of believing in God's providence is for Calvin that it gives "incredible freedom from worry about the future."[65] That the doctrine is so practical for Calvin does not, however, mean that it is so in a straightforward manner. In this section we will discuss some of the practical 'uses' Calvin makes of the doctrine, but also some applications of it by others against which he hastens to warn.

The most important remark that must be made in this context is that for Calvin the doctrine of providence is a doctrine of faith and as such not easily discerned by natural eyes: it often has to be believed amidst the paradoxes of life.[66] Calvin, who vehemently argues against fate and chance, does not shrink from acknowledging that, "however all things may be ordained by God's plan, according to a sure dispensation, for us they are fortuitous."[67] Following this statement, he immediately explains that all things are providential in essence and explains that they are fortuitous *in appearance*:

> But since the order, reason, end, and necessity of those things which happen for the most part lie hidden in God's purpose, and are not apprehended by human opinion, those things, which it is certain take place by God's will, are *in a sense fortuitous*. For they bear *on the face of them* no other appearance, whether they are considered in their own nature or weighed according to our knowledge and judgment.[68]

This statement makes clear that God's providence is not easily discerned in the everyday world. As Schreiner has shown, for Calvin God's provi-

---

64 *Inst*. I.17.11. OS III, 216, 28-30: "… extremum esse omnium miseriarum, providentiae ignorationem; summam beatitudinem in eiusdem cognitione esse sitam." In light of this comment, but also of Calvin's general tone, we agree with Forstman's remark that there is a "tone of ecstacy" in Calvins treatment of providence, Forstman, *Word and Spirit*, 98.
65 *Inst*. I.17.7. OS III, 210, 37: "in posterum incredibilis securitas."
66 Zachman, *Image and Word in the Theology of John Calvin*, 82: Providence "can only be believed in spite of what we see." For Zachman, Calvin's thinking on divine providence is under the constant tension between "the simultaneous manifestation and concealment of God's providence" (76).
67 *Inst*. I.16.9. OS III, 200, 6-7: "Dicam igitur, utcunque ordinentur omnia Dei consilio certa dispensatione, nobis tamen esse fortuita."
68 *Inst*. I.16.9 (emhpasis CvdK). OS III, 200, 10-15: "Sed quoniam eorum quae eveniunt, ordo, ratio, finis, necessitas, ut plurimum in Dei consilio latet, et humana opinione non apprehenditur, quasi fortuita sunt, quae certum est ex Dei voluntate provenire. Non enim aliam imaginem prae se ferunt, aut in natura sua consideratae, aut secundum notitiam nostrum iudiciumque aestimatae."

dence is (often) even more obscure in history than in nature.[69] Calvin's emphasis on the responsibilities of believers in light of their faith in divine providence is in line with this reticence in detecting God's providence in the world. As we saw before, Calvin adopted the distinction between God's revealed and his secret will and repeatedly cites Deut. 29:29.[70] While believing that everything happens according to the will of God, the duty of believers is not to focus on God's secret will but on his revealed will.[71] For Calvin, what has in fact been decreed can only be known after the event.[72] A crucial comment is made on this issue in Calvin's treatise *Concerning the Eternal Predestination of God* where Calvin is discussing God's use of inferior causes:

> Hence, as to future time, because the issue of all things is hidden from us, each ought so to apply himself to his office, *as though nothing were determined* about any part. Or, to speak more properly, he ought so to hope for the success that issues from the command of God in all things, as to reconcile in himself the contingency of unknown things and the certain providence of God.[73]

In this passage, we not only see the aforementioned distinction between believing in providence and perceiving providence, but in fact Calvin states that in order to live an effective Christian life, one ought to accept that the will of God is secret. Zachman states Calvin's point as follows: "Since the future is unknown to us, we must use our prudence and wisdom to direct our lives, even as we acknowledge our lives are governed and directed by the power and wisdom of God."[74] In Calvin's own words: "But rather let them inquire and learn from Scripture what is pleasing to God so that they may strive toward this under the Spirit's guidance."[75]

---

69 Schreiner, *The Theater of His Glory*, 113.
70 The secret things belong to the Lord our God, but the things that are revealed belong to us and to our children forever, that we may do all the words of this law (ESV).
71 E.g. *Inst.* I.17.5.
72 See Helm, *Calvin's Ideas*, 98.
73 Calvin, *Eternal Predestination*, 171. COR III/1, 240, 13-18: "Ergo quantum ad futurum tempus, quia nos adhuc rerum eventus latent, perinde ad officium suum intentus esse quisque debet, ac si nihil in utramvis partem constitutum foret. Vel, ut magis proprie loquar, talem in omnibus, quae ex Dei mandato aggreditur, successum sperare debet, ut in rebus sibi incognitis contingentiam cum certa Dei providentia conciliet."
74 Zachman, *Image and Word in the Theology of John Calvin*, 83. Cf. Helm, *Calvin's Ideas*, 105. There, Helm summarizes Calvin's point in stating that "in order to act effectively we must *believe* that it [God's will, CvdK] is secret, and our actions must be governed not by an attempt to divine God's secret will, but by obedience to his commands and reliance on his promises."
75 *Inst.* I.17.3. OS III, 205, 30-31: "Quin potius ex scriptura, quid Deo placeat inquirent ac discent, ut spiritu duce illuc nitantur."

3.2.8 Conclusion

In this section on Calvin's view of providence, we investigated especially those issues that have important consequences for thinking about divine guidance. We discussed his views on universal and special providence, the various spheres of divine providence, the close relationship between providence and the will of God in Calvin's thought, and the question of God's use of creaturely means. Throughout those sections, references were made to important points related to the issue of divine guidance, and some of these were discussed more explicitly in the last section. In conclusion, three things stand out as particularly important for weighing Calvin's view on divine guidance later on.

First, the will of God is a central theological category throughout Calvin's work and is frequently used almost as a synonym for divine providence. Second, when Calvin speaks about the divine will he makes use of the well-known distinction between the hidden will of God (his decree) and the revealed will of God. Calvin points to God's will as revealed in Scripture as the only ultimate source for good Christian living, although in several places we encountered some ambiguity with regard to the question whether God's providence cannot also be called a source of revelation to a certain extent. Third, wherever Calvin writes about divine providence, his main object is always God's *providentia specialissima*, God's special care for the church and for his children. In various places, Calvin either points to the church, to the elect, or to the (individual) faithful as the object of this most special providence. However, it is clear that all versions convey the idea that God is intimately involved in the details of the lives of his faithful.

Closely related to Calvin's views on divine providence and God's close involvement in all individual lives is his firm belief that God has given all individuals a vocation. It is to his interpretation of vocation that we turn in the next section.

3.3 Calvin on Vocation and Calling

3.3.1 Introduction

An important corrollary of Calvin's emphasis on *providentia specialissima* is his account of vocation. In this section our focus will be on Calvin's use of vocation terminology. We first look at his vision of the entire Christian life as the groundwork underneath his idea of vocation (§3.3.2). We then focus on his exact use of vocation terminology (§3.3.3) with a special focus on the civic use of the term (§3.3.4), followed by a discussion of how vocation is discerned in practice (§3.3.5). We also investigate the specific concerns behind Calvin's stress on the concept of vocation (§3.3.6) before evaluating how the idea of vocation is or can be related to contemporary views on divine guidance and the will of God (§3.3.7).

3.3.2 The foundation of vocation in Calvin's theology

Our account of Calvin's view on vocation must start with a recognition of how the idea of calling and vocation is embedded in Calvin's overall view of the Christian life, which he develops most extensively in the third book of his Institutes.[76] We concentrate on III.7.1, where Calvin describes *self-denial* as a crucial characteristic of the Christian life. Commenting on Romans 12:1-2, he states: "We are not our own, but the Lord's."[77]

This statement emphasizes the importance of Christ's Lordship over the Christian life, an idea that is central to Calvin's theology. Ultimately, we do not master our lives, God does. Calvin applies the first half of the statement in the following way:

> We are not our own: let not our reason nor our will, therefore, sway our plans and deeds. We are not our own: let us therefore not set it as our goal to seek what is expedient for us according to the flesh. We are not our own: in so far as we can, let us therefore forget ourselves and all that is ours.[78]

His explanation of the positive second half takes an identical form:

> Conversely, we are God's: Let us therefore live for him and die for him. We are God's: let his wisdom and will therefore rule all our actions. We are God's: let all the parts of our life accordingly strive toward him as our only lawful goal.[79]

Those two statements combined contain a number of essential points. First, it is clear that for Calvin God is Lord and in a sense owner of the

---

76 *Inst.* III.6-10 form Calvin's central text on the Christian life, often published in separate form as the *Golden Booklet of the True Christian Life*.
77 *Inst.* III.7.1. OS IV, 151, 16: "nostri non sumus, sed Domini..."
78 *Inst.* III.7.1. OS IV, 151, 18-23: "Nostri non sumus: ergo ne vel ratio nostra, vel voluntas in consiliis nostris factisque dominetur. Nostri non sumus: ergo ne statuamus nobis hunc finem, ut quaeramus quod nobis secundum carnem expediat. Nostri non sumus: ergo quoad licet obliviscamur nosmetipsos ac nostra omnia."
79 *Inst.* III.7.1. OS IV, 151, 23-26: "Rursum, Dei sumus: illi ergo vivamus ac moriamur. Dei sumus: cunctis ergo nostris actionibus praesideat sapientia eius et voluntas. Dei sumus: ad illum igitur, tanquam solum legitimum finem, contendant omnes vitae nostrae partes."

entire life and of the Christian life doubly so. Vocation has to be seen as one of the ways in which this Lordship is expressed. Second, we see the influence of Calvin's anthropology and his radical view on the consequences of sin shine through in the way he puts the human will over against the divine will. This is even more characteristic given the fact that those statements appear in a context where Calvin describes the *Christian* life and where, following Romans 12, he speaks about the *transformed* mind of the faithful. Although at times Calvin is much more positive about the possibilities of the renewed Christian mind and will, he always remains hesitant to trust them too much.[80] This will have important consequences for both the way in which vocations are discerned and for the restraining function Calvin gives to the concept of vocation.

We need to add three more remarks that bear on our investigation: First, it is crystal-clear that for Calvin vocation is something that may never become self-centered.[81] As the entire Christian life should have God as its ultimate goal, so should any vocation. Secondly, any account of divine guidance and the will of God that makes the Christian life anything close to a success-story is far removed from the Christian life of self-denial, cross-bearing and pilgrimage Calvin pictures in *Institutes* III.7.1. Finally, it is interesting that at the end of the section, Calvin mentions the guiding work of Christ and the Spirit in the believer as an important way to let them have their proper reign: "But the Christian philosophy bids reason give way to, submit and subject itself to, the Holy Spirit so that the man himself may no longer live but hear [sic] Christ living and reigning within him [Gal. 2:20]."[82] We will return to this remark in our next section on the role of the Spirit in guidance (§3.4).

3.3.3 Calvin's use of vocation terminology
Now that we have seen that Calvin's use of vocation terminology presupposes the Lordship of Christ over the Christian life, we turn to an analysis of his uses of the terminology itself.

---

80 See §3.5 for interesting examples of this distrust in Calvin's personal life.
81 To a certain extent this fact is acknowledged in the contemporary secular use of vocation, where the term vocation often retains the connotation of personal sacrifice for the common good.
82 *Inst.* III.7.1. OS IV, 152, 2-5: "At christiana philosophia illam loco cedere, spiritui sancto subiici ac subiugari iubet; ut homo iam non ipse vivat, sed Christum in se ferat viventem ac regnantem (Gal. 2,20)." There seems to be a spelling mistake in the English translation, as *ferat* should be translated as bear instead of hear. In the context of our investigation this is an important difference.

The terminology of calling and vocation appears in several distinct contexts in the writings of Calvin.[83] Its first and primary use, following the New Testament's most common usage of *kaleo*, is in the context of soteriology: the call to faith in Jesus Christ. According to Calvin, this calling comes in two ways: the external vocation, mainly through the preaching of the Word, and the internal vocation through the *testimonium* of the Spirit. The second way in which Calvin uses vocation terminology, and for our purposes the most interesting one, is its civic meaning, where it points to the different places and roles given to each individual in society.[84] In between those two distinct divine callings, Calvin occasionally mentions a third type of calling: the calling to a spiritual *ministerium*.[85] Similar to the call to faith, this call to the ministry is also twofold, consisting in both an outward and an inward call, although in praxis the actual order seems to be reversed. Calvin unfortunately does not elaborate on the inner call to the ministry.[86]

Thus, both the call to faith and the calling to a ministry consist of an internal and an external call. In light of our overarching research question, it is crucial that for vocations in the civic context, no internal aspect is mentioned by Calvin. Before delving deeper into this issue and its implications for the hermeneutics of vocation, we first need to establish the exact meaning of the civic interpretation of vocation.

3.3.4 The civic use of vocation terminology

The civic meaning of vocation emerged in the Early Reformation period in reaction to Roman Catholic views on monasticism and the difference between clergy and laity, where the contemplative life was preferred over

---

83 Although Calvin is used in our research as one of the primary discussion partners, in the different uses presented here of the conceptuality of vocation and calling he can be seen as representing the broader Reformed and Protestant tradition, especially of the early Reformation period. See e.g. the discussion of the various meanings of vocatio in Heinrich Heppe, *Reformed Dogmatics: Set Out and Illustrated from the Sources*, ed. Ernst Bizer, trans. G.T. Thomson (Grand Rapids: Baker Book House, 1950), ch. 20: "Calling."

84 To refer to this use of vocation as its 'civic' meaning is no standard terminology. However, the existent distinctions are insufficiently clear. Often, a distinction is made between spiritual and external vocation, but this is problematic given the fact that the spiritual vocation can once again be divided in internal and external aspects. See e.g. the discussion of "vocatio" in Richard A. Muller, *Dictionary of Latin and Greek Theological Terms: Drawn Primarily from Protestant Scholastic Theology* (Grand Rapids: Baker Book House, 1985), 329–30.

85 There appears to be some tension between the Reformed emphasis on the equality of laity and clergy, or of the active and the contemplative life, and this emphasis on the need for a special vocation to clerical offices. The tension between rejecting Roman Catholic hierarchical church structures and trying to uphold a high view of church offices is clearly tangible.

86 As Klaus Bockmühl remarks in his *Gesetz und Geist*, "Die innere (arcana) Berufung ... will er jedoch (leider) nicht näher besprechen," *Gesetz und Geist*, 36.

the active life. The problems with and abuses of monasticism asked for a concept to challenge the monastic tradition and its presuppositions.

In his groundbreaking article 'Die Geschichte des Worts Beruf'[87] Karl Holl has shown how vocation terminology was restricted to clerical functions until the late Middle Ages. Then, some tension begins to appear, especially in German mysticism, as a result of "the continual economic and political advance in the productive occupations."[88] Yet, according to Holl, the real shift only takes place in Luther's writings.

Hardy describes Luther's view on vocation as follows: "A vocation is the specific call to love one's neighbor which comes to us through the duties which attach to our special place or "station" within the earthly kingdom."[89] This picture of Luther's mature view on vocation brings to the fore a number of crucial elements. First, the combination of the words *love* and *neighbor* immediately should alert the reader that Luther's view on vocation should be firmly placed within his two-kingdom-framework and Hardy rightly chose to make this explicit by adding a reference to the earthly kingdom. For Luther, a vocation belongs to the earthly kingdom and it has love for the neighbor as its main content, not faith in God. Second, a vocation comes from God but always takes the neighbor as its main object. Thus, vocation and vocational guidance in Luther's conception can never become self-centered. A third important aspect is the idea of the *station (Stand)*.[90] This station, that for Luther is providentially given, points to the places individuals find themselves in. Stations typically include the various ways in which human beings are related to each other. Thus, paid occupations are forms of stations, but so are marriage, parenthood, and social rank. Through each of those stations and the corre-

---

[87] Karl Holl, "Die Geschichte Des Worts Beruf (1924)," in *Gesammelte Aufsätze Zur Kirchengeschichte, Bd. 3* (Tübingen: Mohr, 1928), 189–219. An English translation by Heber F. Peacock was published in *Review & Expositor* 55.2 (1958): 126-154.

[88] Karl Holl, "The History of the Word Vocation (Beruf)," trans. Heber F. Peacock, *Review & Expositor* 55, no. 2 (1958): 136.

[89] Lee Hardy, *The Fabric of This World: Inquiries into Calling, Career Choice, and the Design of Human Work* (Grand Rapids: Eerdmans, 1990), 46. Cf. Paul Althaus, *Die Ethik Martin Luthers* (Gütersloh: Gütersloher Verlagshaus Gerd Mohn, 1965), 43: "Das allgemeine, überall und für alle geltende Liebesgebot besondert sich für den einzelnen je nach dem Stand, in den Gott ihn gesetzt hat."

[90] According to Oswald Bayer, *Martin Luthers Theologie: Eine Vergegenwärtigung* (Tübingen: Mohr Siebeck, 2003), 114, the stations are far more important for Luther than the two kingdoms: "In Luthers Selbstzeugnis kommt der Dreiständelehre ein weit größeres Gewicht zu als der Lehre von den beiden Regimenten." Cf. p. 295. See for discussions of Luthers thought on the stations especially Werner Elert, *Morphologie des Luthertums II* (München: Beck, 1953), 65–79; Althaus, *Die Ethik Martin Luthers*, 43–48; Oswald Bayer, *Freiheit als Antwort: Zur theologischen Ethik* (Tübingen: Mohr Siebeck, 1995), 116–46; Eilert Herms, "Leben in der Welt," in *Luther Handbuch*, ed. Albrecht Beutel (Tübingen: Mohr Siebeck, 2005), 423–35.

sponding duties God calls people in various ways to love the people around them. Fourthly, it is through those vocations and stations in the earthly kingdom that God meets humanity's needs on a day-to-day basis.[91] Thus, fulfilling one's vocation can at the same time be seen as participating in God's special providence. Finally (and this is the real new aspect of Luther's concept of vocation), in this way all human work is charged with religious significance while at the same time the purely contemplative life is denounced as an unloving and unfruitful way of life.[92] Exegetically, Luther's interpretation of vocation is to a large extent dependent on his exegesis of 1 Cor. 7.

Calvin adopts much of the key elements of Luther's view on vocation, although he does not develop them in a two-kingdom context as explicitly as Luther does. Once again, the neighbor is the main object of one's vocation, 1 Cor. 7:20 the main exegetical ground, and the ties with providential language are strong and manifold.

Calvin most explicitly discusses the concept of calling in his *Treatise against the Libertines* and in section III.10.6 of his Institutes. In the *Treatise,* he includes a chapter titled 'On What the Libertines Understand by the Vocation of Believers, and how under this Guise They Excuse Every Form of Villainy.'[93] The chapter starts with a reference to 1 Cor. 7 and the definition of vocation Calvin extracts from it: "Vocation signifies all kinds of living or estates which God has established and founded in His Word."[94] Once again, the estates (cf. Luther's stations) of life gain a crucial place in the concept of vocation and are to a large extent given: "each person ought to continue in his state and rank."[95] In this context, Calvin is mainly concerned with paid occupations, but at the same time makes clear that for example marriage is also considered as a vocation. He repeatedly stresses

---

91 An element that is central to Hardy's depiction of and apology for vocation. His chapter on the concept of vocation and its history is titled "Our Work, God's Providence" and this relation can be interpreted in both directions.

92 The classic study of Luther's concept of vocation is Gustaf Wingren, *Luthers Lehre vom Beruf,* trans. Egon Franz (München: Chr. Kaiser Verlag, 1952). Hagen has recently rightly argued that this is strange, since Wingren's book is polemical in nature and says at least as much about the theological situation in Sweden as about Luther's concept of vocation. See Kenneth Hagen, "A Critique of Wingren on Luther on Vocation," *Lutheran Quarterly* XVI, no. 3 (2002): 249–73. Froehlich emphasizes that Luther did not secularize the term vocation but eliminated the laity, Karlfried Froehlich, "Luther on Vocation," *Lutheran Quarterly* XIII, no. 2 (1999): 201.

93 COR IV/1, 124: "Que c'est qu'entendent les Libertins par la vocation des fideles: et comment soubz ceste couleur ilz excusent toute villanie."

94 Calvin, *Treatises against the Anabaptists and against the Libertines,* 276. COR IV/1, 124: "Or le mot de vocation signifie toute maniere de vivre, ou estat estably de Dieu et fondé en sa parolle."

95 COR IV/1, 124: "que chacun se contienne en sa condition et qualité."

that vocations must always be ruled by the boundaries God has given in his word. In his view, the libertines abuse the concept of vocation to sanctify morally questionable ways of life.

In the passage of the *Institutes,* where his opposition to libertinism is less explicit but still hugely palpable, he writes more elaborately on the concept of vocation itself:

> He [God, CvdK] has appointed duties for every man in his particular way of life. And that no one may thoughtlessly transgress his limits, he has named these various kinds of living 'callings.' Therefore *each individual has his own kind of living assigned to him by the Lord* as a sort of sentry post so that he may not heedlessly wander about throughout life.[96]

Once again we see that vocation is used in the sense of a particular way of life, or a kind of living. Moreover, in this context Calvin explicitly states that this kind of living is *assigned* by God and that this assignment takes place on an individual level. Furthermore, although Calvin does not explicitly mention the neighbor in this specific context, it is clear that vocation is strongly tied to the idea of fruitfulness: humans are not meant to wander heedlessly throughout life.[97] Finally, Calvin emphasizes that this idea of vocation elevates even the most lowly tasks: "no task will be so sordid and base, provided you obey your calling in it, that it will not shine and be reckoned very precious in God's sight."[98] Thus, the Reformed leveling of laity and clergy did not result in a reduction of the importance of the ministry. On the contrary, applying vocation terminology wider than just to the clergy should be understood as sanctifying the life and occupations of ordinary Christians and placing the entire Christian life, in whatever place, class, or occupation, *coram deo*.[99]

---

96 *Inst.* III.10.6 (emphasis CvdK). OS IV, 181, 2-6: "distinctis vitae generibus sua cuique officia ordinavit. Ac ne quis temere suos fines transsiliret, eiusmodi vivendi genera vocationes appellavit. Suum ergo singulis vivendi genus est quasi statio a Domino attributa, ne temere toto vitae cursu circumagantur." Notice that Calvin even attributes the *concept* of vocation to God: He has named them callings.

97 This is one of the points that later developed into the work ethics that became the object of Weber's thesis. In the present study, there is no need to take up that discussion, since it is not directly relevant for our purposes and is discussed extensively in numerous other places. For a recent comparison between Calvin and Weber see Wim van Vlastuin, "Calvin, Weber, and the Soul of Europe: Weber's Thesis Tested and Reapplied," in *Protestant Traditions and the Soul of Europe*, ed. Gijsbert van den Brink and Gerard den Hertog (Leipzig: Evangelische Verlagsanstalt, 2017), 203–15.

98 *Inst.* III.10.6. OS IV, 181, 30-32: "quod nullum erit tam sordidum ac vile opus, quod (modo tuae vocationi pareas) non coram Deo resplendeat et pretiosissimum habeatur."

99 Hence, there is a close link between the Reformed approach to vocation and the insistence on the priesthood of all believers.

Clearly, Calvin largely adopts Luther's concept of vocation and its general contours. Yet, as Aalders remarked, he also went his own way with the concept.[100] The specific Calvinian elements come most explicitly to the fore with regard to Calvin's view on the discernment of vocations and the specific concerns against which he develops his account of vocation.

3.3.5 The discernment of vocations
As mentioned before, Calvin's civic interpretation of vocation lacks the combination of internal and external elements that the other forms of vocation consisted of. This raises the question how civic vocations are to be discerned according to Calvin. Given their shared starting point in 1 Cor. 7, both Luther and Calvin have conservative tendencies in their accounts of vocation.[101] In their reading of Paul, a vocation is something in which the believer is to stay, and consequently, a vocation is a *given* situation and hence there is no need to *search* for it. Whereas vocation is originally a pneumatological term, in its early Reformation form it receives a rather providential interpretation.[102] Common word combinations for Calvin are "responding to our calling" or "following our calling," both emphasizing that for Calvin the main problem was not in knowing what a calling consisted of, but being obedient to it.[103]

As Aalders has shown, in his view on the discernment of vocations, for Calvin vocation and nature are intricately intertwined and as such nature and history (the domains of divine providence) are important means of conveying vocational guidance.[104] Aalders rightly warns against overestimating the status of nature in Calvin, but he cannot deny that for Calvin what is given in nature and history is never independent of God. Calvin is inclined to counsel people to accept the situations in which they find themselves, and take their place (*estat*) in them as good as possible. This place should then be seen as their certain vocation, unless this is impossible because of either God's will or the believers' conscience.[105]

---

100 W.J. Aalders, *Roeping en beroep bij Calvijn*, Mededeelingen der Nederlandsche Akademie van Wetenschappen, Afdeling Letterkunde, 6(4) (Amsterdam: N.V. Noord-Hollandsche Uitgevers Maatschappij, 1943), 3.
101 These conservative tendencies are the main ground of the critique formulated against the concept of vocation in 20th century theology. See for a discussion §6.2, and esp. 6.2.3.
102 Cf. for example Bockmühl, *Gesetz und Geist*, 345. "Beruf und Stand, der damit einhergehende Besitz und die entsprechende Lebensweise hängen für Calvin aufs engste mit der göttlichen *Vorsehung* zusammen."
103 See the examples Aalders lists on p. 18.
104 Aalders, *Roeping en beroep bij Calvijn*, 20. "Men ziet, hoe nauw roeping en natuur hier samengaan."
105 Aalders, 20. "Maar dit neemt niet weg, dat Calvijn in het in de natuur en de geschiedenis gegeven niet een zelfstandige, d.w.z. van God onafhankelijke of aan Hem vijandige macht kan erkennen en er veeleer toe neigt het levens-bestel, dat men bevindt en waarin men

Aalders concludes that in Calvin's view, a Christian does not need to wait for an unmediated call of God, but regularly hears that call through Scripture, hearing what comes to him in the actuality of life as a call from God.[106]

Although to a large extent Aalders' account of Calvin on vocation seems to be a fair representation, on a number of issues Calvin differs from Luther and presents a somewhat less static view.[107] Two aspects stand out and both have to do with what Heiko Oberman named the *Reformation of the Refugees:* the stage of the Reformation in which Calvin operated was a stage in which many Reformed believers were exiles, driven away from their homeland, house, and occupation.[108] This unstable background made it impossible to formulate an account of vocation exclusively in terms of a given situation, a providentially ordered society. Adapting his view in light of the circumstances, Calvin repeatedly emphasizes the importance of gifts in deciding upon an appropriate vocation.[109] Those gifts are then to be so ordered, that they serve the common good in the best possible way.[110] Here, Calvin extends the New Testament imagery of the church as a body in which all members have their proper function to society in general, in which then also all citizens should have a position in which they are able to serve. Furthermore, Calvin showed an increasing awareness that the given order cannot be accepted as entirely God-given, but is itself in need of continual reformation. More than in Luther, with Calvin there is room for not just submitting to the given order, but also transforming it. As Marshall argues, "a certain voluntarism in decid-

---

zich bevindt, te aanvaarden en daarin zijne plaats, zijn status of estat, zoo goed mogelijk in te nemen en daarin zijne "certa vocatio" te zien, tenzij dit om Gods of des gewetens wil volstrekt onmogelijk blijkt."

106 Aalders, 20. "De Christen behoeft dus, om te weten wat hij doen of laten moet, niet van oogenblik tot oogenblik een onmiddellijken roep van God te hooren. Hij hoort dien roep geregeld, hoezeer middellijk, zoowel wat zijn zieleheil betreft als zijn verkeer in deze wereld, als hij de H. Schrift hoort lezen en uitleggen, met haar Evangelie en haar wet, ook met hare voorbeelden in de geschiedenis van het volk Israël en de levens der vrome vaderen, als hij het oor openhoudt voor wat hem in de levenswerkelijkheid als roep van Gods-wege toeklinkt."

107 Paul A. Marshall, *A Kind of Life Imposed on Man: Vocation and Social Order from Tyndale to Locke* (Toronto: University of Toronto Press, 1996), 25. "But Calvin's view was not as static as Luther's. One's given social position was not quite so normative, limiting, or all-encompassing."

108 See e.g. Oberman, *The Two Reformations: The Journey from the Last Days to the New World*, 145–50. For Oberman, it was crucial to take this historical and, for Calvin, pastoral, background thoroughly into account in evaluating his theology. Oberman himself mainly does so with regard to Calvin's doctrine of election and predestination, but it also necessarily has a major impact on his views on vocation and the guidance of the Spirit.

109 Hardy, *The Fabric of This World*, 66.

110 Note another shift with regard to Luther: For Luther the main object of vocation was the (given) neighbor, Calvin points at the overarching category of the common good.

ing on the Lord's calling was appearing" in Calvin's theology.[111] As Preece has argued, in light of recent discussions on the viability of vocation in a world where for many people work is an experience of alienation, this is an important difference.[112]

Calvin's attention for gifts, fruitfulness, and transformation in no way reduce, but only add to Aalders' conclusion that normally God takes an orderly way with individuals, in which what is given through God's providence, either in circumstances or in personal gifts, is His way of guiding an individual into a certain way of life. Calvin's own experiences are in no way to be seen as a normal scheme, but are to be seen as extraordinary.[113] We can understand why Calvin saw such need to emphasize the given order and the ordinary processes against the historical background of his writings.

3.3.6 Concerns in emphasizing vocation
The situation in Europe was not only destabilized by the persecution of Protestants in France, but also by the emergence of various radical groups nowadays subsumed under the heading of the Radical Reformation. Whereas originally the concept of vocation was developed against the background of the Roman Catholic monastic tradition, in Calvin's writing monasticism is no longer his primary opponent. Wherever he writes on vocation, he is in an ongoing discussion with the Libertines or enthusiasts.[114] This accounts for the concerns that seem to drive Calvin in the way he discusses vocation. For example, he repeatedly commends vocation to draw people away from unordered and impulsive lives, to warn against restlessness and human ambition. Too many people, under the appearance of a deeper sort of spirituality, led unfruitful lives and never became reliable and faithful servants. The most repeated advice to believers is to stay in their occupations. Major changes were only justified in extraordinary circumstances.

---

111 Marshall, *A Kind of Life Imposed on Man*, 25. Marshall refers to Troeltsch's statement that in Calvin we encounter "a freer conception of the system of callings." See Ernst Troeltsch, *The Social Teachings of the Christian Churches* (New York: Harper & Row, 1956), II: 611.
112 Preece, *Viability of the Vocation Tradition*, 265–67.
113 Aalders, *Roeping en beroep bij Calvijn*, 38. "Dit [Calvin's own experiences as narrated in the preface to his Psalm's commentary, CvdK] was iets buitengewoons. Gewoonlijk gaat God met den mensch den ordelijken weg. Er bestaan nu eenmaal door de Voorzienigheid Gods zekere onderscheidingen van ordeningen en graden en deze moeten worden in acht genomen. Calvijn gaat hierin zeer ver."
114 Most notably so in his treatises against the Anabaptists and Libertines, but this background is also very explicit in for example the section on calling in the *Institutes*, III.10.6.

Such comments make no sense over against monasticism, but make a lot of sense against the background of the uproars that had happened under influence of radical protestant groups or leaders. Given this specific historical situation, Calvin's concerns seem to be justified and express pastoral wisdom, yet they also reflect Calvin's own personality. For him, nothing was more praiseworthy than an ordered and fruitful life, and nothing more to be feared than chaos and disorder.[115]

The reverse of Calvin's warnings against restlessness, chaos, and ambition is the fact that the concept of vocation gains a crucial place as one of the primary structuring principles of Calvin's ethics. Whereas for Calvin the law of God, his revealed will, provides the content of Christian ethics, as Klaus Bockmühl has shown vocation functions as the primary principle of individuation, through which ethical norms find their specific application in the individual life. One's specific duties flow forth from and are restricted at the same time by one's calling. In Calvin's words, this way "there will be harmony among the different parts of your life."[116]

3.3.7 Implications for Calvin's view on guidance

Having sketched Calvin's view on vocation, and especially on those issues that are most related to our overall aim, it is time to consider what this idea of vocation contributes to our search for Calvin's view on divine guidance.

As will be clear by comparing the different evangelical ideas and views on guidance with Calvin's account of vocation, modern evangelicals make use of a number of insights and beliefs that played important roles in early Reformation theology. The strong conviction of God's involvement in the ordinary daily life of all believers flows directly from the theological choice to apply vocational language to the entire body of believers, instead of exclusively to the clergy. Furthermore, the idea that God gives each person his or her own place and proper duties, the idea that behind what we do in everyday life the divine will is at work is present in both. Finally, in both the Reformed account of vocation and contemporary ideas on guidance God is actively involved in the process as the God who calls, or in more evangelical terms, the God who guides.

---

115 Both chaos and disorder play a major role at the background of Calvin's theology and ethics. William J. Bouwsma, *John Calvin: A Sixteenth-Century Portrait* (Oxford: Oxford University Press, 1988) over-emphasizes those aspects, but the basic "fear" that he found in Calvin is undeniable.

116 *Inst.* III.10.6. Calvin actually negates the opposite, OS IV, 181, 18: "Deinde in ipsis vitae partibus nulla erit symmetria."

At the same time, the distinction in our previous sentence makes clear that there is an important difference between thinking in terms of a God who calls to a (rather) static vocation or a God who is present in the daily process of guiding believers. In Calvin's view, it was the idea of having a vocation that provided the context in which the individual received the necessary guidance as to what were the proper duties to be performed. As said before, Bockmühl nicely expressed this by naming the idea of vocation one of the primary principles of individuation in Reformed ethics.

Given the changed historical and societal situation, the concept of vocation can no longer fulfill the crucial role it played in Reformation theology in an unaltered form.[117] One option is to forget about the idea of vocation and guidance, either by theoretically critiquing it or by practical silence on the relationship between faith and daily life. The other option, and this seems to have happened in evangelicalism, is to lift the idea of guidance out of its static vocational context. Whereas in the original model guidance was given by God in the context of vocation(s) and even through the vocations themselves, in the contemporary view the guidance of the Spirit is no longer found within the structure of vocation, but is necessary to arrive at the proper vocation. That is, the original order of guidance and vocation is reversed, and in the new constellation a decision on vocation has to be made that was absent in the original order.

This is of course a simplified picture, for vocation, even in Calvin, was not the only way in which God guided people. More needs to be said about the role of the Spirit (who was remarkable absent in the current section on vocation) in guiding the believer.

3.4 Calvin on the Spirit as Guide[118]

3.4.1 Introduction
In the first section of the present chapter we asked whether, in his discussions on divine providence, Calvin paid attention to God's plan for the lives of individual believers. It appeared that for Calvin, special providence and God's care for his faithful form the material core of the doctrine of providence. One specific result of that section, which led to the next, was Calvin's attention to the concept of vocations. In our discussion of vocation, it became clear that for Calvin individual vocations perform the crucial function of (ethical) differentiation. At the same time, we

---

117 See §6.2.5 for a discussion of recent attempts of recovering the notion of vocation.
118 Parts of this section were presented at the 7th international RefoRC Conference in Wittenberg, May 11, 2017. I thank the attendants for their helpful remarks.

found that in Calvin's concept of vocation little or no specific role is attributed to the Holy Spirit.

Therefore, in the current section we turn to what can be seen as the focal point of our investigation, namely, the question whether Calvin allowed for a specific guiding role of the Spirit in the individual lives of the faithful. We start with a brief section (§3.4.2) on Calvin's writings against the Libertines to show the boundaries of his position. Next, we review two discussions of Calvin's view on guidance that move largely in line with his criticism of the Libertines (§3.4.3). This picture must however, be complemented because (as shown by the authors we discuss in §3.4.4) there are elements in Calvin's writing that are not done justice in this interpretation. The elements mentioned lead us to two case studies that shed further light on the issue: In §3.4.5 we investigate Calvin's references to the guidance of the Spirit in his *Commentary on Acts* and in §3.4.6 we analyze his use of the word *instinctus*. The section is closed with a brief conclusion (§3.4.7).

3.4.2 The common background: Calvin against the Libertines
Calvin's views on the gifts of the Spirit, fresh revelations, and hence also on guidance are almost exclusively discussed against the same recurring background: the excesses encountered in 16th-century enthusiast movements, in Calvin's case most obviously those he called the *Libertines*.[119] And indeed, in his discussions with the Libertines, explicitly in his *Treatise against the Libertines* and implicitly in many of his other writings, we encounter a number of arguments that are foundational for Calvin's theological approach. A brief survey of his main arguments in the *Treatise* suffices to convey why the issue of guidance is often treated marginally in studies of Calvin's thought.

Basically, what is at stake in Calvin's rebuttal of the Libertines is the relation between Word and Spirit. Discussing their favorite phrase—'the letter kills but the Spirit gives life'– Calvin states that the Libertines want both to go beyond the simplest sense of the text of Scripture and are searching for fresh revelations.[120] However, according to Calvin, the Spirit was not promised "for the purpose of forsaking Scripture, so that we might be led by Him and stroll amid the clouds, but in order to gain its

---

119 For more backgrounds on Calvin's view on the Libertines, see Mirjam G.K. van Veen, "'Supporters of the Devil': Calvin's Image of the Libertines," *Calvin Theological Journal* 40 (2005): 21–32.

120 Calvin, *Treatises against the Anabaptists and against the Libertines*, 222. Later on, he adds the complaint that the Libertines cannot state a sentence without referring to the Spirit, thus using it as a kind of gravy for their talking, COR IV/1, 79.

true meaning and thus be satisfied."[121] When the apostles received the Spirit, their study of the Scriptures increased, instead of decreased.[122] Therefore, it is unwise not to hold to "the pure and plain Word of God, where He has clearly revealed His will to us."[123]

Calvin's tone is especially sharp and ironic when he writes about those who act "under the pretext of being led by God."[124] Returning to the 'cloud-imagery' he used before, he recalls experiences of "those who, desiring to transcend the clouds in their search for God's will, instead of holding to the revelation which contains His will in the Holy Scriptures, have fallen into such churlish absurdities that it is a horror to speak of them."[125] The combination of a lower view of Scripture and the search for the hidden divine will results in a situation in which people regard everything as good and "make it possible for each person to follow the inclination of his own nature and to work and live according to what advances his profit or pleases his heart."[126] In short, this results in a situation in which a person's heart is his or her own master, without asking whether every inclination of the heart is indeed coming from God.

Against this background, which we must certainly keep in mind, it is logical that little room is seen in Calvin for those modern types of divine guidance that come close to the Libertine position. However, it is necessary not to focus solely on the excesses to which Calvin reacted, but also to look for more positive strands in his writings. For that, we turn to a number of authors who have written on the topic of guidance in Calvin's writings.

3.4.3 Two critical treatments: Krusche and Bockmühl
For a theologian often referred to as 'the theologian of the Spirit,'[127] remarkably little attention has been paid to specifics of Calvin's pneumatology

---

121 Calvin, 224. COR IV/1, 77: "Or ce n'est pas à fin qu'en delaissant l'Escriture nous soyons conduis de luy et pourmenez par les nues: mais à fin d'avoir la vraye intelligence d'icelle, pour nous en contenter."
122 Calvin, 224.
123 Calvin, 224. COR IV/1, 78: "Tenons nous, dis ie, à la pure et simple parolle de Dieu, où il nous a pleinement revelé sa volonté."
124 Calvin, 254. COR IV/1, 103: "soubz ombre de se laisser conduire par Dieu."
125 Calvin, 253. COR IV/1, 102: "et nous en avons l'experience en ceux cy, lesquelz voulans monter pardessus les nues, pour chercher la volunté de Dieu, au lieu de se tenir à la revelation qui nous en est faicte en la saincte escriture, tombent en des absurditez si brutalles, que c'est horreur que d'en ouyr parler."
126 Calvin, 276–77. COR IV/1, 124: "pour faire trouver bon que chacun suyve l'inclination de sa nature: et qu'il face et vive selon qu'il luy viendra à poinct pour son profit, ou que son coeur le portera."
127 The title apparently was first used by B.B. Warfield in his "Calvin and Calvinism." See B.B. Warfield, *Calvin and Calvinism*, The Works of Benjamin B. Warfield 5 (New York: Oxford University Press, 1927), 21.

that fall outside the scope of (continental) academic pneumatological studies. One of those issues, which, as we will see, is not marginal for Calvin, is the guiding role of the Spirit. Of the major treatments of Calvin's pneumatology, only Krusche gives explicit attention to guidance.[128] Neither Van der Linde[129] nor Quistorp[130] mention guidance as an issue at all.[131]

As said, in his seminal work on Calvin's pneumatology, Krusche devotes a short section to Calvin's view on 'Obedience and the leading of the Spirit.'[132] In it, he repeatedly stresses that the rule of the Holy Spirit in the faithful primarily leads to the possibility of obedience to God's law; that is, for Krusche guidance is an example of the way Calvin couples Spirit and Word.[133] Based upon Calvin's polemic against the Schwärmer, Krusche explicitly denies the possibility of interpreting Calvin's references to the guidance of the Spirit as going beyond the revealed will of God ("an Gottes Gesetz vorbeiführen").[134]

---

128 Werner Krusche, *Das Wirken des Heiligen Geistes nach Calvin* (Göttingen: Vandenhoeck & Ruprecht, 1957). Krusche devotes pp. 288-294 to the topic of "Gehorsam und Geistesführung."

129 Simon van der Linde, *De leer van den Heiligen Geest bij Calvijn: bijdrage tot de kennis der reformatorische theologie* (Wageningen: H. Veenman & Zonen, 1943). Although Van der Linde's study of Calvin's pneumatology is very insightful, it is somewhat weakened and biased (both with regard to the topics that are being investigated as to the treatment of those topics) as a result of Van der Linde's aim to measure (and disqualify) Barth's theology by a comparison to Calvin.

130 H.J.J.Th. Quistorp, "Calvins Lehre vom Heiligen Geist," in *De Spiritu Sancto: Bijdragen tot de leer van de Heilige Geest bij gelegenheid van het 2e eeuwfeest van het Stipendium Bernardinum* (Utrecht: Kemink en Zoon N.V., 1964), 109–50.

131 I. John Hesselink came to the same conclusion in 1993, and pointed to an appendix in Benjamin C. Milner Jr.'s *Calvin's Doctrine of the Church* as a surprising place to find one of the most explicit treatments of the subject until then. As we shall see, little has changed since the publication of Hesselink's article, I. John Hesselink, "Governed and Guided by the Spirit: A Key Issue in Calvin's Doctrine of the Holy Spirit," in *Reformiertes Erbe: Festschrift Für Gottfried W. Locher Zu Seinem 80. Geburtstag (Band 2)* (Zürich: Theologischer Verlag Zürich, 1993), 161–72.

132 "Gehorsam und Geistesführung." The section is part of the chapter on 'The Holy Spirit and the Church' and appears in a section on sanctification.

133 See e.g. Krusche, *Wirken des Heiligen Geistes*, 289: "Es war wichtig, darauf hinzuweisen, daß die Herrschaft des Heiligen Geistes im Wiedergeborenen sich auswirkt als Ermächtigung zum Gehorsam gegen Gottes Gesetz."

134 Krusche, 290. Krusche points to a difference at this point between Calvin and Bucer, for whom the guidance of the Spirit, even in the smaller issues of daily life, belongs to the essentials of the Christian life. Although Krusche's comparison is slightly biased by his conservative interpretation of Calvin, he seems certainly right that there is at least a gradual difference in this regard between Calvin and Bucer. See e.g. W.P. Stephens, *The Holy Spirit in the Theology of Martin Bucer* (Cambridge: Cambridge University Press, 1970), 85-87. Stephens summarises: "The stress on the guiding of the Spirit expresses the view that the whole life of the Christian is to be lived in dependence on God, that the discerning of God's will is possible only through the Spirit of God, and that there is no situation in which God cannot reveal his will to those who, being children of God, are led by his Spirit" (87).

Yet, Krusche acknowledges that Calvin encountered Biblical narratives that spoke explicitly about forms of special guidance, especially in the stories of the patriarchs and the apostles. Calvin's treatment of those narratives shows three crucial elements according to Krusche: First, Calvin emphasizes the extraordinary character of such guidance and warns not to make these narratives into a general rule. Second, because the patriarchs had no Scripture available to them, theirs is an unrepeatable time. Third, those extraordinary leadings of the Spirit only *seem* to go beyond what is revealed in Scripture – in reality they move inside its borders.[135] Krusche concludes that for Calvin guidance means that the Spirit leads believers by illumining what a concrete rule or prescription of Holy Scripture means in their specific situation, and by inclining their heart to obedience.[136] For Krusche, it is clear that the relation Word (law) – guidance of the Spirit – obedience is closely related to the basic Calvinian scheme Word (gospel) - illumination (by the Spirit) – faith.[137]

Klaus Bockmühl, in his *Gesetz und Geist*,[138] devotes a separate chapter to the issue of *Geistesleitung* in the (early) Reformed tradition. He examines what the Reformed confessions and Calvin have to say about the guidance of the Holy Spirit in the lives of believers.[139] Bockmühl arrives at a similar conclusion as Krusche, although he has more eye for the specifics of Calvin's language on the issue.[140] Whereas Krusche appeared to be

---

135 Krusche, *Wirken des Heiligen Geistes*, 291.
136 Krusche, 293: "Hier wird nun auch deutlich, was Calvin mit der Führung durch den Heiligen Geist meint: der Heilige Geist führt mich, indem er mir klarmacht, was ein bestimmtes Gebot oder eine bestimmte Weisung der Heiligen Schrift in je dieser konkreten Situation von mir fordert, und indem er mir das Herz lenkt ... und bereit macht zum Gehorsam."
137 Krusche, 294.
138 Apparently, Hesselink was not aware of this discussion of Calvin on guidance.
139 Bockmühl, *Gesetz und Geist*, 362: "Was haben die Reformierte Bekenntnisse, was hat Calvin über die Führung des Heiligen Geistes zu sagen, soweit sie unmittelbar die Gläubigen betrifft?" With regard to the Reformed confessions, Bockmühl states that they devote more attention to the work of the Spirit than the Lutheran confessions, and especially to the (active and experienced) indwelling of the Spirit and the guidance and reign of the Spirit. Bockmühl does regret, however, that the guidance is mostly reduced to the Spirit as *Antrieb*, while the *Unterweisung* is relegated to Scripture. For Bockmühl, a problem exists in the confessions with regard to the calling of pastors, as here forms of *unmittelbarer Weisung* seem to be presupposed, shifting the 'problem' of immediacy from all believers to those in a church office. He mentions the Confessio Tetrapolitana as an exception, as there guidance is discussed in the context of Christian freedom and the double love commandment: "ein Jeder ... über sich und Alles, was er hat, dem heiligen Geiste Christi, dem Geber der wahren Kindschaft und Freiheit, die Entscheidung, Leitung, Anordnung und Anwendung zum Besten der Nebenmenschen und zur Verherrlichung Gottes gänzlich überlassen muß" (art. 12). See for the entire discussion Bockmühl, 362-71.
140 Bockmühl himself states that his research confirms Krusche's findings, *Gesetz und Geist*, 420.

relieved that Calvin added many disclaimers to his discussion of extraordinary instances of guidance, Bockmühl criticizes Calvin for this conservative stance.[141] In Bockmühl's view, Calvin solved the tension between his Roman Catholic frontier and his spiritualistic opponents too much in the direction of Rome.[142]

As said, Bockmühl starts with the recognition that there is much vocabulary in Calvin that points to a specific guiding role of the Spirit: for example, he mentions *spiritu duce*,[143] *illuminatio, testimonium internum*,[144] the Spirit as *interior magister*,[145] but above all the numerous instances in which Calvin writes about the Spirit who reigns, guides, teaches, leads.[146] According to Bockmühl however, in the end this guidance of the Spirit is always limited again by Calvin's references to Scripture, Decalogue, vocation, circumstances, or fate.[147] For him, Calvin's language about the Spirit's leading is more formal than material, and its concrete elaboration is a telling example of the depersonalization of the Spirit in western theology.[148] According to Bockmühl, in early Reformed theology, and also in Calvin, we find a reduction of pneumatology in which ultimately the Spirit is silenced.[149] Often, the Spirit is described more as a force than as a person.[150]

Yet, despite Bockmühl's critical stance towards Calvin's conservative position, he points at a number of elements in Calvin's writings that are in some tension with this interpretation and that could point to a different interpretation of Calvin's view on guidance. Not only is there the issue of Calvin's specific word choice, but in 1540 Calvin also starts to end his letters with the wish that the reader may be led by the Spirit.[151] Further-

---

141 Klaus Bockmühl was also discussed in chapter 2 of this study (§2.4.3), and his critique of Reformed theology for its fear of the value of subjective experiences seems to be related to his affinity with evangelicalism. For an analysis of his thought, see Annette M. Glaw, *The Holy Spirit and Christian Ethics in the Theology of Klaus Bockmuehl* (Eugene: Pickwick Publications, 2014).
142 Bockmühl, *Gesetz und Geist*, 406. See also p. 398: "Konfrontiert mit der realen Möglichkeit spiritualistisch-subjektivistischer Anarchie legt der Genfer Reformator alles Gewicht auf die objektive Seite, die Schrift und die Predigt: Nur *durch* diese redet der Geist." (emphasis in original).
143 Bockmühl, 362.
144 Bockmühl, 362.
145 Bockmühl, 372.
146 Bockmühl, 372: "An einer unabsehbaren Zahl von Stellen spricht er von dem Regieren, Führen, Lehren und Leiten des Heiligen Geistes."
147 Bockmühl, 427.
148 Bockmühl, 366; cf. 434.
149 Bockmühl, 427; see also 380.
150 Bockmühl, 366. Bockmühl uses the words *Antrieb* and *Kraft* in the German original.
151 Bockmühl, 372. Calvin continues to do so until his death. For more information, see section 3.5.4. In our reading, it is more precise to say that Calvin started to do so in 1541.

more, for Bockmühl it is clear that in a Reformed perspective the indwelling of the Spirit is not only part of the confession, but also an object of experience.¹⁵²

Both Bockmühl and Krusche point at a number of elements in Calvin's writings that, when elaborated upon, could be interpreted in a way that allows for the possibility of personal guidance by the Holy Spirit today. We proceed to investigate the contributions of three authors that proposed such an interpretation, before working out two case studies that show that Calvin did indeed think of divine guidance in more subtle ways than generally acknowledged.

3.4.4 More is to be said: Milner, Kelly, and Hesselink
A first indication of the importance of the Calvinian terminology of 'the secret impulse of the Spirit' is found in a remarkable place: the appendix to Benjamin Milner's *Calvin's Doctrine of the Church*.¹⁵³ In this brief appendix, Milner emphasizes the importance of this secret impulse in Calvin's writings and makes a number of observations on Calvin's usage. First, he notes that the word combination *arcano instinctu* for Calvin "seems to have the character of a *terminus technicus*."¹⁵⁴ It can be used either collectively or individually and is sometimes even applied to animals.¹⁵⁵

Milner detects two main deployments of the terminology in Calvin's work, namely its influence in the pious and in the ungodly.¹⁵⁶ For our purposes, the first category is most important. Here, Milner points at some of the ways Calvin uses the terminology. He states: "Perhaps the most important references to the 'secret impulse' are those instances in which it seems to take the place of, or to obviate the need for, objective revelation."¹⁵⁷ Furthermore, a number of biblical prayers seem to be instigated by a specific impulse of the Spirit, as are "certain extraordinary and apparently unwarranted actions of the pious."¹⁵⁸ A final instance Milner mentions is the secret impulse that teaches the apostles when to perform

---

152 Bockmühl, 363.
153 Benjamin Charles Milner, Jr., *Calvin's Doctrine of the Church*, Studies in the History of Christian Thought, V (Leiden: E.J. Brill, 1970). The appendix is found on pp. 197-203.
154 Milner, Jr., 197. In a note, Milner adds that the most common combination is *arcano Dei instinctu*, but that the reference to the Deity is dispensable. Furthermore, given Calvin's stylistic flexibility *arcanus* can be substituted by *occultus* and *instinctus* by *impulsus* or *motus*.
155 Milner, Jr., 197. Milner gives an example from the Commentary on Jer. 28:14, see COR II/6-2, 1049, 623-24.
156 Milner, Jr., 197-98.
157 Milner, Jr., 198.
158 Milner, Jr., 199.

miracles. Milner concludes his brief analysis of the secret impulse of the Spirit in the pious with the observation that its function almost without exception is "to authenticate any thought, speech or action of the godly which lacks objective warrant, *i.e.*, objective expression of the divine will – *ordinatio Dei*."[159] With regard to content, Milner states that the person who receives such an *impulsus* experiences "inner certainty of the will of God" although "knowledge in the strictest sense is excluded."[160] This inner certainty (as an experience of God's guidance) points to the main difference of the Spirit's working in the pious and the ungodly, for in the ungodly the impulse functions to execute the divine decree "beyond the purpose of their own minds."[161] In conclusion, Milner points out that the special significance of Calvin's word-choice is found in the many instances referring "to an operation of the Spirit apart from the revealed *ordinatio Dei*.[162]

Almost two decades after Milner's book, two articles were published that dealt with Calvin's view on guidance in a more direct way. The first article, written by Douglas Kelly, deals with Calvin's teaching on guidance in one of his final sermons series, on II Samuel (1562-63).[163] The second article, by I. John Hesselink, deals in a broader way with the specifics of Calvin's language on guidance.

Kelly starts from his assessment that many Reformed thinkers overreact to alleged Pentecostal and Charismatic excesses and end up denying specific guidance.[164] According to Kelly, in his sermons on II Samuel Calvin finds a balance between the objective and the subjective and between the general and the specific when it comes to guidance: "Calvin encourages the people of God with the assurance of a guidance which is characterized both by the warmth of personal relationship and by the chaste, sober practicality needed in a fallen world."[165]

Kelly develops his reading of Calvin in four propositions that struc-

---

159 Milner, Jr., 200 (emphasis in original).
160 Milner, Jr., 200.
161 Milner, Jr., 201. Milner cites the *"trahuntur praeter animi sui propositum"* of Calvin's commentary on Jer. 25:8-9 (COR II/6-1, 924, 373) and mentions as examples of this use Calvin's comments on Cyrus and Darius, Abimelech, and primarily on Pontius Pilate.
162 Milner, Jr., 203.
163 Douglas F. Kelly, "John Calvin's Teaching on Guidance as Expressed in His Sermons on II Samuel," *Reformed Theological Review* 46, no. 2 (1987): 33–42. At the time, Kelly was working on a translation of the sermon series, which appeared in 1992 as Douglas F. Kelly, *John Calvin's Sermons on 2 Samuel: Chapters 1-13* (Edinburgh: Banner of Truth Trust, 1992).
164 Kelly, "John Calvin's Teaching on Guidance," 33. He seems to be pointing at the 'wisdom view' of Friesen by using the label 'modified Deism.'
165 Kelly, 34.

ture his article.[166] First, according to Calvin guidance is as available to contemporary believers as it was in the times of the Old and New Testaments.[167] In this context, Kelly points at Calvin's teaching that through the Spirit believers have the privilege of Christ's real presence and furthermore points at Calvin's depiction of the Holy Spirit as the Spirit of prudence.[168] Second, guidance of God to believers takes place "in the context of their union with Christ."[169] Third, Kelly emphasizes the importance of the Reformed assertion that guidance is always based upon the truth of Scripture.[170] As a consequence, any believer who wants to receive the guidance of God should return again and again to the Scriptures. Finally, Kelly asserts that "the guidance of God to his people today is both specific and personal."[171]

For Kelly, Calvin's view on guidance is an elaboration of the biblical metaphor of the Shepherd and the sheep, in which the sheep need direction from the Shepherd and the Shepherd is willing to provide such guidance.[172] Here, "true Christian guidance may be thought of as the sanctifying of the human understanding by the illumination which the Holy Spirit gives of the truth of God"[173]; yet it also takes place through prayer, circumstances and other means. As Kelly asserts at the end of the article, according to Calvin "remaining uncertain of particulars is proper for sheep, for it reminds them to stay in touch with their Shepherd."[174]

The most extensive and outspoken treatment of Calvin's views on guidance is found in the article written by I. John Hesselink. In it, he presents the government and guidance of the Spirit as a "key issue" in Calvin's pneumatology. Hesselink paints a picture of a Calvin who "speaks again and again of the Spirit as governing, guiding, and leading the Christian in experiential ways that are apparently independent of any concrete scriptural teaching."[175] He hastens to add that "independent of" does in no way mean "contradictory to," for such a position would contravene a number of Calvin's most basic theological instincts. Hesselink starts with a number of introductory remarks to prevent his main point from such a misunderstanding. Crucial

---

166 Although he promises five at the start of the article, the fifth is absent from the article.
167 Kelly, "John Calvin's Teaching on Guidance," 34.
168 Kelly, 37.
169 Kelly, 36.
170 Kelly, 37.
171 Kelly, 39.
172 E.g. Kelly, 42.
173 Kelly, 37.
174 Kelly, 42.
175 Hesselink, "Governed and Guided by the Spirit," 162.

is his double warning that, for Calvin, the Spirit must always be understood as the Spirit of Christ,[176] and that hence no work of the Spirit can contradict the "objective revelation we have in Christ and the Word."[177]

After thus providing the necessary disclaimers Hesselink repeats his point, explicitly countering Krusche's interpretation: "There is massive evidence which indicates that in Calvin's theology the Holy Spirit plays a role that is far more mystical, experiential, and individual than is recognized by most Calvin scholars."[178] In a more positive way, Hesselink defends the following position:

> To state my thesis positively, the abundant references in Calvin's writings to the governing and guiding work of the Spirit suggest that although the concrete truths and injunctions of Scripture may be implied or understood and although Christ is always the model (exemplar) for our lives, Calvin submits that we are given not only faith and assurance by the Holy Spirit but also both general and specific wisdom and direction for our lives quite apart from any explicit instruction in the Scriptures or preaching of the gospel. In short, the Spirit at times gives seemingly independent and secret guidance. The Spirit gives a sort of suprarational insight and understanding.[179]

Hesselink goes on to show how the terminology of *guberno/gouverner, duco, dirigo/conduire* and *rego/moderer* is found throughout the entire corpus of Calvin's writings, including the *Institutes*, his catechisms, commentaries, sermons, polemical writings, and prayers.[180]

According to Hesselink, the idea of guidance for Calvin is "an aspect of the doctrine of sanctification."[181] Although it has close connections to Calvin's views on the Spirit's role in the origin of faith and the illumination of the believer in accepting and understanding Scripture as the Word of God, it is a distinct and independent aspect of the work of the Holy Spirit.[182] Hesselink agrees with Krusche that "the obedience, to which the Holy Spirit frees (us) is ... obedience vis-à-vis (*gegenüber*) God's right-

---

176 Citing Milner, Jr., *Calvin's Doctrine of the Church*, 130.
177 Hesselink, "Governed and Guided by the Spirit," 162.
178 Hesselink, 163. Shortly before this statement, Hesselink briefly described Krusche's interpretation.
179 Hesselink, 163.
180 Hesselink mentions Calvin's correspondence as the sole part of Calvin's writings he did not examine, see note 26, p. 165.
181 Hesselink, "Governed and Guided by the Spirit," 163.
182 Hesselink, 165.

eousness, i.e., vis-à-vis the law of God."[183] Yet he immediately adds that this is not all we find in Calvin. The work of the Holy Spirit is not restricted to inspiring and enabling, but involves providing special guidance, insight and strength. Hesselink goes so far as to say that "for us to maintain stability in the Christian life, a constant, ever-renewing guidance of the Spirit is necessary."[184] From the examples in Calvin's writings Hesselink then concludes that "at times he even seems to come dangerously close to the very enthusiasts (*Schwärmer*) whom he so vigorously attacks and refutes."[185] Once again, to balance his interpretation, he adds that nowhere in Calvin this guidance of the Spirit can be interpreted as new *revelation*.

Given these diverse perspectives on Calvin's interpretation of guidance, and the hints in especially Kelly and Hesselink that Calvin has more to say about special guidance than normally acknowledged by Calvin scholars, Calvin's terminology asks for a more in-depth analysis. Two main ways to proceed are available. First, following in the footsteps of for example Krusche and Kelly, specific writings of Calvin can be analyzed with regard to their content on guidance. Second, Hesselink's approach of studying Calvin's vocabulary could be extended and performed in a more encompassing way. We believe both approaches will yield valuable results, and are perhaps needed to balance each other. As it is impossible to present a complete picture of the issue within the limits of the present chapter, in what follows we present two case studies: The first approach is applied to Calvin's *Commentary on Acts*, while following the second approach we analyze Calvin's use of *instinctus*, elaborating on Milner's brief overview.

3.4.5 Calvin's commentary on Acts

Calvin's commentary on the book of Acts appeared in two volumes in 1552 (chapters 1-13) and 1554 (chapters 14-28).[186] In it, following his usual approach, Calvin provides a verse-by-verse commentary on the Acts of the Apostles. Based upon our question of how Calvin speaks

---

183 Hesselink, 165–66, citing (in own translation): Krusche, *Wirken des Heiligen Geistes*, 228.
184 Hesselink, "Governed and Guided by the Spirit," 166.
185 Hesselink, 169.
186 In his recent dissertation on Calvin's Commentary on Acts, Erik van Alten devotes a brief section to the role of the Spirit as Guide. See H.H. van Alten, "The Beginning of a Spirit-Filled Church: A Study of the Implications of the Pneumatology for the Ecclesiology in John Calvin's Commentary on the Acts of the Apostles" (PhD diss., Theological University Kampen, 2017), 140–46. Most work on Calvin and Acts has been done by Wim Moehn, although his focus is on Calvin's sermons. See esp. Wilhelmus H.Th. Moehn, *"God Calls Us to His Service": The Relation between God and His Audience in Calvin's Sermons on Acts* (Geneva: Librairie Droz, 2001).

about the guidance of the Spirit, a number of elements stand out: 1) several explicit *statements* on guidance, 2) a number of *narratives*, 3) the *names* and *technical terms* used for the Spirit and his work, 4) the *means* of guidance, and 5) some *restrictions* Calvin imposes with regard to guidance.

First, the commentary contains a number of *statements* that underline the importance of divine guidance. For example, Calvin warns his readers that "we must beware that we attempt nothing unless we have him [the Spirit, CvdK] for our guide and governor."[187] The same is found in his commentary on Acts 20:24, where Calvin asserts that "all those go astray who have not God to be the governor of their course. Whereupon it followeth that his calling is unto everyone of us *a rule of good life*."[188] Speaking about Paul, Calvin asserts that "all his life was framed according to God's will and pleasure"[189] and the reader is urged to "learn, by the example of the holy man, not to kick against the Spirit of the Lord, but obediently to give ourselves to him to be governed, that he may rule us at his pleasure after we be as it were bound to him."[190] These statements express on the one hand Calvin's deep faith that "God doth hold the helm of our ship,"[191] yet on the other hand acknowledge a responsibility of believers to be willing to subject and be attentive to God's guidance.

Second, a number of key *narratives* from the book of Acts incite Calvin to more prolonged comments on the nature of guidance. For example, in his commentary on Acts 1:23-26, where a successor to Judas Iscariot as apostle has to be chosen, Calvin answers two questions: What

---

187 *Comm. Acts* 14:23. COR II/12-2, 23, 4-5: "… solicite cavendum est, ne quid nisi ipso duce et praeside tentemus." For a balanced evaluation of such statements, it is crucial to notice that Calvin makes them in his commentary on the guidance of the Spirit *in the context of the church*. Without further evidence they cannot be extrapolated to a more general context.
188 *Comm. Acts* 20:24 (emphasis CvdK). COR II/12-2, 184, 30-31: "sed exemplo suo [Paul, CvdK] docet errare omnes, qui Dominum cursus sui non habent Praesidem. Unde sequitur illius vocationem cuique nostrum recte vivendi normam esse."
189 *Comm. Acts* 19:21. COR II/12-2, 164, 27-28: "totam eius vitam ad Dei arbitrium fuisse compositam."
190 *Comm. Acts* 20:22. COR II/12-2, 183, 25-27: "Porro discamus sancti viri exemplo, non calcitrare adversus Spiritum Dei, sed nos illi obedienter regendos tradere, ut nos quasi devinctos pro suo arbitrio agat." The important subordinate clause "nec tamen violenter trahamur" is missing from the English translation. Cf. e.g. the encouragements in the comments on 18:19-21, where Calvin expresses his wish that "we may learn to give ourselves to be governed at his pleasure" (COR II/12-2, 146, 26: "ut discamus nos eius arbitrio regendos tradere"), and "that we may learn to make our counsels subject to the will and providence of God" (COR II/12-2, 147, 4-5: "ut discamus consilia nostra Dei arbitrio et providentiae subiicere").
191 E.g. *Comm. Acts* 20:1. COR II/12-2, 172, 12: "scientes Deum tenere navis nostrae gubernacula." This is an important analogy for Calvin that is frequently encountered in his discussions of guidance and providence.

made the apostles decide to propose two candidates and why did they decide to cast lots? Calvin explains that the apostles did not simply appoint someone, because it should be known by the people that the one chosen had his authority from God.[192] On a more general level, he asserts that in such weighty matters "the chief judgment should be left unto God."[193] Therefore, the apostles tried to present the two best candidates, but between them cast lots. For Calvin, it is crystal clear, although he explicitly avows that Luke does not say so, that the disciples did not decide upon this particular process themselves, but that "they were moved thereunto by the ... Spirit."[194] Commenting on verse 24, Calvin adds the importance of prayer accompanying the entire process. Interesting is his insight "that the disciples pray that God would bring that to light *which was hidden from men*,"[195] immediately followed by the application that "the same ought to be required even at this day in choosing pastors."[196] Calvin's comments on this passage show an interesting combination of attention for the 'ordinary' processes of prayer, wisdom and discernment of the apostles on the one hand and the reference to the hidden influence of the Spirit (that is in the end fundamental to the legitimacy of the entire process) on the other.[197]

Another key story in Acts, found in chapter 16:6-10, narrates how Paul was 'forbidden' by the Spirit to enter into Asia and the subsequent vision

---

192 *Comm. Acts* 1:23. At the background of Calvin's argument is the difference between the authority of an apostle and that of a pastor. All other apostles had been directly appointed by Christ, so in order that the people would not ascribe less authority to the new apostle he also should be appointed by God, and not just by common consent.

193 *Comm. Acts* 1:23. COR II/12-1, 43, 32-33: "relinqui Deo summum iudicium."

194 *Comm. Acts* 1:23. COR II/12-1, 44, 8-9: "non nisi Spiritus instinctu eos ad sortem confugisse." He repeats the exact phrase in the same paragraph and adds that the apostles were "directed in all the action by the same Spirit" (12-13: "Quemadmodum et totam actionem a Spiritu illis fuisse dictatam, non dubium est"). For Calvin, it is important to be convinced that the disciples did not deal "rashly and disorderly" (6: "temere et praepostere").

195 *Comm. Acts* 1:24 (emphasis CvdK). COR II/12-1, 44, 25-26: "discipuli precantur, ut quod hominibus est absconditum, in lucem proferat."

196 *Comm. Acts* 1:24. COR II/12-1, 44, 27: "Idem et hodie in eligendis Pastoribus petendum est."

197 Calvin's commentary on Acts 13:1-3, where Paul and Barnabas are sent to the Gentiles, contains many elements similar to 1:23-26. Once again, Calvin strongly asserts that there is "no lawful election of pastors, safe wherein God is chief" (COR II/12-1, 363, 27-28: "nullam esse legitimam Pastorum electionem, nisi in qua Deus primas tenet partes"). Yet here also, Calvin emphasizes the singularity of the event in it being the result of a divine oracle. In more ordinary instances, e.g. the appointing of elders over churches in 14:23, Calvin favors election "by the consent of all" ("omnium suffragiis," COR II/12-2, 22, 18), after fervent prayer for "the spirit of wisdom and discretion" ("Spiritu prudentiae et discretionis," COR II/12-2, 22, 23). Calvin's comments on Acts 1 are all the more remarkable given the fact that this is one of the few events in Acts that are pre-Pentecost.

in which he was called to Macedonia.[198] Calvin asserts that it was an encouragement to Paul that the Spirit denied him to preach in some places, because in this way "he knew that the Spirit of God was his guide in his way, and the governor of his actions."[199] With regard to the means of the Spirit's guidance, for Calvin it is clear that Paul received oracles, as he proceeds to ask where contemporary ministers should seek their certainty, "who are certified by no *oracles* when they must speak or hold their peace."[200] Calvin answers that the circumstances of Paul's ministry made this kind of extraordinary guidance necessary, mainly as a result of the immenseness of his task: "Seeing that Paul's province and charge was so wide, he had need of the singular direction of the Spirit."[201] Those who serve in a particular place or region are generally not in need of such singular direction. Just how singular this direction was in the case of Paul is shown by Calvin's remark that "God beckoned unto him, as it were by reaching forth his hand, how far he would have him go, or whither."[202] With regard to the vision that Paul receives, Calvin once again stresses the singularity of the event and, commenting on verse 10, remarks that the persuasion of Paul shows that "it was not bare vision, but that it was also confirmed by the testimony of the Spirit."[203] The reason for this is that satan also regularly makes use of visions to deceive the faithful.

A final type of narrative that sheds light on Calvin's interpretation of the Spirit's work are the miracle narratives in Acts.[204] Whenever a miracle is performed through the service of the apostles, Calvin asks how the apostles could know that God would work a miracle in those specific circumstances. Every time, his answer comes down to the same basic formula: "… so often as the Lord determined to work some miracle by his apostles, he did always direct them by the secret motion of the Spirit."[205]

---

198 This story, as we saw in chapter 2, also plays a major role in many of the contemporary books on divine guidance.
199 *Comm. Acts* 16:6. COR II/12-2, 71, 31-32: "cum Spiritum Dei sibi viae et actionum ducem esse agnosceret."
200 *Comm. Acts* 16:6 (emphasis CvdK). COR II/12-2, 72, 4-5: "qui nullis oraculis redduntur certiores quando loquendum sit vel tacendum."
201 *Comm. Acts* 16:6. COR II/12-2, 72, 5-6: "cum tam late pateret provincia Pauli, opus illi fuisse singulari directione Spiritus."
202 *Comm. Acts* 16:6. COR II/12-2, 72, 10-11: "Deum quasi porrecta manu signum illi dedisse, quorsum tendere eum, vel quousque progredi vellet."
203 *Comm. Acts* 16:10. COR II/12-2, 73, 23-24: "non fuisse nudam visionem, sed confirmatam spiritus testimonio."
204 Of course, many more narratives from Acts could be presented as examples. For instance, Calvin's comments on Acts 20, where Paul goes to Jerusalem against the advice of many other believers, provide ample material to reflect on.
205 *Comm. Acts* 9:39. COR II/12-1, 289, 17-19: "quoties Dominus virtutem suam aliquo miraculo per Apostolos exerere statuerat, arcano Spiritus impulsu eos direxisse." See e.g. also *Comm. Acts* 9:34: "The Spirit who was the author of all miracles … did move his heart by

A telling example of such a miracle story is found in Acts 3, and Calvin's views are especially clear in his comments on verse 4. There, he explains that the apostles did not possess the power to work miracles whenever they wanted to do so, but in this case "Peter doth not thus speak before he be certain of the purpose and intent of God."[206] In answering the lame man, the apostles "had the Spirit of God to be their guide and director," and Calvin adds that they had him also as their guide "in other things."[207] The combination of those stories makes clear, that in Calvin's view the apostles where being guided by the Spirit in a very direct way. On the one hand, he is inclined to stress the singularity and extraordinariness of a number of those events, while on the other hand he pictures the guidance of the Spirit as a reality not restricted to New Testament times and draws specific lessons from the narratives for the church in his own time.

Third, and perhaps most telling, are the *names*, *actions* and *means* Calvin applies to God, and more specifically the Holy Spirit. With regard to the names, common roles attributed to the Spirit throughout Calvin's commentary on Acts are guide (*dux*),[208] governor (*praeses*),[209] director (*director*),[210] and conductor (*auspex*).[211] Often, two of the roles are combined, so that the Spirit is presented as *ducem ac directorem* or *ducem ac praesidem*. In line with this, Christ is compared to the *imperator* and the *dux terrenus* of believers, who move only at his command.[212]

Closely related to those are the corresponding actions ascribed to God (the Spirit). He is presented as guiding (*ducere*), governing (*gubernare*), leading (*praesidere*), reigning (*regere*), calling (*vocare*), directing (*dirigere*) and commanding (*mandare*). What is important about Calvin's use of those names and actions ascribed to the Spirit is that they usually lack an explicit background in the biblical text, but are used by Calvin as a way to *explain* particular events or actions of the apostles.

What is clear by now is that in Calvin's commentary on Acts the guidance of the Spirit is an important and probably even decisive factor. Yet,

---

a secret inspiration." (COR II/12-1, 285, 17-21: "Spiritus quidem, qui miraculorum omnium autor fuit ... cor impulit secreto instinctu.")
206 *Comm. Acts* 3:4. COR II/12-1, 95, 16-17: "Non ita loquitur Petrus, quin de consilio Dei certus sit."
207 *Comm. Acts* 3:4. COR II/12-1, 95, 22-23: "ducem ac directorem habebant Dei Spiritum"; "in aliis rebus".
208 For God/the Spirit as *dux*, see e.g. *Comm. Acts* 7:34, 7:55, 9:39; 11:24, 15:28 and 16:6. According to Van Alten, *dux* is the most frequent designation for the Spirit in the commentary, see Van Alten, "Beginning of a Spirit-Filled Church," 140.
209 *Comm. Acts* 8:16; 8:26; 15:12, 15:28, 16:6 and 19:21.
210 *Comm. Acts* 7:55 and 8:16. The English translation sometimes has *leader* as its translation, see e.g. on 17:11.
211 *Comm. Acts* 9:39.
212 *Comm. Acts* 1:4.

with regard to the *means* of this guidance nothing is clear yet. Once again the most is gleaned from Calvin's vocabulary. Wherever Calvin speaks about the guidance of the Spirit, a number of technical terms frequently appear in his text. Thus, for example, people are led through a motion (*impulsus, motus*),[213] direction (*directio*),[214] inspiration/instinct (*instinctus, afflatus*),[215] and power (*virtus*).[216] Two things stand out with regard to those means of guidance. First, they make clear that for Calvin guidance is something the Spirit works mainly internally, in the heart of believers, moving them towards specific actions. Second, a telling characteristic of Calvin's use of those terms is that he usually combines them with either *arcano, secreto* or *occulto*.[217] This way, Calvin makes clear that this guidance is never something obvious or calculable.[218]

Although this method provides a lot of insight, not everything can be said about Calvin's view on the means of God's guidance by focusing on his vocabulary. Whereas the notions mentioned all have a rather singular character and focus on guidance on a specific moment or in a specific situation, guidance for Calvin also has a more organic side. Following his basic assertion that God is Lord and that He will not only dwell but "reign in us",[219] Calvin can state that God governs the affections of believers,[220] and directs their mind.[221] Combined with his attention for the Spirit as the *spiritus prudentiae et discretionis*,[222] this more organic strand enables Calvin to defend (esp. when writing on things pertaining to church order) that choosing is a legitimate activity and that it is not necessary to wait on the special direction of the Spirit in every situation. Thus, he explicitly

---

213 So, in commenting on Stephen's speech (Acts 7), Calvin asserts that Moses was led out of the palace of pharao towards his people through a "new and unwonted motion of the Spirit" (COR II/12-1, 192, 22-23: "ex novo et insolito Spiritus impulsu"). Apparently, there are differences of intensity in the motions of the Spirit, as some are explicitly labelled as "impulsus vehementes" (9:40).
214 E.g. *Comm. Acts* 8:32. COR II/12-1, 255, 30-31: "occulta spiritus directione".
215 *Comm. Acts* 9:34, 11:28. An important drawback of the translations of the Calvin Translation Society is that they are not always concordant, even within a single volume. This obscures the importance of Calvin's specific wording for those not able to consult the Latin original.
216 *Comm. Acts* 10:44.
217 Cf. Oberman, *The Two Reformations: The Journey from the Last Days to the New World*, 130. There, Oberman mentions the French *secret* and its Latin equivalent *arcanum* as words Calvin was very fond of.
218 This is not to say that this kind of guidance is unclear. For Calvin, one of the primary roles of those hidden motions of the Spirit is to reduce uncertainty, not to increase it. In the examples provided, the apostles were very aware of their specific task.
219 *Comm. Acts* 1:3. COR II/12-1, 19, 25-26: "in nobis regnet Deus."
220 *Comm. Acts* 1:14. COR II/12-1, 35, 15-16: "interiores affectus regit".
221 *Comm Acts* 16:27-28. COR II/12-2, 89, 4: "Dominus animos suorum dirigere solet in rebus perplexis".
222 See e.g. *Comm. Acts* 13:3; 16:16; 17:11.

states that "the church is permitted to choose,"²²³ and the Spirit directs the church *through* its decision-making.²²⁴

Finally, in order to draw a complete picture of Calvin's view on guidance as depicted in his commentary on Acts a few additional remarks need to be made. First, Calvin continues to warn against curiosity and the search for what goes beyond divine revelation.²²⁵ Thus, the impulses of the Spirit cannot (assuming at least this kind of consistency in Calvin) have noetic content in the strictest sense of the word. Second, for Calvin the narratives of Acts show that following the leading of the Spirit is no guarantee to success,²²⁶ but in contrast often leads to hardship, as the life of the apostle Paul clearly shows. Finally, although we have seen that the special guidance of the Spirit plays an important role in Calvin's commentary on Acts, it is important to see that it is balanced by his repeated attention for the wisdom, zeal, and constancy of Paul as important factors in the success of the missionary journeys.²²⁷ In many instances those character traits of Paul play at least as crucial a role as the special and extraordinary influences of the Spirit.

3.4.6 Calvin's use of 'instinctus'

In Calvin's writings, and mainly his commentaries, the world is full of *instincti*, instigations towards specific actions or reactions.²²⁸ In this section we analyze Calvin's use of the term.

With regard to the source of the various promptings mentioned by Calvin, four main origins stand out as important: such promptings can come from the devil (*diaboli/satanae instinctus*), from nature (*naturali/ naturae instinctus*), from the self (*proprio instinctus*) or from God (*Dei/*

---

223 *Comm. Acts* 6:3. COR II/12-1, 166, 15: "electio permittitur Ecclesiae".
224 *Comm. Acts* 6:5. COR II/12-1, 68, 10: "Spiritus ... eligendis iudicia direxerit." Interestingly, in this specific instance Calvin limits the guidance of the Spirit to the choice of six of the seven deacons. Cf. 13:3 and 14:23.
225 See e.g. *Comm. Acts* 1:7-8.
226 Or, in some instances, God withholds the succes in order to test obedience. See e.g. *Comm. Acts* 8:26. COR II/12-1, 250, 18-21: "Atque ita Dominus saepe cum suis agere solet ad probandam eorum obedientiam. Quid facere ipsos velit, demonstrat; hoc vel illud praecipit: successum vero penes se absconditum tenet."
227 See e.g. his comments on Acts 15:36 and 24:24.
228 Around 300 places are found where Calvin uses the word, 80% of which are in the commentaries (28 in the different versions of the *Institutes*, 15 in sermons, 14 in treatises and 5 in personal letters). We already encountered a number of them in our discussion of his *Commentary on Acts*. All instances of the word in Calvin's writings were recovered with the help of the digital version of the *Calvini Opera* prepared at the Institute for Reformation Research in Apeldoorn, the Netherlands. In what follows, we will use the English 'prompting' as our standard translation of the term *instinctus*.

spiritus/coelesti instinctus).[229] Promptings from the first three sources, the devil, nature, and the self, are often placed in opposition to the promptings that come from God. Given our focus on divine guidance, in this section we look at those promptings that have God as their (direct) source. It is, however, important to see that the existence of other sources of *instincti* creates the necessity for discernment.[230]

The promptings that come from God have various objects and in general can be seen as important (if not: the primary) means God uses in the governance of the world. This is not only true with regard to nature, where especially animals are repeatedly described as heeding to God's prompting,[231] but also with regard to history. On the scene of history, Calvin considers major events like wars not as random events, but as ultimately inspired *arcano Dei instinctu*.[232]

In most instances, however, the divine promptings function at the level of the individual human being.[233] Here, a distinction must be made between how God directs people in general and how he guides the faithful. In general, Calvin is clear that God guides the minds and hearts of persons *arcano instinctu* and changes their affections just as he pleases.[234] In many instances, Calvin adds that God bends the hearts of men "hither and thither" (*huc et illuc*) and does so while they are unknowing or unwilling (*vel inscios vel nolentes*).[235] In most instances where Calvin uses the terminology in this way enemy kings or heathen rulers are the objects. Notable examples are the pharaoh of Egypt, Nebuchadnezzar, Belshazzar,

---

229 In most instances where no explicit source is mentioned one of these four sources is discernible as Calvin's intention from the immediate context.
230 Yet, it appears that the origin of divine instincts is often so clear that Calvin saw little need to elaborate extensively on the praxis of discernment.
231 For examples of animals heeding to divine promptings see e.g. the commentaries on Isa. 34:16; Isa. 43:20; Jer. 28:14; Ez. 14:15-16 etc. In some instances Calvin can speak about God's sustenance of his creation as entirely dependent on his *instincti*, e.g. *Comm. Acts* 17:28 (COR II/12-2, 124, 23-24: "quia admirabili Spiritus sui vigore et instinctu Deus quaecunque ex nihilo condidit, conservat") and *Comm. Ez.* 1:19 (CO 40, 47: "nihil accidit nisi ex arcano instinctu, quem nos non perspicimus oculis"). Apart from the animals, the waters are also frequently mentioned as influenced by divine instincts, e.g. *Comm. Ps.* 77:17; *Jer.* 5:22.
232 See e.g. *Comm. Obad.* 1.
233 That the individual and the collective are not entirely exclusive here appears from the fact that many wars are started because of the *arcano Dei instincti* in kings and military leaders.
234 *Comm. Dan.* 1:9. CO 40, 547: "et mentes et corda hominum sic gubernari arcano Dei instinctu, ut mutet affectus, prout visum est." Cf. e.g. *Comm. Josh.* 11:19.
235 For "huc et illuc" see e.g. *Comm. Ps.* 105:25; *Ez.* 9:5-6. For different versions of "vel inscios vel nolentes" see *Comm. Ps* 105:17; *Jer.* 34:22; *Dan.* 5:13-16. In some instances people are told to do things contrary to the wish of their own hearts, as e.g. Balaam, *Comm. Mic.* 6:5.

Darius, Cyrus, and Pilate.[236] Crucial to this use of the word *instinctus* is that it conveys the notion of providential guidance that works in and through people who follow their own hearts unaware of any divine involvement.

This unawareness of being an instrument in the divine hands is the main difference with the way Calvin sees God's guiding work in the faithful. As we shall see from the examples below, the way in which Calvin discusses the promptings in believers shows that believers are necessarily aware of their divine origin. Although we heard Calvin say that God bends the hearts of all men wherever He wants, Calvin nowhere explicitly says so about a believer.

In what contexts does Calvin refer to the divine promptings and to what actions do they incite their recipients? Most references Calvin makes to the *instincti* occur in contexts where Biblical figures act in ways that are unwarranted by prior revelation or knowledge.[237] The promptings incite to the following actions:

Prophecy. In a number of places Calvin makes clear that prophets do not always repeat what they heard from God, but (more freely) speak while moved *arcano spiritus instinctu*. Although in a sense those *instincti* provide more freedom, Calvin reinforces their weight by adding that they go against private insight or carnal feeling.[238]

Name-giving. Closely related to the category of prophecy inspired by divine prompting is a number of instances where Calvin suggests that parents give their children specific (and appropriate) names under influence of a divine instigation.[239]

Speech. On a number of occasions individuals are said to speak in uncommon ways that were directed by the Spirit. Thus, Isaiah was led to ask a severe question, Job ascribed his calamities to God, Moses spoke to the Pharaoh and Joshua delivered a non-standard message to the people

---

236 Pharaoh: *Comm.* Gen. 41:8; Nebuchadnezzar: *Comm.* Dan. 2:47, 3:24-25, 4:1-3, 4:26 and 4:35; Belshazzar: *Comm.* Dan. 5:6, 5:13-16, 5:34; Darius and Cyrus: *Comm.* Jer. 50:21, Zach. 1:12; Pilate: *Comm.* John 19:21.
237 Only in a few instances the word is used in the context of faith and regeneration, e.g. Inst. III.24.13.
238 See *Comm.* Ex. 8:10; Ez. 1:4; Jer. 11:20. Interestingly, the *instincti* not only provide the content of prophecies or Biblical writings, but sometimes also influence their form. Thus, Isaiah is "coelesti instinctu edoctum" to narrate a story very vividly (*Comm. Isa.* 21:5) and Jeremiah is enabled, although he was not taught in the school of the rhetoricians, to adorn his discourse with rhetoric means (*Comm. Jer.* 31:15-16).
239 In general, Calvin notes that names are sometimes given "prophetico instinctu ad notandum aliquod arcanum Dei opus" (*Comm.* Lk. 1:59). See for examples *Comm.* Gen. 5:29; Isa. 7:3; Dan. 1:6-7. In one instance a name is given in this fashion to a place, *Comm.* Num. 11:34.

of Israel at his departure, all following an *instinctus*.²⁴⁰ Specific instances where Calvin uses the terminology are the places where main Biblical figures utter imprecations and indignations to others. Examples of this kind are Noah's reaction to his son Cham and Moses' imprecation of Korah.²⁴¹

Prayer. *Instincti* are said to inspire the act of prayer in general,²⁴² an increased earnestness in prayer in a specific situation,²⁴³ or the content of specific prayers.²⁴⁴ In a number of instances, what appear to be strange or even stubborn prayers are warranted for by particular divine promptings.²⁴⁵

Extraordinary actions. Not these four language-oriented occurrences are most prominent in Calvin, but the places where the promptings incite individuals to concrete actions. In the second book of his *Institutes*, Calvin remarks on these "special activities" he finds for example in the books of Judges and Samuel, that "in every extraordinary event there is some particular impulsion (*specialis instinctus*)."²⁴⁶ Examples of such actions are numerous. Thus, for Calvin there is no doubt that Sarah was led by a prompting of the Spirit when she told Abraham to send Hagar away, as was the case with David when he danced before the Ark, Daniel when he wished to receive a different diet at the court in Babylon, Simeon when he went to the temple to see the Messiah, and Mary when she anointed the feet of Jesus.²⁴⁷

Two examples of this kind of action inspired by a divine prompting stand out for shedding light on Calvin's theological view on guidance. The first is found in Calvin's comments on the war Abram fought against Chedorlaomer and the other kings (Gen. 14). One of the first questions Calvin raises in this context is "whether it was lawful for Abram, as a private person, to arm his family against kings, and to undertake a public war."²⁴⁸

---

240 See resp. *Comm. Isa.* 6:11; *Calumniae*, CO 9,300; *Comm. Ex.* 9:29 and *Comm. Jos.* 24:15.
241 See *Comm. Gen.* 9:24 and Num. 16:5. For similar examples see further *Comm. Ps.* 69:25; Ps 109:17 and Jer. 18:21.
242 *Comm. Ex.* 10:18; Ps. 137:7; Ps. 138:3; Jer. 10:25; Mt. 20:32; Acts 1:20.
243 *Comm. Ex.* 32:9.
244 See e.g. *Inst.* III.20.5. OS IV, 302, 24-25: "significans ita vigere spiritus instinctum ad formandas preces."
245 So the prayer of Eliezer in Genesis 24 (*Comm. Gen.* 24:12) and a prayer of David reflected in Lam. 5:20 (*Comm. Lam.* 5:20).
246 *Inst.* II.2.17. OS III, 260, 9-10: "Denique in eximiis quibusque factis specialis est instinctus." The examples that follow show that for Calvin this was not restricted to the extraordinary events of Judges and Samuel, but applied to the entire biblical corpus.
247 Resp. *Comm. Gen.* 21:10; *Interim Adultero-Germanum*, CO 7, 609; *Comm. Dan.* 1:11-13; Lk. 2:25; and Mt. 26:10.
248 *Comm. Gen.* 14:13. CO 23, 198: "an Abrae homini privato licuerit armare familiam contra reges, et publicum bellum suscipere." Notice how for Calvin as jurist the issue of lawfulness always remains prominent.

At stake is the question whether Abram transgressed "the bounds of his vocation" (*vocationis suae metas*), because private persons were not allowed to fight wars according to Calvin's interpretation of vocation. After putting the question, Calvin hastens to add that Abram "went to war endued with the power of the Spirit," "was guarded with a heavenly command," and that the commendation of Melchizedek that follows is a sign of God's approval. He concludes that this war was undertaken by Abram "under the special direction of the Spirit."[249] No doubt must remain in the reader that "God was his [Abram's, CvdK] Guide and Ruler in this affair."[250]

A similar example is found in the story of Phinehas the priest, who kills the adulterers in the camp of Israel (Num. 25). Once again, Calvin reacts to the suggestion that Phinehas "transgressed the bounds of his calling" when taking up a sword. He counters that "God sometimes requires new and unusual acts of His servants" and in this case Phinehas "was called by the special inspiration of God." God's approval once again indicates that Phinehas acted under the guidance of the Holy Spirit. Applying the passage to his readers, Calvin stresses the importance of normal vocations, but also God's freedom to make exceptions: "God preserves his free right to appoint His servants by privilege to act in His behalf as He shall see fit."[251] What is vital for evaluating such situations is "spiritual prudence" (*prudentia spirituali*) to recognize the Holy Spirit, who "must go before and dictate what is right."[252]

Lots. One final context where the *instincti* occur in the writings of Calvin is wherever lots are cast. These could be seen as specific examples of promptings that inspire extraordinary actions. Calvin generally warns against throwing lots or other divinizing methods, but wherever Biblical figures cast lots Calvin assures that they do so *spiritus instinctu*. He explicitly assures that in all instances where believers cast lots there were divine promptings at work.[253]

In summary, the word *instinctus* occurs in situations where individuals prophesy, give their children 'inspired' names, say remarkable or hard things, pray in particular or remarkable ways, seemingly 'overstep' the boundaries of their functions or vocations, or ask God for specific signs.

---

249 *Comm. Gen.* 14:13. CO 23, 198: "spiritus virtute instructus in bellum descendit;" "coelesti mandato fuisse munitum;" "singulari spiritus directione".
250 *Comm. Gen.* 14:13. CO 23, 198: "Deum illi ducem et autorem fuisse."
251 *Comm. Num.* 25:7. CO 25, 299: "interim tamen manet sua Deo libertas, ut privilegio servos suos ad res gerendas prout visum fuerit praeficiat."
252 *Comm. Num.* 25:7. CO 25, 299: "spiritum sanctum praeire, ac dictare quid rectum sit."
253 *Comm. Jonah* 1:7. CO 43, 220: "Itaque tenendum est, fuisse peculiares quosdam instinctus, ubi servi Dei usi fuerunt sorte." See also *Comm.* Isa. 38:7-8 and Acts 1:23.

Given these uses of the term *instinctus*, in light of our research question it is important to see what functions such promptings have in Calvin's writings. Given the contexts in which *instinctus* is used, it is clear that these divine instigations are an important *explanatory device* in Calvin's exegesis. As his standard advice for believers is to live their lives according to the word of God and their personal vocations, Calvin needs an instrument to account for the multiple Biblical narratives in which those two 'guides' are insufficient to explain the behavior or specific acts of important figures. In all those instances, also in the Old Testament examples, Calvin almost without exception refers to a particular stimulus from the Spirit.[254] As we saw, according to Milner "Calvin adduces this 'secret impulse of the Spirit' to authenticate any thought, speech or action of the godly which lacks objective warrant, *i.e.*, objective expression of the divine will – *ordinatio Dei*. In all of the foregoing cases there is no such, and in some of them *ordination* to the contrary."[255] This statement is confirmed by our own research of Calvin's use of *instinctus*.

Behind Calvin's fondness for the use of *instinctus* and similar words as an exegetical instrument we may surmise his aversion of disorder. In many places where he uses the terminology he explicitly denies that the subjects acted rashly, thoughtlessly (*temere*), spontaneously or based on their own senses, flesh or inner motions.[256] Thus, by referring to the divine *instincti*, Calvin makes clear that the actions of the believers that were instigated by divine stimuli do not belong to the category of the *disorderly*, but of the *extraordinary*. As a result, such actions are to be seen as congruent with the secret will of God, although they are not warranted upon his revealed will.[257]

While it is clear that the divine promptings play a major role, especially in Calvin's exegetical work, it is not yet clear whether those stimuli have a distinct content. Given Calvin's strong conviction that in the Bible we have a *complete* revelation of what God intends to make known, and a

---

254 As said, in this specific case study we focused on the *instinctus*, yet a very similar picture emerges for *impulsus, motus, nutus* and similar terms.
255 Milner, Jr., *Calvin's Doctrine of the Church*, 200. One could discuss whether Calvin's *arcano* could best be translated as 'secret' or 'hidden'. There are instances where the believer who receives the divine prompting is aware of it, yet there are also instances in which this prompting seems to remain secret even to the person who undergoes it unconsciously.
256 For references to the *instincti* as opposed to acting *temere* see e.g. *Inst.* IV.10.25; *Comm.* Gen. 24:12; Ex. 3:3; Isa. 38:7-8 and Dan. 1:11-13. 'Sponte': *Comm.* Jer. 22:7. 'Proprio motu': *Comm.* Ex. 9:29; Dan. 1:11-13. 'Ex suo sensu neque in hominis gratiam': *Comm.* John 1:31. 'Pro carnis libidine': *Comm.* Gen. 24:12, cf. Jer. 10:25.
257 See Milner, Jr., *Calvin's Doctrine of the Church*, 200 for a similar conclusion.

sufficient revelation to base Christian conduct and decision-making upon, it would be difficult to argue that the promptings do have a revelatory content. Furthermore, there is evidence from Calvin's own texts that these divine stimuli have a status that is different from direct revelation. For example, Calvin writes that a particular prophetic message was accompanied by an *arcano instinctu* to add extra weight to it.[258] Such a comment only makes sense when the instinct is something different from the substance of the message itself. This is confirmed by a number of passages where Calvin asserts that an individual was driven to a certain action by a combination of a certain revelation and a divine impulse.[259] Even more telling are those instances where Calvin defends a course of action by stating that the acting person did so either upon an express divine command or a divine stimulus.[260] Thus, the *instincti* clearly lack the status of revelation and are distinct from divine commands, having an experiential content rather than a noetic one. Both Milner and Hesselink seem right in pointing out that, although "knowledge in the strictest sense is excluded,"[261] the Spirit does indeed give "new insights, deeper understanding, empowerment, and concrete applications or directions for our lives."[262]

If this is what Calvin means by a divine *instinctus,* we may ask whether this kind of guidance by divine promptings, granted that no fresh revelation is to be expected, is still occurring in our (or Calvin's) times. In answering this question, we must first remind ouselves of their function: to stimulate to specific actions that are not directly commanded or concretely encouraged in Scripture. Thus, for many decisions Calvin would insist that 'searching' for God's will is unnecessary since this will is already known and available. Yet, important as this basic perspective is, a number of considerations prompt us to think that for Calvin the divine stimuli were not restricted to biblical times, but continued to occur after Pentecost. Perhaps the most important is Calvin's use of the example of Christ.

---

258 *Comm. Isa.* 38:2. In another place, Calvin more generally states that the efficacy of divine words depends on the correlating *instinctus, Comm. Ez.* 2:1-2.
259 So, e.g., Isaiah went to king Hezekiah "instinctus spiritus sancti ac iussi Dei" (*Comm. Isa.* 39:3), Simeon went to the temple to see the Messiah "arcano instinctu et certa revelatione" (*Comm. Lk.* 2:25) and John the Baptist spoke "instinctu spiritus et Dei mandato" (*Comm. Jn.* 1:31).
260 Thus, e.g., Moses spoke to pharao not rashly, but "vel spiritus instinctu, vel certo oraculo edoctum" (*Comm. Ex.* 9:29) and Isaiah named his son Schear-Jaschub "arcano spiritus instinctu vel expresso Dei mandato" (*Comm. Isa.* 7:3).
261 Milner, Jr., *Calvin's Doctrine of the Church*, 200.
262 Hesselink, "Governed and Guided by the Spirit," 170. Hesselink names this "suprarational insight and understanding" (163).

According to Calvin, Christ did nothing out of his human instincts or will, but was continually led by the impulses of the Spirit. A similar statement is made elsewhere about the angels, who have no will of their own, but are governed by the hidden instinct of God.[263] For Calvin it is obvious that following God's guidance is as important for the believer as it was for Christ and is for the angels.

This picture is complemented by Calvin's treatment of the main biblical figures, the applications he makes from their stories and experiences, and especially the way these function as models for contemporary believers.[264] For example, when Calvin states that Moses was led *spiritu instinctu*, because he "was accustomed to inquire what God's pleasure was,"[265] it is clear that Moses' habit is exemplary for every believer. This is reflected in Calvin's method of moving from the narratives to general statements on what 'we' ought to do. A very clear example of such a generalizing statement, that shows that for Calvin the divine impulses are indeed a contemporary form of divine guidance is found in his comments on Psalm 143: "God therefore must be master and teacher to us not only in the dead letter, but *by the inward motions of his Spirit* [arcano spiritus instinctu]; indeed there are three ways in which he acts the part of our teacher, instructing us by his word, enlightening our minds by the Spirit, and engraving instruction upon our hearts, so as to bring us observe it with a true and cordial consent."[266]

Thus, our investigation of Calvin's use of the terminology of *instinctus* shows that for believers those divine stimuli are different from the general stimuli through which God governs the entire world. They are so specifically because the believer is somehow aware of them and through them perceives some kind of divine direction. This direction does not have a distinct noetic content, but leads to insight into the course that should be taken or the decision that is to be made. Such stimuli, according to Calvin, are not restricted to biblical times, but are part of the ongoing reality of God's guidance of his church.

---

263 *Comm. Ez.* 10:8. CO 40, 213: "angelos non habere proprium vel intrinsecum aliquem motum, sed gubernari arcano suo instinctu."
264 Compare for the importance of models and imitation Bouwsma, *John Calvin*, 90–93.
265 *Comm. Num.* 16:5. CO 25, 216: "solitus fuerit sciscitari quidnam Deo placeret."
266 *Comm. Ps.* 143:10 (Emphasis CvdK). CO 32, 404: "Ideoque necesse est Deum nobis non mortua tantum litera magistrum esse et doctorem, sed arcano spiritus instinctu. Imo tribus modis fungitur erga nos magistri officio: quia verbo suo nos docet: deinde spiritu mentes illuminat: tertio cordibus nostris insculpit doctrinam, ut vero et serio consensu obediamus."

This conviction that divine guidance also applies to contemporary reality leads us to the next section, in which we will investigate what then is perceived of this guidance in Calvin's personal life. Do we find traces of Calvin's experience of the guidance of the Spirit in his reflections on his own life?

3.4.7 Conclusion
In this section, we examined Calvin's thought on the guidance of the Spirit. Mostly, as seen in the examples of Krusche and Bockmühl, the possibilities for construing such an account of guidance are severely restricted by presenting Calvin's opposition to spiritual enthusiasm as the complete picture. When this approach is taken, Calvin's emphasis on the relation between Word and Spirit does not allow for specific personal guidance.

Yet, a number of scholars have pointed at a somewhat different strand in Calvin's thought, mainly encountered in his commentaries. In his commentaries, as for example Kelly and Hesselink have shown, Calvin wrestled with biblical narratives that displayed an actively guiding Spirit and did not declare these passages irrelevant for Christian living.

Following these scholars, in this section we performed two case studies: an analysis of Calvin's references to guidance in his commentary on Acts and an investigation of his use of the word *instinctus*. Both case studies yielded a similar result: According to Calvin, the Spirit is very actively guiding the faithful throughout the Biblical narratives, beginning early in the Old Testament. And although Calvin puts several restrictions in place, the lessons he draws from the material show that this guiding role of the Spirit did not end in the time of the Apostles, but continues to be a weighty reality for contemporary believers. This guidance does not take the form of fresh revelations, but, in the wording of Hesselink, should be thought of as suprarational. Whereas God does guide his entire creation according to his decree, his ways with his children are of a different order.

3.5 Guidance in Calvin's Personal Life

3.5.1 Introduction
In the second edition of his biography of Calvin, his disciple Theodore Beza reflects on his life and concludes that "his judgment was so sound and exact on all subjects, that his decisions seemed almost oracular."[267] As

---

[267] Theodore Beza, *Ioannis Calvini Vita*, CO 21, 119-72: 169: "Iudicii, quibuscunque de rebus consuleretur, tam puri et exacti, ut paene vaticinari saepe sit visus…" Beza's biography of Calvin was first appended to Calvin's commentary on Joshua (1564), then published in an enlarged version by Nicolas Colladon (1565), and finally published in a new version in 1575, together with Calvin's correspondence. The version referred to here is the 1575 edition.

is commonly acknowledged, Beza's description of Calvin's life was severely biased, as it gives the impression of being the first protestant hagiography, published only a few months after Calvin's death.

Not only is it difficult to agree with Beza's *laudatio* on every occasion, but little is known about most of the important moments of Calvin's life. Especially his own reflections on these moments are scarce. In his own words: "*de me non libenter loquor.*"[268] References to Calvin's personal life are scarce in his writings and sermons, his letter collection being somewhat of an exception. Yet even in his letters Calvin often focuses on church issues, international politics, and theological debates.

Still, when researching as personal an issue as divine guidance, our treatment would be incomplete without an account of experiences of guidance in Calvin's personal life. As the general picture of Calvin's life is sufficiently documented in a number of biographies, in this section we focus on a few occasions in which the issue of guidance comes to the fore.[269]

In this chapter, we will first take a brief look at Calvin's early years (§3.5.2), followed by discussions of his coming to Geneva in 1536 (§3.5.3), his stay in Strasbourg and the inner turmoil with regard to his calling in the years 1538-41 (§3.5.4) and his eventual return to Geneva (§3.5.5). Finally, we will discuss an example of Calvin's pastoral teaching on guidance in his correspondence with the De Falais couple (§3.5.6), and conclude with a number of observations (§3.5.7).

3.5.2 Important decisions in Calvin's early years
Destined by his father to become a priest, Calvin made a start with his studies in Paris in 1523 at the age of 14. In 1528, following the authority of his father, he was sent to Orleans, not to study theology, but law.[270] Apparently his father, who later on had his own personal conflicts with the church, was driven by financial concerns rather than by theological convictions. The study of law had Calvin's interest and he travelled to various universities to receive teaching from the great teachers of law (for example Pierre de l'Estoile in Orleans and Andrea Alciati in Bourges).

---

268 John Calvin, *Responsio Ad Sadoleti Epistolam*, CO 5, 385-416: 389. See Herman J. Selderhuis, *John Calvin: A Pilgrim's Life* (Nottingham: Inter-Varsity Press, 2009), 29–30 for a number of qualifying remarks on the interpretation of this statement.
269 A detailed and balanced recent biography is Bruce F. Gordon, *Calvin* (New Haven: Yale University Press, 2009).
270 Although Beza suggests, without further information, that the change was also welcomed by Calvin himself, because "having been acquainted with the Reformed faith ... he had begun to devote himself to the study of the Holy Scriptures, and ... to discontinue his attendance on the public services of the Church," Beza, *Vita Calvini*, CO 21, 121.

This period of intense study of law had a lasting influence on Calvin's writings, but as far as known he never pursued a legal career, for "his sole, true passion in 1530 was the humanities."²⁷¹ A picture emerges in which the major early decisions were made under paternal authority, but within their confines Calvin pursued a number of personal interests. It seems that Cottret's evaluation, that Calvin "dallied on his way, wandering into byroads," burdened by the sense of "the need to choose" that confronted his generation, paints a fairly adequate picture of this period of Calvin's life.²⁷²

Even in the years after his somewhat mysterious and oft debated "sudden conversion,"²⁷³ Calvin does not decide upon a place to settle or a career to pursue, although given the amount of work he performed during those years 'dallying' would no longer do justice to his mindset. From our perspective, it is important to know that Calvin is still deeply uncertain about his future when he arrives at Geneva in 1536. The most likely career path at that moment is academia, far from the center of public attention. Calvin had experienced periods of quiet and prolonged study and writing in the preceding years, especially in the library of Louis du Tillet in Angouleme, 1534.

3.5.3 Called to Geneva? On 'providential accidents'
In 1536, during a short and unintended stay at Geneva, "the question of what he was to do with his life was not so much resolved as taken out of his hands."²⁷⁴ The details of the situation still remain obscure, but for Calvin it became undoubtable that he was called by God.

History paints a picture of a restless Calvin who travelled in a short period of time from Basle, to Italy, returning to Basle, moving to Paris in order to then set out for Strasbourg. Obstructed by military unrest, he took a detour through the south and arrived at Geneva, allegedly for a one-night stop. There, either his presence was reported to Guillaume Farel, as in his own account, or he paid a visit to Farel and Viret, as for example Beza narrates.²⁷⁵ Farel took his chance and tried to convince Calvin, who by the time had the name of a promising theologian, to stay in Geneva. Calvin's own words convey how he experienced the situation:

---

271 Bernard Cottret, *Calvin: A Biography*, trans. M. Wallace McDonald (Grand Rapids: Eerdmans, 2000), 53.
272 Cottret, 53.
273 Preface to the *Comm. Psalms*. CO 31, 21: "subita conversione."
274 Bouwsma, *John Calvin*, 18.
275 For Calvin's account, see *Comm. Ps.*, pref. CO 32, 25-26. Beza's version is found in his *Vita Calvini*, CO 21, 125. A frequently encountered suggestion is that Calvin tried to represent the situation in such a way that it reinforced his account of the scholar drawn against his will into an active life, see e.g. Bouwsma, 18-19.

Farel, who burned with an extraordinary zeal to advance the gospel, immediately strained every nerve to detain me. And after having learned that my heart was set upon devoting myself to private studies, for which I wished to keep myself free from other pursuits, and finding that he gained nothing by entreaties, he proceeded to utter an imprecation that God would curse my retirement and the tranquility of the studies which I sought, if I should withdraw and refuse to give assistance when the necessity was so urgent. By this imprecation I was so stricken with terror that I desisted from the journey I had undertaken.[276]

Much can be said about the event: The 47-year old Farel addressing the 26-year old Calvin in such a way; Calvin, "disheartened by exile and unsure of his next step," being "unusually vulnerable to authoritative direction by an older man"; etc.[277] Yet for our purposes it is interesting to see how, although at first he was mostly afraid, later on Calvin would always refer to the event as his divine calling. For example, in 1538, when troubles in Geneva had already begun, he spoke about the church in Geneva as "the church over which the Lord has been pleased to set us."[278] Later, after being banished from and while dreading a return to Geneva, Calvin reflects on his first calling and asserts that "when I first entered upon it I could discern the calling of God which held me fast bound, with which I consoled myself."[279] No mention is made of Farel, Calvin's sole focus is on the call of God, which strengthened him to continue to work in the church while opposition grew. As Cottret observes, Calvin's arrival in Geneva was "one of those providential accidents in which he would detect the will of God."[280] In Calvin's view, Farel only served as an instrument in the divine hands. Such a view, of course, is only possible in retrospect, when "the hidden coherencies and internal rhythms that are bound up with the story" have become clear.[281]

---

276 *Comm. Ps.*, pref. CO 32, 25-6.
277 Bouwsma, *John Calvin*, 18.
278 Calvin to Heinrich Bullinger, Zurich Geneva, February 21, 1538. COR VI/1, 329, 5: "Quae ecclesiam, cui praeesse nos Dominus voluit". For translations of Calvin's letters, unless otherwise remarked, we have made use of the 4-volume edition of *Letters of John Calvin* edited by Jules Bonnet.
279 Calvin to Louis de Tillet, Strasbourg, July 10, 1538. COR VI/1, 411, 38-39: "Car comme lors ie sentois la vocation de Dieu qui me tenoit lié, en laquelle ie me consolois…"
280 Cottret, *Calvin: A Biography*, 118.
281 Cottret, 118–19.

3.5.4 Banished from Geneva: "I know assuredly that our Lord will guide me"
In April 1538, after the situation in Geneva had become untenable, Calvin and Farel were banished from the city. A number of his letters to friends make clear what thoughts occupied Calvin's mind at the time. In a first letter, dated May 20, 1538 and written from Bern, he tells Bullinger that he sets out on a journey to Basle, and asserts that "we look to him [God] in our proceedings, so we commit the success to his wise disposal."[282] As appears from another letter, this time to Viret, while they stayed in Bern some people pressed Farel and Calvin to stay there and serve the church, and "they confidently alleged that we would be unpardonable if we should decline so just a call."[283] Apparently, this time the call did not convince Calvin, for Farel and Calvin wrote with a sense of relief that "the Lord at length has opened an outlet to us."[284]

In July, Calvin's letter to Louis du Tillet shows an interesting combination of uncertainty with regard to the course to be taken and a deep certainty that the Lord will show the way. First, Calvin wrote that he would return to Basle (at the time he was in Strasbourg), "waiting to understand what the Lord would have me to do."[285] In a very revealing remark, he told his friend that,

> nevertheless, I know assuredly that our Lord will guide me in that so very doubtful a deliberation, the more so because I shall look rather to what he will point out to me than to my own judgment, which beyond measure drawing me contrariwise, I feel ought to be suspected.[286]

Here, we encounter a few interesting elements, that return more often in Calvin's letters on personal issues. Firstly, he clearly professes God to be

---

[282] Calvin to Heinrich Bullinger, Zurich Bern, May 20, 1538. COR VI/1, 375-76, 16-18: "Ut enim eum respicimus in agendo, ita successum eius providentiae committimus." Notice that Calvin speaks about God's providence, an aspect that is unfortunately lost in the translation.

[283] Guillaume Farel and Calvin to Pierre Viret [and Elie Corauld], Lausanne Basel, [circa June 6, 1538]. COR VI/1, 379, 10-12: "Quin etiam iactabantur istae voces, nos nulla fore venia dignos si tam iustam vocationem abnueremus."

[284] Guillaume Farel and Calvin to Pierre Viret [and Elie Corauld], Lausanne Basel, [circa June 6, 1538]. COR VI/1, 379, 12: "Dominus tamen exitum nobis aperuit."

[285] Calvin to Louis de Tillet, Strasbourg, July 10, 1538. COR VI/1, 411, 32-33: "attendant ce que le Seigneur vouldra fere de moy."

[286] Calvin to Louis de Tillet, Strasbourg, July 10, 1538. COR VI/1, 411, 42-47: "Neantmoins i'espere que nostre Seigneur me conduira en ceste deliberation tant ambigue, d'autant que ie regarderé plus tost ce qu'il m'en monstrera que mon propre iugement, lequel me tirant au contraire oultre mesure, me doibt estre suspect." Different versions of this letter exist. The version used in the COR edition reads "i'espere" whereas the edition used for the English translation reads "ie sçay" or "ie scé". See CO 10b, 221n9.

his guide.[287] Secondly, he apparently expects God to somehow reveal his will, and in so concrete a way that Calvin can wait for that moment. Thirdly, we see a deep distrust of his own judgments in weighty personal matters.

After a few months Calvin settled in Strasbourg. At first, he declined a number of attempts to let him stay in that place, for, as he writes to Farel, "they [the church leaders, CvdK] could not include you."[288] However, shortly afterwards he went there nevertheless to serve the community of French exiles. Again, Calvin's correspondence with Louis du Tillet provides additional insights. In September 1538 Du Tillet had expressed his doubts about Calvin's calling, thinking that he followed the call of men, not God.[289] Whatever reasons Du Tillet had for his doubts, Calvin responds that "the Lord has furnished me with more firm and stable ones for my confirmation."[290] Those reasons are so convincing for Calvin, that it is not only to his personal satisfaction, but that he can also "approve it to those who are willing to submit their censures to the test of truth."[291] Elaborating upon what happened and referring to his encounter with Bucer, he tells that "the most moderate of them all threatened that the Lord would find me out as he did Jonah."[292] Originally, Calvin had wanted to find a retreat in which he had time and rest to pursue a writing career, but once again he came to the conclusion "that the will of God has

---

287 Interestingly, Calvin writes something similar to (the faithful in) the church in Geneva: "we can willingly commit all to the guidance of his providence who knows the fit opportunity, and sees what is for our real advantage better than we can anyhow conceive," Calvin to the Genevians, Strasbourg, October 1, 1538. CO 10b, 255: "que nous puissions le tout permettre a sa Providence, laquelle congnoist l'opportunité des temps, et veoit mieux ce qui nous est expedient que ne le pouvons concevoir."
288 Calvin to Farel, Basle, August 20, 1538. COR VI/1, 441, 19-20: "quia te adhibere non poteram."
289 For the full correspondence between Calvin and Du Tillet see John Calvin, *Correspondence Française de Calvin Avec Louis Du Tillet, Chanoine d'Angoulême et Curé de Claix Sur Les Questions de l'église et Du Ministère Évangélique: 1537-1538*, ed. A. Crottet (Geneva: Cherbuliez, 1850).
290 Calvin to Louis du Tillet, Strasbourg, October 20, 1538. CO 10b, 270: "que le Seigneur ne m'en donne de plus fermes pour me conferrer en icelle."
291 Calvin to Louis du Tillet, Strasbourg, October 20, 1538. CO 10b, 270: "mais que ie la puisse approuver a ceulx qui vouldront submettre leurs censures a la vérité."
292 Calvin to Louis du Tillet, Strasbourg, October 20, 1538. CO 10b, 271: "Mais quand les plus modérez me menacent que le Seigneur me trouveroit aussi bien que Ionas." In the preface to his *Psalms Commentary*, Calvin makes clear that with "the most moderate" he meant Bucer: "That excellent servant of Christ Martin Bucer, with a remonstrance and declaration similar to those Farel had made before, recalled me to another position. Appalled by the example of Jonah, which he suggested to me, I still persevered in the duty of teaching," OC 31, 26-7.

otherwise disposed."²⁹³ Half a year later, he writes to Farel that he firmly believes that his calling is of the Lord.²⁹⁴

3.5.5 "I am horrified at the mere mention of a recall"- On returning to Geneva

Almost upon arriving in Strasbourg the first references to a possible return to Geneva occur, but early in 1540 these become more serious. Calvin enjoys the peace and fruitful period in Strasbourg,²⁹⁵ but becomes aware of rumours that the Genevans want to call him to return to their church. His first letter to Farel on this issue immediately makes his feelings clear: "rather would I die a hundred other deaths than on that cross, on which one has to die thousand times daily."²⁹⁶ He explicitly asks Farel to oppose a call from Geneva. In October of the same year we learn from a letter to the *Seigneury* of Geneva the official reason Calvin gives for his refusal to come to Geneva, based upon his view of the vocation of a pastor:

> For so I have always believed and taught, and to the present moment cannot persuade myself to the contrary, that when our Lord appoints a man as pastor in a church to teach in his word, he ought to consider himself as engaged to take upon himself the government of it, so that he may not lightly withdraw from it without the settled assurance in his own heart, and the testimony of the faithful, that the Lord has discharged him.²⁹⁷

In this statement, a number of issues from former sections recur. First, we see that for Calvin the vocation of a pastor is very specific. God does not call to be pastor of the church in general, but to a specific place. Secondly, once again we encounter Calvin's fear of doing things *lightly*, that is,

---

293 Calvin to Louis du Tillet, Strasbourg, October 20, 1538. CO 10b, 271: "Mais i'ay iugé que la volunté de Dieu me menoit autre part."
294 Calvin to Farel, March 1539. CO 10b, 330-2.
295 Even so much, that in February 1540 he writes to Farel that "I am so much at ease, as to have the audacity to think of taking a wife," Calvin to Farel, Strasbourg, February 6, 1540. CO 11, 12: "mihi tantum est otii ut de uxore ducenda cogitare audeam."
296 Calvin to Farel, Strasbourg, April 4, 1540, own translation. CO 11, 30: "Sed centum potius aliae mortes quam illa crux: in qua millies quotidiè pereundum esset." Two months later, he still asserts to be "horrified at the mere mention of a recall," Calvin to Farel, Strasbourg, May 1540. CO 11, 38: "me ad solum revocationis auditum exhorrere".
297 Calvin to the Seigneury of Geneva, Strasbourg, October 23, 1540. CO 11, 96: "car iay ainsin tousiours creu et enseigne, et ne me puis encores de present aultrement persuader, que quand nostre seigneur constitue ung homme pasteur en une eglise pour lenseigner en sa parolle, quil se doibt penser estre comme attache au gouvernement dicelle, pour ne sen point facilement retirer, sans avoir certitude en son coeur et tesmoignage devant les fideles, que le Seigneur len ha descharge."

without taking into account that the call of God results in an *engagement* (at the time of writing, Calvin's engagement was with the church of Strasbourg). Finally, we see the combination of internal and external calling, although here the inner assurance seems to have gained primary place.

The somewhat detached tone found in the official letter to Geneva is quite different from Calvin's letter to Farel a few days earlier. In that letter, he reports being "thrown for two days into such perplexity and trouble of mind that I was scarcely half myself"[298] after receiving the summons out of Geneva. Given his ambivalent position, he tells Farel that he grows more and more suspect of his own judgment of the issue,[299] and therefore entrusts his choice to a number of trusted guides: "… I am ready to follow those who, there is some good hope, will prove safe and trusty guides to me."[300]

In the meantime, as a welcome diversion, in November 1540 Calvin is sent as a representative to the diet in Worms. Writing once again to the Senate, he explains that he believes being in Worms "by the will of God,"[301] and that he therefore is not free to come to Geneva to consider their call. The same argument is used when Calvin goes to Ratisbon for the next session of the diet.[302]

In Calvin's correspondence in the crucial months between the summer of 1540 and May 1541 a number of interesting aspects frequently reoccur. There is the repeated assurance that Calvin "shall follow wherever God leads,"[303] because he is "at the disposal of God, and not at my own," and thus "always ready to employ myself thereto in whatsoever it shall seem good to him to call me."[304] The second element that stands out

---

[298] Calvin to Farel, Strasbourg, Oct. 21, 1540. CO 11, 90: "tanta animi perplexitate me aestuasse, ut vix dimidia ex parte apud me essem." He adds that his soul 'shudders' ("toto pectore exhorrescam") at the mere thought of returning.
[299] Calvin to Farel, Strasbourg, Oct. 21, 1540. CO 11, 92: "Nam quo magis ab illa provincia animus meus abhorret, eo magis mihi sum suspectus."
[300] Calvin to Farel, Strasbourg, Oct. 21, 1540. CO 11, 92: "paratus sum eos sequi, quos mihi fidos ac tutos duces fore bona spes est." Farel obviously is one of the intended guides, yet no evidence is available of who Calvin had exactly in mind and how in reality things turned out with this approach.
[301] Calvin to the Senate of Geneva, Worms, Nov. 12, 1540. CO 11, 104-5: "ie suis constitue en ce lieu par la volunte du Seigneur."
[302] Calvin to the Senate of Geneva, Strasbourg, Feb. 19, 1541. CO 11, 158: "nostre Seigneur me tire ailleurs."
[303] Calvin to Farel, Strasbourg, Feb. 19, 1541. CO 11, 156: "Sed Deum sequar qui novit cur mihi hanc necessitatem imponat."
[304] Calvin to the Senate of Geneva, Strasbourg, Feb. 19, 1541. CO 11, 158-9: "ie suis a Dieu et non pas a moymesme, ie suis tousiours prest de memploier la ou bon luy semblera de m'appeller." Cf. e.g. the letter of Calvin to Farel, Aug. 1540, CO 11, 99-100: "But when I remember that I am not my own, I offer up my heart, presented as a sacrifice to the Lord" ("sed quoniam non esse mei iuris memini, cor meum velut mactatum Domino in sacrifi-

is Calvin's firm conviction that the Lord will indeed provide definite guidance. Thus, for example, he can write that he will follow God's calling "as soon as he shall have *opened it up* before me."[305] Thirdly, Calvin elaborates on the way he hopes God will guide him. As we saw before, Calvin looked for counsel of others in this regard and repeatedly refers to them in his letters. In August 1540, he writes to Farel about those "by whom I hope that the Lord himself will speak to me."[306] Previously, he had written about the "friends by whose opinion I had agreed to be guided" that they were to be "sound in judgment and sincerely well-disposed."[307] Finally, at the background of this procedure is the ever-growing suspicion of his own judgment and inclination.[308]

Suddenly, in September 1541, without much further information Calvin returns to Geneva and is welcomed as its pastor. Although there are some hints in earlier letters, his correspondence had not shown any indication that a decision had been taken. One of the first letters after his return shows that somehow Calvin had received convincing guidance, because he urges the Duchess of Ferrara to pray "that he would instruct us in the doing of his will," based on the firm belief that "he will so guide us that he will not let us go astray out of the right path."[309]

Interestingly, from the moment of his arrival in Geneva onwards, Calvin adopts a fresh standard formulation to conclude his letters. From then on many of his letters end with the wish "May the Lord Jesus …

---

cium offero"), and "I submit my will and my affections, subdued and held-fast, to the obedience of God" ("Ergo animum meum vinctum et constrictum subigo in obedientiam Dei").

305 Calvin to Farel, Worms, Nov. 13, 1540 (emphasis CvdK). CO 11, 113: "simul ac mihi fuerit patefacta." Notice how the wording (*patefacta*) conveys the idea that God discloses something that at the moment still is hidden. Cf. the exhortation to Nicolas Parent, Worms, Dec. 14, 1540. CO 11, 132: "Interim rogemus Dominum ut viam nobis demonstret."
306 Calvin to Farel, Aug. 1540. CO 11, 100: "per quos spero Dominum ipsum mihi loquuturum."
307 Calvin to the Pastors of the Church of Zürich, Ratisbon, May 31, 1541. CO 11, 231: "quibus me regendam dederam." At the same time, although the counselors are the main 'instrument' Calvin mentions, he makes clear that he will in everything adhere to the way of lawful procedure (*ordine legitimo*) in the church (as could be expected from the architect of many a procedure) and was prepared "to remove as often as it may be the mind of the Church that I should do so" ("quin paratus sim identidem migrare, quoties ecclesiae iudicio fuerit constitutum"), Calvin to James Bernard, Ulm, March 1, 1541, CO 11, 165-6.
308 See e.g. the letters of Calvin to Parent, Worms, Dec. 14, 1540, CO 11, 130-2 and to the Pastors of the Church of Zürich, Ratisbon, May 31, 1541, CO 11, 229-33.
309 Calvin to the Duchess of Ferrara, Geneva, Oct. 1541. CO 11, 331: "quil nous enseigne a faire sa volunté;" "il nous conduira tellement que il ne nous laissera esgarer du droict chemin." Various proposals as to what made Calvin change his mind are made. Bouwsma, *John Calvin*, 24 focuses on Bucer's role as one of the trusted guides, while Gordon, *Calvin*, 121–2 mentions Viret's role and the involvement of Zurich and Basle.

direct you continually by His Spirit."³¹⁰ Apparently, the intensity of the preceding months had impressed Calvin anew with the continual need of divine guidance amidst the perplexities of life.³¹¹

3.5.6 Correspondence with mr. and mrs. De Falais
Thus far, we have concentrated on the experiences of guidance in Calvin's personal life. Yet, it is also interesting to see the role it played in his pastoral praxis. Multiple examples could be taken, but our focus in this section will be on his correspondence with mr. and mrs. De Falais. De Falais, also known as Jacques de Bourgogne (?-1556), Lord of Falais and Bredam, was the first nobleman from the court of Charles V to leave the Roman Catholic Church, together with his wife Yolande de Brederode.³¹² Starting in 1543, Calvin develops a correspondence with both partners.³¹³ From the start of their correspondence, Calvin tries to convince the couple to leave their Catholic environment and to openly declare their choice for the Reformation. Apparently, Calvin hoped that their example would be followed by more of the aristocracy.

In his first letter, dated October 14, 1543, Calvin lists numerous reasons for leaving to De Falais, and exhorts him to withdraw before it becomes impossible. In an interesting comment, he states that "in such a case you must seize the opportunity when it presents itself, concluding, that when the Lord vouchsafes the means, it is *as though he opened the door for us*; thus *it behoves you* thereupon to enter without further trifling or delay..."³¹⁴ Calvin goes on to explain that the fact that certain "heart-

---

310 Calvin's standard formulation is "Dominus Iesus te/vos spiritu suo ... semper dirigat." According to the matter of the letter he is writing, he sometimes adds more specific wishes for guidance. Calvin had occasionally used similar endings before, but only when the circumstances of the addressee where especially confusing or dangerous. See e.g. his letter to Caroli, Strasbourg, August 10, 1540, CO 11, 75: "Dominus Christus te spiritu consilii et prudentiae gubernet, ut ex istis periculosis scopulis, ad quos impegisti, et tempestuosa iactatione, in portum te cito recipias."
311 Bockmühl also mentioned this standard ending of Calvin's letters, but failed to direct attention to the timing of the change, Bockmühl, *Gesetz und Geist*, 372.
312 For De Falais, see e.g. Philippe Denis, "Jacques de Bourgogne, Seigneur de Falais," in *Bibliotheca dissidentium, vol. 4*, ed. André Séguenny (Baden-Baden: Koerner, 1984), 9–52; Michiel A. van den Berg, *Friends of Calvin*, trans. Reinder Bruinsma (Grand Rapids: Eerdmans, 2009), 185–95.
313 Unfortunately, only Calvin's letters remain. Francoise Bonali-Fiquet suggests that Calvin might have destroyed the letters of the couple after the break of their friendship in 1552; John Calvin, *Lettres à Monsieur et Madame de Falais*, ed. Francoise Bonali-Fiquet (Geneva: Droz, 1991), 33. The suggestion is adopted by e.g. Mirjam G.K. van Veen, "'In excelso honoris gradu': Johannes Calvin und Jacques de Falais," *Zwingliana*, no. 32 (2005): 7; Van den Berg, *Friends of Calvin*, 187.
314 Calvin to Mr. De Falais, Oct. 14, 1543 (emphasis CvdK). CO 11, 629-30: "Car en telle chose, il fault prendre loccasion quant elle soffre, estimant que quant le seigneur nous donne le moien, cest comme sil nous ouvroit la porte: ainsi il convient adoncq entrer sans

ties" that are lately broken, and "the disposedness wherewith he [God] has inclined you" form the ideal circumstances (the 'open door') to make the bold move to openly subscribe to the Reformation.[315] Giving the example of Abraham, Calvin asserts that, although there is no express command to leave the country, the commandment to honour God in their specific situation means that they can apply the words "Go from your country and your kindred" (Gen. 12:1) to themselves.[316] In the remainder of the letter, Calvin comforts Jacques de Falais with the assertion that God will give "wisdom to order your steps aright" and that he himself will pray to God "that he would open your eyes yet more and more, that you may be able to contemplate what he has already in some measure bestowed upon you, giving you, besides, strength of endurance to follow the course which he points out to you."[317] This last statement once again shows that Calvin believes that the Lord is actively pointing out a certain route to follow, which, apparently, is already clear to Calvin but needs more contemplation from De Falais.

In a successive letter, written in June 1544, Calvin once again takes up the example of Abraham. By that time, Jacques de Falais had left Brabant for Cologne and asked Calvin to send him a minister. Calvin does indeed send a minister and leaves it up to Jacques and this minister to agree upon a form of worship. As his 'infallible rule,' he states that "everything ought to tend to edification" and that in such situations discernment is needed, for which the Lord will give wisdom upon request. Returning to the story of Abraham, Calvin promises to pray for De Falais "so that you may be fully conformed to our father Abraham, who not only forsook the country

---

plus delayer." Notice how the terminology of the 'open door,' so characteristic for contemporary evangelicalism, is also found here in Calvin, combined with the suggestion that such an 'open door' constitutes an imperative to enter.

315 Calvin to Mr. De Falais, Oct. 14, 1543. CO 11, 630: "les lyens du cueurs," "la bonne affection quil a esmeue en vous."

316 Calvin to Mr. De Falais, Oct. 14, 1543. CO 11, 630: "Nous navons pas revelation expresse de quitter le pais. Mais puis que nous avons commandement dhonorer Dieu et de corps et dame partout ou nous sommes, que voulons nous plus? Cest doncq aussi bien a nous que ces lettres saddressent: Sorts hors du pais de ta nativite, quant nous sommes la contrainctz de faire contre nostre conscience, et ne pouvons vivre a la gloire de nostre Dieu." Interestingly, in the correspondent letter to Mme. De Falais Calvin uses the example of Sarah, following her husband. The letter gives the impression that Mme. De Falais is more inclined than her husband to leave, but Calvin exhorts her to support and follow him, letter to Mme. De Falais, Oct. 14, 1543, CO 11, 631-2.

317 Calvin to Mr. De Falais, Oct. 14, 1543. CO 11, 630: "ie prieray ce pendant nostre bon pere celeste, quil luy plaise de vous ouvrir de plus en plus les yeulx pour pouvoir contempler ce que desia il vous a donne en partie, vous donnant aussi la force et constance de suivre la voye quil vous monstre."

of his birth to follow God, but on his arrival in the land of Canaan, forthwith raised an altar…"[318]

The De Falais family could not stay long in Cologne, and with the imperial army nearing, withdrew to Strasbourg. Apparently, they still were uncertain about the course to be taken and the place to settle, for Calvin wrote in May 1545 to Jacques de Falais that "now you have as much need as ever of the Divine assistance, as well as to enlighten you as to the course which it will be good and expedient for you to follow, as to strengthen your fortitude …"[319]

Later on, Calvin assists in finding a suitable house for the couple in Geneva. The friendship ends in an unfortunate way in 1552.[320]

This pastoral correspondence of Calvin shows us that he not only believed that God had a special purpose with his own life and would make clear what to do at crucial moments, but that he also believed so for others.[321] In line with this conviction, he gives advice concerning their situation or himself interprets the alleged clues in their situation.

3.5.7 Concluding general observations

The combination of Calvin's reflection on his own quest, especially in his early years as a pastor, and a fragment from his pastoral praxis have shown Calvin's firm conviction that there is a certain course through life that coincides with 'the will of God.' This belief was combined with the confidence that God would at times reveal the right way to proceed. We also saw a number of remarks from Calvin on what to do at such times. Thus, distrusting his personal judgment, he asked for the help of trusted counselors and emphasizes the importance of praying for wisdom and the need for careful discernment.

---

[318] Calvin to Mr. De Falais, June 24, 1544. CO 11, 736: "que soiez pleinement conforme a nostre père Abraham, lequel non seulement abandonna le pais de sa nativite pour suivre Dieu, mais estant venu en la terre de Chanaan dressa incontinent un autel"). To Mme. De Falais Calvin promises to "pray our Lord to guide you always, as he has done hitherto" ("ie prye nostre seigneur de vous guider tousiours comme il a faict iusque icy"), letter to Mme De Falais, June 24, 1544, CO 11, 737-8.

[319] Calvin to Mr. De Falais, Geneva, May 31, 1545. CO 12, 85: "toutefois si avez vous a present aussi bon mestier que iammais quil vous assiste, tant en vous enseignant ce qui sera bon et expedient de faire, quen vous fortifiant en bonne constance."

[320] In the controversy with Jerome Bolsec in 1551, Jacques de Falais chooses the side of Bolsec. For Calvin, there is apparently no other option but a radical break with De Falais, as for example shown in his withdrawal of the original dedication of his commentary on 1 Corinthians (1546) to De Falais. For further background, see Van Veen, "'In excelso honoris gradu': Johannes Calvin und Jacques de Falais."

[321] One could argue that Calvin does make a distinction between the 'common man' and friends from the aristocracy. As we have seen, Calvin always points the common man to the boundaries and duties of their vocation. Apparently, different rules may apply to the aristocracy.

With regard to how Calvin experienced these periods, Cottret sums up well how things worked out in practice:

> His vocation always took an indirect route; it was not a natural bent, fashioned by habit or for comfort, but a sudden eruption, imperative and peremptory, a calling he could not shirk. God decidedly contradicted Calvin; he led him precisely where he did not want to go—to return him finally to his point of departure. Geneva or Basel, Strasbourg or Geneva: the Reformer was on a predestined trajectory.[322]

This clearly is not only Cottret's interpretation, but also Calvin's own. Especially in the Preface to his Psalms Commentary, he attributes almost everything to divine providence, not to personal choices.[323] The way Calvin interprets many episodes of his life gives solid ground for speaking of Calvin's "obsession with calling."[324] It also explains the ongoing nostalgia Calvin displays whenever reflecting upon the comforts and pleasures of the scholarly life he initially pursued.[325] Clearly, if everything had been up to John Calvin to decide, his life would have taken a totally different course.

3.6 Conclusion

In this chapter we brought the questions on divine guidance as we formulated them at the end of the second chapter into conversation with the theology of John Calvin. This conversation turned out to provide fruitful elements for thinking about divine guidance from a Reformed perspective. In our research, we were not only interested in Calvin's explicit reflections on guidance, but also in the underlying theological concerns and emphases. We focused on Calvin's accounts of providence, vocation, and the guiding role of the Holy Spirit. It appeared that Calvin devotes much more attention to the idea of specific guidance than generally acknowledged. This is most clear, not from his systematic writings, but from his commentaries on Scripture.

Our analysis of providence in Calvin made clear that, while he adopts the classical distinction between general and special providence, his focal point throughout is on *providentia speciallissima:* God's specific care for and involvement with the life of the church and the lives of the faithful. One of the primary ways in which God guides individuals according to

---

322 Cottret, *Calvin: A Biography*, 132–33.
323 Cf. Gordon, *Calvin*, 47.
324 Cottret, *Calvin: A Biography*, 154–55.
325 See Cottret, 155.

Calvin is through the vocations. Once again, the stress is on the individual level: God *assigns* certain roles and positions to each individual. This picture was further confirmed by our analysis of Calvin's ideas on the Spirit as guide as encountered for example in his *Commentary on Acts*. Reflections on his personal life once again affirmed that Calvin believed God to personally guide his children. At times, Calvin had such trust in this guidance that he could wait for God to make his ways clear to him.

Yet, our reading of Calvin has also shown a number of constraints he imposed on the way guidance is conceived. First, and most important, is Calvin's strong conviction that the Spirit does not operate apart from the Word and does not provide fresh revelations. Guidance is thus clearly distinct from revelation and should be conceived as a specific kind of application. Furthermore, Calvin makes a strict distinction between the revealed and the hidden will of God and repeatedly warns against curiosity with regard to the hidden will of God. Believers should be content with the revealed will of God and conform their lives accordingly. Thus, believing in God's guidance can in practice mean to live as though there is no providence: taking full responsibility in applying all normal decision-making procedures to the question at hand. Calvin himself, however, seemed at times strikingly familiar with the hidden will of God in complex affairs.

For Calvin, one of God's main guiding instruments was the personal vocation, which in his account received a largely providential interpretation. This vocation, that Calvin presented as a divinely given, was the instrument in the divine hands to assign each person his or her proper duties. Unfortunately, for several reasons Calvin's providential interpretation of vocation is no longer completely tenable in our dynamic modern society. As a result, in order to arrive at a Reformed theology of guidance in the present either the fruitful elements of this concept of vocation should be restored or other strands in his thought must be worked out.

Besides vocation, we did indeed encounter a number of elements that could be elaborated in a contemporary account of vocation. For example, his deep distrust of human inclinations is at times opposed by a deep trust in renewed and sanctified human reasoning. Furthermore, taking up the Pauline metaphor of the church as the body of Christ, Calvin thought of divine guidance not in individualistic terms, and his personal experiences show how his fellow believers were trusted at crucial times as perhaps God's primary way to speak to and guide him.

However, perhaps the most intriguing and promising element is the frequency with which Calvin refers to the guiding Spirit as the Spirit of discernment (*discretio*). Once again, this idea of discernment is not elaborated upon in his writings, but it combines the crucial convictions of the indwelling of the Spirit in believers with the hope that this Spirit equips the church and the faithful with the crucial and increasing ability to discern the ways of God. For a more elaborated account of how discernment could be thought within the basic structure of a Reformed theology we turn to the thought of Jonathan Edwards in our next chapter.

CHAPTER 4:
Jonathan Edwards on Divine Guidance

4.1 Introduction

In this chapter, our primary discussion partner in thinking on divine guidance will be Jonathan Edwards (1703-1758). Following the pattern of the previous chapter, the focus will be respectively on his account of divine providence (§4.2), of vocation (§4.3), of the guidance of the Spirit (§4.4) and on his personal life (§4.6). Given the specifics of Edwards's theology, we will also focus on the role virtues and character formation play in his account of the Christian life (§4.5).

Although it is notoriously difficult to put Edwards into a precise category, we believe it to be sufficiently clear that Edwards's theology in general can be described as an example of Reformed theology.[1] In a number of places Edwards accepts the name of 'Calvinist',[2] describes himself as an apologist for the Reformed tradition,[3] and declares his support for the contents of the Westminster Confession, although as a Congregationalist he did not subscribe to such church documents.[4] That being said, as shown by McClymond and McDermott, there is a number of issues on which Edwards diverged from mainstream Reformed theology and

---

1 And so do McClymond and McDermott in their recent handbook, see Michael J. McClymond and Gerald R. McDermott, *The Theology of Jonathan Edwards* (New York: Oxford University Press, 2012), 663: "His thinking is recognizably Reformed (…)." Yet they felt the need to add the qualifying addition "but with a difference." But see also Amy Plantinga Pauw, "The Future of Reformed Theology: Some Lessons from Jonathan Edwards," in *Towards the Future of Reformed Theology: Tasks, Topics, Traditions*, ed. David Willis and Michael Welker (Grand Rapids: Eerdmans, 1999), 457, who emphasizes that, although this is not always visible in his doctrinal positions, Edwards is often much freer in his handling of Reformed theology than realized by many. Cf. also Kenneth P. Minkema, "A 'Dordtian Philosophe': Jonathan Edwards, Calvin, and Reformed Orthodoxy," *Church History and Religious Culture* 91, no. 1-2 (2011): 241-53.
2 Most notably so in the preface to his *Freedom of the Will*, where he writes he "should not take it all amiss, to be called a Calvinist, for distinction's sake" although he is well aware that the term is mostly used in a derisive way, see WJE 1:131. In this chapter, we will use the common notation for the Yale edition of the works of Edwards: WJE followed by the number of the volume and the relevant page number. When appropriate the title and the year of publication of the specific work will be included in the footnote.
3 McClymond and McDermott, *The Theology of Jonathan Edwards*, 2012, 322.
4 The remark is made in a letter to his Scottish correspondent John Erskine, who had offered Edwards a position in a Scottish (presbyterian) church after his dismissal from Northampton. See WJE 16:355.

developed his own creative insights and arguments.⁵ This can, however, not be an argument for not considering Edwards a Reformed thinker, given the fact that from its very beginnings the Reformed movement has never been a monolithic movement with carefully defined boundaries.⁶

As a result of the difficulty to neatly delineate Edwards's position, in the field of Edwards studies different approaches exist, taking as their point of departure respectively Edwards's philosophical, theological, or experiential interests.⁷

Most of the topics that are investigated in the present chapter have not been at the center of attention of the field of Edwards studies. Hence, in the main text we interact chiefly with primary sources, referring to scholarly debates when appropriate. Given the aims of this chapter, our focus will not be on developments in Edwards's thought.

4.2 Edwards on Divine Providence

4.2.1 Introduction

Little has been written on Jonathan Edwards's views of divine providence, at least as a locus in itself.⁸ Presumably this is the result of the contexts in which the idea of providence appears throughout the writings of Edwards. Apart from a number of *Miscellanies*, providence does nowhere receive a distinct and extended treatment. Furthermore, where it does appear, it often does in the context of his views on the history of redemption, his

---

5 McClymond and McDermott, *The Theology of Jonathan Edwards*, 2012, 667-71. As the areas mentioned by McClymond and McDermott are not in a straightforward way related to the topic of guidance, this is further support for our choice to discuss Edwards as an important Reformed voice on guidance. The only point on which Edwards went a different way from mainstream Reformed theology that will feature in this chapter is his view on continuous creation and his related occasionalism, see §4.2. The question of Edwards's orthodoxy and his relation to the Reformed tradition has been one of the foci of Oliver Crisp's work. See his recent Oliver D. Crisp, *Jonathan Edwards among the Theologians* (Grand Rapids: Eerdmans, 2015), esp. ch. 1 on "Edwards and Reformed Theology."
6 This breadth of even the early Reformation is nowadays a broadly accepted position (perhaps even to be regarded as a historical fact). It still is notoriously difficult to formulate what is and what is not to be considered as 'Reformed' theology. See our discussion in §1.3.2.
7 For a similar observation and examples of the approaches, see Gijsbert van den Brink, "'Scripture with Reason': Een gereformeerde triniteitsleer bij Jonathan Edwards?," in *Triniteit en kerk: Bundel ter gelegenheid van het afscheid van prof. dr. A. Baars*, ed. G. C. Den Hertog, H.R. Keurhorst, and H.G.L. Peels (Heerenveen: Groen, 2014), 118.
8 It is, for example, telling that M.X. Lesser, in the index to his extended annotated bibliography *Reading Jonathan Edwards: An Annotated Bibliography in Three Parts, 1729-2005* (Grand Rapids: Eerdmans, 2008), under the entry "providence" lists only one source, namely Stephen Stein's 1978 article on "Providence and the Apocalypse."

discussions on the freedom of the will, his reflections on types of Christ, or when discussing creation.⁹

We will not treat all venues in which providence features separately, but we move from a sketch of the basics of his views on providence (§4.2.2) to the more specific questions of continuous creation and occasionalism (§4.2.3), the distinction between God's secret and revealed will (§4.2.4), Edwards's reflections on humanity's limited perspective (§4.2.5), and finally the practical implications he draws from his account of providence (§4.2.6).

4.2.2 Edwards on divine providence: two main metaphors

Edwards uses two main images for depicting providence: the machine and the river. Those images show a number of basic elements that are crucial in his interpretation of divine providence.

The first major image Edwards uses as an example of the workings of divine providence is inspired by the vision of Ezekiel: the machine or wheel of providence.¹⁰ In his *Dissertation Concerning the End for which God Created the World*, Edwards wrote:

> The whole universe is a machine which God hath made for his own use, to be his chariot for him to ride in; as is represented in Ezekiel's vision. In this chariot God's seat or throne is heaven, where he sits, who uses and governs and rides in this chariot, Ezekiel 1:22, Ezekiel 1:26-28. … God's providence in the constant revolutions and alterations and successive events, is represented by the motion of the wheels of the chariot, by the spirit of him who sits in his throne on the heavens, or above the firmament. Moses tells us for whose sake it is that God moves the wheels of this chariot … ; and to what end he is making his progress, or goes his appointed journey in it, viz. the salvation of his people.¹¹

---

9 In some of these discussions, divine providence is not even discussed explicitly, but is present as a crucial presupposition of Edwards's positions. His strong emphasis on 'types' for example would be impossibe without a complementary strong belief in divine providence.

10 John Gerstner mentions Edwards's discussion of this image as "Edwards's most comprehensive reflections on divine providence," John H. Gerstner, *The Rational Biblical Theology of Jonathan Edwards*, vol. 2 (Powhatan: Berea Publications, 1992), 298. It is interesting to see that for Edwards the machine has very positive connotations, whereas especially since the Romantic period the machine is used in literature mainly as a symbol of alienation and dehumanization, cf. James Hewitson, "'As Ordered and Governed by Divine Providence': Jonathan Edwards' Use of the Machine as Master Metaphor," *Interdisciplinary Humanities* 24, no. 1 (2007): 6. The reticent stance of theologians towards the machine metaphor can be explained by its connotations with the pagan wheel of fortune, see e.g. Matthias Vollmer, *Fortuna Diagrammatica: Der Rad der Fortuna als bildhafte Verschlüsselung der Schrift* De Consolatione Philosophiae *des Boethius* (Bern: Peter Lang, 2009).

11 WJE 8:508 (The *Dissertation Concerning the End for Which God Created the World* was written during the 1750s but published only posthumously in 1765). See for an extended

Although Edwards's use of the machine metaphor is very detailed and at times highly subtle,[12] the metaphor in itself reveals a number of characteristic and closely related elements of Edwards's account of divine providence. Firstly, in the *Dissertation* Edwards argues that God's ultimate end in all he does is his own glory. Although at times he presents creation as an overflow of the intra-Trinitarian divine love, Edwards more strongly asserts that God created the universe with this clear goal in mind: to show his own glory in and through it. Thus, when we read in the passage on the machine metaphor that God made the universe "for his own use," God's ultimate aim is clearly in view as driving all of his providence. In order to achieve this goal, the second thing that stands out is that Edwards pictures a sovereign God who *governs* his entire creation and is literally depicted as its 'driver'. In the third place, providence for Edwards is at its deepest level driven by teleological motives. It is directed from beginning to end to the salvation of God's people. In this process of governing creation to its *telos*, finally, God is making progress, but this progress is not always easily perceived from the human perspective, since it takes place through constant revolutions, alterations, and motions. These also account for the cyclical patterns that are oftentimes found in history.[13]

These key elements are confirmed and augmented by the second metaphor Edwards likes to use to depict divine providence: the image of the river. In the 30th sermon of his grand series *A History of the Work of Redemption,* Edwards states:

> God's providence may not unfitly be compared to a large and long river, having innumerable branches beginning in different regions, and at a great distance one from another, and all conspiring to one common issue. … The different streams of this river are ready to look like mere jumble and confusion to us because of the limitedness of our sight, whereby we

---

treatment of Edwards's use of the machine image Hewitson, "'As Ordered and Governed by Divine Providence': Jonathan Edwards' Use of the Machine as Master Metaphor," 7. According to Hewitson, the image functions as "a master metaphor to provide a way of comprehending divine history" for Edwards. Furthermore, Hewitson shows how in Edwards's thought the machine metaphor is related to his views on the millennium.

12 The metaphor is used in a number of Edwards's writings, e.g. *A History of the Work of Redemption* (WJE 9), but also *Notes on Scripture* (no. 389, WJE 15:374) and *Images of Divine Things* (WJE 11:125) The subtlety in its use is shown by the fact that Edwards can use the metaphor to draw conclusions on the possibility of multiple fulfillments of types ('rotating wheels'), on the relation between heaven and earth ('the seat' and the 'chariot'), and on the systematic nature of redemption and the measured pace God takes to unfold it.

13 For Edwards, most clearly so in the interchange between periods of revival and periods of decline of the church.

can't see from one branch to another and can't see the whole at once, so as to see how all are united in one. A man that sees but one or two streams at a time can't tell what their course tends to. Their course seems very crooked, and the different streams seem to run for a while different and contrary ways. And if we view things at a distance, there seem to be innumerable obstacles and impediments in the way to hinder their ever uniting and coming to the ocean, as rocks and mountains and the like. But yet if we trace them they all unite at last and all come to the same issue, disgorging themselves in one into the same great ocean. Not one of all the streams fail of coming hither at last.[14]

Once again, God's providence is presented by the use of a vivid picture. In this picture, a number of the elements encountered in the machine metaphor return: that all history is essentially united and moves towards a common goal; that, although this is not always obvious and visible, all parts contribute to this common goal; and that what seem to be reverses in the historical progress of God's work of redemption will ultimately be understood as contributions to this work.

Two new and important elements receive more attention in the use of this metaphor. Here, Edwards emphasizes how even the minor branches that seem negligible ultimately contribute to the final result, reflecting his conviction that God controls and governs even minor details and uses them in surprising ways to further his work of redemption. However, even more important, he adds another element that was absent in the machine-imagery: his stress on what McClymond and McDermott call "the severe limitations of perspective that hampered the human observer."[15] Standing within the historical process, and seeing only a few of the branches of the river of providence, one cannot (expect to) see and understand how the specifics of the historical situation are part of an overarching plan of God. For such an understanding, one needs to be lifted up out of the historical process and view things from a heavenly perspective.

The combination of those two metaphors presents a fairly accurate picture of Edwards's overall view of divine providence. A number of elements need to be developed a little further. In the first place, in analyzing the machine metaphor Edwards's teleological interpretation of divine providence was highlighted. In order to understand this, we need to see

---

14 WJE 9:520 (*A History of the Work of Redemption*; the sermon series was preached from March-August 1739 but published only in 1774).
15 McClymond and McDermott, *The Theology of Jonathan Edwards*, 2012, 240. They interestingly link this element to Edwards's "near obsession with the 'saints in heaven,'" 241.

that for Edwards providence always stands in the service of redemption.[16] David Barshinger rightly detects a link in Edwards between Christ's kingly office, his work of redemption, and his government of creation, citing a sermon on Psalm 2:6 in which the kingly office is presented as "that office by which he Governs & dispenses all things with supream power so as to subserve to the Great design of his Redemption."[17] Thus, the category of divine government is so closely intertwined with Edwards's view of the history of redemption that it needs not be discussed separately.[18] Furthermore, this government of the created order in the service of redemption presupposes a sovereign God, who is able to control everything that happens.[19] From very early on in his thinking Edwards stressed that everything that happened did so under the control and according to the will of God.[20] This high view of divine sovereignty, combined with God's work of redemption, resulted in Edwards's conviction that "the divine will may be thought to manifest itself in a vast concatenation of events, no one of which might not have been since all are ordained for the best."[21] Just how literally we have to take this 'all' becomes clear when Edwards, in his *Freedom of the Will*, challenges Watts' conviction that "the most High wills one thing rather than another, without any superior fitness or preferableness in the thing preferred."[22] Watts defends his claim by referring to the millions of perfectly equal atoms in the world, which yet take different ways through the world. There is no need to discuss the

---

16 In this respect, it is interesting to see that the sermon in which the river metaphor occurred presented the doctrine that "The Work of Redemption is a work that God carries on from the fall of man to the end of the world" and that providence is only presented as one of the subsidiary elements of this thesis, *HWR*, sermon 30, see esp. WJE 9:515.
17 David P. Barshinger, *Jonathan Edwards and the Psalms: A Redemptive-Historical Vision of Scripture* (Oxford University Press, 2014), 211. For the sermon, see WJEO 62, sermon 745 (June 1744).
18 It is, e.g., interesting to see how the chapter on 'Providence and History' in McClymond and McDermott, *The Theology of Jonathan Edwards*, 2012, 138–39 deals exclusively with Edwards's *History of the Work of Redemption*.
19 That the sovereignty of God plays a major and decisive role throughout Edwards's theology is undeniable. Marsden even mentioned sovereignty as the central principle of Edwards's thought (George M. Marsden, *Jonathan Edwards: A Life* (New Haven: Yale University Press, 2004), 4), but Plantinga Pauw seems right in emphasizing that (divine) love is at least as central to Edwards's thought, Amy Plantinga-Pauw, *"The Supreme Harmony of All": The Trinitarian Theology of Jonathan Edwards* (Grand Rapids: Eerdmans, 2002), 6–8, 13–14.
20 Thus, in analyzing Edwards's apocalyptical writings until 1724 (age 21!) Stephen Stein concluded from Edwards reading of Rev. 4 that "the orderly progression of the chapter reflects the reality of divine providence, that all things begin and end in God, that they are arranged and administered in accord with his will," Stephen J. Stein, "Providence and the Apocalypse in the Early Writings of Jonathan Edwards's," *Early American Literature* 13 (1978): 250.
21 Paul Ramsey, "Editor's Introduction," in *Freedom of the Will*, WJE 1 (New Haven: Yale University Press, 1957), 99–100. The statement occurs in Ramsey's discussion of the differences of opinion on contingency between Isaac Watts and Edwards.
22 WJE 1:387.

details of Edwards's argument, but for our purposes it is important to see that Edwards is deeply convinced that each atom, however equal to others, is given its distinct place in direct accord with the divine will.[23] Even the smallest details take place according to divine providence and in the service of redemption.

The idea of God's government of single atoms returns in a different but interesting context. In Edwards, we do not find a distinction of various spheres of layers of divine providence, as we encountered in the writings of Calvin. Yet, what we do find is the same underlying conviction that God takes special care of his faithful. In the early *Miscellany ff*, Edwards argues that "by virtue of the believer's union with Christ, he doth really possess all things."[24] In explaining the meaning of this statement, Edwards writes that "*[e]very atom* in the universe is managed by Christ so as to be most to the advantage of the Christian, every particle of air or every ray of the sun ...."[25]

In this section we have seen a number of key features of Edwards's concept of divine providence. One technical aspect that did not follow from the two metaphors presented here has been the subject of some scholarly debate over the past few years: the relation between creation and providence in Edwards's writings. To this we turn in the next section.

4.2.3 The universe created out of nothing every moment
One of the most striking aspects of Edwards's view on divine providence is that for him providence is synonymous with God's act of creation out of nothing: "The universe is created out of nothing every moment."[26] Although this kind of continual creation is a non-standard position in both Reformed theology and Edwards's personal theological environment, he "taught it fervently and made it a fundamental concept."[27] Following his firm belief that there is no strength in created being to uphold itself, he asserts that "therefore the existence of created substances, in each

---

23 WJE 1:388: "Therefore what the will of God determines, is this, namely, that there should be the same figure, the same extension, the same resistance, etc., in two different places. And for this determination he has some reason. There is some end, for which such a determination and act has a peculiar fitness, above all other acts. Here is no one thing determined without an end, and no one thing without a fitness for that end, superior to anything else."
24 WJE 13:183 (*Miscellany ff: Union with Christ*). The miscellanies are a collection of Edwards's personal notes that often functioned as the basis on which he wrote his books. The early miscellanies are named in alphabetical order, later on Edwards used a numerical method. In the Yale edition, the miscellanies are published in the volumes 13, 18, 20, and 23.
25 WJE 13:184.
26 WJE 6:241.
27 Gerstner, *The Rational Biblical Theology of Jonathan Edwards*, 2:191.

successive moment, must be the effect of the *immediate* agency, will, and power of God."[28]

What is often discussed under God's act of preservation is just an extension of the act of creation, and not really a distinct act of God. For,

> upholding the world in being, and creating it, are not properly distinct works; since it is manifest, that upholding the world in being is the same with a *continued creation;* and consequently, that creating the world is but the *beginning* of upholding it, if I may so say—beginning to give it a supportive and dependent existence—and preservation is only continuing to give it such a supported existence.[29]

In Reformed theology, the link between creation and providence has always been a close one, as we saw for example in Calvin, but by most theologians providence was still seen as a distinct work of God.[30] For Edwards, influenced by early enlightenment thinkers, this was not the case, and creation and providence were not only inseperable, but identical acts of God.[31]

By formulating his account of providence in this fashion, Edwards tried to uphold the absolute dependency of creatures on God and a view of nature as "a system established and constantly renewed by the sovereign will of God."[32] However, in doing so, a number of related questions were raised. In defining God's preservation as a continuous creation, the traditional categories of divine *gubernatio* and *concursus* also have to be seen in a different light, since genuine secondary causality is difficult to maintain within a continual creation model.[33]

---

28 WJE 3:401 (*The Great Christian Doctrine of Original Sin Defended* (1758), emphasis in original).
29 WJE 23:608 (*Miscellany* "Concerning the Reasonableness of the Doctrine of the Imputation of Merit").
30 The link between the doctrines of creation and providence is often so close that it is difficult to draw a clear line between theologians who see them as distinct works of God and those who think of providence in terms of continual creation. See e.g. the various nuances in the authors Heppe cites in his *Reformed Dogmatics: Set Out and Illustrated from the Sources*, esp. 257-58.
31 See for the link between Edwards's occasionalism and Early Enlightenment thinkers Oliver D. Crisp, "Jonathan Edwards and Occasionalism," in *Abraham's Dice: Chance and Providence in the Monotheistic Traditions*, ed. Karl W. Gibersen (Oxford: Oxford University Press, 2016), 195–212.
32 Clyde A. Holbrook, "Editor's Introduction," in *Original Sin*, WJE 3 (New Haven: Yale University Press, 1970), 57.
33 See Stephen A. Wilson, *Virtue Reformed: Rereading Jonathan Edwards's Ethics* (Leiden: Brill, 2005), Ch. 3 for a recent treatment of secondary causality in Edwards.

There has been some discussion on whether Edwards's view on the relation between creation and providence does make his theology occasionalistic. McClymond and McDermott deliberately choose a careful formulation in stating that "in various passages, Edwards showed a *tendency toward occasionalism*, or the idea that all events are effects of God's agency and that creatures are not properly capable of producing effects on one another."[34] Sang Hyun Lee instead argued for understanding Edwards as advocating a dispositional ontology,[35] but Crisp has shown in an analytical essay that it is difficult to evade the conclusion that ultimately Edwards was an occasionalist.[36]

What has become clear throughout the last two sections is the crucial role the will of God plays in Edwards's theology.[37] As this is a crucial concept for our research, we will turn to Edwards's use of it in our next section.

4.2.4 Providence and the secret will of God

As we have seen thus far, for Edwards the sovereign will of God is at work behind all we see and experience. However, we have not yet seen how Edwards conceptualizes God's will and what distinctions he draws with regard to it.

Throughout his writings, Edwards accepted and defended the traditional (Reformed) distinction between the secret and the revealed will of God, or "more properly expressed, our distinction between the decree and law [of God]."[38] In his early *Miscellany no. 7* he defends the division against the ridicule of the Arminians by pointing to a number of biblical narratives, concluding that "we do certainly and absolutely know there is such a thing [a distinction between the wills, CvdK], so that it is the greatest absurdity to dispute about it."[39]

---

34 McClymond and McDermott, *The Theology of Jonathan Edwards*, 2012, 109 (emphasis CvdK). Cf. Elizabeth A. Cochran, *Receptive Human Virtues: A New Reading of Jonathan Edwards's Ethics* (University Park: Penn State University Press, 2010), 16, who judges that Edwards was "at least on some level an occasionalist."
35 See e.g. Sang Hyun Lee, *The Philosophical Theology of Jonathan Edwards* (Princeton: Princeton University Press, 1988), which is entirely devoted to arguing for this position.
36 Oliver D. Crisp, "How 'Occasional' Was Edwards's Occasionalism?," in *Jonathan Edwards: Philosophical Theologian*, ed. Oliver D. Crisp and Paul Helm (Aldershot: Ashgate, 2003), 61–77.
37 Thomas Schafer somewhere mentions Edwards as "a champion of the absolute, inscrutable, and unconditioned will of God," Thomas A. Schafer, "Editor's Introduction," in *The "Miscellanies": (Entry Nos. a-z, aa-zz, 1-500)*, WJE 13 (New Haven: Yale University Press, 1994), 19.
38 WJE 13:203-4 (*Miscellany 7: 'Will of God'*). Elsewhere Edwards uses the terminology of "disposing and preceptive will," e.g. WJE 1:407.
39 WJE 13:204.

Edwards not only defends the distinction, but also consistently applies it throughout his writings and does keep the two clearly distinct. As a result, he presents God's secret will, his providence and plan with his creation, as secret on purpose, whereas our lives are to be arranged according to the "revealed mind and will of God."[40] It is important to understand that the two wills of God are more properly to be seen as "dissimilar exercises of the divine will," expressions of one will that are not inconsistent with each other, but have different objects.[41]

With regard to God's secret will, Edwards tries to avoid the accusation of arbitrariness by emphasizing that God's will is determined by supreme wisdom and love.[42] He thus tries to avoid a purely voluntarist position, but maintains the conviction that the divine will governs everything that happens. Even in seemingly inexplicable situations, like the crucifixion of Christ or the continued existence of satan, it is beyond doubt for Edwards that nothing happens outside the secret will of God.[43]

The revealed will of God, according to Edwards, has been given throughout history by various means and was supported by signs and miracles. This will of God was most deeply revealed in Christ through his words, acts, and sufferings.[44] However, with the completed canon of Scripture God gave to the church "an established written revelation of the mind and will of God, wherein he had so fully revealed his mind and will, a standing rule to his church in all ages."[45] With God's will so completely revealed, it is clear for Edwards that miracles and miraculous gifts are no longer necessary and that no additional revelation is to be expected.[46]

Edwards frequent use of the distinction between the secret and revealed will of God has major repercussions for the question of divine guidance. We discuss a number of these implications in section 4.2.6, but first we need to turn to a more critical question: If Edwards does believe that God's providential will is secret, does he indeed abstain from drawing inferences based on providential circumstances? Does his awareness

---

40 See e.g. WJE 25:285.
41 WJE 1:406-7.
42 For wisdom, see e.g. WJE 1:380, where Edwards states that "God's will is determined by his own infinite all-sufficient wisdom in everything." See Plantinga-Pauw, *The Supreme Harmony of All*, 7, who challenges the view of Edwards as a theologian who celebrates divine power and complements this view with a focus on love.
43 For Christ's suffering, see e.g. WJE 15:173. For Satan's continued existence, see WJE 3:426.
44 See e.g. WJE 9:315-6.
45 WJE 8:357 (*Charity and its Fruits,* the sermon series was preached in 1738 and published in 1852). For Edwards, the extraordinary gifts of the Spirit belonged to the period of the infancy of the church and were no longer necessary after Scripture had been given. See on Edwards's cessationism e.g. McClymond and McDermott, *The Theology of Jonathan Edwards*, 2012, 138-39.
46 WJE 8:357.

of the limitations of the perspective of the individual believer with regard to divine providence result in reticence in drawing conclusions from it?

4.2.5 Human perspective and the will of God

When Edwards described providence as a big river with many branches, one of the key elements he emphasized was the limited perspective of the individual believer on the workings of divine providence. This notion of limited perspective was then theologically accounted for by his adoption of the distinction between the secret and the revealed will of God, where providence is explicitly placed in the domain of God's secret will.

In this light, it is remarkable that in an early review of his *A History of the Work of Redemption,* the anonymous reviewer described Edwards as "an intoxicated visionary presuming to see the will of God."[47] And indeed, especially when reading Edwards from a modern point of view, he seems to be remarkably sure how to interpret historical events. But what presumably gave rise to the reviewers' remark is Edwards's inclination to predict future events. Behind his concrete expectations of how history will unfold is his strong interest in apocalyptic themes, an interest already present very early in his intellectual development.[48]

In order to understand the ambiguity in Edwards's writings on this point a distinction should be made between interpreting providence on the level of the meta-narrative of the history of redemption, and interpreting providence on the personal level from the limited perspective of the individual. With regard to the meta-narrative, Edwards did indeed believe it was possible to see the hand of God in and underneath the actual events of history (as he showed extensively in his *History of the Work of Redemption*), as long as this was done informed by the characteristics of the work of redemption taken from the Bible.[49] This approach towards providence and history perhaps found its culmination in

---

[47] See *Monthly Review*, 52 (London, 1775), article 6, pp. 117–20 (cited e.g. in WJE 9:86). Remember that the same charge was levelled against Calvin, as we saw in the previous chapter. Apparently, it is difficult to maintain the restraint that should logically flow forth from the idea that providence belongs to God's secret will, and not his revealed.

[48] As shown, e.g., by the fact that Stein's 'Providence and the Apocalypse' takes mid-1724 (Edwards was 21 at the time!) as its *terminus ad quem*. Edwards's earliest references to apocalyptic themes are found a.o. in the early miscellanies k, hh, uu, ww, xx, yy, and 26 (all written somewhere in 1722-23).

[49] This emphasis in Edwards's theology is also behind the interest in historical events around the world that drives a lot of his correspondence. He is not only interested in personal circumstances and theological discussions, but always also in actuality, political developments and the situation of churches all over the world. This can be seen as an attempt to (partly) overcome the limitations of the perspective of the individual believer in order to get an improved view of the proceedings of providence.

Edwards's *History*, but could be seen as an important influence of his puritan heritage on his worldview.[50]

This tendency to identify the hand of God behind specific events is perhaps most clearly seen in Edwards's references to 'providences' as those specific events in which God's providence shines clearly through. Wallace Anderson gives a number of examples of Edwards's predecessors who pointed at specific events as 'illustrious providences' that somehow conveyed God's will to his covenant people.[51] Edwards adopted the concept of 'providences' and used it especially in his sermons.[52] Most of the time, those 'providences' are natural disasters that are interpreted as awakening and awful providences used by God to warn his people. However, the providences functioned also at a more historical level. After the Babylonian exile, God "built the Jewish church again in their own land" and did so "by a series of wonderful providences."[53] In his own time, especially in the war with the French army Edwards noticed a lot of "remarkable providences" that showed God's care for his church and that functioned as positive encouragements to pray for new works of God.[54] Given Edwards's conviction that the French, as a Catholic nation, represented the anti-Christ, he could give nationalistic interpretations of 'providences' as evidence of the proceeding work of redemption. Thus, the combination of the puritan heritage of providentialism and Edwards's own interest in types and the Apocalypse resulted in his attempts to trace the hand of God through history. It was on this level that the reviewer of the *History of the Work of Redemption* accused Edwards of presuming to know the will of God.[55]

On the personal level, however, Edwards was diametrically opposed to the socalled enthusiasts who pretended to know the will of God for

---

50 See e.g. Michael P. Winship, *Seers of God: Puritan Providentialism in the Restoration and Early Enlightenment* (Baltimore: Johns Hopkins University Press, 2000) for an account of providentialism in the Puritan tradition.
51 Wallace E. Anderson, "Editor's Introduction to 'Images of Divine Things' and 'Types,'" in *Typological Writings*, WJE 11 (New Haven: Yale University Press, 1993), 22.
52 See the remarks of Kenneth P. Minkema, "Preface to the Period," in *Sermons and Discourses: 1723-1729*, WJE 14 (New Haven: Yale University Press, 1997), 33, who describes it as a common practice among "the providentialist-minded people of New England." It is interesting that on the manuscript of Edwards's *Images of Divine Things* an alternative title is suggested (by Edwards): 'The Book of Nature and Common Providences', see WJE 11:35.
53 WJE 3:180.
54 See e.g. WJE 5:449.
55 It is also on this meta-level that McClymond and McDermott note a departure of Edwards from his Reformed predecessors. They contrast Calvin, who was content with mystery ('abyss') with Edwards who "filled his notebooks with reflections on the providential meaning of current events around the world," McClymond and McDermott, *The Theology of Jonathan Edwards*, 2012, 668–69. However, as we saw in the previous chapter, Calvin could sometimes rightly be accused of 'presuming' to know the will of God as well.

their lives from extra-Scriptural sources or unreasonable applications of Scripture.[56] From the perspective of the doctrine of providence, Edwards answered the question whether personal circumstances or providential events should be seen as 'indicators' of God's will in the negative. He explicitly warned that "there are innumerable ways that persons may be misled, in forming a judgment of the mind and will of God, from the events of providence."[57] That brings us to the question to be answered in our next section: Given Edwards's perception of divine providence, what are the implications for the praxis of the Christian life, and especially for the idea of divine guidance?

4.2.6 The praxis of providence

We closed our last section with Edwards's warning that judgments from circumstances can be very misleading. The warning occurs in a section of his *Some Thoughts Concerning the Present Revival of Religion in New England* (1743) where Edwards challenges the idea that a minister's success testifies to "God's approbation of those persons and all the courses they take."[58] Edwards supports his warning by pointing to our limited understanding of providence, citing Ps. 77:19 on God's 'unknown footsteps' and concluding that the events of providence "are too little understood by us *to be improved by us as our rule.*"[59] Consistently following his distinction between God's hidden and his revealed will, Edwards accepts only "one rule to go by" and that is God's Word: "They who make what they imagine is pointed forth to 'em in providence their rule of behavior, do err, as well as those that follow impulses and impressions: we should put nothing in the room of the Word of God."[60]

Statements like this underline Edwards's high view of Scripture as a "standing revelation of the mind and will of God" that functions for him as the "rule of faith and practice through the ages."[61] Thus, in those places

---

56 We will return more in depth to this issue in section 4.4, where we discuss Edwards's concept of guidance and his discussion with the enthusiasts.
57 WJE 4:451 (*Some Thoughts Concerning the Present Revival of Religion in New England*, 1743).
58 WJE 4:451.
59 WJE 4.451 (emphasis CvdK). It is important that 'to improve' in Edwards has the meaning of 'to make useful, to turn into profit,' and not the contemporary meaning of bringing something into a more desirable condition.
60 WJE 4:452. In the immediate context, Edwards admits that "indeed, there is a voice of God in his providence" but the explanation he gives moves in line with the distinction made in the previous section: Providence can be 'improved' through observation, experience, human histories and the opinion of eminent men to recognize God's outworking of his redemption (the 'meta-narrative') but only as long as this is "brought to one rule, viz. the Word of God."
61 WJE 25:285.

where Edwards uses the words "the will of God" in the sense of the revealed will, he uses it repeatedly as an exact synonym for the commandments of God.[62] It is not surprising that one of the common verbs Edwards combines with 'the will of God' is *doing*: the divine commandments should be done, and Christian conduct should be first of all 'agreeable' to the will of God.

Interestingly, when it comes to those instances where the secret will of God is meant, Edwards's usual verbs are *resigning* and *submitting*. For him, our response to God's secret will should be one of resignation and submission, whereas God's revealed will is to be done. Repeatedly, Edwards's highlights the submission to the will of God that Christ showed in the garden of Gethsemane as the supreme example to follow. There, Christ shed his blood "in the exercise of a holy submission and entire resignation to the will of God."[63] Other examples in this regard are the young missionary David Brainerd, who was so "wholly resigned to the will of God that God might do with him what he pleased",[64] and Edwards's own wife, Sarah, who when she was on the brink of death as the result of illness, was "assisted to an unmoved resignation to the will of God."[65] More generally, in his *Charity and its Fruits*, Edwards argues how the virtues of love and humility tend to produce such submission to the will of God: "Love will dispose the heart to submission to the will of God" and "true Christian humility of heart tends to make persons resigned to the will of God, patient and submissive to his holy hand under afflictions."[66]

Edwards's use of the *conditio Jacobi* moves in line with his emphasis on submission to the will of God: he uses the condition only in cases where he has a rather fixed plan but wants to express that ultimately he himself

---

62 See e.g. Schafer's summarizing statement that "doing the will of God, taking on Christ's yoke, means keeping God's commandments, all of them, every day, for the rest of one's life," WJE 13:33.

63 WJE 25:671; see also 1:290, 9:321, 13:184, 15:173, 18:489, and 25:338. In another place, discussing the consequences of union with Christ for the believer, Edwards does not only present Christ as an example, but asserts that "the Christian shall have everything managed just according to his will; for *his will shall so be lost in the will of God*, that he had rather have it according to God's will than any way in the world" (emphasis CvdK), WJE 13:184.

64 WJE 7:181. See also 7:282, 412, 520, and 549. David Brainerd (1718-1747) was a missionary to the Native Americans, stationed near Stockbridge in Massachussets. Brainerd suffered from chronic tuberculosis and died in the Edwards home after being nursed there for several months. In 1749 Edwards published his *An Account of the Life of the Late Reverend David Brainerd*, based upon Brainerd's diaries. It has been Edwards's most popular publication. See for further background Joseph K. Tyrpak, "Brainerd, David (1718-1747)," in *The Jonathan Edwards Encyclopedia*, ed. Harry S. Stout, Kenneth P. Minkema, and Adriaan C. Neele (Grand Rapids: Eerdmans, 2017), 75.

65 WJE 16:543-44. The same is said about one of the 'two converts' Edwards describes at the end of his *Faithful Narrative* (1737), see WJE 4:196, 198.

66 See WJE 8:135 and 304 respectively.

is not in control. Thus, he can for example write that he is planning "by the will of God to preach three or four more lectures" on a theme,[67] or that he is "by the will of God about to set out on my journey in a few days."[68]

Thus, a rather clear picture emerges with regard to Edwards's view on the practical consequences of divine providence: A firm belief in divine providence is crucial for the Christian faith, but our personal interpretation of this providence should not become a rule or guide for the praxis of the Christian life. As believers, we should *do* the will of God as revealed in his Word, and submit to God's secret will when we encounter circumstances beyond our control.

4.2.7 Conclusion

Given the aim of our interaction with Edwards, this is a moment to pause and ponder the implications of his perception of divine providence for his thinking about divine guidance. It is undeniable that Edwards had a firm belief in the utter sovereignty of a God who controls and guides everything that happens in the universe. This belief was so profound that Edwards grounded the dependence of creation on God in his concept of continual creation. Yet, God's guidance of his creation belongs to the sphere of the secret will of God, a sphere that is secret on purpose and no rule for the Christian faith or practice.

Instead, Edwards repeatedly warns against putting too much trust in our limited interpretations of circumstances and instead points to the revealed will of God as the ongoing source of guidance. And indeed, when Edwards directly addresses the question of how to know the will of God, he states that this will is "manifested either by the light of reason or by his Word" and is "the proper rule of men's actions."[69]

When stressing the Word of God as the only rule of Christian praxis, a new question arises: Is there (a need for) a principle of individuation of the divine command? In the previous chapter we saw how in the Reformation and in Calvin's writings the concept of vocation functioned as precisely such a 'principle of individuation.' We now turn to the question whether this also applies to Edwards.

---

67 WJE 16:322.
68 WJE 16:737, Cf. 16:622, and, for Brainerd's same use of the condition, 7:443.
69 WJE 19:520. We will later return to the relation between reason and the Word of God in Edwards's thinking. For Edwards, there is no doubt that "between these there is the most perfect harmony and agreement."

4.3 Edwards on Vocation

4.3.1 Introduction
In this section, our focus will be on the question whether Edwards used the concept of vocation, and if so, what the implications of his use are for the idea of divine guidance. As we will see, Edwards does not use the concept of vocation much, but traces of it are found throughout his writings (§4.3.2). One particular example that Edwards gives on vocation to the ministry will further help us in thinking about Edwards's view on divine guidance (§4.3.3).

4.3.2 Traces of vocation thought in Edwards's writings
Whereas in the Early Reformation period, and as we saw in the previous chapter especially in Calvin, the concept of (civic) vocations was a close corollary of the doctrine of divine providence, in Edwards it is nearly absent, at least in any explicit way. Edwards does not provide us with a detailed account of what vocation entails and how it is discerned. Accordingly, little to no research on this concept in Edwards's thinking exists.[70]

This does not, however, mean that the concept is entirely absent. In a number of places the impression is conveyed that the idea of vocation functions as a presupposition for Edwards views on societal order. Perhaps the clearest example of this is found in Edwards's use of the Lutheran concept *station*. The word 'station' in Edwards's writings can be used with a range of interconnected meanings, including the place where one lives, the rank one has in the societal order, or one's daily work. In most cases where Edwards uses the concept it is not possible to indicate one of those as the exclusive meaning.[71]

In his use of the term as denoting the complex of relations in which one is placed, it becomes clear that for Edwards providence is at work behind those placements. Only in a number of passages Edwards does explicitly state that a station is something an individual should consider a

---

[70] It is, for example, telling that no reference is made to vocation or calling in Lesser's extensive bibliography of research on Edwards. There is some research into the vocation to the ministry according to Edwards, but it mostly focuses more on the contents of the ministerial task than on the *event* of vocation. See e.g. Helen Westra, *The Minister's Task and Calling in the Sermons of Jonathan Edwards* (Lewiston: Edwin Mellen, 1986).

[71] Edwards sometimes uses 'station' with more separate and particular meanings. The most notable example is his use of the term to describe the intra-trinitarian relations, especially so in *Misc. 1062* "Economy of the Trinity and Covenant of Redemption". Another use of the word that seems to be particularly Edwardsean is the way it is not only used to denote the societal order on earth but also the order in heaven, in which each one will receive their own "particular station and circumstances God sets 'em in in heaven, the degree and place they stand in in the heavenly society," *Misc. 822* "Decrees of Glory".

"station in which God hath set him."[72] Yet, this aspect becomes clearer in the implications Edwards draws from the various stations. Here, he moves in line with what we encountered previously in the Reformed accounts of vocation. Thus, for example, the idea of having a specific station is connected to a plea for contentment, and depicted as the context for showing what is appropriate behavior.[73] Furthermore, someone's station also will define what counts as true humility for that person. Most importantly however, the stations teach us what our major duties are. One of the effects of godliness then will be to "dispose every one in whatever station to be faithful in doing the duty of his place."[74]

In a number of places Edwards's use of the concept of stations reflects the changing circumstances in New England. Two elements are important to mention, because they highlight possible reasons why the direct link between providence and vocation proved difficult to maintain. Firstly, in his writings Edwards hints at situations of (upward) social mobility. Thus, when emphasizing contentment and humility in one's station, he uses the case of a relative who has been promoted or who has increased in wealth as a mirror for self-reflection: do such situations produce envy and jealousy in our hearts?[75] Secondly, as indicated by Kenneth Minkema, this upward social mobility was limited to certain families and generations. By the time Edwards settled in Northampton, land ownership was "concentrated in the hands of a minority of very affluent individuals" and the others "were likely to live out their lives in the stations in which they were born," a situation that often led to "inter-generational tensions."[76] Thus, while Edwards's use of the concept of 'stations' shows his allegiance to the Reformed tradition and the practical implications of his view on divine providence, his use of the terminology is relatively scarce and given his social context not unchallenged.

---

72 E.g. WJE 8:136.
73 WJE 8:136. In another place, Edwards mentions discontent with their God-given station as the prime fault of the fallen angels, *Misc. 1261* "Occasion of the fall of the angels".
74 WJE 17:365.
75 WJE 8:227: "And possibly some others whom heretofore we used to look upon as our equals, with whom we used to be mates, and used to look upon ourselves and others used to look upon us as good men as they; yea, it may be formerly we were above them, but after that we have seen them rise above us, they have grown in wealth faster than we, and we have seen them promoted and advanced, while we have been left behind and now see them in a station much superior to us. It may be there have been such trials time after time through a great part of the course of our lives." Especially the last sentence underlines the apparent frequency of such situations in Edwards's environment.
76 Minkema, "Preface to the Period," 10, in: WJE 14.

4.3.3 Vocation to the ministry as a telling example

One notable exception where Edwards does freely speak about vocation, calling, the will of God, and their correlation with divine providence is when he writes about the ministry. Because his advice in this case sheds some light on our general topic, the question how God guides, we will devote a separate section to it.

In his controversial book *An Humble Inquiry into the Rules of the Word of God, Concerning the Qualifications Requisite to a Complete Standing and Full Communion in the Visible Christian Church* (1749), Edwards discusses situations in which there are both arguments for and against taking a certain course of action.[77] In the context of the book, Edwards is concerned with the question of who can or cannot partake of the Lord's Supper. He argues that letting the 'uncertainties' prevail over the 'certainties' is not the default option but that "in such a critical situation, a man must act according to the best of his judgment on his case."[78] Examples of such 'critical situations' abound, but Edwards decides to discuss one example: the calling to the ministry.[79]

After starting out with the general remark that we do not take this 'honor' to ourselves, because "a man ought not to take upon him the work of the ministry, unless called to it in the providence of God," Edwards gives the example of a young man with a good education but "at a loss whether it is the will of God that he should follow the work of the ministry."[80] The young man subjects himself to thorough self-examination, seriously weighs all arguments ("considers his circumstances" and "weighs the appearances in divine providence") and prays continually, but does not arrive at a definite conclusion. Training for the ministry looks to him the best he can do, but is that enough to enter the ministry, or is it presumption?

In no uncertain terms Edwards makes clear that in all such cases (the ministry in this case is only an example of the 'innumerable' critical situ-

---

77 Over the 1740s, the relations between congregation and pastor had become more and more difficult. When Edwards refused to accept someone as a new 'full member' of the church in 1748 based upon his changed insights, things grew worse. The intense discussion on the qualifications for partaking of the Lord's Supper that was raised by Edwards's change of perspective eventually led to his dismissal as pastor of the Northampton congregation in 1750. It is this specific pastoral situation and the discussion surrounding it that led Edwards to write his *Humble Inquiry*.
78 WJE 12:296.
79 Note that it is already telling that for Edwards such a vocation is a 'critical situation,' and that he does not expect the calling to the ministry as something that should always be crystal clear.
80 WJE 12:296.

ations in human life[81]) it is our duty to follow our consciences, and not to shun our responsibility out of a fear of presumption: "If he neglects it under these circumstances, he neglects what according to his own best judgment, he thinks God requires of him, and calls him to; which is to sin against his conscience."[82]

Basically, Edwards states that, when confronting a difficult decision, our task is to carefully weigh the options and make an informed judgment. This judgment, in its turn, we should consider as that what God calls us to. Not acting upon our judgment out of a fear to act according to our own will instead of God's will is not pious caution, but in the strong words of Edwards, sin against our conscience. For Edwards, in those so-called 'critical situations', "it is equally dangerous to neglect on uncertainties, as to take on uncertainties. In such a critical situation, a man must act according to the best of his judgment on his case; otherwise he willfully runs into that which he thinks the greatest danger of the two."[83]

4.3.4 Conclusion

Although the concepts of calling and vocation do not occupy a central place in Edwards's thought, as we have seen they are often present as a presupposition. Furthermore, in the example of the calling to the ministry, given by Edwards in the context of critical decisions in general, a number of central elements in Edwards's ideas on guidance became clear. Thus, for Edwards it is clear that with regard to important decisions ('critical situations') part of our human condition is that we often end up with valid arguments for various, sometimes opposite, courses. In such situations, after the hard work of evaluating all aspects of the decision, our judgment "must govern and determine us"[84] and thus should be acted upon. In forming a good judgment, the human conscience is an important instrument according to Edwards.

At the same time, however, this raises a number of questions. For is presenting guidance and vocation in terms of good judgment and conscience not too indirect an approach? Should we not look for more immediate instances of divine direction? We will turn to those questions in the next section.

---

81 Once again, the fact that Edwards's speaks about 'innumerable' critical situations could reflect the increased (social) mobility of his time.
82 WJE 12:297.
83 WJE 12:296.
84 WJE 12:296.

4.4 Edwards on the Guidance of the Spirit

4.4.1 Introduction
After our discussion of Edwards's views on providence and vocation, in this section we turn to the central issue of the Spirit's role in guidance. Edwards's remarks on guidance, as we will see, appear mainly in his writings on the Great Awakening. In those writings, Edwards attempts to find a balanced position between the extreme critics of the awakenings (the 'old lights') and those who accepted the awakenings and all surrounding events without reserve (the 'new lights'). To find such a balanced position, Edwards avidly sought for ways to test and recognize truly religious experiences. In the first section (§4.4.2) we will discuss Edwards's remarks on what is not characteristic of the leading of the Spirit, followed by his interpretation of what it is to be 'led by the Spirit' (§4.4.3). This will lead us to short investigations of the 'distinguishing taste' (§4.4.4) and beauty (§4.4.5). We return to the topic of guidance in our discussion of the indwelling of the Spirit (§4.4.6). Finally, we will draw some conclusions (§4.4.7).

4.4.2 On impressions, texts, and the leading of the Spirit
The most mature and extended result of Edwards's quest for balance between critics and advocates of the awakenings is found in his *Treatise Concerning Religious Affections* (1746). In it, he describes a number of 'characteristics' of what in his eye qualify as sincere religious experiences. Along the way, he obviously also needs to show what experiences can be, but are not necessarily, important religious experiences.[85]

One of the sections in which Edwards objects against an experience too often judged as a deep and convincing (even honorary) encounter with God is found in his discussion of the fourth sign of sincere religious affections: "Gracious affections do arise from the mind's being enlightened, rightly and spiritually to understand or apprehend divine things."[86]

In explaining what it means to be enlightened by the Spirit, Edwards develops a prolonged argument against those who think it to be spiritual knowledge "for persons to be informed of their duty, by having it immediately suggested to their minds, that such and such outward actions or

---

85 The book consists of three parts. In the first part, Edwards formulates the 'nature' of religious affections and defends their due place in Christian spirituality. In the second part, he criticizes a number of 'signs' often regarded as signs of conversion that are not necessarily signs of the work of the Spirit. In the final part, Edwards introduces what he considers as the 'distinguishing signs' of the work of the Spirit.
86 WJE 2:266 (*Religious Affections*, pt. 3, sign IV).

deeds *are the will of God*."⁸⁷ Edwards first argues that, even if God's normal way of dealing with people would (still) be by immediate suggestions, this does in no way prove that the receiver is spiritual; for, as Edwards is keen to mention, Balaam received such clues continually. One important conclusion Edwards draws from this is that when the New Testament speaks about saints being *led by the Spirit* (Rom. 8:14, Gal. 5:18), something different must be meant. In the New Testament, the objects of guidance are always the saints.

Edwards then goes on to criticize the practice of drawing conclusions about the will of God from 'receiving' specific texts that at face value seem to fit the individual's situation precisely. He describes an example that could as well have come from a recent book on guidance:

> As for instance, if a person in New England, on some occasion, were at a loss whether it was his duty to go into some popish or heathenish land, where he was like to be exposed to many difficulties and dangers, and should pray to God that he would show him the way of his duty; and after earnest prayer, should have those words which God spake to Jacob, Genesis 46, suddenly and extraordinarily brought to his mind, as if they were spoken to him; "Fear not to go down into Egypt ... and I will go with thee; and I will surely bring thee up again."⁸⁸

If, says Edwards, this person perceives these words as having a meaning beyond what they had in their original setting, and that "by Egypt is to be understood this particular country he has in his mind, and that the action intended is his going thither, and that the meaning of the promise is that God would bring him back into New England again," this is a gross misunderstanding of divine guidance, for "there is nothing of the nature of a spiritual or gracious leading of the Spirit in this."⁸⁹

The reason that such events are not the guidance of the Spirit according to Edwards, is that what happens in this case has nothing to do with illumination. As Edwards argues, when the Spirit enlightens the believer,

---

87 WJE 2:279 (emphasis CvdK).
88 WJE 2:280.
89 WJE 2:280. A very similar example is given by Edwards a few years earlier in his 'Thoughts': "As for instance, suppose that text should come into a person's mind with strong impression, Acts 9:6, "Arise, and go into the city; and it shall be told thee what thou must do." And he should interpret it as an immediate signification of the will of God, that he should now, forthwith go to such a neighbor town, and as a revelation of that future event, viz. that there he should meet with a further discovery of his duty." For Edwards, it is clear that "[t]his is quite a different thing from the Spirit's enlightening the mind to understand the precepts or propositions of the Word of God...," WJE 4:435.

he enlightens *the mind,* thus leading to a deeper *understanding* of what was *already in the text* of Scripture before the event.[90] None of those three elements, crucial to Edwards, are present in the all too common example he describes.

In the course of his discussion of this example, Edwards mentions two (apparently) common and closely related experiences that are in his view deceptive and not to be conceived of as enlightenment by the Spirit: interpreting strong and sudden impressions as suggestions or errands from God, and randomly applying specific Bible verses to one's personal situation. Both 'errors' seemed to have disconcerted Edwards, as he returns to them in several places in his work, and mentions them already in 1743 as major excesses of the awakenings and dangers for the continuing work of God.[91] The intensity with which Edwards attacks these notions suggests their widespread occurrence and acceptance, and Edwards explicitly mentions his amazement that "many well disposed and religious persons … fall in with and hold fast this notion [of guidance through impressions, CvdK]."[92]

With regard to guidance through 'sudden impressions', Edwards rejects the notion that "'tis God's manner now in these days to guide his saints, at least some that are more eminent, by inspiration, or immediate revelation; and to make known to 'em … what it is his will that they should do, by impressions that he by his Spirit makes upon their minds …"[93] What is at stake here is those situations in which people claim to have spiritual insight in things that are known exclusively through this "revelation by immediate suggestion" and not confirmed by other arguments. Edwards does not only reject this kind of guidance because he is a cessationist, but also points at a number of other problems.

In the first place, on the practical level, since the beginning of the awakenings until the publication of Edwards's reflections, there have been so many "plain instances of the failing of such supposed revelations" that Edwards does not understand that they "don't open everyones eyes."[94]

---

90 See e.g. WJE 2:280-81.
91 See esp. WJE 4:432: "And one erroneous principle, than which scarce any has proved more mischievous to the present glorious work of God, is a notion that 'tis God's manner now in these days to guide his saints, at least some that are more eminent, by inspiration, or immediate revelation; and to make known to 'em what shall come to pass hereafter, or what it is his will that they should do, by impressions that he by his Spirit makes upon their minds, either with or without texts of Scripture."
92 WJE 4:433.
93 WJE 4:432. See for similar remarks WJE 8:168, 364 (*Charity and its Fruits*).
94 WJE 4:433.

Furthermore, the notion of this kind of guidance tends to make people incorrigible and impregnable for critique, "for what signifies it for poor blind worms of the dust to go to argue with a man, and endeavor to convince him and correct him, that is guided by the immediate counsels and commands of the great Jehovah?"[95] Thirdly, Edwards critiques this notion for its emphasis on the 'manner of producing the effect' instead of on the content. For Edwards, it is clear that truly spiritual experiences always are so primarily because of their content and effect, and not because of their appearance, however strong and unexpected the impressions.[96] Fourthly, according to Edwards people who expect this kind of divine guidance are at an enormous risk of self-deception. How logical is it, Edwards argues, for someone who is at a loss what course to take and prays to God to guide him in his will, to follow "the first extraordinary impulse that they shall have, groundlessly concluding it is from God," or to have an overactive imagination 'awakened and quickened' by their strong expectation.[97] Finally, he argues that a focus on extraordinary experiences leads people to neglect and contempt the Bible and causes some "to esteem the Bible as a book that is in a great measure useless."[98]

Edwards shows how trusting in impressions can lead to two different reactions toward Scripture, that are similar in the sense that, for Edwards, both are forms of disrespect. Often, when Edwards challenges the importance of impressions, he at the same time challenges the idea that Biblical texts that come suddenly in the mind are direct messages from God. We saw this concern in the examples discussed earlier, where people used texts to justify their decisions. For Edwards, texts that come to the mind, seemingly without occasion, even when they do so in a 'stream', are not to be considered as messages from God that gain a meaning in one's particular circumstances they did not have in the original.[99]

Underneath this mistaken use of Scripture is a high view of Scripture, from which the wrong inference is drawn that "therefore, those experiences which come from the Scripture must be right."[100] In answer to it, Edwards makes a distinction between experiences that arise *on occasion*

---

95 WJE 4:432-3.
96 See for this distinction e.g. WJE 2:227.
97 WJE 4:438-9.
98 WJE 4:432.
99 Edwards repeatedly objects against this idea of a 'stream of texts' as more convincing than a single text being 'presented' to the mind.
100 WJE 2:143. Edwards explicitly says that this mistake is especially common among "the less understanding and considerate sort of people."

of Scripture and those that are *agreeable* to Scripture.[101] Thus, "a scripture coming to the mind proves no more to be true than reading it proves. If reading any text of Scripture at any time, and at all times, as it lies in the Bible does not prove such a thing, then its coming suddenly into the mind does not prove it."[102] Thus, what goes wrong in concluding from Acts 9:6 that it is "God's mind and will that such a person by name should arise at such a time, and go from such a place to such a place, and that there he should meet with discoveries" is that new propositions are read into the text that have as less to do with Acts 9:6 as with Genesis 5:6.[103] Edwards regards such farfetched applications from Scripture as instances of new revelations and denies their validity. His reflections on the issue bring Edwards to the lament:

> And why can't we be contented with the divine oracles, that holy, pure Word of God, that we have in such abundance and such clearness, now since the canon of Scripture is completed? Why should we desire to have anything added to them by impulses from above? … And why should we desire to make the Scripture speak more to us than it does?[104]

All this does not, however, mean that Scripture does play no role in guidance. For Edwards, it is clear that "God may and doubtless often does direct persons' thoughts to such and such Scripture,"[105] but he does so in order for believers to apply what is meant in the text in a meaningful way to their situations. Edwards repeatedly stresses that illumination has nothing to do with sudden impressions, but that by illumining our minds the Spirit opens our eyes for what is already contained in the Word.[106] The Spirit, in enlightening, brings the mind to understand the meaning of the text, the consequences that can be drawn from it, and the way it applies to the particular case and circumstances.[107] Thus, Edwards's reflections on what is *not* the leading of the Spirit ultimately result in his positive view on what it is instead. To this we turn in our next section.

4.4.3 Being led by the Spirit
After his discussion of the most common misconceptions he frequently

---

101 Note the similarity between this distinction and the earlier distinction between "the effect" and "the manner of the effect" when it came to impressions.
102 WJE 8:168.
103 The example is Edwards's, see WJE 4:435.
104 WJE 4:434.
105 WJE 8:170.
106 WJE 2:230.
107 WJE 4:435.

encountered during the times of the awakenings, Edwards moves to a positive account of how the phrase 'being led by the Spirit' (Rom. 8:14 and Gal. 5:18) should be interpreted. Both in his *Thoughts Concerning the Revival* and in his *Religious Affections* he explicitly discusses the meaning of those Bible texts. Instead of supporting the enthusiast view, Edwards thinks these texts oppose it. It is clear in both texts that the leading meant is a gracious leading, "peculiar to the children of God."[108] As impulses and texts can be given to everyone, the meaning of being led by the Spirit must be something different and deeper for Edwards. It is worth citing Edwards more fully here:

> There is a more excellent way that the Spirit of God leads the sons of God, that natural man cannot have, and that is by inclining them to do the will of God, and go in the shining path of truth and Christian holiness, from an holy heavenly disposition, which the Spirit of God gives them, and enlivens in them which inclines 'em and leads 'em to those things that are excellent and agreeable to God's mind, whereby they are 'transformed by the renewing of their minds, and prove what is that good, and acceptable, and perfect will of God,' as in *Romans 12:2*. And so the Spirit of God does in a gracious manner teach the saints their duty; and teaches 'em in an higher manner than ever Balaam, or Saul, or Judas, were taught, or any natural man is capable of while such [*sic*]. The Spirit of God enlightens 'em with respect to their duty by making their eye single and pure, whereby the 'whole body is full of light' [Matthew 6:22]. The sanctifying influence of the Spirit of God rectifies the taste of the soul, whereby it savors those things that are of God, and naturally relishes and delights in those things that are holy and agreeable to God's mind .... And thus the Spirit of God leads and guides the meek in his way, agreeable to his promises; he enables them to understand the commands and counsels of his Word, and rightly to apply them.[109]

A number of elements stand out that make the kind of guidance Edwards proposes higher and more excellent in his view than in the view he opposes. For our ultimate purpose of formulating how guidance can be conceived from a Reformed perspective the following aspects are most interesting and central to Edwards's argument. In the first place, gracious leading of the Spirit is leading *internal to* the believer, and not just guidance through external directives. In other words, the guidance mentioned

---

108 WJE 4:436.
109 WJE 4:436-37.

in Rom. 8:14 and Gal. 5:18 is transformative in nature, and not (just) informative, given Edwards's reference to Romans 12:2. Secondly, the leading of the Spirit does not primarily concern singular events, but works a lasting change in believers. It has more to do with a deepened 'way of life' than with the concrete 'way to go'. Finally, as the logical consequence of the preceding elements, for Edwards the guidance of the Spirit does perhaps fit best within the locus of sanctification.[110]

In his *Religious Affections* Edwards paints the same picture of the leading of the Spirit but introduces a helpful further distinction. In his view, the gracious leading of the Spirit consists of two basic elements: *instruction* in our duty and powerful *inducement* to comply with that instruction.[111] He then proceeds to elaborate on the form the instruction by the Spirit takes, and writes that "so far as the gracious leading of the Spirit lies in instruction, it consists in a person's being guided by a spiritual and distinguishing taste of that which has in it true moral beauty."[112] As this statement contains a number of components that play a central role in Edwards's entire theology, we need to make two crucial digressions before we return to Edwards's account of guidance. Thus, we turn briefly to the meaning and function of the 'spiritual and distinguishing taste' in Edwards's theology and to the role the concept of beauty plays in his metaphysics and ethics.

4.4.4 'A spiritual and distinguishing taste'

When Edwards uses the word 'taste' in his description of what the guidance of the Spirit entails, he uses a concept that plays a major role in his theology, and especially in his view of conversion and sanctification. For Edwards, what best describes the transformation that takes place in conversion is receiving a new 'sense of the heart' or a new taste.[113] This new sense opens for the believer the possibility of spiritual sensible knowledge, a kind of knowledge that enables its subject not only to speculati-

---

110 We return to this observation in §4.5, where we discuss Edwards's view on virtue ethics and character.
111 WJE 2:281.
112 WJE 2:281.
113 See on the sense of the heart Terrence Erdt, *Jonathan Edwards: Art and the Sense of the Heart* (Amherst: University of Massachussets Press, 1980); John E. Smith, "Religious Affections and the 'Sense of the Heart,'" in *The Princeton Companion to Jonathan Edwards*, ed. Sang Hyun Lee (Princeton: Princeton University Press, 2005), 103–14; William J. Wainwright, "Jonathan Edwards and the Sense of the Heart," *Faith and Philosophy* 7 (1990): 43–62. Caleb Henry states that in his discussion of the sense of the heart Edwards is most reflective of Locke, see Caleb Henry, "Locke, John (1632-1704)," in *The Jonathan Edwards Encyclopedia*, ed. Harry S. Stout, Kenneth P. Minkema, and Adriaan C. Neele (Grand Rapids: Eerdmans, 2017), 354. The exact nature of Edwards's dependence on Locke is still oft-debated.

vely know spiritual truths, but to experience them, apprehend and contemplate them, engaging both mind and heart.[114] Through the new sense or taste of the heart, a different and deeper knowledge of God and spiritual truth is possible, in which the believer has an "inward tasting or feeling, of sweetness or pleasure, bitterness or pain" that arise out of the contemplation of the object of knowledge in the mind.[115] Besides sense and taste, another image Edwards frequently employs is the image of light. When the divine light shines upon the soul of a person, he or she gains a new vision of God and divine things. Through this new light, the 'saint' is enabled to see "things in a new appearance, in quite another view, than ever he saw before: ... he sees these things by an eye of faith, and by a new light that was never before let into his mind."[116] Thus, both the new ability to see and the new taste for spiritual things are expressions of the new sense of the heart 'created' in the moment of conversion.

In trying to understand what Edwards meant by the leading of the Spirit and the form of instruction contained in it through this new sense, we need to emphasize the radicality of the newness wrought in the moment of conversion. In his 1723 sermon 'A Spiritual Understanding of Divine Things Denied to the Unregenerate', in which Edwards "contrasts the knowledge of divine things that the unregenerate and regenerate have," we can see how for Edwards conversion places believers "on an entirely different epistemological level."[117] Here it becomes most clear how deep conversion changed the nature of men according to Edwards. For, "the believer hath got such a sight and such a knowledge of things that, ever since, *he is become quite another man than he was before. It has exceeding altered his internal tempers and disposition.*"[118] The radical

---

114 See Robert W. Caldwell III, *Communion in the Spirit: The Holy Spirit as the Bond of Union in the Theology of Jonathan Edwards* (Eugene: Wipf & Stock, 2007), 145–48 for a helpful introduction into the distinctions Edwards makes between 'mere cognition', 'speculative knowledge', and 'sensible knowledge' and the further distinction between 'natural sensible knowledge' and 'spiritual sensible knowledge'. Especially this last category of 'spiritual sensible knowledge' is relevant for our discussion.
115 WJE 18:459 (*Miscellany 782*: 'Ideas. Sense of the Heart. Spiritual Knowledge or Conviction. Belief.'). The standard imagery Edwards uses for explaining the new sense or taste is that of honey: "It is not he that has heard a long description of the sweetness of honey that can be said to have the greatest understanding of it, but he that has tasted," WJE 14:76 (Sermon 'A Spiritual Understanding of Divine Things Denied to the Unregenerate').
116 WJE 14:79. The importance of the image of light also explains why in Edwards the concept of illumination, that we encountered before, gets a prominent place.
117 Kenneth Minkema in WJE 14:67. Cf. McClymond and McDermott, *The Theology of Jonathan Edwards*, 2012, 673, who discuss the two epistemologies in Edwards, namely that of the regenerate and of the unregenerate.
118 WJE 14:81 (emphasis CvdK). The notion of changed internal tempers and disposition will be taken up in §4.5, where our focus will be on the ideas of character and virtues in Edwards's ethics.

change is further elaborated upon when Edwards remarks that the "innermost principles" are changed and that the converted has received "an heavenly temper and an angelical mind."[119]

Furthermore, this new sense of the heart has such a transformative impact that Edwards repeatedly emphasizes its spontaneity or immediacy. By giving, among others, the examples of someone with "a rectified musical ear" who does not need the "trouble of reasonings of a mathematician, about the proportion of the notes," Edwards tries to show how the believer who has a new sense of the heart does not need to go through "the trouble of a train of reasoning" to know what is good or the right course of action, but senses this in an immediate way in his or her heart.[120] Thus, the holy disposition and spiritual taste given to the believer "enable a soul to determine what actions are right and becoming Christians, not only more speedily, but far more exactly, than the greatest abilities without it."[121]

One final observation must be made on the nature of the new sense of the heart that plays such a crucial role in Edwards's account of the Christian life, and thus of guidance. The sense is, for Edwards, dependent on the work of the Spirit, as it is "given and maintained by the Spirit of God, in the hearts of the saints."[122] There, it works more or less easy and accurate as the saints have "more or less of the Spirit of God dwelling in them."[123] Before we return to Edwards's view on guidance and this correlated notion of the indwelling of the Spirit, we first need to make another detour and look at the importance of the concept of 'beauty' in his theology.

4.4.5 The concept of beauty in relation to guidance
As we have seen earlier, for Edwards guidance consists "in a person being guided by a spiritual and distinguishing taste of that which has in it true moral beauty."[124] In the previous section we focused on the meaning of the 'spiritual and distinguishing taste.' Here, we turn to the meaning of the concept of *beauty* that is the object of this new taste.

---

119 WJE 14:81. This almost euphoric language of Edwards on the radical transformation taking place in conversion does not mean that he has lost sight of the often disappointing reality of the Christian life or works with a perfectionist view of sanctification.
120 WJE 2:281. Cf. Caldwell III, *Communion in the Spirit*, 150 for a similar kind of 'immediacy' in Edwards' thought about believers 'seeing God', where Caldwell also points at the lack of need for "any intermediary support, such as a rational syllogism …."
121 WJE 2:283.
122 WJE 2:283.
123 WJE 2:283.
124 WJE 2:281.

The concept of beauty is at the heart of Edwards's theology.[125] As McClymond and McDermott state, the concept of beauty is

> fundamental to his understanding of God, as the first of God's perfections, as key to the doctrine of the Trinity, as defining aspects of the natural world, as basic to the phenomenon of conversion, as visible in the lives of saints, and as marking the difference between the regenerate and the unregenerate mind.[126]

For our purposes, it is crucial to understand, as underscored by for example Alan Heimert, that for Edwards beauty is a motivating force that combines the instructive and inducive elements mentioned before: "It was not ratiocination, but an aesthetic perception of the good, that according to Edwards determined human action."[127] At the deepest level, not the most rational course of action, but what reflects the ultimate beauty of the divine will influence and motivate Christians to pursue a particular choice or path.

Thus, when we return to Edwards's discussion of guidance in his *Religious Affections,* we see how this combination of a spiritual sense and its object, beauty, works out in his view on guidance. Edwards lists a number of examples that show how those who have a 'rectified taste' can judge about certain objects "without being at the trouble of a train of reasoning"[128]: An artist knows art by looking at it, not reasoning about its proportions; a musician knows harmony by listening and needs no rational analysis of the chords; a gastronomer does not need physical knowledge to delight in a beautiful dish. In the very same way a believer does not need "the trouble of a train of reasoning" to discern between holy and

---

125 Ortlund's recent *Edwards on the Christian Life: Alive to the Beauty of God* (Wheaton: Crossway, 2014) takes the concept of beauty as the structuring element for his entire book on Edwards' view of the Christian life. Many Edwards-scholars stress the importance of beauty in Edwards's theology. See e.g. McClymond and McDermott, *The Theology of Jonathan Edwards,* 2012, 93–101; Roland Delattre, *Beauty and Sensibility in the Thought of Jonathan Edwards: An Essay in Aesthetics and Theological Ethics* (New Haven: Yale University Press, 1968), 1; Louis Mitchell, *Jonathan Edwards on the Experience of Beauty* (Princeton: Princeton Theological Seminary, 2003), ix. Some even mention it as the characteristic of Edwards's theology that is most original and distinguishes him from older Calvinistic or Puritan theologians. See e.g. Douglas J. Elwood, *The Philosophical Theology of Jonathan Edwards* (New York: Columbia University Press, 1960), 3. Cf. McClymond and McDermott, *The Theology of Jonathan Edwards,* 2012, 94: "There are many reasons to regard Edwards as an original and venturesome thinker. Yet his placement of beauty at the heart of his theology may have been the boldest stroke of all."
126 McClymond and McDermott, *The Theology of Jonathan Edwards,* 2012, 93.
127 Alan Heimert, *Religion and the American Mind: From the Great Awakening to the Revolution* (Cambridge: Harvard University Press, 1966), 194.
128 WJE 2:281.

unholy, good and evil: "When a holy and amiable action is suggested to the thoughts of a holy soul; that soul, if in the lively exercise of its spiritual taste, at once sees a beauty in it, and so inclines to it, and closes with it."[129] After this explanation of what it means to have a 'taste' for what is the right course of action in particular circumstances, Edwards concludes with an answer to the question what it means to be *led by the Spirit*:

> Thus a holy person is led by the Spirit, as he is instructed and led by his holy taste, and disposition of heart; whereby, in the lively exercise of grace, he easily distinguishes good and evil, and knows at once, what is a suitable amiable behavior towards God, and towards man, in this case and the other; and judges what is right, as it were spontaneously, and of himself, without a particular deduction, by any other arguments than the beauty that is seen, and goodness that is tasted.[130]

Interestingly, he combines this conclusion with a reference to a biblical text we frequently encountered before, Romans 12:2, and states that there "the Apostle seems plainly to have respect to this way of judging spiritual beauty."[131] Before, we showed how the new sense of the heart worked in an immediate way. Here, from the perspective of beauty, we should add that this is only true insofar the object perceived more or less reflects the ultimate beauty that for Edwards is only to be found in God and his excellences.

Our discussion of Edwards's critique of the claim of the 'enthusiasts' that they were 'led by the Spirit', as well as our analysis of his positive account of guidance, uncovered a number of crucial aspects of Edwards's conception of divine guidance. Firstly, and characteristic for Edwards's overall view on guidance, extraordinary experiences and sudden inspirations are not indications of something being a profound spiritual event. The depth of experiences is to be found in their content, not in their form. Secondly, being guided by the Spirit requires a spiritual sense or taste that is only received in conversion. Thirdly, when speaking about guidance Edwards is not so much concerned with finding the particular 'will of God' or singular right choice in a situation, but with deciding whether a particular

---

129 WJE 2:281 (the forementioned examples of the artist, musician, and gastronomer are all Edwards's own).
130 WJE 2:282. The language of this quote suggests that Edwards thinks primarily of explicitly moral choices. Yet the examples he provides clearly show that Edwards includes those situations in which it is not *a priori* clear whether something is a moral choice, or a choice between several good options.
131 WJE 2:282.

course of action that is suggested to the believer is a fruitful course to take. Finally, while dismissing irrational accounts of guidance, Edwards simultaneously opposes overly rational accounts in insisting on the new sense. Although this sense is not irrational, its defining quality certainly is not rationality, as the affections play a primary role.

One important question needs to be addressed in this section, before we turn to an investigation of the role character formation and virtues play in Edwards's theology and ethics. For, as we have seen, the new sense is given to believers in conversion. However, when they 'have' this sense afterwards, what ongoing role is there for the Spirit to actually *guide*? Is the Spirit silenced once again after his moment of fame? In order to answer this question, we need to consider Edwards's account of the *indwelling* of the Spirit.

4.4.6 The indwelling of the Spirit

One final time, we return to Edwards's statement that "the sanctifying influence of the Spirit of God rectifies the taste of the soul." Thus far, we investigated the meaning of the 'taste' and the object of this taste, beauty. However, we still need to consider the question what Edwards meant with the 'sanctifying influence', and therefore we turn to his view on the indwelling of the Spirit in the believer.[132]

We closed the previous section with the question whether an ongoing role exists for the Spirit once the believers have received the 'new sense of the heart'. For Edwards, who had a deep interest in the ways of the Spirit in the soul,[133] this would not have been an alarming question. In his view, the new sense of the heart, or the operation of grace in the heart, is not

---

[132] The notion of the indwelling of the Spirit has featured in some recent research on closely related issues. See for examples the recent works on Edwards' virtue ethics (Wilson, *Virtue Reformed*; Cochran, *Receptive Human Virtues*), on his idea of communion with God (Caldwell III, *Communion in the Spirit*; William M. Schweitzer, *God Is a Communicative Being: Divine Communicativeness and Harmony in the Theology of Jonathan Edwards* [London: Bloomsbury T&T Clark, 2012]), and on his concept of participation in God (Seng-Kong Tan, *Fullness Received and Returned: Trinity and Participation in Jonathan Edwards* [Minneapolis: Fortress Press, 2014]; Kyle C. Strobel, *Jonathan Edwards's Theology: A Reinterpretation* [London: Bloomsbury T&T Clark, 2014]; W. Ross Hastings, *Jonathan Edwards and the Life of God: Toward an Evangelical Theology of Participation* [Minneapolis: Fortress Press, 2015]).

[133] See the interesting and correct remarks of Robert Caldwell III, who states that "Edwards's pneumatology profoundly shaped his entire theology," that he was fascinated by "the ongoing pneumatological realities of the Christian life" and that, although we do not find a systematic treatment of sanctification in Edwards's writings, "sanctification, broadly considered, was one of the theological concerns he was most passionate about," Caldwell III, *Communion in the Spirit*, 138–39.

something distinct from the Spirit, but is the Spirit himself.[134] In regeneration, the Spirit "enters"[135] the soul of the believer, unites himself to the soul and remains present in it. As a result of this "vital indwelling" of the Spirit[136] no strong distinction can be made between the Spirit and his operations, and an emphasis on the saints 'having' the new sense of the heart without the continuing active presence of the Spirit is unthinkable.

That the Spirit's presence in the soul is an active presence, also after the moment of conversion, is most clear from the verbs Edwards uses to describe this activity. As Caldwell writes: "At every turn of his thought on the subject [sanctification, CvdK] we find the Spirit's presence influencing, communicating, loving, affecting, etcetera."[137] With regard to the precise mode of this activity of the Spirit, Edwards writes that the Spirit "unites himself with the mind of a saint, takes him for his temple, actuates and influences him *as a new, supernatural principle of life and action*. ... The Holy Spirit operates in the mind of the godly, by uniting himself to them, and living in them, and exerting his own nature in the exercise of their faculties."[138] The key concept in this sentence is that the Spirit becomes a new 'principle' within the believer when united to the mind, operating within its faculties.[139] Interestingly, Caldwell mentions especially the faculties of understanding and willing that are influenced through the Spirit's indwelling the soul.[140] For Edwards, it is important to distinguish between the Spirit as a new principle and the faculties of the human soul, and he emphasizes that we should not think of regeneration

---

134 At the background of this is a discussion among Edwards-scholars on the notion of 'created grace,' sparked originally by Anri Morimoto, *Jonathan Edwards and the Catholic Vision of Salvation* (University Park: Pennsylvania State University Press, 1995). Morimoto's view has been criticized by many Edwards-scholars, see e.g. Caldwell III, *Communion in the Spirit*, 110; Tan, *Fullness Received and Returned*, 282. However, Strobel's reaction seems the most promising: He avoids the language of created and uncreated grace because it is foreign to Edwards, but alleges that if pressed to place Edwards in the debate he would side with 'uncreated grace,' because in Edwards grace is often synonymous with the Spirit, see Strobel, *Jonathan Edwards's Theology*, 190n56.
135 So e.g. WJE 14:407.
136 WJE 2:236, cf. Strobel, *Jonathan Edwards's Theology*, 197.
137 Caldwell III, *Communion in the Spirit*, 139. Note the interesting similarity between Calvin and Edwards on this point. Sometimes when speaking about God, and especially the Spirit, the choice of verbs might say more about the underlying theology and spirituality than the explicit contents of what is said.
138 WJE 17:411 (emphasis CvdK). See Tan, *Fullness Received and Returned*, 283 for a discussion of how Edwards can at the same time maintain that the Spirit indwells the saints as a new, supernatural principle and operates in them as a natural principle.
139 Cf. Caldwell III, *Communion in the Spirit*, 149.
140 Caldwell III, 102. Given Edwards's description of instruction and inducement as the main elements of the Spirit's leading this is an important insight.

or the new sense as the addition of a new faculty.[141] In this way, Edwards could uphold that the Spirit does not "overpower" the human faculties, but "treats people as people."[142]

This background makes Edwards's use of the concept of principle all the more important in trying to understand his notion of indwelling. For Edwards, a principle is a relative phenomenon in that it functions as a source of actions that flow forth from it. Thus, a principle of grace like a source flows forth in a stream of gracious actions.[143] When the Spirit, who is the divine Love itself, dwells in the soul as a governing principle, he changes the desires and loves of the believer at the deepest level.[144] What the Spirit ultimately desires and loves, "the saint now desires in finite, yet increasing, degrees."[145] In this light, it comes as no surprise that Tan finds "very clear instances where Edwards identifies the new disposition of the regenerate with the Holy Spirit."[146]

An important implication from Edwards's depiction of the Spirit's primary role as principle is that for him the work of the Spirit is internal to the soul. This is not only true in regeneration, where Edwards objected against an external or 'suasive' model of the Spirit's role,[147] but also applies to what Caldwell dubbed "the ongoing pneumatological realities of the Christian life."[148] That this is also true for Edwards's view on guidance is clear from his suggestion that the enthusiast view on guidance is based on a "false notion of communion with God, as though it were carried on by impulses, and whispers, and external representations, immediately made to their imagination."[149] Instead, by communion with God, through the indwelling of the Spirit, the believer is transformed from within.[150]

---

141 See esp. Strobel, *Jonathan Edwards's Theology*, 189, who links this with Edwards' "trinitarian psychology of being."
142 Strobel, 192.
143 See the remarks in WJE 8:298.
144 There is clearly a strong Augustinian influence here in Edwards's theology. Strangely enough, no extended research has been devoted to the Augustinian influences in Edwards's thought. Most authors simply refer to Niebuhr's description of Edwards as 'America's Augustine.' See H. Richard Niebuhr, *The Kingdom of God in America* (New York: Harper, 1959), xvi.
145 Caldwell III, *Communion in the Spirit*, 113.
146 Tan, *Fullness Received and Returned*, 284. Aside from the comparison between disposition and the Spirit as new principle, a comparison is sometimes made between Edwards's idea of a new principle and the Lockean notion of a 'simple idea'. See e.g. Strobel, *Jonathan Edwards's Theology*, 189.
147 See Caldwell III, *Communion in the Spirit*, 108.
148 Caldwell III, 138.
149 WJE 2:246.
150 As Strobel remarks, for Edwards "equally disconcerting as the Spirit communicating his essence is the idea that the Spirit only communicates externally, as he does with the unredeemed," Strobel, *Jonathan Edwards's Theology*, 203.

One could object that Edwards paints an oversimplified and overoptimistic picture of the holiness of the saints after conversion that moves close to a perfectionist view on sanctification. Although it is undeniably true that Edwards is more optimistic in this area than much of the Reformed tradition,[151] two qualifiers should be made. First, Edwards is increasingly aware of the remaining corruption in the hearts of even the greatest saints and second, in writing on the Spirit's indwelling he repeatedly asserts that the Spirit can be given in different degrees.[152] This is, however, not to be subtracted from his conviction that "by the Spirit who reigns in the heart, Christ governs the saints."[153]

4.4.7 Conclusion
In this section we investigated how Edwards thought of divine guidance ('the leading of the Spirit'). For him, this guidance is not to be found in spectacular impulses or fresh applications of biblical material, but in a deep and lasting transformation through the indwelling of the Holy Spirit.

Through this transformation, the believer receives a new spiritual sense that enables him or her to weigh actions from a spiritual perspective. In this weighing, the application of Scripture plays a crucial role, but not through impulses or sudden impressions. Whoever is at a loss concerning a decision that is to be made, should "pray to God to direct them, and make known to 'em his mind and will", but then, instead of waiting on special guidance, he or she should expect "to be directed, by being assisted in consideration of the rules of God's Word, and their circumstances, and God's providence", being "enabled to look on things in a true light, and justly to weigh them."[154] This way, a decision is to be made using all the God-given natural faculties, while the guidance takes place through the transforming work of the Spirit in the heart.

4.5 Edwards on virtues and character formation

4.5.1 Introduction
We ended the last section with an analysis of Edwards's thinking on the indwelling of the Holy Spirit. In that section, we noticed how Edwards

---

151 See e.g. his remarks in WJE 2:100, where he allows for various 'degrees' of true grace, but states that "everyone that has the power of godliness in his heart, has his inclinations and heart exercised towards God and divine things, with such strength and vigor, that these holy exercises do prevail in him above all carnal or natural affections, and are effectual to overcome them."
152 WJE 13:468 (*Misc. 403*: "Rewards. Degrees of Glory.")
153 Tan, *Fullness Received and Returned*, 287, cf. WJE 14:422.
154 Cf. WJE 4:438-39.

stresses the transformation the Spirit works in the believer. In the current section, we will further investigate the nature of this transformation through a discussion of Edwards's views on virtues and character formation. We start out with a section on the relation between virtue, grace, and justification in Edwards's thought (§4.5.2), followed by an analysis of his most extended discussion of what virtue entails, his book *The Nature of True Virtue* (§4.5.3). Then, we turn to the concepts of habits, disposition, and character in their relation to the virtues (§4.5.4). With that groundwork laid, in the fourth section our focus will be on the acquisition and maintenance of virtues as described by Edwards (§4.5.5).

4.5.2 Virtues, grace, and justification

In order to understand Edwards's view on ethics and especially the role of the virtues, it is important to point out from the start that his thinking about virtues takes place within the contexts of his thinking about grace, justification, sanctification and the nature of God, and is inseparable from his views in those areas. Because of this, we will first sketch the contours of Edwards's view on ethics.

Most importantly, with Elizabeth Cochran we need to stress that given Edwards's strong dichotomy between the regenerate and the unregenerate, when we speak about virtues we always speak about *receptive* virtues: virtues are always necessarily received from God.[155] Although with regard to the virtues Edwards has a lot in common with Aristotle, his theological concerns are not compatible with Aristotle's view of virtues as a cultivated state of character.[156]

This emphasis on grace and conversion as decisive moments in Edwards's account of the virtues brings us back to the theme of the previous section: Edwards's view on what virtues entail is closely intertwined with his view on the indwelling of the Spirit, as the Spirit itself is "the only principle of true virtue in the heart."[157]

Through the connection between virtues and the indwelling of the Spirit, Edwards gives communion with God a central place in his account

---

155 Cochran, *Receptive Human Virtues*, ix.
156 See esp. §4.5.4 on the discussion whether Edwards's view on habituation is in line or at odds with Aristotelean habituation. Cochran mentions this aspect of Edwards's incorporation of grace in his view on the virtues as the most promising element a retrieval of Edwards's ethics has to offer to modern Christian virtue ethicists, Cochran, 11.
157 WJE 21:197. Cf. William J. Danaher Jr., *The Trinitarian Ethics of Jonathan Edwards* (Louisville: Westminster John Knox Press, 2004), 114. Danaher rightly stresses that for Edwards the indwelling of the Spirit is decisive for the moral life.

of the virtues.¹⁵⁸ Through their intimate fellowship with God, believers somehow share in God's nature, concerns, and dispositions.¹⁵⁹ In this context, Edwards repeatedly uses the concepts of *theosis* or participation in God. In order rightly to understand him it should be noted that Edwards distinguishes between God's essence and his nature and rejects any notion of participation in which sharing in God's essence is meant.¹⁶⁰ Through sharing in God's nature, by the indwelling of the Holy Spirit, believers participate in the ultimate source of virtue and only in this way can be said to be virtuous themselves.¹⁶¹

Those basic tenets of Edwards's account of human virtues and the different theological *loci* that function at their background show the rightness of Cochran's statement that Edwards developed "a careful and complex theory of virtues," while it is also true that he "does not treat them systematically,"¹⁶² returning to the topic of virtues in a number of his writings. In our next section, we turn to his most extensive treatment of virtue, his treatise on *The Nature of True Virtue*.

4.5.3 The Nature of True Virtue

In his posthumously published *A Dissertation Concerning the Nature of True Virtue* (1765) Edwards makes a distinction between *true* virtue, and "others which only seem to be virtuous."¹⁶³ Edwards defines true virtue as "benevolence to Being in general," or more precisely, "that consent, propensity, and union of heart to Being in general, that is immediately exercised in a general good will."¹⁶⁴ Edwards defines 'Being in general' as the primary object of virtuous love, but hastens to add that not only acts that have 'Being in general' as their direct and immediate object are truly virtuous. Instead, he means that "the nature of true virtue consists in a disposition to benevolence towards Being in general: though, from such

---

158 Danaher also pointed at the importance of communion with God when he wrote that "in the *Religious Affections* Edwards develops a theological anthropology that places communion with God at the center of the moral life, which in turn informs his understanding of the nature of virtue, duty, and practice," Danaher Jr., 8.
159 Cf. Wilson, *Virtue Reformed*, 132.
160 In recent years, a number of publications have dealt extensively with Edwards's account of participation. See e.g. Strobel, *Jonathan Edwards's Theology*; Tan, *Fullness Received and Returned*; Hastings, *Jonathan Edwards and the Life of God*. For a more specific focus on Edwards's account of *theosis* see Kyle C. Strobel, "Jonathan Edwards's Reformed Doctrine of Theosis," *Harvard Theological Review* 109, no. 3 (2016): 371–99.
161 How the human virtues are in various ways reflections of divine virtue is excellently shown trough the multiple categories of human virtues that form the basic structure of Cochran's depiction of Edwards's virtue ethics.
162 Cochran, *Receptive Human Virtues*, ix.
163 WJE 8:539-40.
164 WJE 8:540.

a disposition may arise exercises of love to particular beings, as objects are presented and occasions arise."[165] What he does want to achieve with this formulation, however, is that "no affection limited to any private system ... can be of the nature of true virtue."[166]

In the second chapter, Edwards immediately draws the conclusion that for 'Being in general', we should read God. At it deepest level, true virtue "must radically and essentially, and as it were summarily, consist in this," namely, love to God.[167] Drawing upon his Trinitarian thought, and especially his use of the social analogy of the Trinity, Edwards proceeds that divine virtue "must consist primarily in *love to himself*, or in the mutual love and friendship which subsists eternally and necessarily between the several persons in the Godhead."[168] For humans, virtuous love to others is dependent upon their love to God and must seek "above all things ... the glory of God" and make this the "supreme, governing, and ultimate end."[169]

In the remainder of the book, Edwards distinguishes this true virtue that ultimately consists in love for God from many other things that are "erroneously confounded with real virtue."[170] He explains how they are different and how their similarities with real virtue lead people to mistake them for true virtue.

From Edwards's account of the role of virtues in the Christian life in *The Nature of True Virtue* three key elemements flow forth. In the first place, Christian virtue is inseparably linked with and flows forth from the character of God and is most clearly manifested in time in the life of Jesus Christ.[171] Secondly, for Edwards virtue is "not a set of distinct habits but a unified, single virtue of love of which more particular virtues are denominations."[172] According to Cochran, Edwards follows Augustine in his emphasis that "love unifies all the virtues so that each quality we might identify as a virtue ... is both distinct from love and, simultaneously, a form of love that reveals a particular dimension of love's character."[173] Thirdly, in *True Virtue* Edwards shows that what ultimately differentiates sanctified charity from its semblances is its "unique motive-structure."[174]

---

165 WJE 8:541.
166 WJE 8:556.
167 WJE 8:551.
168 WJE 8: 557.
169 WJE 8:559.
170 WJE 8:561.
171 Cf. Danaher Jr., *The Trinitarian Ethics of Jonathan Edwards*, 119.
172 Danaher Jr., 40.
173 Cochran, *Receptive Human Virtues*, 21.
174 Wilson, *Virtue Reformed*, 84.

This motive-structure, expressed in Edwards's use of terms like habits and dispositions, will be our focus in the next section.

4.5.4 Habits, dispositions, and character formation

The concepts Edwards uses in his account of human virtues can perhaps best be understood against the background of his use of the practical syllogism. In order to 'know' whether one is saved, Edwards points to the fruits of the Spirit: the actions in daily life that show forth whether one really believes in God's grace and lives in accordance with that faith. The most telling deeds, in this regard, are not those that are singular events, but those that are repeated continuously: the *habits*. Those habits or consistent good actions manifest the inner *dispositions* of the heart, and especially whether the actions ultimately flow forth from a virtuous love of God.

There has been some debate on whether Edwards moves in line with the standard Aristotelean model of habituation. For Aristotle, through repetition of good acts (habits) a person gradually cultivates the virtues, in the same way people learn a craft. According to Wilson, in his major study of Edwards's virtue ethics, Edwards works with a "standard Aristotelean meaning of habit."[175] Yet, Wilson's position has been strongly opposed by both Danaher and Cochran. According to Danaher, "Aristotelean habituation runs counter to the basic tenets of Edwards's moral anthropology"[176] and Cochran specifies this statement by pointing at Edwards's understanding of original sin and the essential place of grace in his theology as basically at odds with Aristotelean habituation.[177]

Instead of an Aristotelean model of habituation, in Edwards the spiritual sense that is given in conversion is the source behind virtuous dispositions. Adopting Hutcheson's ideas of apprehension and approbation Edwards presents a view of the virtues in which the spiritual sense instills in believers a disposition that approves divine things and finds its joy in acting them out. Thus, in the elect judgments follow "from their dispositions' response to the world they apprehend rather than as cultivated through repeated actions."[178] For Edwards, trusting in cultivation through habituation without the mortification of corrupt nature is the same as throwing up a stone and trusting it to fly.[179]

---

175 Wilson, 4.
176 Danaher Jr., *The Trinitarian Ethics of Jonathan Edwards*, 143.
177 Cochran, *Receptive Human Virtues*, 12.
178 Cochran, 114.
179 WJE 2:396.

In this way, a person's consistent practice manifests his or her inner dispositions and reflects whether these dispositions, the deepest expressions of a person's character, derive from a virtuous love to God. Danaher rightly characterizes Edwards's position in stating that "normative in each act, in each decision, in each movement of the heart, is not merely to pursue what is good or to do what is right, but to become complete persons."[180]

Thus far, we have seen how for Edwards the moment of conversion, where the Spirit 'enters' the human soul, is crucial in his account of becoming virtuous. At that moment, a person's deepest dispositions are changed and a love for God is distilled into the heart. However, from this perspective it is insufficiently clear how those virtues are actually maintained and even enhanced after conversion. To those issues we turn in the next section.

4.5.5 Maintenance of and growth in virtues

As discussed, for Edwards in the moment of conversion the Spirit enters the believer's heart and transforms her or his deepest dispositions. Yet, as Edwards makes clear in his sermon series *Charity and its Fruits*, this does not mean that at that same moment all the virtues come to full fruition. Instead, the seeds of all 'graces of Christianity' are present: "A convert at the same moment that he is become such is possessed of all holy principles, all gracious dispositions. There is a seed of every kind of holy behavior towards God, and towards men."[181] He emphasizes this point so strongly that he is able to say that "there are as many graces in a true Christian as there are in Jesus Christ himself."[182]

Those strong statements are immediately followed by a passage in which Edwards further explains how those graces are present as *seeds*. Comparing the 'new birth' with a normal birth, he explains that all graces are present in the Christian in the same way as a fetus in its mother's womb "has all the parts of a man," though "in a very imperfect state."[183] This means that although present, the virtues have to be cultivated and maintained, and this has to be done "against the downward trajectory of

---

180 Danaher Jr., *The Trinitarian Ethics of Jonathan Edwards*, 66. Cochran, *Receptive Human Virtues*, 10, states something similar: "Edwards presents an ethic for which character, rather than law, is primary." However, Danaher's statement is more precise, for there is little evidence in Edwards's for the opposition of law and character Cochran's statement presupposes.
181 WJE 8:334.
182 WJE 8:334.
183 WJE 8:334.

the fallen human nature."[184] Through the indwelling of the Spirit, and the "perpetual reinvigoration"[185] of the virtues the Spirit provides, the believer is enabled to transform the inner dispositions into outward actions and habits of love. In a typical Reformed fashion, and distinct from Aristotelean habituation, in Edwards the possibility of virtue is given in conversion and the cultivation and strengthening of the virtuous disposition remains dependent on divine assistance.[186] In this process, "God's Spirit is united with the human disposition in such a way that God's actions through human beings are also the actions of the human beings themselves."[187]

Thus, whereas Edwards view on habituation differs from those of Aristotle and Aquinas, there is undeniably a component of duty and diligent practice involved in the process of transforming the disposition given in conversion into the active presence of virtues. However, even this tendency towards activation is present in the transformed disposition itself:

> The first thing is a new heart, a new sense and inclination that is a principle of new life, a principle that, however small, is active and has vigor and power, and, as it more beats and struggles, thirsts after holiness, aims at and tends to everything that belongs to the new creature, and has within it the foundation and source of the whole. It aims at perfection, and from thence are the issues of life. From thence the various things that belong to the new creature all proceed and branch forth and gradually appear, *and that more and more*. And this principle, from its first existence, never ceases to exert itself, until the new creature be complete and comes to its proper perfection.[188]

The potentiality given in conversion is actualized when the renewed disposition is translated into virtuous acts, both inward and outward acts.[189] At it deepest level, the resulting growth in love, which is none other than the indwelling Spirit, is a growth in communion with and participation in the loving nature of God. Only in this way a believer forms his or her character into a godly character.

---

184 Wilson, *Virtue Reformed*, 266.
185 Wilson, 266.
186 Cf. Cochran, *Receptive Human Virtues*, 22.
187 Lee, *The Philosophical Theology of Jonathan Edwards*, 231–32.
188 WJE 11: 122-23 (*Images of Divine Things*, emphasis CvdK).
189 Cf. Lee, *The Philosophical Theology of Jonathan Edwards*, 232, who states: "… the actuality of a regenerate person is realized when his or her newly transformed disposition is exercised in and through all the inward and outward, perceptual and volitional (affectional) dimensions of the self."

Such a transformation from virtues that are present in the believer as seeds to a saint who is able to conclude his or her salvation from a virtuous character needs not only the ongoing stimulus of the Holy Spirit and the sustained effort of the individual, but it also needs a supportive community. As Wilson states, for Edwards "the church ... is the normal context for post-conversion habituation"[190] and, in Danaher's words, "the primary locus for living the Christian life."[191]

4.5.6 Conclusion

Although the above account of Edwards's view on virtues and character formation is brief and inevitably incomplete, it reveals at least one significant aspect of Edwards's thought that is related to our overarching search for an account of guidance: his emphasis on the relation between the indwelling of the Spirit and the transformation of the believer.

As Danaher states, Edwards "places considerable stress on personal transformation"[192] and the way he does this is mainly through the venues of dispositions and virtues. As discussed, a new disposition is given in conversion and it exercises and actualizes itself in the life of the believer. The main virtue for Edwards is love (charity) for God and for others, and this transformed and transformative love in its turn becomes the major source of influence on the Christian way of life.

With regard to guidance, Edwards stresses communion over communication and relates the indwelling of the Spirit more to transformation than to information.

4.6 Guidance in Edwards's Personal Life

4.6.1 Introduction

In this chapter, we traced, via the venues of providence, vocation, the leading of the Spirit, and the notions of character and virtues, how Edwards conceived of the nature and possibilities of divine guidance. In this final section we complement this picture with an investigation of the praxis of decision-making and the experience of guidance in Edwards's personal life. We start with a number of more general remarks (§4.6.2)

---

190 Wilson, *Virtue Reformed*, 296. According to Wilson, this emphasis on community is also behind's Edwards's slightly ambiguous position towards Brainerd and his process of achieving assurance of salvation. Brainerd's melancholic tendencies increased the difficulty of discerning between his psychological disposition and his spiritual disposition and this was only amplified by the lack of a Christian community in Brainerd's life as a missionary.
191 Danaher Jr., *The Trinitarian Ethics of Jonathan Edwards*, 68.
192 Danaher Jr., 44. Cf. p. 17-8.

before focusing on a few concrete moments in which an important decision had to be made: the early pastorate in Bolton, the move to Yale as tutor, and the move to Northampton (§4.6.3), the dismissal from Northampton and consequent move to Stockbridge (§4.6.4), and finally the decision to become president of the College of New Jersey (§4.6.5).

4.6.2 Guidance in Edwards's life: general remarks

As we have seen in the section on divine providence, Edwards conceived of this world as a "God-willed reality" and was delighted by that idea.[193] This deep conviction had a major influence on the life of the Edwardses, resulting in a household characterized by Marsden as "a household where the highest goal was to subordinate one's will to God's."[194] We already considered the practical implications of divine providence in §4.2.6, where we emphasized that one important consequence of Edwards's strict adherence to the distinction between the secret and the revealed will of God was that the secret will of God is foremost something to submit and resign to. We also discussed there that Edwards's use of the *conditio Jacobi* moves in line with this submission to the providential will of God.[195]

Three additional remarks can be made to get an impression of the interaction between his theological convictions and his personal life. In the first place, as a young college student, Edwards was often anxious to fail in his spiritual and intellectual duties. Especially in the summer of 1723, when his M.A. oration was approaching, he seemed to have struggled with intense doubts. Here, his diary entries shed an interesting light on the way the young Edwards handled those doubts. On Friday August 9, he wrote:

> With respect to the important business which I have now on hand, resolved, to do whatever I think to be duty, prudence and diligence in the matter, and to avoid ostentation; and if I succeed not, and how many disappointments soever I meet with, to be entirely easy…[196]

In the remainder of the entry, he explicitly points to his 57th resolution, in which he resolved "when I fear misfortunes and adversities, to examine whether I have done my duty, and resolve to do it; and let it be just as providence orders it, I will as far as I can, be concerned about nothing but

---

193 Cf. Marsden, *Jonathan Edwards*, 443.
194 Marsden, 323.
195 Although we also had to stress that Edwards himself was not always as consequent in applying the distinction in his interpretation of historical events.
196 WJE 16:778. Edwards's *Diary*, published in the volume containing *Letters and Personal Writings*, contains personal reflections written between Dec. 1722 and Mar. 1724.

my duty and my sin."[197] Here, we see how Edwards determines not to fret about missed opportunities or past choices, but to work diligently at the task at hand and accept that not every circumstance and outcome can be controlled. The insightful combination of duty, prudence, and diligence is in line with what we saw thus far of Edwards's approach to guidance.

Secondly, when Edwards had formed his convictions on a certain issue, we see how he did not hesitate to oppose even those whom he esteemed highly. In the section on the leading of the Spirit we saw how Edwards opposed people trusting on impressions as messages from God. Just how deep Edwards's fear of and opposition to this practice went is seen from the discussions Edwards had with George Whitefield. In general, Edwards was very sympathetic to Whitefield and generously supported his work. Yet, in their private conversations, Edwards did not "put politeness above principle"[198] and told Whitefield what he thought. It was Whitefield's custom to pray intensely about a decision and then to believe that God was telling him what to do through his impressions. As we have seen, for Edwards this resulted in following the (fearsome) imagination, and not "impulses from above."[199] As Marsden reports, after Whitefield had left New England, Edwards believed he "had been used of God to spark a new awakening among his congregation, but he was determined to cultivate it carefully by his own methods."[200] Under the influence of Whitefield and Gilbert Tennent a few years later the custom of trusting impressions to come from God resulted in the excesses Edwards so vigorously opposed.[201]

Finally, in a number of places we see how a sense of calling drives Edwards's writings and especially his choice of topics. His *Account of the Life of David Brainerd* is the most significant in this respect. A year before,

---

[197] WJE 16:757. The resolutions Edwards wrote functioned as maxims to be followed in his life, and were used by Edwards for self-examination. All 70 resolutions were written between December 18, 1722, and August 17, 1723. For a helpful introduction see George Claghorn's "Inroduction" to the personal writings in WJE 16:741-52.

[198] Marsden, *Jonathan Edwards*, 211.

[199] For Edwards's reflections on the discussion, see esp. his *Letter to a Friend*, WJE 16:153-162, in which Edwards publicly defends himself (and Whitefield) against the charge of Thomas Clap that Edwards told him of Whitefield's plan to replace all New England ministers by more pious pastors from England, Scotland, and Ireland. For Whitefield's reflections, see George Whitefield, *George Whitefield's Journals* (Edinburgh: Banner of Truth, 1960), 476 (October 17, 1740).

[200] Marsden, *Jonathan Edwards*, 212.

[201] Most prominently in the unrest caused by itinerants like Davenport, Wheelock, Buell and Pomeroy, but also through laypeople claiming all kinds of experiences and the corresponding spiritual authority, resulting in a lack of respect for the clergy. However, Edwards kept seeing these as excesses of something that was principally positive, differing in this from the likes of e.g. Charles Chauncy (cf. Marsden, 269.).

Edwards had written to John Erskine about his plans to write "something particularly and largely on the Arminian controversy,"[202] referring to a planned discourse on moral agency and free will. However, shortly after the death of Brainerd this plan was postponed because, as Edwards wrote to Erskine, he was diverted "by something else that divine providence unexpectedly laid in my way, and seemed to render unavoidable."[203] Although a discourse against Arminianism was a high priority issue for Edwards, apparently the *Life of Brainerd* was even more important for promoting the international awakening. Edwards had just finished his promotion of the transatlantic Concert of Prayer for revival, and he somehow experienced writing the biography of Brainerd as the next step providence urged him to take.[204] Apparently, Edwards experienced something of a 'burden' to write his account of Brainerd's life before finishing his long-planned rejection of Arminianism. This sense of calling with regard to his writing projects once again features in his letter to the Princeton trustees when he describes his major plan of writing a 'History of the Work of Redemption'. There, he states: "*I have had on my mind and heart ... a great work, which I call* A History of the Work of Redemption, *a body of divinity in an entire new method, being thrown into the form of an history ...*"[205] Once again, his wording suggests that the choice is not a purely rational one, but derives from a sense of urgency.

4.6.3 Pastor at Bolton, tutor at Yale, pastor at Northampton

There are a number of periods of transition in Edwards's life that are interesting to look into to see how he reflected on particular choices to be made. The first period appears right after his graduation from Yale College in 1723. Apparently, Edwards hoped to return to New York, where he had been in the pastorate for a few months, or to become preacher somewhere around New Haven. However, only an opportunity at the small village of Bolton arose.[206] Around the time, Edwards wrote in his diary:

---

[202] The letter is quoted in Dwight's *Life of Edwards*, 250, but the original is not included in the collection of letters in WJE 16, and is apparently lost.
[203] WJE 16:249.
[204] Cf. Marsden, *Jonathan Edwards*, 330, who speaks in even stronger terms of a "providentially sanctioned sequel." The *Concert of Prayer* was an agreement between ministers from Britain, Scotland, and New England to engage in united prayers for the spreading of the Gospel over the earth. Edwards, who was an early advocate of the movement, published a treatise promoting it, *An Humble Attempt to Promote Explicit Agreement and Visible Union of God's People in Extraordinary Prayer* (1747), published in WJE 5.
[205] WJE 16:727 (emphasis CvdK).
[206] In late 1722, the first contacts between the committee from Bolton and Edwards were established, presumably at the urging of his father Timothy Edwards. According to George Claghorn, Timothy apparently "relished the idea of having his son settled in a town close at hand," George S. Claghorn, "Editor's Introduction," in *Letters and Personal Writings*,

> Have this day fixed and established it, that Christ Jesus has promised me faithfully, that, if I will do what is my duty, and according to the best of my prudence in the matter, that my condition in this world, shall be better for me than any other condition whatever …; And if I find need of faith in the matter, that I will confess it as impiety before God.[207]

Although his discomfort with his 'condition' is manifest, Edwards apparently resolved to do what he thought his duty in the circumstances. In November 1723, he moved to Bolton and agreed to be the pastor of the village.

After a short period, in late May 1724, he "received news that provided escape from Bolton."[208] His former college in Yale offered him a position as tutor. Taking little time to consider the offer, within two weeks Edwards had moved to New Haven. No personal reflections or letters from the period exist that shed light on Edwards's motives. His time as a tutor at Yale was a period full of responsibilities and spiritual despondencies. In the meantime, the position, a short-term occupation, did not relieve the stress of his ambition and further career. Thus, when rumors spread that the church of his old grandfather Solomon Stoddard in Northampton planned to appoint an assistant, this heightened Edwards's inner turmoil. After Israel Chauncy was temporarily appointed as assistant, in August 1726 the church of Northampton invited Edwards to come and serve among them. Once again, little is known about Edwards's considerations, but in October of the same year he arrived in Northampton. After a few months, on February 15, 1727, Edwards was officially ordained as permanent pastor to assist Stoddard.[209]

4.6.4 From Northampton to Stockbridge

After a prolonged pastorate in Northampton, the struggles around admission to the Lord's Supper resulted in a request from his congregation that Edwards should be dismissed from his pastoral duties. As was the custom, after a lot of debates on the participating churches a committee of neighboring churches was formed to investigate the issue. In June 1750, Edwards was dismissed immediately from his pastorate.

WJE 16 (New Haven: Yale University Press, 1998), 8.
207 WJE 16:781. Note how the "according to the best of my prudence" is in line with what Edwards wrote on the calling to the ministry, see esp. 4.3.2.
208 Marsden, *Jonathan Edwards*, 101.
209 See Marsden's account, Jonathan Edwards, 110. Unfortunately, few personal writings exist from the period 1723-35, and no single letter of the period remains that could shedd further light on Edwards's considerations.

Although he did not show this to the congregation, Edwards was deeply disturbed by the events resulting in his dismissal and doubted his pastoral skills.[210] Furthermore, he was concerned about his family now that his income disappeared. In the months that followed a number of options were presented to him, among them offers to come to Scotland, requests by his supporters to start a new church in Northampton, and an invitation to settle as pastor and missionary in the frontier village Stockbridge. Edwards expressed his concerns about moving to Scotland, but left the door open, as he did with the option of forming a new congregation in Northampton. Yet he felt most attracted to the position in Stockbridge, hoping that the relative isolation it would give him would enable him to focus on his writing projects. To come to a decision about the complex situation, Edwards "followed what he believed the proper procedure whenever contemplating a move: he agreed to convene an ad hoc council of clergy that would meet in May [1751] to advise him what to do."[211] Such a council investigated the different options, and inquired into the motives behind personal preferences in order to come to a balanced decision. The council concurred with Edwards's preference of Stockbridge and advised him to accept the invitation. Arriving early in the summer, Edwards was officially installed in Stockbridge in August 1751.

4.6.5 From Stockbridge to Princeton
In September 1757, shortly after the sudden death of his son-in-law, Aaron Burr, who was president of the College of New Jersey at the time, Edwards was approached by the trustees to become the new president of the college. In an extensive and very personal letter, dated October 19, Edwards acknowledges his surprise and thanks the trustees for the honor

---

210 In a letter to John Erskine, shortly after his dismissal as pastor of Northampton, Edwards laments: "I am fitted for no other business but study," WJE 16:355. His letters from the period also reflect a deep awareness of being dependent upon God's guidance, see e.g. WJE 16:309: "I need God's counsel in every step I take and every word I speak."
211 Marsden, *Jonathan Edwards*, 365. The ad hoc councils were a custom of the congregational churches of New England as a remedy against oppression. In case of insoluble problems (most often cases of excommunication or problems with pastors) a number of neighboring churches were chosen with mutual satisfaction and invited to send delegates to give advice on the situation. In a public hearing ("as publick an hearing as they can have," Ratio Disciplinae 160), the council was expected to investigate the case, to weigh it, and to give an advice. The exact jurisdiction or authority of the councils is unclear. In the context of Edwards's decisions, it is important to know that pastors could only be ordained with the consent of a council and could not be disposed without council. Neither could a pastor decide all by himself to leave his community when called by another church or a college. See esp. Cotton Mather, *Ratio Disciplinae Fratrum Nov Angelorum: A Faithful Account of the Discipline Professed and Practiced in the Churches of New England* (Boston, 1726), chap. IX "Of Councils upon Emergencies." I thank Margaret Bendroth for pointing me to this source.

conferred upon him, but he mainly expresses his doubts "whether I am called to undertake the business."[212] After mentioning a number of practical concerns, for example the difficulty of moving his family, which was just growing accustomed to Stockbridge, Edwards mentions his two major concerns: His first concern is about his qualifications for the heavy demands of the job. Edwards lists different doubts with regard to his health, energy, his being an introvert not fitted for conversation, and his deficiencies in some parts of the curriculum.[213] Yet, his biggest concern is that he will not be able, when accepting the position of president, to work his numerous notes into coherent books. He describes his plans to write a *History of the Work of Redemption* and *The Harmony of the Old and New Testament* along with a number of other projects on which he has made progress. As he indicates, "if divine providence favor," all his years of thinking would lead to a number of major publications from his study, "which have long engaged, and swallowed up my mind, and been the chief entertainment and delight of my life."[214] This last concern could be levied if his teaching duties would not be as heavy as those of his predecessor. Edwards ends his letter with the confession that "on the whole, I am much at loss, with respect to the way of my duty in this important affair."[215] As he is afraid to make a decision he would later regret, he promises the trustees to take the matter into serious consideration by asking advise from those he esteems "wise, friendly and faithful" and to investigate whether his Commissioners in Boston are willing to absolve him from his duties in Stockbridge.[216]

Acting upon his promises, once again Edwards entrusts the decision to a council of local ministers. When the council convenes, it is quickly decided that Edwards must accept the offer from the trustees and go to Princeton. According to his friend Samuel Hopkins, Edwards is deeply moved by the decision against his objections, but after composing himself says "he would cheerfully follow what he saw as God's will and his duty."[217] Once settled in Princeton, Edwards confided to his daughters that, notwithstanding his earlier scruples, he now sees his task as a calling that he could happily pursue.[218]

---

212 WJE 16:725.
213 WJE 16:726.
214 WJE 16:726.
215 WJE 16:729.
216 WJE 16: 729-30.
217 Marsden, *Jonathan Edwards*, 431.
218 According to Samuel Hopkins, "The Life and Character of the Late Reverend Mr. Jonathan Edwards," in *Jonathan Edwards: A Profile*, ed. David Levin (New York: Hill and Wang, 1969), 79.

4.6.6 Conclusion

This section on guidance in Edwards's personal life has shown the interplay between Edwards's theological convictions and his personal life. A few elements stand out from our analysis. In the first place, it is interesting to see how Edwards, while opposing immediate forms of guidance in his theological writings, still shows his deep awareness for the need of divine guidance in his personal writings. Clearly, rejecting the validity of certain forms of divine guidance does not result in rejecting the entire idea of guidance for Edwards. In the second place, it is important to see that when it comes to the crucial decisions, Edwards does not restrict guidance to the personal communication between God and the individual, but sees guidance as a community issue, in which others are to be involved and are perhaps even better enabled to make prudent decisions. Thirdly, Edwards's distinction between guidance as consisting of instruction and inducement reappears in his personal writings. Especially in his choice of writing topics his reflections portray a sense of burden and urgency that could be interpreted as the inducement he wrote about earlier. Finally, when it comes to concrete decisions in his personal and family life, Edwards's concern is not to find the specific way God points out, but to find a place where his gifts can be made useful for the future spread of the Gospel.

4.7 Conclusion

In this chapter, we brought the questions on divine guidance as we encountered them in our second chapter into conversation with the theology and life of Jonathan Edwards. Living and writing in an age of awakenings, enthusiasm, but also the rise of Enlightenment philosophy, his thought proved to be a fruitful source in thinking about divine guidance from a Reformed perspective.

Our investigation included his views on divine providence, on vocation, on guidance and the indwelling of the Spirit, and on virtues and character formation. The theological analysis was complemented by a section on Edwards's personal life and his reflections on guidance relating to it. Our search in this chapter yielded a number of important insights that will help us in formulating a contemporary account of guidance from a Reformed perspective.

Like Calvin, Edwards is deeply convicted that God is sovereign and that the entire creation is subjected to God's will and decree. Nothing, not even a single atom, is in a place where God did not consciously will it to be. However, like Calvin, Edwards adopts the distinction between the revealed and secret will of God, and concludes from the distinction that the events of providence are not to be used as indicators of the divine will in the same way Scripture is. Although, especially in his apocalyptic writings, Edwards could be accused of concluding a lot from the events of providence, when it comes to guidance in personal decisions his rejection is firm.

Edwards's use of the terminology of vocation, an important concept in the early Reformation and in Calvin, is scarce. Yet in his hierarchical views on the order of society and especially in his use of the term 'station,' a number of elements can be traced that suggest Edwards's thought moves in line with the Reformed concept. An example on the vocation to the ministry showed Edwards's awareness that 'critical' decisions are never crystal clear and often require a decision based on partial knowledge. Here, the role of conscience proved important.

Edwards's discussion with enthusiasm, and especially his reflections on whether certain impressions, either combined with specific Bible verses or not, are to be regarded as specific divine guidance, proved helpful for our overall research aim. Here, Edwards was not only critical because of the 'risks' he perceived in this approach, but more profoundly because he thought focusing on this kind of guidance thought too low, and not too high, of the nature of God's guidance. In his view, trusting impressions to be God's way of guiding amounted to regarding the work of the Spirit as transitory and superficial. The work of the Spirit in the believer leaves a deeper imprint than the wind over the water does.

Thus, in the positive account Edwards offered of divine guidance, the idea of *transformation* proved to be important. In regeneration, believers receive a new sense or taste that teaches them to value the good and beautiful as derived from God's goodness and beauty. Through the continual indwelling of the Holy Spirit the believer is transformed more and more, as are his or her will, dispositions, and priorities. The idea of transformation was further developed in Edwards's account of the virtues and of character formation.

Finally, this theological picture was complemented by elements from Edwards's biography and personal reflections. Always subjecting his life to the will of God, Edwards was not seeking to find this will in order to make his decisions. Instead, he thought for ways to make his gifts fruitful and did so, especially in crucial situations, with the help of a council of wise, mature, and trusted believers.

CHAPTER 5:
Intermediate Conclusion and Transition

5.1 Introduction

Our analysis of contemporary evangelical literature on divine guidance and our interaction with the thought of both John Calvin and Jonathan Edwards have brought us to an important point in the argument of this study: we are now in a position to take stock and formulate a preliminary answer to our main research question. In this brief chapter, we will focus on the question which view on guidance is most coherent with the concerns and emphases found in the writings of Calvin and Edwards and can hence function as the best point of departure in formulating a contemporary Reformed account of divine guidance.

In order to do so, we will first look backward and return to the typology formulated in chapter 2 (§5.2), followed by an account of the most pressing and relevant material from the chapters on Calvin and Edwards (§5.3). In combination, these sections lead us to a concise framework of what we consider a fruitful and theologically robust contemporary account of divine guidance coherent with the broader outlines of Reformed theology (§5.4). Based upon this framework, we will look forward to the next chapter by considering how this approach to guidance raises a number of questions that need to be answered in order to arrive at a theology of guidance that is both theologically deeper rooted than the popular evangelical accounts and that moves beyond Calvin and Edwards in integrating more recent theological discussions (§5.5).

5.2 Models of guidance: information, intimation, or transformation?

In chapter 2, after analyzing a number of popular evangelical books on guidance published between 1980 and 2010, we developed a typology of views consisting of three basic models: guidance through information, through intimation, and through transformation.[1]

In the first and most common model, God guides believers by providing them with crucial *information* on his will for their lives. At the core of this model are the twin convictions that a) God has a detailed will or plan for every individual believer and b) that He does reveal (parts of) this plan to them. Throughout their lives, and especially at crucial junctures,

---
1 See esp. §2.6 for more detailed accounts of the three models of guidance.

God will provide 'road-signs' to show individuals which way to take. What is asked of believers is a continual awareness to the pointers God may provide ('searching' God's will is a common expression) and reflection on whether these pointers correlate, since God often speaks 'in stereo'. In many cases, concrete steps are prescribed to arrive at a certain level of certainty with regard to God's will.

In the second model of guidance, God invites believers into an intimate relationship with himself, enabling them to get accustomed to his subtle 'nudges' and his 'still, small voice' in their hearts. Proponents of this model believe that God has a distinct will for the individual believer and at times makes this will known to them. Yet the focus is no longer on 'searching' the will of God, but on growing into an intimate relationship with God in Christ. The result of this growth will be an ever-increasing awareness of the indwelling of the Spirit in the heart of the believer and a growing ability to recognize his voice ('His sheep know his voice'). Practically, in this model the concept of discernment plays an important role. Because discernment is recognized as a human activity, the results of the process of discernment are presented as less certain than the results of following the 'steps' in the first model.

In the third model of guidance, God guides primarily through *transforming* believers into people able to make wise choices in the service of his Kingdom. In this model, the distinction between God's secret and revealed will plays a key role. Although the details of individual lives are included in God's hidden will, there is neither reason nor promise to expect additional divine revelation or communication. This does not mean, however, that no guidance is possible; what it does mean is that guidance is conceived less concrete and more process-oriented, as an aspect of sanctification. God's guiding presence is thought more as transformative than revelatory in nature. As a result, in practice the main responsibility shifts from finding the will of God to making wise decisions and bearing full responsibility for them. Wisdom and spiritual maturity are both gracious gifts of God and the result of certain spiritual disciplines.

Since our discussion of these models in chapter 2, we developed an extended conversation with John Calvin and Jonathan Edwards on key theological assumptions behind each view on guidance. In the next section, we will summarize the key points that emerged from our interaction with their theologies.

5.3 Learning from Calvin and Edwards
In two major chapters, we investigated aspects of the discussion on guidance encountered in the writings of Calvin and Edwards. We looked for

characteristic concerns and emphases that could point to essential tenets of a Reformed account of guidance. Priority was given to their views on providence, vocation, and the indwelling of the Spirit. In Edwards, this also led to an investigation of his account of the virtues and character. Although in a number of places we noticed links between the models of chapter 2 and the writings of both Calvin and Edwards, in this section we will do so in a more explicit and systematic way.[2]

With regard to the idea of a divine plan or will for the lives of individuals, our interaction with both Calvin and Edwards presented us with the following perspective: In their accounts of divine providence, both authors stress that nothing, not even seemingly minor details, happen without the will of God (e.g. 3.2.3, 4.2.2), and that the church and the faithful receive the most specific care of God (esp. 3.2.4). For both Calvin and Edwards, however, the history of redemption, or God's will and plan with his entire church, take centre stage, not individual histories of believers. Thus, if we want to maintain the idea of a 'plan' of God for each believer, it should always be stressed that it only exists as part of an overarching 'council' of God in which' service it stands, not as something independent.

Furthermore, both authors strongly emphasized the distinction between the revealed and secret aspects of the divine will, and, referencing Deut. 29:29, stressed that we should not inquire curiously into God's secret will. Calvin explicitly warned against searching for God's secret will (3.2.5) and combined an emphasis on providence as a doctrine of *faith* with the admonition to live as though nothing were determined (3.2.7). Edwards highlighted the limited perspective of the individual and stressed that circumstances and providence are not to be "improved as our rule" (4.2.6).

Although Calvin devoted more attention to the concept of vocation than Edwards did, in both accounts we encountered the strong conviction that God gives each person a proper place in which to serve (e.g. 3.3.3 and 4.3.2). Both accounts focused on the content of vocation, not on the event. In Calvin, vocations are strongly tied to the social order and are to a large extent given; in Edwards we found more recognition of the fact that often good reasons exist for various possible paths and that in the end the process of deliberation must be concluded with a definite choice based upon partial knowledge (4.3.3).

Both Calvin and Edwards were actively engaged in discussions with spiritualists or enthusiasts. Advocating a strong connection between Word and Spirit, they objected to a one-sided appeal to impressions as

---

[2] We will refer to the specific sections of chapters 3 and 4 by putting the section numbers in brackets in the text.

communications of God's will (3.4.2 and 4.4.2). Yet for them this did not mean that any speech of guidance by God or of being led by the Spirit became obsolete. Instead, they object that an interpretation of guidance that focuses solely on new information and divine communication is superficial. Both authors stressed transformation over information and communion over communication. In Edwards, this was most explicit through his use of the concept of the 'new sense' (4.4.4) and the close ties between the indwelling of the Spirit, the virtues, and character formation (4.5). Interestingly, in both accounts of the Christian life Romans 12:1-2 with its reference to the 'transformation of the mind' played a crucial role. In conclusion, one could say that, for both, living a Christian 'way of life' is a more pressing concern than choosing a specific 'path to go'. That being said, we have seen that in various places Calvin betrays his deep conviction of the reality of spiritual stimuli and divine influences. This aspect of his thought is not done full justice to in the field of Calvin studies, since there most attention goes to his interactions with the Libertines.

One final point of interest is the awareness both Calvin and Edwards showed of the need for guidance in moments of important personal choices. Our investigation of these moments in their lives showed an interesting similarity: both authors invited others (the 'trusted guides' of Calvin (3.5.5), and 'the wise, friendly and faithful' Edwards invited for an ad hoc council, 4.6.4) to advice them in weighty matters. Both showed on the one hand how they distrusted their own judgments in such situations and on the other how guidance is not strictly a personal responsibility, but also a community issue.

5.4 A Reformed approach to guidance

Given the main points we have drawn from our interaction with Calvin and Edwards, which of the models of guidance can best function as our point of departure in formulating a Reformed perspective on guidance?

In order to answer this question in a satisfactory way, we need to understand first which venues were precluded by our previous investigations and which we hence must avoid in our own proposal. Taking Calvin's and Edwards's thought as a heuristic means, a Reformed account of guidance agrees with all three models in the conviction that there is some divine 'plan' behind whatever happens in the world, and that the individual lives of believers are not only part of this plan but important focal points.[3] The main differences with the models that conceive of guidance

---

3 This basic agreement on divine intentionality behind what happens in the world does not, however, mean that in a Reformed account of guidance this is to be thought of as some kind of 'blueprint,' an image regularly encountered especially in accounts of the first model of guidance. Cf. Schuurman, *Vocation*, 126.

as information or intimation arise with regard to the second premise underneath them: according to both Calvin and Edwards there is no reason to believe that God intends (let alone promises) to reveal the relevant parts of this plan to the individual believers *before* its actual execution. In some places they even censure attempts to find out the divine will as unwarranted curiosity. In this light, any account of divine guidance that presents a 'method' for finding the will of God is not only impossible, but presumptuous. It follows that a Reformed account of guidance would avoid the popular phrases of 'searching', 'finding', and 'discovering' the will of God. These phrases do not only misrepresent the nature of God's will, but also the certainty that is to be acquired: the end results is always based upon a (fallible) human interpretation, conclusion, and decision.

This major point excludes the information model as the basis for a Reformed account of guidance, while pointing to problematic aspects in the intimation model. With that model, however, there are also points of agreement, especially with regard to the importance of discernment. While the premise that God is constantly intimating his will to the human soul is unwarranted (although especially Calvin sometimes seems close to suggesting this, see 3.4.5 and 3.4.6), this does not mean that no spiritual dimensions are influencing our decisions. The main difference concerns the role of these spiritual influences in the decision-making process. In the intimation model, the divine communication in the soul is the central moment of guidance and ultimately decisive. In both Calvin and Edwards, spiritual influences have their proper place, but *within* the ordinary decision-making process. They have to be carefully weighed[4] in the final decision, but do not *a priori* overrule other considerations.

For these reasons, a Reformed account of divine guidance can best be developed in close interaction with the transformation model. In doing so, the following pitfalls present in much of the evangelical accounts must be avoided, both in the contours we sketch here and in the elaboration presented in the next chapter:

In the first place, we should avoid the impression that moments of choice are unconnected episodes that can be detached from their context and be approached as discrete entities. In this regard, many accounts of divine guidance suffer from what Alisdair MacIntyre called an atomistic approach to human life.[5] This problem is only intensified in those accounts

---

[4] Especially Calvin emphasized that spiritual influences can come from different sources and hence have to be evaluated carefully, see §3.4.6.
[5] See esp. Ch. 15. 'The Virtues, the Unity of a Human Life and the Concept of a Tradition' in Alasdair MacIntyre, *After Virtue: A Study in Moral Theory*, 3d edition (London: Bloomsbury Academic, 2013), 237–62. Cf. Hahnenberg, *Awakening Vocation*, 162.

of guidance that choose to focus on 'crucial decisions' while acknowledging that for day-to-day decisions no special guidance is required. This approach does not only detach the 'crucial decisions' from their context, but also wrongly supposes that it is possible to specify in advance which decisions will turn out to be crucial.

The second pitfall to be avoided is a direct result of the isolation of moments of choice from the rest of an individual's life: the risk that the important topics of conversion and transformation are not a primary part of an account of guidance.[6] In what follows, we must resist such atomization and stress the narrative dimensions of life, placing transformation at the heart of our account of divine guidance.

The third pitfall we must avoid is the result of another form of isolation: this time not of moments of decision from their context, but of the individual from her or his social context. An account of guidance can never focus exclusively on the individual believer and his or her decisions, as each individual is always involved in a myriad of social networks.[7] This is even more urgent from a Christian perspective, as love must be central and this means that sometimes "the urgent need to act is postponed in the interests of others' actions."[8]

A fourth pitfall we must steer clear of in thinking about divine guidance is the danger of focusing too much on future possibilities at the neglect of the present. Focusing on the socalled 'major decisions' might focus an individual more on the speculative opportunities of next year than on the immediate needs of today.[9]

Finally, we should avoid the impression that guidance always leads to movement and change: many of the accounts discussed earlier draw an implicit connection between God's guidance and a movement away from one's current location: guidance is often guidance towards something

---

6 Cf. Hahnenberg, *Awakening Vocation*, xiii: "the principal weakness of choice—as a fundamental framework for the spiritual life—is the way it can so easily short-circuit personal transformation."
7 In relation to the concept of vocation, Wingren rightly remarked that the isolated individual exists only *coram deo*, but not on earth. See his *Luthers Lehre vom Beruf*, 17.
8 Oliver O'Donovan, *Entering into Rest*, Ethics as Theology 3 (Grand Rapids: Eerdmans, 2017), 2. O'Donovan describes a number of features of love as "restraint of competitive self-assertion, acceptance of others' activities and initiatives, flexibility in waiting upon them, and readiness to give them time and space."
9 Cf. O'Donovan, *Finding and Seeking*, 146: "We should not be so beguiled by futures as to miss the note of present immediacy in the word 'today' … The expansive exercise of imagination has its own proper part to play, but it is essentially speculative, and our thought will fail to make the transition from speculation to practicality, if it does not shorten its focus from the open universe of indeterminate futures to the determinations of the present future, the future of today rather than the futures of tomorrow."

new.¹⁰ One could overemphasize staying in and accepting one's current position, but in the present age a point can be made for the importance of *stabilitas loci*.

The above considerations issue in the following concise account of divine guidance, in which the basic contours of a Reformed perspective on guidance are sketched. As we do so, the coherence with the transformation model will become more explicit.

A Reformed account of divine guidance, as developed in conversation with Calvin and Edwards, will have the following dogmatic theses as its theological basis:

1. The doctrine of divine providence is an expression of God's care for his creation that finds its culmination in the history of salvation and its most intense focus in the church.
2. The conviction that "for those who love God all things work together for good" (Rom. 8:28) means, among other things, that God guides the lives of individual believers, often in mysterious ways.
3. The classic distinction between the hidden and revealed aspects of the divine will is crucial and must be maintained.
4. Providence is a doctrine of faith, and should not be solidified into a worldview (the danger of providentialism).
5. Qualifying one's own plans, priorities, and decisions by use of the Jacobean condition is more pertinent than searching for the will of God or executing a purportedly 'found' will of God.
6. The concept of vocation is still one of the most promising means for Reformed theology to express a belief in concrete divine guidance.
7. A contemporary account of vocation must take into account the highly complex and dynamic nature of (post)modern societies and can in no way reduce its scope to paid professions.¹¹

---

10 Cf. Schuurman's comments on Luther's position, Schuurman, *Vocation*, 126: "Luther was less concerned that we might miss God's call to a new job or social location than that we might fail to respond obediently to the many and constant callings reaching out to believers all the time." David S. Cunningham, *Christian Ethics: The End of the Law* (Abingdon: Routledge, 2008), 110, nicely summarizes these problems in his discussion of the metaphor of life as a path with multiple forks in the road: "But our progress through life isn't like that— not at all. We are not alone; there is no path; our lives are not defined by a series of forks in the road; and, to whatever extent we do actually choose a particular direction, we will probably not be able to determine whether it is the right one until it is far too late to retrace our steps."

11 The tension between the static and the dynamic has been present in discussions of vocation from the very beginning. As we have seen, Calvin moved beyond Luther in stressing dynamic factors, and Edwards was forced by social-economic circumstances to address the dynamic side even more. More on this will be said in §6.2.

8. A Reformed approach to divine guidance requires robust notions of Christian wisdom and discernment that on the one hand indicate the particularity of Christian decision-making and on the other hand leave the full freedom and responsibility for the chosen path with the individual.
9. Hence, referring to divine guidance behind one's own choices in no way reduces the personal responsibility for those choices.[12]
10. Ultimately, sanctification is the field or *locus* within which guidance is to be discussed.[13]
11. Formation and transformation take place on the individual level, but are impossible without the constant support and influence of a Christian community, which can be of great aid in the important tasks of deliberation and discernment.
12. Guidance by the Spirit primarily takes place in and through ordinary human decision-making processes, as daily life is the normal workplace of the Spirit, not exclusively the extraordinary experiences.[14]
13. Extraordinary instances of divine guidance may put ordinary decision-making processes in perspective; these extraordinary instances are indeed *extra*-ordinary and rest upon divine initiative. Hence, they cannot be part of a heuristic procedure to 'find' the will of God.

5.5 Areas for further development

In the account described above, and especially in the theses that form the basis of a Reformed account of guidance, I singled out a number of concepts that were encountered either in the original evangelical models of guidance and/or in the chapters on Calvin and Edwards. Yet, these concepts were either described in insufficient detail or they need development beyond what we found in Calvin or Edwards. Thus, in order to make our proposed account of guidance theologically more robust and geared to the times, in the next chapter these theses will be fleshed out in conversation with different conversation partners. As theses 1-4 are common ground between the various models and thesis 5 expresses the core

---

[12] The risk of reducing one's responsibility for the own decision-making and the resulting decisions through reference to divine guidance is most pressing in those accounts of the information model that outline a precise method which leads one necessarily to the will of God.

[13] In their recent introduction to dogmatics, Gijsbert van den Brink and Cornelis van der Kooi argue for using the term transformation over the more traditional sanctification. Like them, when I use transformation in what follows this is closely related to the traditional *locus* of sanctification. See Van den Brink and Van der Kooi, *Christian Dogmatics*, 686–87.

[14] It is a typical Reformed move to stress the importance of ordinary life. See e.g. Chapter 13 "God Loveth Adverbs" in Charles Taylor, *Sources of the Self: The Making of the Modern Identity*, 10th ed. (Cambridge: Harvard University Press, 2001), 211–33.

conviction of the transformation model, in what follows we focus on the content of theses 6-13.

Thus, in theses (6) and (7), we returned to the concept of *vocation*. In our chapter on Calvin, we indicated already that the concept of vocation underwent major changes and received a lot of criticism during the last century. In the next chapter, we will therefore need to focus on vocation and ask whether it is still fruitful to use this concept as an important tool. We will analyze and evaluate some recent attempts to reimagine it.

In thesis (8) we mentioned *wisdom* as an important venue of guidance, but we have not answered the questions what this wisdom looks like and whether it is possible to speak in particular about *Christian* wisdom.

Also in thesis (8), the idea of discernment was introduced. We encountered this concept a number of times in chapters 2-4, but we nowhere explicitly discussed its possible meanings and the role it could play in an account of divine guidance.

The notions of on the one hand *transformation* and *character*, and on the other hand *community*, introduced resp. in theses (9-10) and (11), were only hinted at in the previous chapters. In the next chapter, the issues of character transformation, and the formative influence of community will receive more focused attention than could be given to them in previous chapters.

Finally, we referred to the role of the *Holy Spirit* in theses (12) and (13); in the final section of the next chapter we will reflect on this role in the process of guidance as proposed in that chapter.

CHAPTER 6:
Towards a Reformed Account of Divine Guidance

6.1 Introduction
As argued at the end of the previous chapter, for a deeper understanding of how to think of divine guidance from a Reformed perspective, a number of crucial concepts need to be retrieved or developed in a more detailed fashion than we have done thus far. Therefore, in the current chapter we will focus on the concept of vocation (§6.2), on Christian wisdom (§6.3), on discernment (§6.4), on character formation and transformation (§6.5), on the importance of the Christian community in guidance (§6.6), and finally on the role of the Holy Spirit (§6.7). Our aim is to devise a theologically robust account of divine guidance from a Reformed perspective.

Given this aim, in this final chapter, our method will be different from the method of the earlier chapters, especially those on Calvin and Edwards. There, the main aim was to understand *their* thought, whereas in this chapter we develop our own account. In doing so, we will engage the writings of various theologians, not all necessarily Reformed, and without always trying to do full justice to the backgrounds against and contexts in which they developed their thought. The main criterion for engaging with their writings is the way in which they help us formulate or develop the concept in question.

6.2 Vocation as a Key Concept for a Reformed Account of Guidance

> *Thesis 6: The concept of vocation is still one of the most promising means for Reformed theology to express a belief in concrete divine guidance.*
> *Thesis 7: A contemporary account of vocation must take into account the highly complex and dynamic nature of (post)modern societies and can in no way reduce its scope to paid professions.*

6.2.1 Introduction
As stated in the theses above, in this section we are looking for a 'contemporary account of vocation' that takes into consideration 'the highly complex and dynamic nature of modern society.' Such an account of vocation

can serve as the basis of the interpretation of guidance developed in this chapter.

In order to arrive at a fresh articulation of vocation, we will first return to the original Reformed concept of vocation (§6.2.2). We will then discuss the criticisms that were leveraged against this interpretation of vocation (§6.2.3). We then argue why, in light of those criticisms, it is still possible and important to retain the essentials of the original Reformed concept of vocation while taking the critique deeply serious (§6.2.4). In dialogue with a number of recent interpretations of vocation, we present an account of vocation we think theologically fruitful (§6.2.5). Finally, we will return to the relation between vocation and guidance and reflect on the implications of our view of vocation (§6.2.6).

6.2.2 The classic Reformed account of vocation
In our discussion of Calvin's view on guidance, we have seen how the idea of vocation was the primary bridge between universal principles and the particularity of one's individual situation (see §3.3). As such, vocation is the locus in Reformed theology most directly related to contemporary models of guidance. To assess whether the concept of vocation is still useful, we first need a clear picture of the original meanings the concept did and did not have.

Vocation as described by Luther and adopted by many other early Reformers must be understood against the background of the Medieval distinction between the active and the contemplative life, and the relative appreciation given to each. Thus, vocation was meant to deconstruct the dominant two-tiered hierarchy of the spiritual and the mundane life, and to invest the daily life of laity with spiritual significance. It was no longer seen as exclusively related to monastic and clerical roles, but as a descriptor for the different roles of all individual lives.[1]

This also means that originally the word was not restricted to paid professions, but was a more expansive notion.[2] Vocation in Luther was a "function of love,"[3] and as such transformed "all spheres and activities into so many callings."[4] The relationships in which the individual was 'placed' were the sites of vocation, and vocation in this light focused on the interpretation of the given more than on the search for a meaningful

---

[1] Cf. Hahnenberg, *Awakening Vocation*, 4; 12.
[2] Schuurman, *Vocation*, xiii. Cf. O'Donovan, *Finding and Seeking*, 224, who emphasizes that this aspect needs to be stressed in contemporary uses of the concept of vocation.
[3] Gary D. Badcock, *The Way of Life: A Theology of Christian Vocation* (Grand Rapids: Eerdmans, 1998), 38; 123. Cf. Hardy, *The Fabric of This World*, 46 who stresses the importance of the neighbor in Luther's concept of vocation.
[4] Schuurman, *Vocation*, 35.

occupation.[5] As Hahnenberg puts it, "vocation is the call to serve God and one's fellow human beings in and through one's station in life."[6] This interpretation of vocation was quickly adopted among Reformed theologians. So much so that, according to Marshall, not many thorough early discussions of vocation exist because the concept was so generally accepted.[7] Marshall adds that, as a drawback of this general adoption of vocation language in the 16th and 17th centuries, "many people consistently worked with the notion without having a very clear sense of what they were saying nor what it might imply. They often thought that they were reiterating a well-established view when in fact they were saying something quite different. Post-Restoration divines in England assumed that they were repeating the views of a century earlier; but meanwhile, several subtle and not-so-subtle shifts of meaning had taken place."[8]

One important implication of the way vocations were linked to the given is that there was no need to 'search' for a vocation.[9] Wingren even uses this as a complaint against contemporary anguish around 'finding' a proper vocation: "Uncertainty as to whether one is called is often due to regarding oneself as an isolated individual, whose 'call' must come in some inward manner. But in reality we are always bound up in relations with other people; and these relations with our neighbors actually effect our vocation, since these external ties are made by God's hands."[10] Although he detects subtle changes in this regard in the early Reformation period, Marshall affirms that little attention was devoted to discovering one's vocation.[11] Only with Perkins' work on vocation a real tension starts to exist between abiding in a given calling and a kind of voluntarism with regard to calling that was only hinted at in Calvin.[12]

This close conjunction between vocation and the medieval and feudal idea of society as a social organism in which each individual had an ascribed role is at the same time one of the main reasons why the concept has fallen under critique and why there is no easy transition from the

---

5 Schuurman, 117.
6 Hahnenberg, *Awakening Vocation*, 15.
7 Marshall, *A Kind of Life Imposed on Man*, 29–30.
8 Marshall, 30. The same could be said about contemporary uses of vocation and guidance: as our analysis of vocation and guidance in contemporary evangelical books showed these terms are widely established but often without being supported by a clear view of their (theological) background and connotations.
9 Hahnenberg, *Awakening Vocation*, 15.
10 Gustaf Wingren, *Luther on Vocation*, trans. Carl C. Rasmussen (Eugene: Wipf & Stock, 2004), 72.
11 Cf. the differences we saw between Luther and Calvin (esp. §3.3.4).
12 Marshall, *A Kind of Life Imposed on Man*, 40–42. Marshall refers to William Perkins, *A Treatise of the Vocations, or, Callings of Men, with the Sorts and Kindes of Them, and the Right Use Thereof* (Cambridge: John Legat, 1605).

early Reformed concept of vocation to a fruitful contemporary version.[13] In order to attempt such a transition we need first to listen more carefully to the critique.

6.2.3 Vocation as a disputed concept
As said, the concept of vocation has fallen under a shadow of critique since the beginning of the 20th century, and this critique focuses not only on the medieval social background of the concept's original articulation. We will see how it is challenged on the problematic popular use of the concept, on its difficult relation with a number of contemporary socio-cultural phenomena, on its lack of biblical basis, and most fundamentally on a number of underlying theological problems.

The most general objection to the viability of the concept of vocation concerns the connotations the word has in contemporary society. If vocation and paid work can be unproblematically used as synonyms,[14] and if the awkwardness of the combination 'choosing a vocation' is no longer felt,[15] the concept of vocation may well be beyond salvage.[16]

Even more than the connotations of the word, the society in which the concept is invoked has changed. Especially in its Lutheran form the idea of vocation was closely tied to the relatively static medieval society and its hierarchies. Luther's emphasis on 'remaining' in one' s calling was understandable in this organic society, but is "rather naive in the face of our global economic system."[17] Add to this the growth in unemployment;[18] the fact that for many people (especially outside the West) vocational choice is an illusion;[19] processes of alienation, instrumentalization, and dehumanization in contemporary industrial environments, especially in developing countries,[20] and it will be clear that the concept of vocation must be fundamentally rethought to serve any function at all.

---

13 Cf. Badcock, *The Way of Life*, 40, 44.
14 See e.g. how avocation has become serious antonym for vocation, expressing the hobbies one does in addition to one's true vocation. Cf. similar remarks of Schuurman, *Vocation*, 1; W. R. Forrester, *Christian Vocation* (London: Lutterworth Press, 1951), 15–16.
15 Hardy, *The Fabric of This World*, 80.
16 Hahnenberg, *Awakening Vocation*, 23 calls the contemporary use of the word vocation "the great irony of the Protestant doctrine of vocation" because "Luther's attempt to highlight the sacredness of work led to a secularization of the concept of the calling."
17 Hahnenberg, 110. Miroslav Volf, *Work in the Spirit: Toward a Theology of Work* (Eugene: Wipf and Stock, 2001), 108–9 stresses that vocation has difficulty adapting to a society in which the standard is moving towards both diachronic and synchronic plurality of employments.
18 Preece, *Viability of the Vocation Tradition*, xiv. Cf. Louis T. Almen, "Vocation in a Post-Vocational Age," *Word and World* 4, no. 2 (Spring 1984): 136.
19 Jacques Ellul, *The Ethics of Freedom* (Grand Rapids: Eerdmans, 1976), 457–60; Preece, *Viability of the Vocation Tradition*, 193.
20 Hahnenberg, *Awakening Vocation*, 23; Hardy, *The Fabric of This World*, 29.

Besides those 'external' challenges, vocation also became disputed as its exegetical basis was challenged. In Luther, it was primarily based upon his reading of 1 Cor. 7:17-24, but the interpretation of this passage seems to give little occasion to think of work as a vocation. According to Jacques Ellul, "nothing in the Bible allows us to identify *work* with *calling*".[21] Instead, *klesis* in the New Testament primarily refers to the call to faith, and if it is related to specific functions, those are functions of a religious nature.[22] Even among those who are favorable to a form of worldly vocation, many admit that it has no direct exegetical basis, at least not in 1 Cor. 7.[23]

The most fundamental critique of vocation in its Early Reformation form has, however, been based upon underlying theological problems.[24] A major concern is that by using the concept of vocation no justice is done to the post-fall condition of work. Ellul dubbed the term vocation a "superfluous spiritual decoration" for a reality of work that has mainly the function of survival.[25] Given the harsh reality of most work, it is difficult if not impossible to incarnate a vocation concretely in a work environment and it can only be seen as a special kind of grace if such incarnation is possible.[26] Stanley Hauerwas raised similar concerns, stating that attributing spiritual significance to work "risks making it demonic as work then becomes an idolatrous activity."[27] A second major concern is that, in its attachment to the given order, vocation "promotes conservative conformity to the coercive powers of this evil age and selfish constrictions of Christian love."[28] Authentic Christian discipleship would thus not be stimulated, but constrained by the idea of secular vocations. Therefore, vocation is said to encourage the restriction of our commitments to a

---

21 Jacques Ellul, "Work and Calling," *Katallagete* 4, no. 2-3 (Fall-Winter) (1972): 8.
22 Badcock, *The Way of Life*, 106; Ellul, "Work and Calling," 8.
23 So for example Marshall, *A Kind of Life Imposed on Man*, 14. There are also some authors who interpret 1 Cor. 7 in a way that allows for wordly vocations, but those form a small minority. See e.g. Schuurman, *Vocation*, 33; Preece, *Viability of the Vocation Tradition*, 297.
24 Most recent books on vocation include a description of those, either ordered by theologians or by themes. See e.g. Hahnenberg, *Awakening Vocation*, 24–26; Marshall, *A Kind of Life Imposed on Man*, 67–71; Schuurman, *Vocation*, 83–116.
25 Ellul, "Work and Calling," 8.
26 Ellul, 12, 14. The use of incarnatory language is based upon Ellul's article. In general, I prefer to preserve it to refer to the incarnation of Jesus Christ in order to emphasize the exclusivity of that event.
27 Stanley Hauerwas, "Work as Co-Creation: A Critique of a Remarkably Bad Idea," in *Co-Creation and Capitalism: John Paul II's Laborem Exercens*, ed. J.W. Houck and O.F. Williams (Lanham: University Press of America, 1983), 48.
28 Schuurman, *Vocation*, 87.

limited group,[29] and becomes "a cover for egoism, nationalism, racism, and other tribalisms."[30] A third concern is that vocation does not only stimulate a flawed direction of love, but actually supports societal injustice. The injustice supported by vocation comes in at least three different forms: In the first place, the combination of acknowledging the world as fallen into sin and encouraging people to accept the limitations of their callings results in a strong conservative tendency that leaves little room for transformation of the status quo.[31] In the second place, in stressing the need to heed the appropriate borders of one's calling, there is a risk of isolating societal spheres from dimensions that could challenge their inherent injustice.[32] Thirdly, the original formulations of vocation stressed the divine origin of hierarchical orders, and hence potentially sanction hierarchical relations that support injustice.[33]

This concern that various forms of injustice are unchallenged or even upheld by reference to vocation is raised most often and experienced as the most pressing. The core problem is found in an unresolved tension at the heart of Luther's account of vocation, dubbed by Volf its 'dangerous ambiguity':

> In his [Luther's, CvdK] view, spiritual calling comes through the proclamation of the gospel, while external calling comes through one's station (*Stand*). It has proven difficult for Lutheran theology to reconcile the two callings in the life of an individual Christian when a conflict arises between them.[34]

Volf goes on quoting Moltmann to show how in the end vocation came to affirm the status quo:

---

[29] John H. Yoder, *The Priestly Kingdom: Social Ethics as Gospel* (Notre Dame: University of Notre Dame Press, 1984), 138 and esp. 210n9. See also Leo Tolstoy, *On Life and Essays on Religion*, trans. Aylmer Maude, The World's Classics (London: Oxford University Press, 1934), 100–104.
[30] Schuurman, *Vocation*, 90.
[31] See e.g. the incisive questions Barth puts to Luther, *KD III/4*, 645.
[32] Schuurman mentions the way Kuyper's notion of 'sphere sovereignty' was used in South Africa to immunize state policy from critique by the churches, see Schuurman, *Vocation*, 102.
[33] This third aspect is most forcefully brought forward by a number of feminist theologians. See e.g. Dorothee Soelle, *To Work and to Love: A Theology of Creation* (Philadelphia: Fortress Press, 1984), 13–14, 77; Rosemary R. Ruether, *Sexism and God Talk: Toward a Feminist Theology* (Boston: Beacon Press, 1983), 72–82.
[34] Volf, *Work in the Spirit*, 107. Preece names Volf's as the most thorough critique of the Lutheran concept of vocation, Preece, *Viability of the Vocation Tradition*, 295. Against Volf, one could argue that the 'unresolved tension' might also be more positively understood as a healthy form of dialectic.

The history of Lutheranism as well as Lutheran ethics shows that Luther's bold identification of vocation [i.e., *vocatio externa*] with the call [i.e., *vocatio spiritualis*] led again and again to the integration of the call into vocation and vocation into occupation, and thus to the consecration of the *vocational-occupational structure*.[35]

At the heart of all theological critique two central issues seem to be at stake: (1) the discongruence between the first interpretation of *klesis* as the call to salvation and its second interpretation as worldly calling, and (2) the strong, at times even exclusive, protological basis of the concept of vocation, and thus its inherent conservatism.

In the light of all this critique, we may wonder whether there is any reason to try to 're-awaken' the protestant notion of vocation. We will address this crucial question in the next section.

6.2.4 On the value of maintaining the concept of vocation
Given the problems surrounding the notion of vocation, why are some authors trying to recover it, and why do I think it can serve a constitutive function in a Reformed account of guidance? In this section I will argue that there are several reasons for this: the concept (1) expresses divine intentionality in relation to 'ordinary life'; (2) has a strong integrative force, preventing the fragmentation of life; (3) strongly articulates the particularity of the individual person; and (4) has the potential to challenge a number of dominant, dubious patterns in contemporary culture and Christian spirituality.[36]

In the first place, the idea of vocation expresses the belief that behind the seemingly contingent aspects of each life there is some kind of divine intentionality, the same belief that is the presupposition of the idea of divine guidance.[37] Thus, vocation conveys both the "sense of the world being under the control of God and the sense that each life has a purpose in such a world."[38] As such, it also provides people with a sense of dignity

---

35 Jürgen Moltmann, *On Human Dignity: Political Theology and Ethics*, trans. M. Douglas Meeks (London: SCM Press, 1984), 47. Quoted in Volf, *Work in the Spirit*, 107-8.
36 A very pragmatic further argument could be that the notion of vocation is so deeply ingrained in Christian speech that instead of 'theoretically' discarding it we can better think of ways to speak of it in a way that makes sense.
37 Hahnenberg, *Awakening Vocation*, 93.
38 Forrester, *Christian Vocation*, 113. Cf. Hahnenberg, *Awakening Vocation*, xiv: "To speak of call is to acknowledge a caller, to see that God's gracious initiative precedes all of our projects and our plans, that our individual journeys have a goal. Our freedom does not hover supreme over an infinite number of options (the fundamental paradigm of choice). Our freedom stands under and before the transcendent, always being drawn up and out into the source of our being (the basic pattern of call)."

in what could otherwise be experienced as a random and meaningless life.

In the second place, the concept of vocation has the potential to function as a means of integration, resisting the all too common division between faith and daily life. In this sense, it also does justice to the notion of the narrativity of human life brought so forcefully to attention by MacIntyre.[39] In stressing the narrative unity of life, the concept of vocation resists the tendencies to view periods of decision-making as unconnected episodes,[40] and to sever vocation from personal transformation.[41]

In the third place, vocation is one of the concepts in Reformed theology that enables us to do full justice to the particularity of all persons.[42] Alongside generic principles, vocation enables one to express the conviction that God's call meets us in the specificities of our lives, the particular situations we find ourselves in, and the complex combinations of possibilities and limitations provided by our circumstances. As such, the concept of vocation fulfills an important role for which few if any alternative concepts exist, highlighting that God calls us to service "where we are, as we are."[43]

Finally, the concept of vocation has a strong potential to challenge a number of ambiguous patterns both in contemporary culture and contemporary Christian spirituality. Two of the more important (and closely related) of those patterns are individualism and an overemphasis on choice. Vocation, with its emphasis on love and service, its attention for the concrete neighbor, and its simultaneous embeddedness in a number of different narratives (personal, communal, but also the personal narratives of those with whom the individual is involved in relationships) challenges the exclusive focus on the individual and his or her self-actualization. While emphasizing particularity, the notion of vocation resists the isolation of the individual, the impression of a solitary quest, and the focus on detached subjects.[44] Furthermore, vocation terminology offers a "constructive alternative to our contemporary cultural default, namely,

---

39 MacIntyre, *After Virtue*, 239. For the link between MacIntyre and vocation, see also Hahnenberg, *Awakening Vocation*, 165; Eleonora D. Hof, *Reimagining Mission in the Postcolonial Condition: A Theology of Vulnerability and Vocation at the Margins* (Zoetermeer: Boekencentrum Academic, 2016), 250.
40 Cf. MacIntyre's critique of atomized lives, *After Virtue*, 237–38. Cf. Schuurman, *Vocation*, xiv, who sees vocation as a powerful concept against the fragmentation of life.
41 Hahnenberg, *Awakening Vocation*, xiii.
42 Karl Barth considered this as the greatest contribution of the concept and one of his main reasons for upholding a concept of vocation while being aware of its abuses and shortcomings; see Barth, *Kirchliche Dogmatik III/4*, 692.
43 Hahnenberg, *Awakening Vocation*, 125.
44 Hahnenberg, 159–61.

choice."⁴⁵ Vocation conveys the sense of coherence and consistency to our commitments that choice as the primary lens of framing reality and spirituality lacks.⁴⁶

As argued, there are good reasons for trying to formulate a theological account of vocation for the 21st century. In doing so, however, we should take the profound criticism described in the previous section fully serious. Gordon Preece has forcefully articulated the challenge for such a contemporary account of vocation:

> If the Reformed concept of vocation is to retain validity and relevance for working life today it will need reforming itself … in the light of Volf's critique and alternative [of replacing vocation with pneumatology and a focus on gifts, CvdK] in order to: demonstrate its biblical credentials; shed itself of the remnants of immutability, singularity and one-sided protological and conservative emphases; distinguish itself from post-sixteenth century vocational secularization; provide resources to attack alienation from work in industrialized or 'post-industrialized' societies; and engage the rising role mobility of modern information societies.⁴⁷

We cannot, as Preece does in his book, take up this full challenge, but as part of a Reformed approach to guidance, in the next section I will sketch a number of key features of what I think is vital to a contemporary account of vocation.

6.2.5 *Essentials of a concept of vocation*

Back in 1996, Paul Marshall lamented the strange situation in which the idea of vocation received more attention from "sociologists, economic historians, and political theorists (…) than of theologians *per se*."⁴⁸ Since then, however, a number of theologians have written extensive accounts of vocation, most notably Gordon Preece (1998), Douglas Schuurman

---

45 Hahnenberg, xii (emphasis in original).
46 Cf. Hahnenberg, xii. Hahnenberg's account is strongly influenced by Robert Wuthnow's analysis of American spiritual life, see Robert Wuthnow, *After Heaven: Spirituality in America since the 1950s* (Berkeley: University of California Press, 1998).
47 Preece, *Viability of the Vocation Tradition*, 4–5. Cf. identical challenges formulated by Hahnenberg vis-à-vis protestant accounts of vocation, *Awakening Vocation*, 233–34: "In our increasingly instrumentalized, commodified, and militarized world – a world so profoundly split between the rich and the poor – can such a conception of vocation continue? Is such a view of calling too quick to confirm one's place in the world, in society, in a certain occupation or line of work? Is it capable of confronting our fallen condition, our unjust economic structures, our comfort in conforming to a dehumanizing system?" See also p. 45.
48 Marshall, *A Kind of Life Imposed on Man*, 3.

(2004), and Edward Hahnenberg (2010).[49] In this section, we will interact with them and a number of other authors to detect essential elements of a contemporary account of vocation.

Following Oliver O'Donovan, we think vocation can be defined as "the ensemble of worldly relations and functions through which we are given, *in particular*, to serve God and realize our agency."[50] O'Donovan's concise definition contains a number of crucial elements. It makes immediately clear that the term vocation should not be narrowed to professional careers. Instead, it challenges an overemphasis on paid work in precisely the same way as Luther's account of vocation challenged the monastic life: as a severe neglect of other and equally important parts of the 'ensemble.' Likewise, O'Donovan's formulation precludes any interpretation of vocation in which it is possible to have or not to have 'a vocation,' or the tendency to think in terms of before and after the vocation.[51] As O'Donovan himself asserts, vocation refers primarily not to the *event* of the calling but to its *object*.[52] Not only does vocation as such have no starting point, there is also no end to vocation as there would be with retirement when vocation and profession did coincide.[53]

Furthermore, O'Donovan's definition makes clear that one is always primarily called to serve God, and only in a derivative sense to do so in particular ways, and the two can never be played off against one another.[54]

---

49 See §1.2.4 for brief discussions of each of these books.
50 O'Donovan, *Finding and Seeking*, 224 (emphasis in original). Cf. Douglas J. Schuurman, "To Follow Christ, to Live in the World: Calling in a Protestant Key," in *Calling in Today's World: Voices from Eight Faith Perspectives*, ed. Kathleen A. Cahalan and Douglas J. Schuurman (Grand Rapids: Eerdmans, 2016), 58, who speaks about vocation in terms of "the complex and distinctive social matrix of an individual's life."
51 Hof, *Reimagining Mission*, 270; Schuurman, *Vocation*, xi.
52 O'Donovan, *Finding and Seeking*, 224.
53 Cf. O'Donovan, 225. As we have seen, in the evangelical literature the biblical stories of extraordinary callings that mark a break between a 'before' and an 'after' play an important role. However, we think most of these are precisely not meant to be paradigmatic, not designed to encourage us to see our experiences as somehow analogous. The exact opposite might be more true. The absence of both starting point and end of vocation is emphasized by an intriguing recent book, Cahalan and Miller-McLemore, *Calling All Years Good*. In it, the authors approach vocaction from a 'lifespan perspective.' One of the conclusions is that "engaging vocation across the span of our lives demands a more nuanced theology than previous interpretations of calling offered in the Christian tradition, especially when we consider it outside the framework of speech, rationality, and choice, as with a newborn or a person with dementia" (2).
54 Barth deeply felt the problematic tension between the two aspects of vocation and ensured the primacy of God's *klesis* by distinguishing between *Beruf* and *Berufung*. For all the richness of his resulting account of vocation, following Hahnenberg, *Awakening Vocation*, 123, we believe that Barth finally leaves us with "an unresolved tension between the human vocation (Beruf) and the divine summons (Berufung)." For a helpful overview of Barth's account in KD III/4 and IV/2 see Rhys Kuzmič, "Beruf Und Berufung in Karl Barth's Church Dogmatics: Towards a Subversive Klesiology," *International Journal of Systematic Theology* 7, no. 3 (2005): 262–78.

The primacy of discipleship means that an account of vocation and guidance cannot do without a proper account of (trans)formation.

This approach to vocation does also take seriously the fact that, to a much greater extent than as modern (Western) 'autonomous' people we want to acknowledge, our lives are given.[55] From our birth onwards we inhabit what Bonhoeffer called 'places of responsibility,'[56] starting points from which basic roles and obligations are given to us.[57] Especially Barth has offered a powerful account of the 'given' in his description of *Beruf*. He presents the various given dimensions of life as so many limitations (*Beschränkungen*) on the ways our vocation takes shape. Although more could be said about his precise interpretation of all those areas, his insights that (1) life-stage (*Lebensalter*), (2) special historical situation (*besonderer geschichtlicher Standort*), (3) personal aptitude (*persönlicher Tüchtigkeit*), and (4) sphere of operation (*Wirkungskreis*) present each individual with both limitations and opportunities are realistic yet profound.[58] While criticizing Luther's concept of orders, Barth still takes the 'given' aspects of life deeply serious.

Two further benefits flow forth from Barth's description of the 'limitations' through which we are given our particularity. First, this way of conceiving the given enables us to do more justice to the inherent dynamics of the 'given,' one of the main problems of the original Lutheran interpretation. Second, although the word 'limitation' may have mainly negative connotations to the modern ear, Barth presents them at least in part as blessings. Through the limitations given to each of us, we are invited to accept our places of responsibility and thus 'to serve God and realize our agency.'[59]

---

55 Cf. Hof, *Reimagining Mission*, 255–56. Referring to MacIntyre, she states that "[h]is viewpoint is particularly valuable in a cultural climate in which the choices of a disembodied self are stressed to the extent that every individual is solely responsible for crafting her/his own future and happiness."

56 Bonhoeffer discusses vocation (*Beruf*) under the heading 'The Place of Responsibility', see DBWE 6:289.

57 MacIntyre, *After Virtue*, 205: "I inherit from the past of my family, my city, my tribe, my nation, a variety of debts, inheritances, rightful expectations and obligations. These constitute the given(s) of my life, my moral starting point. This is in part what gives my life its own moral particularity." Schuurman also stresses the high level of givens even in the most free kind of modern life, Schuurman, *Vocation*, 120.

58 Preece even calls Barth "the author of the best 20th century theology of vocation," Preece, *Viability of the Vocation Tradition*, 19.

59 The sense of invitation and the positive acceptation of the given are clearly present in O'Donovan's definition, in particular in his wording "through which we are *given* to serve God..." (emphasis CvdK).

An important question we still need to answer is whether this approach to vocation has a biblical basis. We agree with the critics that there is no direct scriptural basis in 1 Cor. 7 for thinking about particular callings in the way Luther and later Reformers suggested.[60] Yet, with Schuurman we hold that there are biblical patterns that present elements of what we have come to designate as vocation.[61] Throughout both the Old Testament and the New, people are called to special places of responsibility and in numerous places attention is given to giftedness. Besides these extraordinary callings, the "comprehensive character of the covenant relationship" as presented especially in the Torah warrants seeing the more mundane roles and tasks as instilled with a sense of sacred duty. This comprehensive Old Testament pattern is reiterated in the New Testament, especially in the housetables, where the roles mentioned are clearly not exclusively intra-ecclesial roles. In Schuurman's words, "the call to love and serve the Lord, made active in a person's life, transforms all spheres and activities into so many callings."[62] Finally, restricting vocation to church functions is at odds with the expansive notion of the Kingdom presented in the New Testament. The comprehensiveness of the notion of the Kingdom allows for an account of vocation that extends beyond the church.

Addressing the critique described before exclusively through conceptual clarifications will, however, prove insufficient. We also need to formulate a number of ongoing challenges that have more to do with the practical embodiment of vocation than with its theoretical formulation.[63]

A first demand for living out one's vocation is the ongoing discernment needed to find a balance between accepting the given by taking up one's roles within it and attempts to transform the given because of the injustice contained in it. Vocation lived out in the mixed reality of goodness and fallenness can never be exclusively a source of comfort or of challenge, but needs elements of both.[64] As Preece indicated for a theol-

---

60 Badcock takes an intermediary position by affirming that callings are only to ministerial roles, thus acknowledging the Biblical basis for particular vocations but restricting it to church offices and activities. See esp. Badcock, *The Way of Life*, 106.
61 See Schuurman, *Vocation*, 29–37.
62 Schuurman, 35. Although Schuurman contends that in the New Testament the church is the primary domain of vocation, he is right in stating that it is not the exclusive domain.
63 As we have seen, Ellul summarized his critique of the strong ties between vocation and professional career with the claim that it was not 'incarnatable' in a modern world. We choose to use the verb 'embodiment' instead, as we think the use of the word 'incarnation' in contemporary theology draws away attention from the uniqueness of Christ's incarnation. Cf. Van den Brink and Van der Kooi, *Christian Dogmatics*, 576.
64 Cf. Hahnenberg, *Awakening Vocation*, xviii, who states that we need "a language of call that speaks to each of us and challenges all of us." Hahnenberg later repeats that comfort and challenge need to go intertwined, 195.

ogy of work, an account of vocation "must not be merely descriptive and neutral but liberating and transformative."[65]

In light of the critique discussed in §6.2.3, two main challenges need to be raised continually with respect to the transformative aspect of vocation. The first is the challenge to criticize unjust hierarchies, those hierarchies to which the original concept of vocation was too closely bound.[66] Thus, those elements of vocation that criticize hierarchies based upon gender, race, or class must be emphasized. They include "the ground vocation establishes for resisting and reforming authority," its "positive vision of domestic roles and general revaluation of mundane roles and relations," and its "affirmation of authority as service."[67] The second and closely related challenge for faithfully embodying vocation is the presence of 'the poor.'[68] Embodying vocation should be done with a sense that imbalances of wealth and power should be moving "towards symmetry and mutuality."[69] A deep desire to be an instrument of this move towards justice should be coupled with the awareness that it is often through the experience of severe 'need' that vocations are discerned.[70]

Those practical challenges could be summarized positively in Badcock's condition that the values and patterns "of the Kingdom must thus inform and even determine the shape of Christian vocation."[71]

6.2.6 Implications for guidance

In this section, we investigated the critique leveraged against the idea of vocation, as well as the reasons why we think it important to maintain the concept, and we provided an account of vocation and the accompanying practical challenges which we think does justice to the critique while at the same time retaining its strengths. Now, we need to come back to our

---

65 Preece, *Viability of the Vocation Tradition*, 189.
66 However, in support of the original concept, we think Schuurman is right in pointing out that at its heart the concept of vocation opposes the dualisms sustaining sexist hierarchies, like sacred/secular, public/private and mind/body in its insistence that all people have a vocation and that this vocation includes all worthwhile tasks. See Schuurman, *Vocation*, 109.
67 See for a more elaborate discussion of those Schuurman, *Vocation*, 111-116 and in a more recent version Schuurman, "To Follow Christ," 76–79.
68 As Hahnenberg rightly states, "to ignore this fact [the massive and unjust suffering of the poor, CvdK] in our treatment of vocation would be to ignore the world within which Christian discernment occurs," Hahnenberg, *Awakening Vocation*, 194. See also Hof, *Reimagining Mission*, 281–88.
69 Schuurman, *Vocation*, 115.
70 Cf. the oft-quoted maxim of Buechner: "The place God calls you to is the place where your deep gladness and the world's deep hunger meet." Frederick Buechner, *Listening to Your Life: Daily Meditations with Frederick Buechner* (New York: Harper Collins, 1992), 95.
71 Badcock, *The Way of Life*, 52.

overall aims and ask what the implications of this account of vocation are for our view on divine guidance.

In the previous chapter (esp. §5.4) we sketched the basics of a Reformed account of guidance and the pitfalls encountered in some evangelical models that should be avoided. The concept of vocation as presented here deepens the previous account in a number of ways. Most importantly, it stresses the narrative unity of life and functions as a strong parapet against different kinds of isolation that threaten contemporary accounts of guidance: isolation of the individual from the web of relationships he or she is already involved in; isolation of particular areas of life (mainly work or church) as the crucial area at the neglect of other dimensions of life; isolation of specific decisions as if they are disengaged and objectifiable events. All these isolating tendencies are counteracted by a conscientious embodiment of vocation.

Besides, vocation as described here enables one to take the given dimensions of life fully seriously without precluding that those 'givens' might often be in acute need of transformation themselves. Furthermore, with the categories Barth used to describe the 'limitations' given to each individual, he also provided grounds for "fallible yet redeemable choices"[72] that do justice to the 'trial and error' often involved in discerning one's vocation and that take fully into account that our knowledge and discernment are provisional and incomplete.

Finally, congruent with our preliminary conclusion that a Reformed account of guidance should take its point of departure in the model of guidance through transformation, vocation as presented here does not focus on moments of choice or on the event or process that leads to vocation, but on vocation as an ensemble that is always already present. As such, vocation does not normally have a clearly delineated 'before' and 'after' but asks for a continual reevaluation of actual engagements and a reordering of priorities. For this ongoing task, the virtue of (practical) wisdom is indispensable. Therefore, it will be treated in the next section.

6.3 Wisdom as an integral part of guidance

Thesis 8: A Reformed approach to divine guidance requires robust notions of Christian wisdom and discernment that on the one hand indicate the particularity of Christian decision-making and on the other hand leave the full freedom and responsibility for the chosen path with the individual.

---

72 Preece, *Viability of the Vocation Tradition*, 176.

6.3.1 Introduction
In chapter 5, I argued that interpreting guidance in terms of transformation is most in line with Reformed convictions as encountered in Calvin and Edwards. In this model of guidance-through-transformation, often labeled the 'wisdom view', the concept of wisdom plays a crucial role.[73] Yet, the idea of wisdom itself, as well as the distinctive nature of *Christian* wisdom, has thus far received insufficient attention. Given its central place in the proposed model of guidance, and its indispensability for embodying vocation, a more elaborate account of wisdom must be developed. We will proceed in the following way. We will first briefly return to Friesen's account of wisdom and guidance in order to evaluate his stance on the nature of wisdom and see where his account is lacking (6.3.2).[74] We then turn to the concept of *phronesis* or *prudentia*, and we will show how and why this concept deepens our understanding of guidance (6.3.3). With this groundwork laid, we will ask after the specific nature of *Christian* wisdom because for an account of divine guidance a general notion of wisdom will prove to be insufficient (6.3.4). Following this depiction of Christian wisdom, we will evaluate how Samuel Wells and Kevin Vanhoozer flesh out such a notion of wisdom in their theo-dramatic accounts of the Christian life and Christian ethics (6.3.5). In the concluding section we will reflect on the relation between wisdom and divine guidance (6.3.6).

Two further comments on our method are needed here: (1) The transition from 6.3.3 to 6.3.4 shows a move 'from the general to the special.' Traditionally, this move is met with great suspicion, especially in forms of theology influenced by Karl Barth. In explanation, I would like to point to the following considerations. First, I am not opting for this ordering of the material in a naive way, as if Christian wisdom is just a special instance of wisdom at large, involving only some minor qualifications. As will become clear in section 6.3.4, I distinguish both continuities and discontinuities between wisdom at large ('pagan' wisdom) and Christian wisdom. Second, many classical Reformed confessions typically show a similar movement; the Belgic confession, for example, starts with some fairly general theistic considerations in order to then move on, in the second part of article 2 and in article 3, to a more specific Christian view of

---
73 See §2.6.7 for the reason why I think it more insightful to discuss the model, despite the prominent role played by the notion of wisdom, under the overarching label of transformation.
74 Friesen's book is taken as our point of departure because, among the authors advocating guidance through transformation, he devotes most explicit attention to the concept of wisdom. If his account of wisdom proves to be conceptually thin, this will most likely apply to the other accounts as well.

God. Third, the order followed in this chapter serves a pragmatic function: By starting with *phronesis* the connections with the topic of guidance can be made clear from the start; moreover, this order enables us to connect our search to currents in theological ethics.[75] As to the notion of wisdom, the fact that according to mainstream biblical scholarship considerable parts of the Old Testament wisdom literature stem from other parts of the Ancient Near East (esp. Egypt), may make us pause here. (2) In the account of Christian wisdom below, I will not focus exclusively on explicitly Reformed thinkers (though the two authors singled out for special discussion in section 6.3.5 are, in any case from a material point of view, Reformed in their thinking). What makes the view of Christian wisdom proposed and elaborated here Reformed—that is, not exclusively Reformed but still typically Reformed—I would argue, is its explicit embeddedness in and drawing on the history of salvation.

6.3.2 'Wisdom' in Friesen's wisdom view of guidance

As discussed in §2.3.3, Garry Friesen was at the start of a discussion among evangelicals on the nature of divine guidance with the publication of his *Decision Making and the Will of God* (1980). In this book, he proposed a 'wisdom view' of guidance as an alternative to the 'traditional view.' Friesen rejected the existence of an 'individual will' of God and presented his alternative: through his commandments, God has delineated the sphere of proper Christian behavior. Within that sphere, believers have both freedom and responsibility to make their own choices. This responsibility, however, presupposes some kind of accountability, and accountability presupposes a basis on which one can be held accountable. According to Friesen, *wisdom* functions as "the single controlling factor" when it comes to this accountability.[76]

Friesen then proceeds to show how "the pursuit of wisdom in decision making permeates the entire Bible."[77] He appeals to the examples of Old Testament leaders, the biblical wisdom literature, the life of Jesus, the decisions taken by the church in Acts, and the teaching of the epistles.[78]

---

75 That is, in our account we *use* elements of the ancient tradition but do not build our account on them. The distinction between using and building upon is taken from Hauerwas and Pinches, *Christians among the Virtues*, 68, who clarify their choice for *using* the ancient virtue tradition: "To use requires that one apply a thing within a framework significantly other than the one in which it originally appears, which is precisely what Christianity requires insofar as it refounds human life on the life, death, and resurrection of Jesus Christ, God made flesh."

76 Friesen and Maxson, *Decision Making*, 2004, 174.

77 Friesen and Maxson, 160.

78 See esp. chapters 10 and 11 of Friesen and Maxson, *Decision Making*, 2004.

As convincing as Friesen's arguments from the biblical material may be, given the importance of wisdom in his approach to guidance it is strange that he makes only a few minor comments on the nature of such wisdom. Friesen approves of J.I. Packer's definition of wisdom as "the power to see, and the inclination to choose, the best and highest goal, together with the surest means of attaining it,"[79] and of A.W. Tozer's shorter version of wisdom as "sanctified common sense,"[80] without further commenting on them. Complementing these definitions, Friesen suggests that 'spiritual usefulness' should be the goal of wisdom; that our own happiness is an important ingredient; and that wisdom is often "spiritually opportunistic."[81] Finally, he describes how wisdom is acquired through prayer, the reading of Scripture, inspection of the circumstances, counselors, and life experience. Wisdom is not given in a single instant, but "progressively as a component of spiritual growth."[82]

This brief return to Friesen shows that wisdom plays a crucial role in his account of divine guidance, yet also that his description of wisdom is substantially too thin to bear this weight. Therefore, in what follows we will elaborate on the nature and role of wisdom. We start our inquiry with an investigation of the ancient concept of *phronesis* or *prudentia*.

6.3.3 Phronesis or prudence as starting point

With the revival of virtue ethics in both philosophy and theology, a renewed attention has emerged for the role of (practical) wisdom among the virtues. In classical and medieval philosophy, this type of wisdom was discussed under the name *phronesis* (Greek) or *prudentia* (Latin).[83] What is at stake is a kind of wisdom that is distinct from *sophia* or *theoria*, speculative knowledge. As we are discussing wisdom in the context of decision-making and guidance, this type of wisdom oriented on praxis seems most appropriate for our investigations, and it *a priori* excludes the primarily intellectual connotations wisdom might have in common usage.[84]

---

79 Friesen and Maxson, 175, referring to J.I. Packer, Knowing God, 80.
80 Friesen and Maxson, 175, quoting A.W. Tozer, "How the Lord Leads," *Alliance Weekly*, January 2, 1957.
81 Friesen and Maxson, 175, 178, 179. With 'spiritually opportunistic', Friesen means that wisdom makes the most of "specific opportunities that come up from time to time."
82 Friesen and Maxson, 181.
83 E.g., various authors have pointed to Aquinas's use of *prudentia*, which is mainly an extended discussion of Aristotle's interpretation of *phronesis*; Aquinas is clearly convinced that he is discussing exactly the same phenomenon. See e.g. Linda Trinkaus Zagzebski, *Virtues of the Mind: An Inquiry into the Nature of Virtue and the Ethical Foundations of Knowledge* (New York: Cambridge University Press, 1996), 212.
84 Therefore, when I refer to wisdom in what follows what I mean is practical wisdom: *phronesis* or prudence. For convenience sake I decided to refer to those simply as wisdom.

The primary function of practical wisdom in ancient philosophy is to mediate between universals and the particularity of a given situation.[85] As such, it moves in exactly the same domain as guidance. The particulars of our lives confront us with situations in which "good judgment cannot always be reduced to the following of a decision procedure specifiable in advance of the situation in which action occurs."[86] Hence, an instrument is needed that helps us form good judgments in those situations nonetheless. Wisdom is the concept used to fill this gap.

As Linda Zagzebski has argued, in order to fulfill this bridging role, for both Aristotle and Aquinas wisdom functioned as a higher-order virtue.[87] Zagzebski presents three arguments for the necessity of a virtue that is able to somehow 'govern' the moral and intellectual virtues: First, in cases where virtue can be considered as a mean, wisdom is needed to resolve what is the mean between extremes.[88] Second, in each situation different features are relevant for different virtues, and therefore one must be able to mediate between and among the various virtues. Only wisdom can serve this function.[89] Finally, wisdom is needed because in most cases the weighing of evidence does not result in a decisive answer either in relation to a course of action or a belief; and thus in the end good and wise judgment needs to be exercised.[90]

Charles Allen has defined the higher-order virtue of prudence as the "historically implicated, communally nurtured ability to make good sense of relatively singular contexts in ways appropriate to their relative

---

85 Cf. David F. Ford, *Christian Wisdom: Desiring God and Learning in Love* (Cambridge: Cambridge University Press, 2007), 2: "Any wisdom needs to take seriously the desire both for some sense of overall meaning and connectedness and also for guidance in specific situations."
86 Zagzebski, *Virtues of the Mind*, 220. Cf. Kevin J. Vanhoozer, *The Drama of Doctrine: A Canonical Linguistic Approach to Christian Doctrine* (Louisville: Westminster John Knox Press, 2005), 325, who describes the task of practical wisdom as "forming judgments about what to do in situations for which there is no guaranteed theory, method, or technique."
87 Zagzebski, *Virtues of the Mind*, 229. See for a brief summary of her argument James S. Spiegel, "Wisdom," in *Being Good: Christian Virtues for Everyday Life*, ed. Michael W. Austin and R. Douglas Geivett (Grand Rapids: Eerdmans, 2012), 55–56.
88 Zagzebski, *Virtues of the Mind*, 221. The idea of virtues being a mean between an extreme of excess and an extreme of deficiency is a central Aristotelian insight. For Zagzebski, this does not apply to all virtues, but when it does, the need for wisdom arises: "It takes *phronesis* to know *how persevering* one should be to be persevering, *how careful* one should be to be careful, *how self-sufficient* one should be to be autonomous, and so on" (emphasis in original).
89 Zagzebski, 221–24. Zagzebski sketches a situation in which "there are salient features of the situation that pertain both to courage and to humility" (222). The decision whether in this particular situation courage or humility should prevail is a decision only wisdom is able to reach.
90 Zagzebski, 224–26.

singularity."[91] His definition presents us with a number of key elements and functions of wisdom. First of all, wisdom is presented as a crucial virtue for navigating the universal and the particular, where questions about the good life and the right course of action become questions about the good life *for me* and the right course of action *in this situation,* the same area in which questions about divine guidance are experienced.[92] In his elaboration, Allen makes clear that in these situations universal principles are necessary but insufficient.[93] As an instrument for navigating the universal and the particular, wisdom consists of two aspects: a cognitive and a deciding aspect.[94]

According to Allen, such wisdom is communally nurtured.[95] Aristotle's *phronesis* and Aquinas's *prudentia* are deeply communal virtues, both with regard to the way they are acquired and to the way in which they operate.[96] Without some kind of community, gaining and exercising wisdom is almost impossible.[97] The community of which one is a member offers the examples, practices, and sources from which wisdom can be learned, while at the same time it offers resources for accountability and self-criticism.[98]

---

91 Charles W. Allen, "The Primacy of 'Phronesis': A Proposal for Avoiding Frustrating Tendencies in Our Conceptions of Rationality," *The Journal of Religion* 69, no. 3 (1989): 363.
92 Cf. the description of such situations in §1.1.2.
93 Allen, "Primacy of Phronesis," 364: "Phronetic sense-making presupposes that particulars in their full particularity are capable of making sense in a way that universals cannot fully anticipate and that furthermore affects the way in which universals are to be actualized in that instance."
94 Cf. Josef Pieper, *The Four Cardinal Virtues: Prudence, Justice, Fortitude, Temperance* (New York: Pantheon Books, 1954), 11–12. Aquinas, in ST II-II.47.8, mentions three acts of prudence: to take counsel, to judge of what one has discovered, and to command ("applying to action the things counselled and judged").
95 In §6.6 a more extended evaluation of the connection between guidance and community will be provided. Here, we briefly mention a few connections between wisdom and community that will be more fully developed in the section on community.
96 Aristotle, NE VI.8.1142a12-21 for example mentions for the following aspects: wisdom is learned by imitation, depends upon the presence of people with wisdom in the community, and (hence) is not found in the young. The version used is Aristotle, *The Nicomachean Ethics*, trans. David Ross, J.L. Ackrill, and J.O. Urmson, Oxford World's Classics (Oxford: Oxford University Press, 1998).
97 In their account of prudence, Hauerwas and Pinches argue for the importance of a specific kind of community: "a cross-generational community in which a tradition of practices is passed on, sustained, and modified." See Stanley Hauerwas and Charles R. Pinches, *Christians Among The Virtues: Theological Conversations with Ancient and Modern Ethics* (Notre Dame: University of Notre Dame Press, 2015), 96.
98 Allen, "Primacy of Phronesis," 364.

In addition, an important aspect of wisdom is that it has the nature of a virtue, a learned capacity.[99] From the perspective of wisdom as virtue, decision-making cannot be reduced to the application of a procedure. In order to become prudent, one has to develop "habits of attitude and feeling" through which one is enabled to make good judgments in singular situations.[100] As such, wisdom has everything to do with transformation (§6.5).[101]

Two final components of Allen's definition are important from the perspective of guidance: his insistence that wisdom is 'historically implicated' and his insight that wisdom deals with situations that are *'relatively singular.'* The *historical boundedness* points to the fact that *phronesis*, more than *sophia*, is always practically engaged with a specific spatial and temporal situation, and thus in a sense limited. It often has to proceed with "unacknowledged conditions and unintended consequences" while at the same time it must always be aware of "the various forms of self-deception" prevalent in a specific time and culture.[102] The *relative singularity* of the situations that call for wisdom points to the double fact that moments of decision are always related to and informed by other contexts (hence *relative* singularity) while at the same time they contain elements that provide them with a definite singularity.[103] As a result of this combination, making a wise decision will always be a somewhat unsettling experience, especially as those situations that are 'relatively singular' are often also "relatively transient."[104] One important implication of both the practical engagement and the relative singularity of situations that call for wisdom is the uncertainty about its result: "In the decisions of prudence, which by the very nature of prudence are concerned with things concrete, contingent, future … there cannot be that certainty

---

99 We follow Zagzebski's fuller definition of a virtue as a "a deep and enduring acquired excellence of a person, involving a characteristic motivation to produce a certain desired end and reliable success in bringing about that end," Zagzebski, *Virtues of the Mind*, 137. Cf. Rosalind Hursthouse and Glen Pettigrove, "Virtue Ethics," ed. Edward N. Zalta, *The Stanford Encyclopedia of Philosophy* (Metaphysics Research Lab, Stanford University, Winter 2016), https://plato.stanford.edu/archives/win2016/entries/ethics-virtue/: "A virtue is an excellent trait of character. It is a disposition, well entrenched in its possessor—something that, as we say, goes all the way down, unlike a habit such as being a tea-drinker—to notice, expect, value, feel, desire, choose, act, and react in certain characteristic ways."
100 Cf. Zagzebski, *Virtues of the Mind*, 226.
101 This works in both ways, as each wise decision is result of the virtue, but also reinforces it.
102 Allen, "Primacy of Phronesis," 364–65.
103 Cf. Allen, 365–66.
104 Charles W. Allen, "The Recovery of Phronesis: Its Implications for the Role of Practical Reason in Theology" (PhD diss., University of Chicago, 1987), 366, http://www.therevdrcharleswallen.com/page2.html.

which is possible in a theoretical conclusion."¹⁰⁵ In the context of guidance this acknowledgment means that certainty should not be expected where it cannot exist, and also that one should not be deceived by false certainties.¹⁰⁶

6.3.4 The distinctive nature of Christian wisdom

Since wisdom as presented above has its background in ancient philosophy, the question how *Christian* wisdom differs from this account comes up quite naturally. Given that Paul contrasts the wisdom of God and the wisdom of the world in 1 Corinthians, this question becomes even more pressing: Can the above account be helpful at all? As we indicated already in §6.3.1, however, there are both continuities and discontinuities between these accounts of wisdom. The Bible not only contains Paul's sharply contrasting notions of God's wisdom vis-à-vis the 'wisdom of the world', but also includes many wise proverbs that had a background in the ancient Middle East.

In line with Aquinas' adoption of the general structure of Aristotle's account of *phronesis*, we think the differences between 'pagan' and Christian wisdom are of a material, not a formal nature: the operation of practical wisdom as described does not change.¹⁰⁷ What makes Christian wisdom different is that it works within another view of (ultimate) reality, has distinct priorities, is influenced by other sources, and pays attention to different aspects of the relevant situation.¹⁰⁸ In the words of David Ford:

> Above all, theology desires a wisdom that is true to God and God's desires; that lives in the midst of life while hoping in God's future; that takes as its main guide the scriptures interpreted in the Spirit and in community

---

105 Cf. Pieper, *Cardinal Virtues*, 18, who refers to Aquinas' statement in ST II-II.47.9: "Non potest certitudo prudentiae tanta esse quod omnio solicitudo tollatur."
106 Pieper, *Cardinal Virtues*, 18.
107 For example, the four ingredients listed by David Ford (knowledge, understanding, good judgment, and far-sighted decision-making) are congruent with the account of wisdom of the previous section. See Ford, *Christian Wisdom*, 1.
108 Pieper also argues that what makes prudence into *Christian* prudence is not a radically different conception of prudence itself, but "the throwing open of this [the natural, CvdK] realm and ... the inclusion of new and invisible realities within the determinants of our decisions," Pieper, *Four Cardinal Virtues*, 37. See also James M. Gustafson, "Moral Discernment in the Christian Life," in *Norm and Context in Christian Ethics*, ed. Gene H. Outka and Paul Ramsey (London: SCM Press, 1969), 17–36. Gustafson, who considers discernment and wisdom as synonyms, emphasizes that "no special affective capacities, logic, or rational clarity can be claimed by Christians," (26) but that their discernment works from a different perspective, including a different self-understanding, interpretation of the world, and set of values and preferences (28-30).

with Christians and with others who seek wisdom; and that seeks to ring true to the great cries that arise in scripture and in life.[109]

As such, there is much that is distinctive of *Christian* wisdom.[110] The most basic distinctive of Christian wisdom is its radically different framework, characterized first and foremost by God's revelation in Christ. No Christian wisdom is thinkable apart from the message, life, death, and resurrection of Christ, who *is* the wisdom of God (1 Cor. 1:30).[111] As such, the wisdom learned from Christ is cruciform wisdom, deeply involved with the pain of the world and of other human beings.[112] As cruciform wisdom, it may lead to choices that are indeed foolish in the eyes of the 'world'.

This wisdom does not only participate in fallen creation, but also in its "reordering in Christ through the Spirit."[113] Through that reordering, wisdom is involved in a reality that is opened to the eschatological horizon. Hence, Christian wisdom works with a fundamentally different teleology but is also influenced by eschatological hope.[114]

Operating within a Christian framework and informed by Scripture, Christian wisdom operates with its own set of priorities, which could be summarized as the priorities of the Kingdom Jesus proclaimed and established. In order to become wise, one's desires and priorities are in need of purification and transformation in line with this Kingdom.[115] What does this mean on a practical level? First, there will always be *a close connection between wisdom and love*. One of the principal determinants for the choices wisdom makes is what, in a given situation, is the most loving way to proceed.[116] Second, it means that wisdom is directed to a specific set of goods: "the *salus* of the individual, the *shalom* of the community, the glorification of the *shema*."[117] Beyond these fundamental priorities of

---

109 Ford, *Christian Wisdom*, 50.
110 Cf. Daniel J. Treier, *Virtue and the Voice of God: Toward Theology as Wisdom* (Grand Rapids: Eerdmans, 2006), 31.
111 Cf. Treier, 65; Ford, *Christian Wisdom*, 153.
112 Treier, *Virtue and the Voice of God*, 48. Christian wisdom could be described as traumatized wisdom, contrasted with the "untraumatized wisdom" displayed by the friends of Job; Ford, *Christian Wisdom*, 102.
113 Vanhoozer, *The Drama of Doctrine*, 255.
114 Treier, *Virtue and the Voice of God*, 52. The distinction between teleology and eschatology here signifies that as human beings Christians make their distinctions with a specific set of priorities and goals in mind, but also reckon with God's eschatological intervention.
115 Cf. Ford, *Christian Wisdom*, 159, 163.
116 Cf. the intimate connection there is in Aquinas between the virtues of *prudentia* and *caritas*, Pieper, *Cardinal Virtues*, 36-37.
117 Vanhoozer, *The Drama of Doctrine*, 329. Vanhoozer's account of wisdom will be further analyzed in the next section.

Christian wisdom, there is, third, what Pieper calls the "astonishing" insight from Aquinas that prudence is "specially opposed to covetousness."[118] In order to be really wise, and hence receptive to the particulars of each situation, the crippling strategies of *sinful* anxiety, self-preservation, and concern for security, status, and comfort need to be abandoned. A close corollary of this is, fourth, David Ford's insight that in the Bible wisdom is closely linked to cries:[119] "If Jesus embodies wisdom, then wisdom is vitally concerned to hear and respond with compassion to the cries of those who are suffering."[120] Fifth, in its opposition to covetousness and its attentiveness to the needs of the world, Christian wisdom can be nothing but *humble* wisdom.[121] It is a pervasive Biblical pattern that the simple are made wise and that God grants understanding to those who humble themselves.[122] The humble, while granted wisdom by God, know that "it eludes control and bears a certain humility cognizant of limitation."[123]

Christian wisdom does not only *operate* from its own overarching narrative and the corresponding priorities and values, it is also *acquired* in a way distinct from ancient wisdom. While habits and practices play an important role in the cultivation of wisdom, Christian wisdom knows that its ultimate source lies outside the individual in God. Hence, wisdom is to be vehemently sought in prayer.[124] Given the promise that those who pray for wisdom will receive it (Jas. 1:12), wisdom and prayer are parts of a virtuous circle, in which seeking wisdom results in gaining it, which in turn enables one to seek for it wisely.[125] As an answer to prayer, wisdom is

---

118 Pieper, *Four Cardinal Virtues*, 21.
119 See esp. the entire first chapter of his *Christian Wisdom*, which opens with the statement: "Prophetic scriptural wisdom is inextricably involved with the discernment of cries," p. 14.
120 Ford, *Christian Wisdom*, 20. On page 50-1 Ford expounds what this means for doing theology wisely, but it also extends to wise Christian living: "Theology is called to be ceaselessly attentive to these cries – articulate, inarticulate, or even silent – and to exercise discernment while being gripped by them, with the purpose of shaping life – worship, arts, science, ethics, politics, economics, friendships, and the heart of each person – for the love of humanity, of all creation, and of the God of compassion, wisdom, and blessing."
121 Treier, *Virtue and the Voice of God*, 52, mentions humility as one of the distinctive features of Christian wisdom.
122 Cf. Spiegel, "Wisdom," 57, who refers to Ps. 19:7; Ps. 25:9; Prov. 1:4; and Prov. 11:2.
123 Dorothy C. Bass et al., *Christian Practical Wisdom: What It Is, Why It Matters* (Grand Rapids: Eerdmans, 2016), 8.
124 Ford, *Christian Wisdom*, 51, mentions "crying out for wisdom" as the "core activity" for acquiring it. Cf. Treier, *Virtue and the Voice of God*, 54: Phronesis finds its true home in prayer.
125 Cf. Treier, *Virtue and the Voice of God*, 63. Spiegel, "Wisdom," 71 points to another such virtuous circle in showing that trusting in God is both crucial in the process of becoming wise and a sign of wisdom. Note that 'seeking for wisdom' in the proposed view of divine guidance is a helpful alternative for the more common 'searching for the will of God.'

primarily Spirit-cultivated[126] and nurtured by the reading and re-reading of Scripture.[127] Furthermore, Aristotle already argued that wisdom cannot be learnt apart from a community, and the appropriate community to learn Christian wisdom is the church. Daniel Treier provides a balanced summary of the way Christian wisdom is acquired: "Phronesis is nurtured by the Spirit in response to prayer, who hones it through habits of obedience, and informs it by Scripture and Christian teaching."[128]

In conclusion, Christian wisdom is not so much different from ancient *phronesis* in its operation, but by the story it is involved in and lets itself be informed by. This formal exposition of Christian wisdom does, however, beg the question what this overarching story looks like and how it influences the nature of both wisdom and guidance. In order to gain an answer to this question, in our next section we will turn to two proposals for understanding wisdom within the overarching Christian narrative, or, as both authors prefer, drama.

6.3.5 Wisdom in the theo-dramatic accounts of Wells and Vanhoozer
As stated before (see e.g. §5.4), a Reformed approach to divine guidance shifts the focus from the life of the individual to the overarching context of salvation-history, as this context is key to making wise choices on the micro-level. Following our description of Christian wisdom in the previous section, here we will turn to two depictions of such wisdom that are explicitly placed in the encompassing divine drama of redemption: the accounts of Samuel Wells and Kevin Vanhoozer.[129]

As both authors acknowledge, the metaphor of drama is inspired by the multi-volume work of Von Balthasar, but in their case more immediately by N.T. Wright.[130] In an article on the authority of Scripture, Wright invites his readers into a thought experiment:

> Suppose there exists a Shakespeare play whose fifth act had been lost. The first four acts provide, let us suppose, such a wealth of characterization, such a crescendo of excitement within the plot, that it is generally agreed

---

126 Cf. Vanhoozer, *The Drama of Doctrine*, 308.
127 Cf. Treier, *Virtue and the Voice of God*, 53. David Ford has pointed to the importance of re-reading as a crucial Christian practice, e.g. *Christian Wisdom*, 66.
128 Treier, 55.
129 In what follows, I will frequently refer to the notion of a theo-drama. I consider it an helpful metaphor for several reasons: It draws the attention to the overarching framework of the history of salvation and of God's work throughout history; in doing so, it relativizes the tendency to focus only on God's plan *for my life*, the ego-drama; and it enables one, as especially Vanhoozer argues, to draw close ties between doctrine and discipleship.
130 Samuel Wells, *Improvisation: The Drama of Christian Ethics* (Grand Rapids: Brazos Press, 2004) discusses Von Balthasar on pp. 46-51.

that the play ought to be staged. Nevertheless, it is felt inappropriate actually to write a fifth act once and for all: it would freeze the play into one form, and commit Shakespeare as it were to being prospectively responsible for work not in fact his own. Better, it might be felt, to give the key parts to highly trained, sensitive and experienced Shakespearian actors, who would immerse themselves in the first four acts, and in the language and culture of Shakespeare and his time, *and who would then be told to work out a fifth act for themselves.*[131]

In the resulting situation, the first four acts would clearly be authoritative for the improvisation of the fifth, as characters need to behave consistently and plots and themes need to be resolved properly. Thus, authors are required to understand the essentials of the preceding acts and then to enter into the drama in a responsible manner. Their mission would be to speak and act "with both innovation and consistency." Wright then applies his example to the issue of the authority of Scripture.

This model could and perhaps should be adapted further; it offers in fact quite a range of possibilities. Among the detailed moves available within this model, which I shall explore and pursue elsewhere, is the possibility of seeing the five acts as follows: (1) Creation; (2) Fall; (3) Israel; (4) Jesus. The New Testament would then form the first scene in the fifth act, giving hints as well … of how the play is supposed to end. The church would then live under the 'authority' of the extant story, being required to offer something between an improvisation and an actual performance of the final act.[132]

Wells considers the general framework that Wright proposes helpful and "immensely promising,"[133] but disagrees with Wright on four points: (1) he considers it wrong to put the church at the end of the story as this suggests that it is the church's responsibility that the story ends well; (2) Wright's model insufficiently distinguishes between church and eschaton;

---

131 Wright first introduced the idea in N. T. Wright, "How Can the Bible Be Authoritative?," *Vox Evangelica* 21 (1991): 18–19 (emphasis in original). This article is cited by Wells, *Improvisation*, 51-55, and mentioned in Vanhoozer, *Drama of Doctrine*, 2. Wright has later developed his proposal in N. T. Wright, *The New Testament and the People of God*, 4th ed. (London: SPCK, 1997), chap. 5, and N. T. Wright, *Scripture and the Authority of God*, rev. and exp. edition (London: SPCK, 2013), 121–27.
132 Wright, "How Can the Bible Be Authoritative?," 19. Vanhoozer and Wells are not the only ones to adopt Wright's proposal. See e.g. Craig G. Bartholomew and Michael W. Goheen, *The Drama of Scripture: Finding Our Place in the Biblical Story* (Grand Rapids: Baker Academic, 2004), who structure their entire book around six acts.
133 Wells, *Improvisation*, 52.

(3) Jesus should be in the middle of the story; and (4) for Wells the separation of creation and fall into different acts is not sufficiently justified from the scriptural treatment of these themes and risks the misunderstanding that the fall is an act of God.[134] Wells' own version, revised in light of those problems, consists of the following acts: creation, Israel, Jesus, church, and eschaton.[135] Kevin Vanhoozer accepts Wells' re-interpretation and hence a fundamental insight underneath both their proposals is that the church is invited to take up its role in Act 4 of a five-stage drama.[136] In what follows, we will investigate these proposals within their dramatic framework and focus on how these can be interpreted as embodying the kind of Christian wisdom sketched above.

In his book *Improvisation: The Drama of Christian Ethics*, Wells introduces a view of Christian ethics that focuses on embodying the Christian faith "in the practices of discipleship all the time" (15). In doing so, he tries to move from ethical 'issues' to habits and practices as the core of Christian ethics (19).[137] After presenting drama as a fitting metaphor for the history of God's interaction with the world, Wells proposes that what the church is called to in the fourth act could best be understood as improvisation:[138] "When Christians, whether scholars in a colloquium or parishioners in a house group, whether bishops in a retreat house or aid workers in a field station, gather together and *try to discern God's hand in events and his will for their future practice*, they are improvising, whether they are aware of it or not" (65, emphasis CvdK).

---

[134] Wells, 52–53.
[135] Wells, 53.
[136] See Vanhoozer, *The Drama of Doctrine*, 2n4. Cf. p. 57. See for a later and more comprehensive evaluation of the various interpretations Kevin J. Vanhoozer, *Faith Speaking Understanding: Performing the Drama of Doctrine* (Louisville: Westminster John Knox Press, 2014), 96–98.
[137] In another place, Wells writes that ethics should be about "forming lives of commitment, rather than informing lives without commitment" (30). The view Wells opposes, which he later explicitly labels as 'quandary ethics,' portrays "the majority of life, run by habit [as] rudely interrupted from time to time by quandaries, which require concerted moral effort to resolve" (77). There are interesting resemblances between this form of quandary ethics and the view on divine guidance focusing on information and moments of important decisions. Since in the type of ethics Wells proposes there is no fundamental boundary between moral and nonmoral decisions, this is an additional reason why his insights are relevant to the topic of guidance.
[138] Wells considers 'performing' inadequate, since (1) the expectation that the script provides all the answers cannot be met; (2) it suggests that the whole narrative of the church is already encompassed in the Bible; (3) it might suggest the notion of a 'golden era' to which the church should continually strive to return; and (4) a comprehensive story "needs no dialogue partner" and could hence go on without genuine engagement with the world. See Wells, 62-63.

Using the metaphor of improvisation, Wells sets out to show that improvisation is not about being original but about being obvious in the given context: "Being obvious means trusting that God will do what only God can do, and thus having the freedom to do what only the disciple can do. Being obvious means trusting that the practices of discipleship, shaped by the Holy Spirit, are enough – there is no need for a 'second blessing,' whether in the form of further revelation or in a flash of spontaneous insight or inspiration at a moment of crisis" (67). Furthermore, the playful connotations of improvisation should not be covered up, but welcomed, as they remind the church that it is in act four, and not in the decisive acts three or five. There is, for the church, no need "to be more solemn than God" (69).[139]

Learning to live wisely, like learning to improvise, has more to do with honing the right instincts and habits than with making the right choices per se (75). With these instincts and habits trained, believers can welcome the "offers," the invitations to respond, with trust. Moving beyond the standard responses of "blocking" or "accepting" offers (106), Wells suggests that the proper Christian attitude is to "overaccept" (113). Inverting the ethical distinction between givens and gifts, Wells considers God as the only relevant given and circumstances (time, death, sin, bodily limitations) as gifts (124).[140] Considering these as gifts, as offers, the primary responsibility to find a use for the gift lies with the receiver.[141] The way to do this is through 'overaccepting': "accepting in the light of a larger story" (131).[142]

Although Wells does nowhere draw an explicit connection between improvisation and *phronesis,* comparing his account with the description of *phronesis* earlier in this chapter, the type of improvisation Wells depicts

---

139 Later on, Wells explains: "The key to keeping the story going is for disciples to remember that the story does not belong to them. The story is not just *their* story. The originality is already in the story: the decisive elements in the story have already been performed. The church cannot do anything so bad that it could pervert the whole story" (105).
140 Wells shows how the task of Christian ethics is often portrayed in terms of adapting to the so-called 'givens' prevailing and competing in the world (e.g. Reinhold Niebuhr). In this framework, the givens take centre stage and God's role is often an afterthought. Instead, for Wells "the only given is God's story, the theo-drama, the church's narrative: all else is potentially gift" (125).
141 Once again, Wells makes the differences with quandary ethics clear (130). In such an approach, the assumption is that "there *is* a right thing to do in each circumstance." Hence, the receiver of a gift desperately wonders what the gift is *for*. In Wells' own approach, the question a receiver asks is instead "How do I want to *receive* this gift?"
142 Wells convincingly shows how much of the ministry of Jesus could be interpreted with reference to overaccepting the reactions of the people he meets, 135-140. In the remainder of his book, Wells shows what overaccepting could look like with regard to a number of areas of ethical reflection, e.g. human evil (ch. 11), disability (ch.12), cloning (ch. 13), and genetic modification (ch. 14).

could not only be seen as a proposal for Christian ethics, but also as a contemporary reformulation of *phronesis*. Interestingly, this link with *phronesis* is made more explicit in Kevin Vanhoozer's *The Drama of Doctrine*. Vanhoozer opposes the "fatal" dichotomy between theory and practice (13) and reformulates the role of doctrine within a 'dramatic' framework. In his proposal, theology could be compared to dramaturgy, Scripture to the script, understanding to performance, the church to the company, and the pastor to the director (xii).[143] Within this framework, Vanhoozer argues "that doctrine, far from being unrelated to life, serves the church by directing its members in the project of wise living" (xii).[144]

Informed and shaped by doctrine, believers must learn to "perceive and participate rightly in the order of creation and its reordering in Christ through the Spirit" (255). What should be aimed at in life is "Christo-dramatic fittingness" (256), a way of life that is consistent and coherent with the movement of the theo-drama. The ultimate aim is "to cultivate the mind of Christ and a way of life that embodies the wisdom of God" (263).

In order to learn what is coherent with the drama, believers need both *scientia* and *sapientia*. Knowledge is needed to understand the script, to grasp the basic contents of earlier acts of the drama.[145] *Scientia* alone however is insufficient for those called to live in the final, unscripted scenes of act four (307). What is needed is "Spirit-cultivated wisdom" for discerning how to be faithful to the script in unscripted situations (308). In this context Vanhoozer introduces the concept of *phronesis* as part of a theology that, as "canonically instructed practical reason, is prosaic, phronetic, and prophetic" (309).

Leaving aside the prosaic and prophetic dimensions here, we focus on Vanhoozer's concept of 'phronetic' theology. Vanhoozer, who refers to Aritstotle's employment of *phronesis* for ethics and Gadamer's use of it for hermeneutics, points out that their treatments need to be transformed in a number of areas (329). First, he works with a different conception of the good: "*Phronesis* is thus the virtue that directs us toward realizing theo-dramatic goods: the *salus* of the individual; the *shalom* of the community;

---

143 Vanhoozer seems less concerned with the concept of 'performance' than Wells.
144 "Thinking of doctrine in dramatic rather than theoretical terms provides a wonderfully engaging and integrative model for understanding what it means to follow—with all our mind, heart, soul, and strength—the way, truth, and life embodied and enacted in Jesus Christ" (16).
145 An important aspect of Vanhoozer's depiction of *scientia*, in line with Wright's aforementioned article, is his insistence on the richness of the theo-dramatic script and his rejection of an exclusively propositional approach to theology as this tends to neglect the scriptural richness: "The theo-dramatic script is a rich dialogue between various genres that sometimes complement, sometimes contrast with one another, rather than a stable and static monologue that endorses a single system of propositions" (287).

the glorification of the *shema*, or name of God" (329). Second, not only is our judgment affected by finitude, as Gadamer pointed out, but also by fallenness. Within the frame of the divine drama, however, there is also reason for trust: the work of the Holy Spirit.[146] Thirdly, whereas Gadamer was mainly concerned with the conversation between interpreter and text, within a dramatic construal we become part of a conversation that started already within the canon itself. By becoming an apprentice of canonical conversations and having the capacity for judgment (involving imagination, reason, emotion, and volition) transformed, one develops the ability to interpret the world and to do "what is Christo-dramatically fitting in our own situations" (331). Modifying the definition of Allen discussed in §6.3.3, Vanhoozer defines *phronesis* as "the canonically nurtured ability to say and do the 'fit in Christ' in relatively singular contexts in ways appropriate to their relative singularity" (332). To be able to do so, two sapiential virtues are crucial: the *perception* that enables one to see the relevant features of a given situation and the sense of *perspective* to see how it fits within the bigger story. Here, Vanhoozer compares *phronesis* to the practice of improvisation.[147] Two pitfalls threaten good improvisation: preplanning and trying to be original (337).[148] If one succeeds in avoiding both, true wisdom can be expressed in one's actions.

6.3.6 Concluding reflections

We started this section with the observation that the idea of Christian wisdom plays a major role in our preferred model of guidance-through-transformation. Yet, it turned out that the concept was insufficiently developed in accounts advocating that model, as was shown from Friesen's book. Therefore, we investigated the topic of *phronesis* or *prudence*, the distinctiveness of *Christian* wisdom, and we finally introduced two authors unpacking this notion of wisdom. How does all this help us in developing a theologically informed, contemporary account of divine guidance?

Our investigation has confirmed the appropriateness of relating guidance to practical wisdom: wisdom is needed to discern God's guidance in situations characterized by a complicated interplay between universals and particulars, factors that are contingent and future, and the need to reach a practical decision. The fruitfulness of thinking of guidance in

---

146 Hence, it follows that *phronesis* is not a matter of effective historical consciousness (Gadamer) but of "effective *pneumatic* consciousness" (330).
147 Acknowledging that he received a prepublication preview of Wells' book, *Drama*, 336n94.
148 In the context of guidance, especially the notion of preplanning is interesting: one is only able to improvise well when not trying to control the future (338).

terms of wisdom was further accentuated by the fact that wisdom is most needed in situations in which there is no single right way to proceed, but various good options coexist, and absolute certainty is precluded. Furthermore, our investigation of wisdom reaffirmed the need to think through the relations between guidance and community and guidance and transformation in later sections.

Our discussion of the nature of *Christian* wisdom more particularly underscored the importance of placing questions of guidance right from the start in the bigger perspective of the overarching Christian narrative. Shaped by this narrative, Christian wisdom has its own priorities and values and is nurtured in its own way: most fundamentally by the Spirit, through Scripture, in answer to prayer.

By introducing two more detailed accounts of Christian wisdom, those of Samuel Wells and Kevin Vanhoozer, the nature of Christian wisdom was further elucidated, and a few additional insights emerged. It was acknowledged before that a Reformed account of guidance places the individual life and its quest for guidance within the broader perspective of God and his plans with his creation. The metaphor of a theo-drama proved helpful as a further development of this insight. It emphasizes from the start that what we are concerned with is not our personal story, so that we are not the ones to make or break it. As the most fundamental decisions have already been made, we can proceed with a sense of trust and gratitude. This perspective reduces the anxiety believers can experience around difficult decisions. It was also argued that the search for guidance cannot be limited to episodes of decision-making, but has to do with the whole of life. Not the moments of decision-making, but the preparation for them throughout one's life should be the proper focus of an account of guidance. Finally, through the introduction of wisdom as improvisation and the related ideas of 'offers' and 'overaccepting,' Wells was able to provide a helpful reformulation of the importance of givens as gifts that challenges receivers to find fruitful uses for these gifts instead of asking for the intended meaning of the givens, while Vanhoozer deepened the relation between wisdom and script(ure).

6.4 Discerning the Will and the Way

> *Thesis 8: A Reformed approach to divine guidance requires robust notions of Christian wisdom and discernment that on the one hand indicate the particularity of Christian decision-making and on the other hand leave the full freedom and responsibility for the chosen path with the individual.*
>
> *Thesis 9: Hence, referring to divine guidance behind one's own choices in no way reduces the personal responsibility for those choices.*

6.4.1 Introduction
In the previous section, practical wisdom was presented as a virtue that is indispensable to a Reformed account of divine guidance. As explained, such wisdom often resembles a form of improvisation when it comes to making concrete decisions. Whereas wisdom, even in its practical mode, is of a rather general nature, the closely related idea of discernment denotes the capacity to perceive why we should choose one way over the other, to distinguish between wise and unwise, fruitful and unfruitful, loving and unloving ways to proceed. As such, discernment belongs to the category of practical wisdom but is one specific dimension of such wisdom.

In this section, we will develop an account of discernment in which several questions need to be anwered. For example, what does a Christian account of discernment look like, and by what sort of considerations and attitudes is it characterized? How does it compare to moral discernment as a common human task? And to what extent is discernment applicable in situations in which choices have to be made that are not explicitly moral choices? We will set out to answer those questions by interacting with three important voices in Christian ethics. First, we will study how in the writings of Dietrich Bonhoeffer (6.4.2), the concept of discernment (*Prüfung*) is closely related to the important (biographical) decisions he had to make (§6.4.2). Our interaction with James Gustafson will then add further insight to the specific nature of *Christian* discernment (§6.4.3), while our analysis of Oliver O'Donovan's thought on discernment will focus on discernment with regard to non-moral decisions (§6.4.4). We will end the section with a conclusion in which we relate our findings to key notions from the evangelical literature analyzed in chapter 2 (§6.4.5).

6.4.2 Dietrich Bonhoeffer on discerning the will of God
For those who know Bonhoeffer from his stress on simple obedience to Christ (best known from his *Nachfolge*) it might come as a surprise that in his *Ethics* Bonhoeffer devotes serious attention to the concept of discernment (*Prüfung*).[149] Although the concept itself does appear only in the last stage of his writing, in a sense the question of discernment plays

---

149 Only recently a more detailed study of the role of discernment in Bonhoeffer appeared: Joshua A. Kaiser, *Becoming Simple and Wise: Moral Discernment in Dietrich Bonhoeffer's Vision of Christian Ethics* (Eugene: Pickwick Publications, 2015). Before, discernment in Bonhoeffer was studied mostly in other contexts, as in the works of Bartel, Muers, and Dahill (Michelle J. Bartel, "The Rationality of Discernment in Christian Ethics" (Princeton Theological Seminary, 1998), 83–128. Rachel Muers, *Keeping God's Silence: Towards a Theological Ethics of Communication* (Malden: Wiley-Blackwell, 2004), 170–72. Lisa E. Dahill, *Reading from the Underside of Selfhood: Bonhoeffer and Spiritual Formation* (Eugene: Pickwick Publications, 2009), 87–92.

a role throughout his adult life.¹⁵⁰ His most sustained reflections on discernment are found in the *Ethics* manuscript 'Die Liebe Gottes und der Zerfall der Welt.'¹⁵¹

That the concept does appear in his late writings should be understood in light of Bonhoeffer's intense struggles with discerning God's way during the year 1939.¹⁵² In June 1939, Bonhoeffer accepted Reinhold Niebuhr's invitation to come to the United States, an invitation inspired by Niebuhr's (and other's) worries about Bonhoeffer's safety in Germany. Whereas doubts about his future in Germany made him decide to go to America, it is upon arrival there (June 12, 1939) that these doubts intensify.¹⁵³ On his second day in America, he writes in his diary that he does not understand why he is there;¹⁵⁴ and three days later he adds that he would not have thought it possible that at his age and after so many years abroad he could be so seriously homesick.¹⁵⁵ Not feeling able to make such a weighty decision himself, his diary contains sighs like "God, in the next week give me clarity about my future…"¹⁵⁶ On June 20, Bonhoeffer decides to return to Germany. In his diary he reflects on this day:

---

150 That the concept itself appears only late is shown by both Kaiser, *Becoming Simple and Wise*, 2, and Lisa E. Dahill, "Probing the Will of God: Bonhoeffer and Discernment," *Dialog: A Journal of Theology* 41, no. 1 (Spring 2002): 43. On the importance of discernment throughout his life, see Kaiser, 1: "The question of discernment occupied the mind of Dietrich Bonhoeffer throughout a large portion of his adult life."

151 Dietrich Bonhoeffer, "Die Liebe Gottes und der Zerfall der Welt," in *Ethik*, ed. Ernst Feil et al., Dietrich Bonhoeffer Werke 6 (Gütersloh: Gütersloher Verlagshaus, 1992), 301–41. For a sustained analysis of this section, see Kaiser, *Becoming Simple and Wise*, chap. 2. According to Kaiser, of the 100 appearances of *prüfen* in Bonhoeffer's oeuvre, 50 are in this manuscript (39). Further references to Bonhoeffer's writings will be in the standard form of DBW vol:page, or when the English translation is cited to DBWE vol:page. The manuscripts collected in the *Ethics* were written in the final years of Bonhoeffer's life and were his preparations for an Ethics volume. *Liebe Gottes* was presumably written in the second half of 1942. See the editor's preface for more background information.

152 Schuurman uses the same episode to illustrate the Protestant (esp. Lutheran) idea of vocation in Schuurman, "To Follow Christ," esp. 52-55. See also Bethge's account of this period in his biography of Bonhoeffer: Eberhard Bethge, *Dietrich Bonhoeffer: Theologian - Christian - Man for His Times*, ed. Victoria J. Barnett, revised (Minneapolis: Fortress Press, 2000), 648–62. Earlier experiences from his life could also have been chosen as an illustration. E.g., Bonhoeffer doubted for a very long time whether his vocation was in academia or as a pastor in the church (Bethge, *Bonhoeffer*, 120, 128).

153 See Bethge, *Bonhoeffer*, 636 about the questions that made Bonhoeffer go to the USA. On the ship that brings him back to Germany, Bonhoeffer describes his experience in America as "innere Entzweiung über die Zukunft," July 9, DBW 15:240. Cf. Bethge, *Bonhoeffer*, 650.

154 DBW 15:222.

155 Diary June 15, 1939 (DBW 15:222). On June 21, he writes on this homesickness: "And is this lingering homesickness, which is almost incomprehensible to me and till now remains almost completely unfamiliar, an accompanying sign from above, which should make the refusal easier?" (DBWE 15:228)

156 Diary June 18, 1939 (DBWE 15:226).

With that the decision has been made. … It is strange that in all my decisions I am never completely clear about my motives. Is that a sign of lack of clarity, inner dishonesty, or is it a sign that we are *led* beyond that which we can discern, or is it both? … God certainly sees how much personal concern, how much fear is concerned in today's decision, as courageous as it may appear. The reasons that one puts forward to others and oneself for an action are certainly not sufficient. … In the end one acts out of a level that remains hidden from us.[157]

The diary entry is closed with the following words: "At the end of the day, I can only pray that God may hold merciful judgment over this day and all decisions. It is now in God's hand."[158] When reading 2 Timothy 4:21 ("come before the winter") a few days later, Bonhoeffer considers this a confirmation of his choice and does not consider it an abuse of Scripture to read it in this way.[159] Bonhoeffer never regretted his decision to return to Germany.[160]

What Bonhoeffer writes on discernment in his 'Die Liebe Gottes und der Zerfall der Welt' must be understood against the background of his decision to return to Germany. In the manuscript, Bonhoeffer discusses two competing approaches to ethics: one that is based upon the distinction between good and evil and one that is based upon the unity (*Einheit*) of the divine will. In line with his earlier writings, Bonhoeffer starts with the assertion that Christian ethics cannot, like all other ethics, take as its point of departure the knowledge of good and evil, but must 'supersede' it.[161] As humanity lived in unity with God before the fall and through

---

[157] DBWE 15:226-27. Bonhoeffer's acknowledgment of the immense complexity of one's decisions is crucial for the account of discernment he develops. While a sense of guidance is clearly present in this quote, all simple accounts of such guidance are precluded.

[158] DBWE 15:227.

[159] 26 Juni (DBW 15:234). The text from 1 Timothy was the days' motto from the *Hernnhütter Losungen*. On Bonhoeffer's use of the *Losungen*, see Hans Kronenburg, "'De dagteksten zijn mijn dagelijkse vreugde.' Over een vergeten aspect van Bonhoeffers praxis pietatis," *Kerk en Theologie* 66 (2015): 274–85. and esp. Peter Zimmerling, *Die Losungen: Eine Erfolgsgeschichte durch die Jahrhunderte* (Göttingen: Vandenhoeck & Ruprecht, 2014), 107–22. Although he was at times critical of the *Sprüchfrommigheit* triggered by the *Losungen* and the risk that believers lose sight of the bigger framework of Scripture, Bonhoeffer used the *Losungen* throughout the later years of his life.

[160] See his letter of December 22, 1943 to Bethge, DBWE 8:236: "You should know, by the way, that not for a single moment have I regretted my return in 1939, nor anything of what has then followed."

[161] "Die christliche Ethik hat ihre erste Aufgabe darin, dieses Wissen aufzuheben," DBW 6:301. The verb *aufheben* is notoriously difficult to catch in English. 'To supersede' is the choice of the translators of DBWE but in my opinion this does not catch fully what Bonhoeffer wanted to say. In Hegel-studies 'to sublate' is the more common translation of *aufheben*.

redemption is enabled to live in unity with God in Christ once again, the state of disunity (*Entzweiung*) that is a result of the Fall cannot be the primary reality from which Christian ethics thinks.

It is in Jesus' confrontations with the Pharisees that the two approaches are seen in their full difference.[162] Bonhoeffer portrays the Pharisee as an admirable human being whose entire life is arranged in terms of good and bad. In order to be able to navigate the continual conflict between good and bad, the Pharisee is constantly thinking through the myriad of possibilities to predetermine that what is good. Jesus, however, does not allow the Pharisees to pull him into their reality based upon good and bad. For him, "there are never several possibilities, conflicts, or alternatives, but always only one. Jesus calls this one option the will of God. … He lives and acts not out of knowledge of good and evil, but out of the will of God."[163]

Although he stresses the unity of the divine will and the need to simply obey it, Bonhoeffer warns that a theological, not a psychological simplicity is involved. Thus, psychologically it is possible that the simple obedience to Christ involves very complex reflection.[164] Indeed, he asserts, the Bible speaks about both a necessary searching after the will of God and a necessary self-examination.[165] Texts like Romans 12:2, Phil, 1:10, and Eph. 5:9 show the importance of discernment for the Christian life.[166] The primary object of discernment is the will of God, but this will does not force itself upon the human heart or is easily recognized as such. Instead, it often lies deeply hidden under the many possibilities.[167] As the

---

162 DBWE 6:309: "It is the encounter of Jesus with the Pharisees that most clearly highlights the contrast of the old and the new. The proper understanding of this encounter is very important for understanding the gospel as such …." For Bonhoeffer, the Pharisees function not as a historical phenomenon, but as "the epitome of the human being in the state of disunion [Entzweiung]" (310).
163 DBW 6:315.
164 See DBW 6:323. For the distinction between psychological and theological simplicity see also Kaiser, *Becoming Simple and Wise*, 37. As Kaiser convincingly shows, the combination of simple obedience and complex reflection should not be understood as an irresolvable incoherence but as a tension in Bonhoeffer's thought that is ultimately resolved.
165 DBW 6:322. In his working notes on Bewährung (*dókimos*), written in 1938-39, Bonhoeffer distinguished three forms of discernment: of the will of God, of the situation, and of oneself. In the *Ethics*-manuscript, the first two forms are combined, for as we will see, discerning the will of God has everything to do with discerning the situation. See DBW 15:345 and Kaiser, 40.
166 DBW 6:323-24. According to Kaiser, *Becoming Simple and Wise*, 53, Bonhoeffer saw discernment as the central task for the Christian life. Dahill, *Underside of Selfhood*, 87, concurs, viewing Bonhoeffer's as a "spirituality radically dependent on discernment."
167 DBWE 6:321: "The will of God may lie very deeply hidden among many competing possibilities."

will of God is a living reality it cannot be caught in a set of rules, but must ever be sought anew in every new situation.

Once the importance of discernment is established, Bonhoeffer considers the *how* of discernment. He first mentions a number of mistaken views that result from interpreting simple obedience in terms of psychological simplicity: thinking that the will of God is known through intuition, through the exclusion of all deliberation, or through the naive following of the first thought or feeling that arises.[168] Later on, he adds three more fundamental errors for which there should be no place: the dread of facing insoluble conflicts, the arrogant conviction that one can master every conflict, or the enthusiastic expectation or even claim that one will receive immediate inspiration from God.[169]

With these misunderstandings cleared up, Bonhoeffer sketches the basic contours of what discernment does entail.[170] Among the guidelines he offers are first that in the complex task of discernment heart, intellect, good observation and experience must work closely together.[171] Apart from each other, neither of these is sufficient, but together the heart, the intellect, the capacity for observation, and attentive perception of the context work fruitfully together. In the process, there is also a modest place for personal experience to weigh in.[172] Warning once again against counting on or waiting for immediate inspirations (as these might easily lead to self-deception), Bonhoeffer states that a high level of soberness should be involved in the entire process, taking fully into account the possibilities and consequences.[173] Summarizing his own guidelines, he concludes that the entire apparatus of human capacities must be involved. Kaiser renders Bonhoeffer's position as follows:

---

168 DBWE 6:320-21: "These verses [Rom 12:2 and Eph. 5:9, CvdK] thoroughly correct the notion that a single-minded [einfältige] discerning of the will of God must occur in the form of intuition, by abandoning all reflection, by naively grasping the first thought or feeling that insinuates itself, that is, any psychologizing misunderstanding of the simplicity of the new life that has begun in Jesus."
169 DBW 6:324: "But in all of this there will be no place for the torment of being confronted with insoluble conflicts, nor the arrogance of being able to master any conflict, nor also the enthusiastic [schwärmische] expectation and claim of direct [unmittelbarer] inspirations." See for a helpful discussion about the possible opponents against who those warnings might be directed Kaiser, *Becoming Simple and Wise*, 46.
170 Kaiser, *Becoming Simple and Wise*, 45. writes: "For him, discernment is not a matter of method, but a matter of faith, and this means there is no blueprint for discernment, but rather some general guidelines."
171 DBW 6:324.
172 DBWE 6:324: "Prior experiences will raise encouraging or cautionary notes."
173 DBW 6:326.

While discernment is a spiritual activity, it is not a mystical and disembodied activity; rather, discernment is an activity deeply rooted in the reality of the world: an activity that remains faithful to God precisely by making good use of the best of human ability in order to discern God's will.[174]

When approaching the task of discernment in a spirit of genuine humility, one can truly believe that God will make his will known.[175] It is clear that for Bonhoeffer this remains a conviction of faith, and he warns against the inclination to incorporate some other kind of immediate certainty in the process after a decision has been taken. In line with his own reflections following the decision to return to Germany in 1939, Bonhoeffer contends that in the end two things are required: an actual decision and the confidence and trust that ultimately it is God who ensures that his will will be done.[176] Resisting the temptation to return to the division between good and bad, after having made a decision one must not fear to have gone wrong but trust in the grace of God in Jesus Christ and let the good or bad be hidden in the knowledge and mercy of the Judge.[177] After the decision has been made, simple obedience is asked for: "One must ultimately surrender all evaluation and judgment of an action to God and depend on God's grace in discernment."[178]

As said before, for Bonhoeffer discernment not only has God's will as its object, but also the self (*Selbstprüfung*).[179] This should not be a kind of

---

174 Kaiser, *Becoming Simple and Wise*, 47. Cf. p. 55, "there is a sense throughout the manuscript that moral discernment is a human activity" and Michelle Bartel, who likewise points out that discernment for Bonhoeffer is a human endeavor, Bartel, "Rationality of Discernment," 122.
175 Bonhoeffer explicitly mentions the importance of humility twice, DBW 6:326-7.
176 DBW 6:327: "es wird dan nach allem ernsten Prüfen auch die Freiheit zur wirklichen Entscheidung da sein und in ihr die Zuversicht, daß nicht der Mensch sondern Gott selbst durch solches Prüfen hindurch seinen Willen durchsetzt." The English translation makes the final part of the sense a little too passive for conveying Bonhoeffer's meaning: "that it is not the human but the divine will that is accomplished through such discernment" (DBWE 6:324).
177 DBW 6:327. One could argue that, in his rejection of the division between good and bad, Bonhoeffer places (in Kierkegaardian terms) the religious perspective above the ethical perspective. This could also mean that an individual is called to actions that are seemingly immoral (think of his own struggles about participating in plots against Hitler). Such decisions can only be taken at the individual level and can never be prescribed to others.
178 Kaiser, *Becoming Simple and Wise*, 44. There is an interesting similarity here to the idea of praying for God's 'overruling' in case a wrong decision has been made that we encountered in some evangelical books.
179 DBW 6:327. As Dahill has rightly pointed out, this is "one of the instances in Bonhoeffer where *selbst-* is used in an unambigiously positive sense," Dahill, *Underside of Selfhood*, 88.

pharisaic introspection,[180] but a daily renewal of the faith that "Jesus Christ is in us."[181] Yet, although this aspect is almost hidden behind Bonhoeffer's focus on Christ being in us, there is also an element of discerning one's faith and work.[182] The importance of knowing oneself in decision-making and discernment is more readily seen in 'Die Geschichte und das Gute [Zweite Fassung].'[183] There, in his discussion of concrete responsibility, Bonhoeffer argues that it is important to examine one's motives and heart,[184] and later, when discussing criteria for self-examination (*Maßstäbe zur Selbstprüfung*), he adds that knowing our habitual inclinations is important as a guard against following them too easily.[185]

In one of his circular letters to his former seminarians, we get a glimpse of how discernment worked out in practice. In the letter, dated in early 1942, Bonhoeffer answered the questions he received on the legalisation of seminarians as pastor in the *Reichskirche*. He provides his seminarians with three rules for times of uncertainty:[186]

---

180 Bonhoeffer explains the difference between pharisaic and Christian self-examination as follows: "There is not only a pharisaical kind of self-examination. There is also a Christian self-examination, which, rather than focusing on one's own knowledge of good and evil and its realization in practical life, daily renews the knowledge that 'Jesus Christ is in us'" (DBWE 6:325).
181 DBW 6:327, referring for this notion to his own *Nachfolge*, DBW 4:230, 235. The important point for Bonhoeffer is that in self-examination the temptation should be resisted to look at one's own faith and works from a point of view independent from Christ who through the Spirit lives in the believer: "In examining themselves, the Christians' focus is thus not diverted away from Jesus Christ and onto their own selves. Instead, it remains completely focused on Jesus Christ. But given this premise that Jesus Christ already is and acts in us, and is one of us, the question can and must arise, of course, whether and how we belong to, believe in, and obey Christ in our daily lives" (DBWE 6:325).
182 DBWE 6:324-25: "Paul's admonition to examine one's own faith and work."
183 The manuscript was presumably written in the first half of 1942. Bonhoeffer takes over parts of an earlier manuscript with the same title but significantly rearranges it. For an analysis of the differences between the two versions of the manuscript, see Wilken Veen, "'Verantwoordelijkheid' als omslagpunt in Bonhoeffers ethiek: Het verschil tussen de eerste en tweede versie van 'Die Geschichte und das Gute,'" in *Schuld en vrijheid: Opstellen aangeboden aan prof.dr. G.C. den Hertog* (Zoetermeer: Boekencentrum, 2017), 284–93.
184 DBWE 6:268: "… we must attempt seriously to examine our own motives and our own hearts."
185 DBWE 6:294: "if, according to my character traits, I know that I tend to be a reformer, a know-it-all, a fanatic, one who does not heed any limits, there I run the risk of expanding my responsibility arbitrarily, and confusing my natural desire with the call of Jesus; if I know myself to be cautious, anxious, insecure, and legalistic, there I must be carefully not to equate the call of Jesus Christ with my limiting responsibility to a narrow domain …." With regard to the criteria for self-examination, Bonhoeffer immediately adds "though they cannot provide complete certainty about one's own self." Notice that the primary function of *Selbstprüfung* for Bonhoeffer is negative, recognizing and unmasking the sinful tendencies that might disrupt wise decision-making.
186 It is important to understand that Bonhoeffer is speaking here more precisely on "Unsicherheit über den *kirchlichen* Weg", DBW 16:252 (emphasis CvdK).

a. I should never make a decision out of uncertainty; that which already exists takes precedence over change, unless I discern with certainty the necessity of the change.
b. I should never act alone, first, because I need the counsel of the brothers; second, because they need me; third, because there are church rules that I may not carelessly disregard.
c. I should never rush to a decision or allow myself to be forced. If today a door is closed to me, God will open another if God wills it.[187]

Here, several of the elements considered before reappear: Bonhoeffer's insistence that discernment is no solitary quest, that rushing is always unwise, and that one should not be reigned by the anxiety of missing chances. Hence, when it comes to discernment we see a close interplay between self-examination and weighing the relevant aspects of the situation. Lisa Dahill provided a succinct and balanced summary of Bonhoeffer's view:

> Involving focused attention on one's diverse intellectual, emotional, and spiritual intuitions as these 'collaborate' in the prayerful sifting of experience and observation, discernment clearly requires a high degree of self-awareness as well as the simultaneous capacity for attunement to the fluid, shifting movements of the grace of God.[188]

One further aspect of Bonhoeffer's account of discernment needs to be mentioned. Before turning to the practical aspects of discernment, Bonhoeffer focuses on a crucial and decisive presupposition underlying his entire interpretation: discernment is only possible based upon a 'metamorphosis,' a radical transformation, "overcoming the form of the fallen human being, Adam, and con-formation with the form of the new human being, Christ."[189] In the next section (6.5), we will return to the nature and necessity of transformation, but our analysis of Bonhoeffer's view on discernment would be incomplete without mentioning it.

---

187 DBWE 16: 264-65.
188 Dahill, "Probing," 44. With "the fluid, shifting movements" Dahill does not deny Bonhoeffer's insistence on the unity of the will of God, but tries to convey his emphasis that, as the will of the *living* God, the object of discernment can never be something static. See e.g. DBWE 6:323.
189 DBWE 6:322: "Here the decisive and clear prerequisite is that such discernment can take place only on the basis of a 'metamorphosis,' a complete inner change of the existing form, a 'renewal of the mind (Rom. 12:2), to living as children of light (Eph. 5:9)." As a conclusion to the 'Voraussetzung' he adds: "Discerning the will of God is possible only on the basis of knowing the will of God in Jesus Christ" (323).

Although Bonhoeffer's account adds depth to the notion of discernment and excludes a number of common misinterpretations, there are three aspects that need to be further discussed and that are insufficiently accounted for in his writings. In the first place, Bonhoeffer does not address the question how the specifically Christian account of *Prüfung* he develops is related to discernment in general. In the second place, although he touches upon the subject, Bonhoeffer does not explain sufficiently how discernment in personal decisions is rooted in character, experience, and personal history. Finally, in Bonhoeffer's specific historical setting all decisions were so strongly morally loaded that we need further reflection on the question how discernment applies in situations were several seemingly equal options exist. For the first two questions, we turn to an article by James Gustafson (§6.4.3), and for the last question to the thought of Oliver O'Donovan (§6.4.4).

6.4.3 James Gustafson on general and Christian discernment
Bonhoeffer's account of discernment raises the question how such *Christian* discernment is related to discernment in general. In his article 'Moral Discernment in the Christian Life,' James Gustafson discusses exactly this point.[190] In the first part of the article, Gustafson traces how the concept of discernment is used in common speech by delineating five attitudes that are *not* meant when we call a person discerning in any specific field.[191] First, we would not describe someone as discerning who applies an analytical scheme or method to whatever the concrete situation entails. What such a person lacks, are "the qualities of empathy, appreciation, imagination, and sensitivity that seem to be involved in discerning perception and judgment."[192] Second, a movement from first principles to the actual situation or a deduction from universals to particulars does not in itself show good discernment. Third, a skill to gather all relevant information does not necessarily equal discernment, as discernment seems to point beyond the gathering to the sifting of the information. Fourth, someone who is "articulate in giving their emotive and expressive reactions to a

---

190 The article was first published as James M. Gustafson, "Moral Discernment in the Christian Life," in Norm and Context in Christian Ethics, ed. Gene H. Outka and Paul Ramsey (London: SCM Press, 1969), 17–36. It was reprinted in James M. Gustafson, *Moral Discernment in the Christian Life: Essays in Theological Ethics*, ed. Theo A. Boer and Paul A. Capetz, Library of Theological Ethics (Louisville: Westminster John Knox Press, 2007), 25–40. Page references are to the original edition.
191 Although he himself is concerned with the question of moral discernment, Gustafson uses examples of what it means to be discerning as a literary critic, critic of liberal arts, student, musician etc. There are interesting parallels here to the examples Edwards presented in his discussion of the 'new sense', see esp. §4.4.4.
192 Gustafson, "Moral Discernment in the Christian Life," 20.

subject"[193] might be able to give a quick response to many different situations, but is not necessarily discerning. Finally, someone who adheres to the same given basis for making all judgments would not be called discerning.[194] Instead, discernment seems to require at least some "sensitivity and flexibility, some pluralism of consideration."[195]

In the light of what discernment is *not*, Gustafson sketches a few "common elements" of discernment.[196] What, according to Gustafson, are the elements necessary to call someone discerning? In the first place, there must be a more or less sophisticated 'reading' of the actual situation. Here, Gustafson emphasizes that such a reading is always done from a particular perspective and that it is this perspective that explains how "different persons accent the importance of different aspects."[197] In the second place, actual persons are involved in the process of discernment, and these are persons with histories that influence their discernment. Gustafson points out that these personal histories lead to certain "moral dispositions," "moral sensitivities or sensibilities," and "certain commitments" (or their absence) and how these dispositions, sensibilities, and commitments in turn influence one's discernment.[198] Thirdly, a person brings a number of basic beliefs, rules, and principles to the act of discernment.[199] Gustafson describes the ideal picture of discernment as follows:

> There is a discriminating and accurate reading of the situation, and an understanding of the relations of elements of the situation to each other, and of its relations to other situations. There is a stipulation of the more and less important factors, an empathy for its 'inner' character as well as a description of its external character. There is a refined moral sensitivity that registers subtle nuances not only of fact but of value, that is not just emotion or sentiment, but appears to contribute to the perception of what one ought to do. Moral sensitivity seems to contribute in the 'discerning'

---

193 Gustafson, 22.
194 Here Gustafson gives the example of 'moralistic critics of literature' who judge all literature based upon for example its level of profanity or sexual content, disabling themselves to appreciate other aspects of the literature under critique (22).
195 Gustafson, "Moral Discernment in the Christian Life," 23.
196 Before doing so, he remarks that discernment is so closely linked to the discerner that these basic elements can take more rational or more emotional forms depending upon the temperament of the discerner (23).
197 Gustafson, "Moral Discernment in the Christian Life," 24.
198 Gustafson, 24–25.
199 "At the minimum, however, discernment involves a reading of the case at hand, an expression of what constitutes the character and perspective of the person, and some appeals to reason and principles both to help one discern and to defend what one discerns." Gustafson, 25. Here, more than Bonhoeffer did, Gustafson accounts for the influence of character, experience, and personal history in the process and results of discernment.

moral man an intuitive element that leads to accuracy in moral aim, judiciousness in evaluation, and compelling authenticity in deed.[200]

After this general account of discernment, Gustafson focuses on the meaning of discernment in the *Christian* life. He sets out with a series of negations: the human processes involved are not different, faith does not ensure excellence in discernment, and the Christian does not have "faculties or capacities" at his disposal that non-Christians do not have.[201] These denials do not, however, mean that there is no difference at all between discernment in general and *Christian* discernment. Taking Romans 12:1-2 as the starting point for his discussion, Gustafson argues that from the perspective of faith "*man [sic] is to discern what God enables and requires him to do.*"[202] Christians do so from a certain perspective, and most fundamentally this perspective can be described as that of "a people who have offered themselves up to God,"[203] or, in the words of Paul, *living sacrifices*. Thus, Christians do not just have a different set of convictions about the world and draw inferences from those, but "their 'very selves' are given to him [God]."[204]

Hence, Christian discernment involves a different self-understanding and a renewed interpretation of the world. This changed perspective in turn has consequences for the values, ends, longings, desires, and preferences that the Christian brings to the process of discernment.[205] Here, a place of primacy goes to love. Yet not only one's sensibilities are involved, but also one's ratio: "If Christians are to discern what God enables and requires them to do, they are involved in rational discrimination as well as sensible response."[206] A person's beliefs and ethical principles influence her discernment. Thus, for Gustafson accounts of discernment in which immediate 'sensitivity' of what God wants or a clear and direct command from God are ruled out[207] and he stresses that discernment is "a human act made with reference to human statements about God."[208] Since discernment is a human act, one must beware not to equate the own judgment with the will of God. The one who does so forgets about his or her

---

200 Gustafson, 25–26.
201 Gustafson, 26.
202 Gustafson, 27 (emphasis in original). Later on, he explicitly speaks about "the discernment of God's will" (34).
203 Gustafson, 27.
204 Gustafson, 28.
205 Gustafson, 30.
206 Gustafson, 31.
207 He explicitly mentions Lehmann and Barth as proponents of such views, p. 32, although his discussion is way too short to make true on this claim, that seems rather far-fetched.
208 Gustafson, "Moral Discernment in the Christian Life," 32.

own partialities, and about the "tendency to discern what is fit and acceptable for one's own gratification or the gratification of one's own group rather than fit and acceptable to God."[209] In order to counteract such tendencies, continual self-reflection is a necessary part of discernment.[210]

As a final but crucial element of Christian discernment Gustafson mentions that the community in which discernment takes place is the Christian community, both the congregation to which an individual belongs and "the historical community that has lived the moral life as Christians in the past."[211] Gustafson ends his article by comparing his account of discernment with prudence and suggests that discernment is "perhaps … only another way of talking about the virtue of prudence."[212] Finally, he returns briefly to Romans 12:1-2 to suggest that, in light of his stress on the humanness of discernment, it would be wise in practice to modify what Paul says there into the modest hope that "by offering oneself up to God, and by formation in prudence informed by love and faith and hope, 'Then you *might* discern the will of God.'"[213]

6.4.4 Oliver O'Donovan on finding one's path
Both accounts of discernment discussed thus far share one 'problem' for our aims in this chapter: In Gustafson the focus is explicitly on *moral* discernment and in the case of Bonhoeffer his situation was so morally loaded that (despite his attempts to go beyond the ethical), the focus was still on decisions between morally good and bad options.[214] Can we still speak of discernment in cases where several good options coexist? Exactly this focus is found in the dense final chapter on 'Discernment' in Oliver O'Donovan's *Finding and Seeking*. In this book, O'Donovan presents an 'ethics in the Spirit'[215] and early on points at the importance of the "competent discernment of God's will" in the life in the Spirit.[216]

---

209 Gustafson, 34.
210 "Reflection is necessary because Christians, like others, tend to be conformed to the expectations of their own desires and to the ethos of the time in which they live …" Gustafson, 34. Notice how, as for Bonhoeffer, the primary function of self-reflection is negative.
211 Gustafson, "Moral Discernment in the Christian Life," 34. We will return to the role of the community in section 6.6.
212 Gustafson, 35.
213 Gustafson, 36. Romans 12:1-2 will be discussed more extensively in §6.5.2.
214 Kaiser discusses discernment in Bonhoeffer under the title 'moral discernment.' Both his discussion, though, and Bonhoeffer's own experience with discernment show that in many instances discernment has to do with important personal (biographical) decisions that are not always *a priori* moral decisions, or at least that a clear distinction is often impossible.
215 O'Donovan, *Finding and Seeking*, 1.
216 O'Donovan, 8. Cf. 10: "the masterful discernment for which the Spirit equips us."

O'Donovan starts his discussion of discernment with the recognition that the process of moral deliberation (the focus of his preceding chapter) does not result in a decision for each situation, since as humans we often encounter major decisions that are not covered by any moral law.[217] In situations where humans experience seemingly arbitrary options in important matters, they tend to "look for, and may very well pray for, a sequential ordering or direction in the complex of circumstances, objective and subjective, which comprise our narrative situation."[218]

In this context, O'Donovan utilizes what he considers an apt metaphor to describe this quest: the path or the way.[219] When asking whether something is a path, we are interested in the question whether it has a direction, whether it is going somewhere. Summarizing the force of the metaphor, he states:

> That is why this metaphor is so potent in talk of practical attention to the future. In acting, we set off into the future with a purpose and a degree of anticipation, but though we may, and must, form anticipations and purposes, we know that these are projections only and that we have no clear sight of the actual future where our action will fetch up a *fait accompli*. The path, its direction abstracted from its goal, mirrors the purposiveness and uncertainty of action. In following it we do not use it as an instrument, turning it to serve purposes of our own; we commit ourselves to its direction, trusting that where it leads is where we want to go. We rely upon the direction it presents to us, and hope to be led somewhere consistent with our overall purpose.[220]

In order to find such a 'path,' we must reflect upon ourselves and our circumstances to see whether the limits of our possibilities, the expectations and duties that bear on us, and our personal mission coincide with each other "to afford a precise opening" that can either be seen as "an obligation imposed on us" or as "a happy opportunity."[221] The idea of congruence is crucial for O'Donovan.[222] The ultimate decision is not taken based upon

---

217 O'Donovan's account of what we called 'the situation of guidance' is discussed in more detail in §1.1.2.
218 O'Donovan, *Finding and Seeking*, 216.
219 O'Donovan develops his interpretation in close interaction with the article of J. K. Aitken on *derek* in the *Semantics of Ancient Hebrew*, ed. T. Muraoka, vol. 6 (Leuven: Peeters, 1998), 11-37.
220 O'Donovan, *Finding and Seeking*, 218.
221 O'Donovan, 220.
222 This could be an interesting similarity between O'Donovan's thought and the evangelical idea that God often speaks 'in stereo' and that the different signs need to 'line up.'

a feeling (not even inner calm) nor upon deductive reasoning,[223] but upon congruence: "In searching for a path, we search for a congruence of normativities, where the ordered demand of the creation, the agential powers which we are conscious of possessing, and the moment of opportunity into which we are thrust all flow together."[224] Discerning such a form of congruence is important, because it suggests purpose to us. The question whose purpose this might be becomes relevant, but for O'Donovan it is interesting in itself that this is a meaningful question to be asked.[225] Believers are even "taught to wait and pray for such indications, ready to recognize in them the leading of God."[226] Pointing to Acts 16, O'Donovan shows how even there discernment was involved, as Luke clearly shows how deliberation and a decision follow Paul's vision.[227]

Although it is sometimes possible to discern a 'congruence' and have a sense of purpose, the end of the process of discernment does always remain a "moment of dangerous opportunity,"[228] where risk and opportunity come very close, as there is no certainty that the path that opens is the right path and no *a priori* verification that the purpose we seem to detect is God's purpose. In the final instance, the outcome of the human process of discernment must remain "an object of hope"[229] and security must not be sought in our decisions but in the promise of God alone.[230]

6.4.5 Discernment beyond evangelical misunderstandings

In this section, we explored the notion of discernment first of all through the writings of Bonhoeffer. Gustafson added insight on the particularity of Christian discernment whereas we used O'Donovan's thought to reflect on discernment in 'nonmoral situations'. More than anywhere before in this chapter we moved close to the literature studied in chapter 2. What results does our inquiry yield for our account of divine guidance?

All three authors reject a number of interpretations of discernment we also detected in many contemporary evangelical accounts of guidance.

---

223 Cf. Vanhoozer, *The Drama of Doctrine*, 241, who contrasts discernment with calculus.
224 O'Donovan, *Finding and Seeking*, 220–21.
225 "If no combination of circumstances could invite such a construction [the idea of being led by God, CvdK], it would be meaningless to wonder whether we were misled in this or that instance. The question would be vacuous, and a good deal of commonplace moral experience would have to be written off as superstition," O'Donovan, 221.
226 O'Donovan, 221.
227 "The verb 'concluding' is all-important; the call was not the dream as such, but what the dream, taken with all the other circumstances, permitted them to recognize." O'Donovan, 221.
228 O'Donovan, 222.
229 O'Donovan, 229.
230 O'Donovan, 223.

On the one hand, views of discernment that stress immediacy, be it through intuition, inspiration, sensitivity, or direct command, are criticized. Indeed, any view of discernment that excludes or undervalues deliberation cannot qualify as genuine discernment. On the other hand, discernment cannot be reduced to a method or be a simple deduction from basic principles. Sufficient justice must be done to the enormous complexity of those situations in which discernment is asked for, as well as to the role of flexibility and sensitivity in such situations.

Positively, we learn from all three, but especially from Bonhoeffer, that discernment must be practiced in a spirit of sober realism: the situation must be 'read' accurately, constraints must be acknowledged honestly, and possibilities and consequences must be thought through in sofar this is possible. All ordinary human processes must be included and the entire person is involved, including his or her ratio, affections, personal history, character, beliefs, and current relations and obligations. This raises the need for continual self-reflection, especially in order to ensure that one is not misled by wrongful inclinations. No objective outsider perspective is possible, because both an accurate perception of the situation and an honest self-evaluation must take their point of departure in understanding oneself as a *living sacrifice* to God.

Discernment, when practiced in this mode, searches for a sense of purpose, a 'path' behind which divine intentions might be suspected.[231] Yet in the end, as all three authors point out, no absolute certainty can be expected that through the very human act of discernment the path one has found is indeed the path of God. A sense of risk ('*Wagnis*', 'moment of dangerous opportunity') will always remain. Good discernment does not free us from the responsibility to make an actual decision. After a decision has been made, however, as both Bonhoeffer and O'Donovan argued, one may rest once again, entrusting one's decision to God's judgment and care without continually looking back and fearing that the right path has been missed.

---

231 O'Donovan is most hesitant in this regard, whereas both Bonhoeffer and Gustafson tend to speak of this intentionality as 'the will of God.'

6.5 'Be Transformed': On Guidance, Character, and Transformation

Thesis 10: Ultimately, sanctification is the field or locus within which guidance is to be discussed.

6.5.1 Introduction
In section 5.4, we outlined a Reformed approach to divine guidance based upon central Reformed convictions as derived from our interaction with Calvin and Edwards and in (critical) dialogue with the various evangelical models of guidance. Since then, in this chapter we developed three concepts crucial to this approach: vocation, wisdom, and discernment. In doing so, we encountered two more fundamental notions that we did not address in sufficient detail: vocation, wisdom, and discernment presuppose a certain form of *transformation* on the one hand, and the support of various forms of (Christian) *community* on the other. In this section, we focus on transformation, while the next section (6.6) will deal with community.

In order to understand where further thought is necessary, a quick review of where and how the idea of transformation has appeared throughout this book is in order. Most fundamentally, the model of guidance we took as our point of departure was the one which is based upon the notions of transformation and wisdom. Furthermore, in our interaction with Calvin and Edwards we repeatedly encountered the importance of transformation. In the case of Edwards, this was further highlighted by his account of virtue.

In the current chapter, our discussions on vocation, wisdom, and discernment stressed the need for transformation once again. Vocation, in the dynamic sense developed in §6.2, presupposes transformation in emphasizing the need for continual reevaluation and reordering of priorities and engagements. In order for this to make sense without undermining the unity of an individual's life, some constancy of character is required. As our account of wisdom (§6.3) was developed against the background of virtue ethics, transformation was implied from the start. More concretely, Christian wisdom, with its particular worldview and corresponding priorities, implies the transformation and purification of mind and desires. Finally, with regard to discernment we saw how the entire apparatus of human capacities is involved in the discernment process. The intimate link between discernment and discerner asks for an undergirding account of character transformation.

In what follows, we will discuss aspects of transformation that are most relevant to our account of guidance. We first turn to a biblical text that has been used by almost all authors we interacted with up to this point, Romans 12:1-2 (§6.5.2). From our exegesis, we will turn to a brief discussion of the notions of character and heart (§6.5.3) before turning to two concepts that bridge the gap between a theoretical concept of transformation and the practical need for decision making: desires (§6.5.4) and imagination (§6.5.5). We will end this section with a critical and typically Reformed counter-question: but what about sin? (§6.5.6).

6.5.2 Romans 12:1-2 and the transformation of the mind
We will take our starting point in Romans 12:1-2, a text we encountered in numerous places throughout the preceding chapters.[232] In these verses, we find a strong link between transformation and discernment of the will of God. A careful exegesis of the passage will aid us in thinking through the notion of transformation as related to guidance.

Romans 12:1-2 is generally regarded as a summary or thesis statement of the paraenetic section of the letter, Romans 12:1-15:13.[233] There is, however, some debate about the scope of the verses: most commentators apply the verses without any explanation to 'the Christian life' in general,[234] whereas some take the other extreme and restrict their meaning to 'Paul's epistolary purpose,' namely, to "gain the cooperation of the Roman house churches for Paul's missionary project."[235] Whereas Paul might have had his need for the support of the Romans (cf. 15:24) in mind when urging them to present themselves as living sacrifices, there is no textual reason to restrict the scope of the verses to this sole purpose. Another

---

[232] We have encountered references to Romans 12:1-2 in almost every chapter. For a number of evangelical authors, it is a key text in their account of guidance. With regard to Calvin, the crucial passage of *Institutes* III.7.1 (discussed in 3.3.2) is basically an extended discussion of these verses. In Edwards the words from Romans play an important role in his discussion on the guidance of the Spirit (see esp. §4.4.5), and finally, in the present chapter all authors we discussed in the section on discernment referred to Romans 12:1-2.

[233] Craig S. Keener, *The Mind of the Spirit: Paul's Approach to Transformed Thinking* (Grand Rapids: Baker Publishing Group, 2016), 143n1. For a brief overview of the consensus on the role of these verses see Robert Jewett, *Romans: A Commentary* (Minneapolis: Fortress Press, 2007), 724.

[234] So e.g. Richard N. Longenecker, *The Epistle to the Romans: A Commentary on the Greek Text* (Grand Rapids: Eerdmans, 2016), 912: "The admonitions of 12:1-8 ... speak directly to the core of every Christian's thought and life." James D.G. Dunn, *Romans 9-16* (Waco: Word Books, 1988), 707: "Paul begins with an exhortation ... which sets out the basis for all Christian lifestyle and relationships ...." Douglas J. Moo, *The Epistle to the Romans* (Grand Rapids: Eerdmans, 1996), 748: "Here Paul succinctly and with vivid imagery summarizes what the Christian response to God's grace in Christ should be."

[235] Jewett, *Romans*, 726. Jewett sees Paul's purpose as primarily "diplomatic and missional" and agrees with C.J. Bjerkelund, *Parakalô: Form, Funktion und Sinn der parakalo-Sätze in den Paulinischen Briefen* (Oslo: Universitetsforlaget, 1967), 173, in seeing "Paul's epistolary purpose rather than some abstract theological framework as the key to understanding what precisely is being urged."

point of discussion among interpreters is the relation between verses one and two. Whereas some argue that in verse 1 Paul's focus is somatic and in verse 2 mental,[236] we consider it more helpful to think of verse 2 as subordinate to verse 1, explicating "how what is requested in 12:1 is to be brought about."[237]

The first important aspect of Romans 12:1-2 is that it is in the plural throughout. Hence, a merely individualistic interpretation of the verses is precluded.[238] Although the plural 'your bodies' necessarily implies that all of them need to be sacrificed individually,[239] the general focus of the text, including its emphasis on discernment, is corporate.[240] As such, what Paul writes about transformation and discernment both presupposes the new community that has come into being in Christ[241] and "forms how believers think about themselves in the context of the Christian community, shaping their relationships there."[242]

Paul appeals to the Roman believers "to present their bodies as sacrifices." Following a Greco-Roman tradition, Paul uses the language of sacrifice as "a metaphor of personal devotion."[243] By using this metaphor, Paul urges his readers to commit themselves entirely to God's purposes and to try to act in ways consistent with the divine will.[244] The radical nature of Paul's language stresses that a life thus devoted to God involves considerable personal costs, and hence these words should not be too

---

236 See e.g. Joseph A. Fitzmyer, *Romans: A New Translation with Introduction and Commentary* (New York: Doubleday, 1993), 638–39; Jewett, *Romans*, 731.
237 Longenecker, *Romans*, 922. Cf. Moo, *Romans*, 754–55. One final introductory issue that cannot be discussed in detail here is the contrast of Romans 12:1-3 with Romans 1:18-32. See for a helpful overview Keener, *Mind of the Spirit*, 155.
238 Although his wording is rather strong, we concur with the tenor of Jewett's critical statement that "both imperatives [of 12:2, CvdK] are in the plural, which seems to be overlooked by commentators bound by the individualizing ethical tradition of the Western world." Jewett, *Romans*, 731n56.
239 As even Jewett, who stresses the plural verbs most, p. 729, has to admit.
240 Jewett, *Romans*, 727, 733; Dunn, *Romans 9-16*, 715.
241 Longenecker, *Romans*, 915. In that context, Longenecker points to Pheme Perkins, "Paul and Ethics," *Interpretation* 38, no. 3 (1984): 269, where Perkins states that "Pauline ethics presupposes that a new community of moral discernment has come into being in Christ."
242 Keener, *Mind of the Spirit*, 167–68.
243 Jewett, *Romans*, 727. Cf. Longenecker, *Epistle to the Romans*, 920, who describes it as "an act of personal devotion." Dunn, *Romans*, 710, relates Paul's phrase not to Greco-Roman traditions but to Paul's Jewish background: "The thought of sacrifice has been transposed across a double line - from cultic ritual to everyday life, from a previous epoch characterized by daily offering of animals to one characterized by a whole-person commitment lived out in daily existence."
244 Cf. Longenecker, *Epistle to the Romans*, 920. See also Keener, *Mind of the Spirit*, 145: "They are thus to be totally consecrated for God's purposes."

easily applied to the 'earthiness' of everyday worldly service.[245] The reference to the body stresses that the entire person is involved,[246] with an emphasis on corporeality,[247] concrete relationships in and with the world,[248] thus preventing the sacrifice to be interpreted in terms of "a mere unworldly pietism or enthusiastic dualism."[249]

In the second verse, then, Paul explains that "the way one offers one's body as a sacrifice to God is rationally, through reason."[250] To do so, it is crucial that the believers "don't let the world around [them] squeeze [them] into its own mould,"[251] but that they be transformed. Given the combination of the renewal of the mind with the offering of the bodies as sacrifices, this transformation must be understood as "a complete inner change of thought, will, and desires ... resulting in a recognizable external change of actions and conduct."[252] Although Paul stresses the responsibility of the Roman believers to work at their transformation,[253] most commentators agree that, while any direct reference to the Spirit is absent in this context, in light of earlier parts of the letter Paul must have thought of the Spirit as the ultimate source of renewal.[254]

It is noteworthy that for Paul the primary locus of transformation is a renewal of the *mind*.[255] "For Paul, the mind is central to Christian character:

---

245 See for this point esp. Jewett, *Romans*, 728, who criticizes the "frequent celebrations of the ideal of worldly service in submission to the Lordship of Christ" because "in emphasizing the totality, earthiness, and quotidian aspects of such obedience, the dramatic urgency of Paul's language is obscured by vaguely uplifting sentiments."
246 Moo, *Romans*, 751; Longenecker, *Romans*, 920.
247 For Longenecker, *Romans*, 920 the bodies here point to "the sacrifice of one's entire person in all its created vibrancy and aliveness."
248 Dunn, *Romans 9-16*, 709; Moo, *Romans*, 751; Ulrich Wilckens, *Der Brief and die Römer: 3. Teilband, Röm 12-16*, 3d ed. (Zürich / Neukirchen: Benziger Verlag / Neukirchener Verlag, 2003), 3.
249 Dunn, *Romans 9-16*, 717.
250 Keener, *Mind of the Spirit*, 152. We omit a discussion of the words 'which is your spiritual/rational worship" here, as they are not directly relevant for our purposes. For a helpful overview of the various difficulties and the interpretative options see Moo, *Romans*, 751-54.
251 As J.B. Phillips renders the verse in his translation of the New Testament. In light of our earlier focus on improvisation and the story it presupposes it would also make sense to translate it as "don't let the world around you squeeze you into its own story/stories."
252 Longenecker, *Romans*, 923.
253 So e.g. Moo, *Romans*, 756.
254 Keener, *Mind of the Spirit*, 157. Dunn, *Romans 9-16*, 714: "The immediate source of the renewal is not specified, but if asked Paul would almost certainly have referred to the Spirit."
255 See e.g. the critical remarks N.T. Wright makes in this context with regard to contemporary Christianity, in N. T. Wright, *After You Believe: Why Christian Character Matters* (New York: HarperOne, 2010), 158: "Part of the problem in contemporary Christianity, I believe, is that talk about the freedom of the Spirit, about the grace which sweeps us off our feet and heals and transforms our lives, has been taken over surreptitiously by a kind of low-grade romanticism, colluding with an anti-intellectual streak within our culture, generating the assumption that the more spiritual you are, the less you need to think."

virtue is the result of thought and choice."[256] But how is the mind renewed? According to both Keener and Wright Paul's language alludes to the 'new life' that is the result of the union with the risen Christ (cf. 6:4) and of the work of the Spirit (cf. 7:6). Hence, the new mind "is affected by its foretaste of the coming world in Christ."[257] The renewed mind learns to view the world from an eschatological perspective, evaluating present choices from their eternal consequences and not just from 'the patterns of this world.'[258] Paul seems to have confidence in the transformed mind of the Christian to be able to discern the will of God. This is, however, no unbounded confidence in the *mind*, but fundamentally an unbounded confidence in the work of the *Spirit*.[259]

What exactly Paul means by the phrase 'the will of God' is difficult to establish. Jewett once again restricts its meaning to the specific occasion for which Paul wrote his letter,[260] whereas Moo speaks broadly of "moral direction."[261] The clue is perhaps to be found in the function of the words "good, acceptable, and perfect." Most commentators agree, firstly, that there is no ascending order in the words,[262] and secondly, that they should be interpreted as appositions to, not as attributes of, the divine will.[263] That is, God's will can be discerned by a transformed person who recognizes "what is good, what pleases God, and what is 'perfect' or 'complete.'"[264] Thus, through the transformation of the renewed mind, one is

---

256 Wright, 154. Earlier, Wright states that "unless the mind is fully involved, not only are you not growing up as a fully (and fully integrated) human being; you are not engaging in virtue at all" (p. 150-51). Cf. Dunn, *Romans 9-16*, 718: "for Paul spiritual renewal ... must include not least the person's power of thought and reason."
257 Keener, *Mind of the Spirit*, 154, cf. Wright, *After You Believe*, 69, who speaks of "learning in advance the language of God's new world."
258 Cf. Keener, *Mind of the Spirit*, 154-55. "A renewed mind, then, evaluates matters of this age in light of the coming age, valuing God's opinions rather than the world's and valuing what counts eternally." Wright, *After You Believe*, 158: "The more genuinely spiritual you are ... the more clearly and accurately and carefully you will think, particularly about *what the completed goal of your Christian journey will be* and hence *what steps you should be taking, what habits you should be acquiring, as part of the journey toward that goal, right now*" [emphasis in original].
259 Moo, *Romans*, 757.
260 Jewett, *Romans*, 734.
261 Moo, *Romans*, 757.
262 So e.g. Keener, *Mind of the Spirit*, 161.
263 See esp. Jewett: "'the good and acceptable and perfect' should not be understood as three attributes of the will of God but rather as an apposition providing traditional guidelines to evaluate alternate courses of action as consistent or inconsistent with the divine will." (734) Cf. Keener, 165; Moo, *Romans*, 641.
264 Keener, *Mind of the Spirit*, 165. Keener goes on to explain that "Paul speaks here in general terms, but he will define (or provide examples of) this way of thinking more concretely in the following context." Cf. C.H. Dodd, *The Epistle of Paul to the Romans* (London: Hodder and Stoughton, 1932), 193: "that kind of life which the renewed mind of the Christian man [sic] can see to be good in itself, satisfying, and complete."

enabled to discern the will of God by perceiving what is 'good, acceptable, and perfect' in light of the Kingdom of God.[265]

What do we learn from this passage with regard to guidance? Most fundamentally, that for Paul the will of God is not something hidden in the clouds, but something that can be discerned by a believer whose mind is transformed, making him or her look for that which is good and pleases God. This is, moreover, said to the Roman believers as a community. Apparently, discerning the will of God is not an individual activity according to Paul. Furthermore, in order to be able to discern, costly transformation ('sacrifice') is required, in which not the pattern of the world but the pattern of God's mercy becomes definitive for one's decisions.

6.5.3 On the object of transformation

At the basis of our argument in the present chapter is the suggestion that God guides believers at the most fundamental level by making them into a particular kind of persons who are able, in their specific circumstances, to decide which course of action is most in line with the divine 'drama', answers the needs of the situation, and fits with the kind of person one thinks oneself to be. In this account, being transformed by God is crucial, and we saw how Paul emphasized the transformation of the *nous*. Given the connotations of both this term, and its common translation *mind*, we need a more comprehensive term than mind to denote the object of transformation. Would it help our cause to speak about the transformation of *character*, as many theologians, especially ethicists, tend to do?[266]

One of the first theologians to turn to character was Stanley Hauerwas. In his groundbreaking book *Character and the Christian Life*, Hauerwas analyzes "how the self acquires unity and duration in relation to the Christian's conviction that Christ is the bringer of God's kingdom."[267] He emphasizes that persons are self-determining beings, whose beliefs,

---

265 These terms cannot be neatly described or delineated. Paul incorporates leading notions of Jewish and Greco-Roman ethics that "evoke disparate and at times overlapping fields of discourse in the Greco-Roman and Jewish world and thus function in an inclusive manner," Jewett, *Romans*, 734. Most commentators agree that Paul sets up in broad and inclusive terms what he will later make more concrete in chapters 12-16.
266 Of course, character as such is not a theological concept, bus has been used in a wide variety of disciplines. For a recent interdisciplinary discussion of many aspects of character from the perspectives of psychology, philosophy, and theology see Christian B. Miller et al., eds., *Character: New Directions from Philosophy, Psychology, and Theology* (Oxford: Oxford University Press, 2015). See esp. the article by Christian B. Miller and Angela Knobel, "Some Foundational Questions in Philosophy about Character," 19-40, for an overview of crucial questions.
267 Stanley Hauerwas, *Character and the Christian Life: A Study in Theological Ethics*, 3d ed. (San Antonio: Trinity University Press, 1985), 1.

intentions, and actions are transformed through deliberative action, thus forming their character. For Christians, this character-formation should be determined by their "basic commitments and beliefs about God."[268] Christian character acquires its orientation from Christ and his Kingdom, not from the values of the world. Such a notion of character is more comprehensive than the mind, yet otherwise moves largely in line with what we found in Romans 12.

Yet, Hauerwas's account is not without problems of its own. In focusing on the bridge between story and character he works with an underdeveloped notion of character itself, not pausing to answer the question what character *is*.[269] A number of theologians have followed Hauerwas in devoting attention to the importance of character without developing a sufficient account of what character is.[270]

In his reaction to Hauerwas, Richard Bondi proposed a phenomenology of character in which he approached character as a configuration of a number of "fundamental aspects of human existence which are formed or combined in a characteristic way of being in the world."[271] In particular, he specified four of such aspects: a capacity for intentional action, involvement with the affections and passions, appropriation of the given, and the capacity of the heart.[272] Although his approach contains a number of insightful elements (we will return to his description of *the heart*), the elements he selects are disparate phenomena, and for example the relationship between 'character' and 'heart' is made insufficiently clear.

Whereas theologians either circumscribe character or appeal to its intuitive ring, but mostly do not define its nature, do other disciplines offer help? Fleeson and his colleagues have shown that in the field of psy-

---

268 Hauerwas, 203.
269 See especially Richard Bondi, "The Elements of Character," *The Journal of Religious Ethics* 12 (1984): 201–18. In his introduction to the 3d edition of his book, Hauerwas mentions Bondi's article as the "most telling critique of as well as the most constructive response to my notion of character," Hauerwas, *Character*, xvi, n3.
270 In this regard, we mention among others N.T. Wright and David S. Cunningham. In his *After You Believe*, Wright states that "human 'character' … is the pattern of thinking and acting which runs right through someone" and then turns to the notion of transformation. Cunningham, in his *Christian Ethics*, presents an ethics focused on character but only presents a brief discussion of character that is largely functional: "Our character determines what kinds of things we will take for granted, what will seem natural to us, and the degree to which we even bother to stop and think about an action before we undertake it." See Wright, *After You Believe*, 27; Cunningham, *Christian Ethics*, 31.
271 Bondi, "Elements," 204. The idea of character as 'configuration' is crucial, creating the possibility to mark a certain character off from others and to account for changes in character as a reconfiguration of the aspects over time: "the content of these elements and their precise combination differs with each of us and within each of us as time goes by."
272 See Bondi, 204-12. Bondi's use of the distinction between affections and passions seems a problematic aspect of his account.

chology character has been used in at least six different classes of ways.[273] Of these, five emphasize that character denotes not just personality, but also an evaluation of personality. Differences between classes reflect the various subsets of characteristics that are selected for the evaluation. In their own definition, they stress moral characteristics: "those characteristics that are descriptive of actions, cognitions, emotions, and motivations that are considered to be relevant to right and wrong according to a relevant moral standard."[274] In the field of (theological) ethics, Christian Miller comes closest to this approach in stressing that "a person's character primarily consists of her character traits and the relationships between them,"[275] where character traits are further defined in terms of dispositions. Interestingly, Miller lists a number of functions such character traits fulfill: they provide grounds for understanding ourselves and others; they are a basis for explaining (in part) why we do what we do; they help us predict what a person will likely do in the future in certain situations; they help us to evaluate persons and imitate them.[276] Yet the most important point to be taken from those definitions is that they no not try to get behind the character traits to the essence of character, but find its essence precisely in the traits.[277] Apart from those, 'character' is an elusive concept.

In light of the above, will it be of any help if we specify transformation as the transformation of character? We answer this question positively, as long as we keep in mind that in speaking of character we speak of an 'assemblage' of character traits.[278] This means that we will not search for the 'essence' of character that needs to be transformed, while the notion of character can still perform an important integrative function. In this light, Bondi's insight that the biblical metaphor of the heart is important in thinking of character is helpful. In that context, Bondi draws on

---

273 William Fleeson et al., "Character: The Prospects for a Personality-Based Perspective on Morality," *Social and Personality Psychology Compass* 8, no. 4 (2014): 179. Cf. William Fleeson et al., "Personality Science and the Foundations of Character," in *Character: New Directions from Philosophy, Psychology, and Theology*, ed. Christian B. Miller et al. (Oxford: Oxford University Press, 2015), 42, where they speak of at least four classes.
274 Fleeson et al., "Character," 181.
275 Christian B. Miller, *Moral Character: An Empirical Theory* (Oxford: Oxford University Press, 2013), 4. For the detailed conceptual background of discussions of character, see also the introductory chapter of his *Character & Moral Psychology* (Oxford: Oxford University Press, 2014).
276 Miller, *Moral Character*, 12–13.
277 This might also be the reason why, although many theologians speak about character, the more common ethical approach is still through the route of the virtues.
278 The term 'assemblage' is taken from Marcia Homiak, "Moral Character," ed. Edward N. Zalta, *The Stanford Encyclopedia of Philosophy* (Metaphysics Research Lab, Stanford University, 2016), https://plato.stanford.edu/archives/fall2016/entries/moral-character/.

a longstanding metaphor which uses the heart to describe the center of our being, that about us which unites intellect and feeling on a fundamental and telling level. The heart is the seat of our deepest memories, of our imaginative exploration of other lives and times, of our yearning for union both of the self and with other people, ideals, and possible ways of life. I am suggesting we can also use the heart to describe the way stories offer us the symbolic language to ponder who we are, who we have been, and who we might become in the possible worlds of the future. Character and story are inherently connected because stories beckon the heart.[279]

Stressing the metaphor of the heart as an expression of the integrative function of character enables us to acknowledge that in our decision-making our affections play a major role and are in as much need of transformation as our mind. Strong and lasting feelings towards situations of injustice, specific groups of people, or any other situation remain one of the primary ways in which God guides people through the transformation of their character. In our heart, "the center of our being,"[280] we find the deepest convictions, motives, and intentions that ultimately influence our decisions. In our heart we recollect earlier decisions and the mistakes we made with them, but also the good ones and the people and things that influenced us. In our heart, stories 'beckon' us, and as we are confronted again and again with the story of God, Israel, Jesus Christ, the church, and the Kingdom, we are offered language to "ponder who we are, who we have been, and who we might become in the possible worlds of the future."[281]

Hence, if God guides believers through transforming their character, their 'heart', he influences their decisions at a profound level without diminishing their responsibility. At the same time, this approach enables us to focus on those elements of character that help us understand more concretely how the transformation of character may lead to the choice for specific actions, choices referred to in faith as made 'under God's guidance': the transformation of our desires and of our imagination.

6.5.4 The transformation of our desires

We have argued that the notion of the *heart* can be used to express the unifying function of the idea of character. As such, the heart is the place

---

[279] Bondi, "Elements," 210. On the role of story, he adds: "I am suggesting that the language of character and the vocabulary of story are the closest we can come to telling others what is in our hearts and to hearing what is in, not only theirs, but our own as well" (211).
[280] Bondi, 210.
[281] Bondi, 210.

where the transformation worked by the Spirit has the most profound impact. As a next step, I will argue that it is especially through transforming our desires that God guides us towards making specific decisions, as we are defined by what we ultimately love and desire at least as much as by our rational considerations and deliberations. We will use the work of Reformed philosopher James K.A. Smith as a starting point for our reflection on the relation between guidance and desire.[282]

In his book *Desiring the Kingdom*, Smith sets out to communicate a view of Christian learning in terms of formation and discipleship.[283] In order to do so, he paints an Augustinian picture of human beings as primarily affective and desiring: "our hearts are oriented primarily by desire, by what we love."[284] Instead of 'thinking things,' human beings are ultimately lovers. In speaking about our *ultimate* loves and desires, what Smith has in mind is "that to which we are fundamentally oriented, what ultimately governs our vision of the good life, what shapes and molds our being-in-the-world—in other words, what we desire above all else, the ultimate desire that shapes and positions and makes sense of all our penultimate desires and actions."[285]

Now if it is true, as Smith insists, that as human beings we are defined by what we love, this supports our suggestion to think of God's guidance primarily in terms of the transformation of our character, and most fundamentally the transformation of our ultimate loves and desires. This statement needs to be further unpacked, and although Smith is not directly concerned with this specific question, his writings point to a number of ways in which we can see the transformation of desire as a 'thick' description of guidance.

According to Smith, our loves and desires form our "most basic attunement to the world,"[286] and as such they provide meaning, purpose,

---

[282] Although we decided to take Smith's work as our point of departure, it is good to remember that we encountered the topic of desire at a number of earlier places in this book, for example: Edwards posed a close relationship between the indwelling of the Spirit and the transformation of desire (§4.4); in our account of wisdom and especially in the discussion of David Ford's book we pointed out how wisdom presupposes a purification and transformation of one's desires and priorities in line with the Kingdom (§6.3.4). Remember also the subtitle of Ford's *Christian Wisdom*: 'Desiring God and Learning in Love.' Notice how Smith draws a close connection between heart and desire: "the heart as the fulcrum of your most fundamental longings – a visceral, subconscious *orientation* to the world." James K.A. Smith, *You Are What You Love: The Spiritual Power of Habit* (Grand Rapids: Brazos Press, 2016), 8.
[283] Cf. James K.A. Smith, *Desiring the Kingdom: Worship, Worldview, and Cultural Formation* (Grand Rapids: Baker Academic, 2009), 11.
[284] Smith, 25.
[285] Smith, 51.
[286] Smith, 25.

understanding, and orientation to our lives.²⁸⁷ These, in turn, prime us to a certain way of living in the world, to value certain things over others, to aim for particular goals, to devote our best efforts to pursue specific dreams and projects.²⁸⁸ At a more practical level this basic orientation to the world flowing from our deepest desires functions as a "wellspring from which our actions and behavior flow."²⁸⁹ Throughout his books, Smith uses a number of metaphors to show how our loves and desires elicit corresponding decisions and actions, often in ways we find ourselves unable to explain precisely:

> There is a sort of drive (or pull, depending on the metaphor) that pushes (or pulls) us to act in certain ways, develop certain relationships, pursue certain goods, make certain sacrifices, enjoy certain things. And at the end of the day, if asked why we do this, ultimately we run up against the limits of articulation even though we 'know' why we do it: it's because of what we love.²⁹⁰

In yet another metaphor, Smith compares our desires to gravity: they carry us "in the direction into which we are weighted,"²⁹¹ issuing forth in actions that are in line with the particular version of the good life that we desire. Interestingly, both functions of our ultimate desires—providing a basic attunement and pulling us towards specific actions in line with that attunement—are described by Smith in terms that remind us of the two elements of guidance pointed out by Edwards (see esp. §4.4.3): "the longings of our heart both *point* us in the direction of a kingdom and *propel* us toward it."²⁹²

Beyond these two functions of our ultimate desires that explain how God guides believers through transforming their desires, focusing on the affective and often unconscious dimension of decision-making helps us overcome two problems inherent in almost all popular contributions on divine guidance. First, they tend to overestimate the importance of thinking and conscious deliberation.²⁹³ Many decisions, and not only trivial

---

287 Smith, 27.
288 Smith, 25.
289 Smith, *You Are What You Love*, 2.
290 Smith, *Desiring*, 51–52. Cf. Bonhoeffer's comments on how the deepest motives behind our choices are never fully clear to us, §6.4.2.
291 Smith, *You Are What You Love*, 14.
292 Smith, 12. Edwards spoke of the twin functions of *instruction* and *inducement* (§4.4.3).
293 This problem is further intensified in light of much recent research into the function of the unconscious. See also Smith, 33. For Smith, this is a symptom of all traditions of Christian spirituality that approach human beings primarily as 'thinking things.' Smith criticizes the (American?) church for following modernity by still aiming primarily at people's head

ones, are taken without such careful deliberation but in a profound way reveal our deepest priorities.[294] Second, by stressing the importance of the transformation of desires as a crucial part of the process of divine guidance, we do not need to isolate the supposedly important decisions from the myriad of daily decisions that in the end might well be more weighty than the ones we deemed to be so.

Smith's primary aim is to convince his readers that, if our desires play such a fundamental role in the life of discipleship, on the one hand we need to see how our world is full of liturgies driven by antithetical kingdoms,[295] and on the other hand we need to think through how the church can be a place of 'counter-formation.'[296] While our hearts need a lot of 'unlearning,'[297] above all we need a church that functions as an "affective school"[298] and an "imagination station,"[299] in which our loves and longings "need to be restored, recalibrated, and realigned by an affective immersion in the story of God in Christ reconciling the world to himself."[300] The church's worship is the most intensive site of such formation, although not the exclusive one.[301]

6.5.5 Imagination and guidance

Thus far, we have seen how it makes sense to speak of divine guidance in terms of transformation and how desires are a crucial venue for such guidance. We need, however, one additional step to understand how transformed desires bring us to specific decisions: Bondi mentioned that some *imagination* is required to transpose ultimate desires into concrete actions in line with God's kingdom purposes. When speaking of the imagination, we do not refer to the human capacity to produce baseless or

---

(forgetting about embodiment and temporality), whereas all kinds of secular liturgies successfully aim at our hearts. Although he certainly has a point, he risks posing too strong a dichotomy between desiring and thinking, which in the end will prove equally unhelpful. See also Kevin J. Vanhoozer, *Pictures at a Theological Exhibition: Scenes of the Church's Worship, Witness and Wisdom* (London: Inter-Varsity Press, 2016), 25. Cf. our earlier discussion of Paul's emphasis on the *mind* and N.T. Wright's comments in that context.

294 Smith, *Desiring*, e.g. 54.
295 See esp. Smith, chap. 3.
296 Smith, 88.
297 Smith, *You Are What You Love*, 22.
298 Smith, *Desiring*, 205. Cf. Ford, *Christian Wisdom*, 252, who speaks of the church as a "school of desire and wisdom."
299 Smith, *You Are What You Love*, 180.
300 Smith, 180.
301 Cf. Smith, *Desiring*, 150. Smith helpfully lays out a view of worship as formation over against the more popular view of worship as expression. The primary actor of the church's worship is God. See esp. Smith, *You Are What You Love*, 79–80. Cf. p. 77: "Worship is the arena in which God recalibrates our hearts, reforms our desires, and rehabituates our loves. Worship isn't just something we do; it is where God does something *to* us."

fanciful mental creations, but to "a cognitive faculty for conceiving what we cannot see ...."[302]

We need the imagination, for instance, for the act of *deliberating* about the future, because it enables us to imagine future consequences of our actions.[303] The crucial role of the imagination is captured very clearly in John Dewey's description of the process of deliberation. Dewey describes deliberation as

> the imaginative rehearsal of various courses of conduct. We give way, in our mind, to some impulse; we try, in our mind, some plan. Following its career through various steps, we find ourselves *in imagination* in the presence of the consequences that would follow: and as we like and approve, or dislike and disapprove, these consequences we find the original impulse or plan good or bad.[304]

Besides enabling us to deliberate about the future, imagination is also required to wisely appropriate the given dimensions that define major aspects of our life. Wells's practice of 'over-accepting',[305] learning to see our personal limitations as gifts of God that we may creatively put into his service requires a lot of imagination. Furthermore, through our ability to imaginatively explore other lives and times we might be invited to imitate other's choices, appropriate their ideals and consider their ways of life as sources of personal inspiration. Their stories offer us material to "ponder who we are, who we have been, and who we might become."[306]

As the above makes clear, the imagination is crucial to decision-making in general, but we need to inquire deeper into the question whether the transformation of the imagination can also be seen as a way God guides Christians in their decision-making. As we have argued, from a Reformed perspective the question 'How do I find the will of God for my life?' should be reformulated from the reverse perspective: What is God doing in the world and how does my life 'fit in' with that? In order to answer the

---

302 Vanhoozer, *Pictures*, 18. Vanhoozer complains about the 'captive evangelical imagination' that thinks of imagination as "a factory for producing images of things that are not there, rather than a cognitive faculty for conceiving what we cannot see," obviously referring to Calvin's image of the human heart as a factory of idols.
303 John Dewey, *Human Nature and Conduct* (New York: Modern Library, 1957), 190: "deliberation is a dramatic rehearsal (in imagination) of various competing possible lines of action."
304 John Dewey, *Theory of the Moral Life* (New York: Holt, Rinehart and Winston, 1966), 135 (cited in Hauerwas, *Character*, p. 213n50).
305 See §6.3.5.
306 Bondi, "Elements," 210.

first part of that question, it takes the synthetic function of the imagination to see how the very diverse parts of Scripture can be understood as a meaningful whole.[307] Furthermore, it takes the 'eyes of faith' to see how this metanarrative of salvation history develops in our own time: "Only the imagination ... enables us to 'see' God and the Kingdom of God at work in the world."[308] As we have seen, the renewal of the mind Paul mentioned in Romans 12:1-2 required an eschatological perspective, and, if anything, living with an eschatological perspective requires imagination. Hence, seeing the world—past, present, and future—in terms of a single overarching theodrama requires a robust, biblically informed imagination.[309]

Yet, imagination is not only important to understand what God is doing in Christ in the world, but also what this has to do with our small lives and how this gives them meaning. This does not require in the first place a correct 'application' of the text to our situation, but learning to see our situations, our life and times, in the light of and as part of the story of God's redemption.[310] Interestingly, this is exactly what Richard Hays describes as the 'conversion of the imagination' that Paul tried to effectuate in gentile believers: "Gentiles needed to be initiated into reading practices that enabled them to receive Israel's Scripture as their own."[311] What is needed is a 'theodramatic transposition,' "the ability to imaginatively view one's current situation as caught up in the very same story as that of ancient Israel, or, more to the point, the early church."[312] If we succeed in

---

307 Vanhoozer, *Faith Speaking Understanding*, 4: "Yet synthesis - keeping the big picture in mind - is just as important and requires imagination: the ability to incorporate the individual parts of Scripture into unifying patterns."
308 Vanhoozer, *Pictures*, 27.
309 This could be seen as a summary of Vanhoozer's various works: "I want the church to recover the power of the *biblical* imagination. The challenge is to read Scripture, the 'living and active' word of God (Heb 4:12) so that it fuels, forms and reforms our imaginations (...). The goal is to see the triune God at work in the world, making all things new, and to foster a desire to participate in the renewal of all things in Christ through the Spirit" (34). Hence Vanhoozer's frequent complaint that "many Christians are suffering from malnourished imaginations" (e.g. *Pictures*, 20). From the perspective of our current project, it might be possible that the way many believers search for clear-cut and undoubtable guidance is partly due to an inability to imaginatively relate to the 'theodrama.'
310 Cf. Vanhoozer, *Faith Speaking Understanding*, 133: "Instead of asking how the text 'applies' to us in our day and age, as if the important thing is to discover hoe the text relates to our world, it is better to think in terms of inserting oneself into the world of the biblical text, which is the true story of our world."
311 Richard B. Hays, *The Conversion of the Imagination: Paul as Interpreter of Israel's Scripture* (Grand Rapids: Eerdmans, 2005), viii. Cf. p. 10: "an imaginative projection of their lives into the framework of the Pentateuchal narrative." Hays considers this an important example for the church to follow, viii.
312 Vanhoozer, *Faith Speaking Understanding*, 200. The words "or, more to the point" can be misleading, as Vanhoozer clearly means that both are part of the same story. What he hints at is that some form of 'weighted authority' must apply, in which material from later 'stages' of the story is brought to bear on earlier material.

relating our lives to the story of God and his kingdom, we need imagination once more to see how our often minor decisions can contribute to *shalom*. It takes some imagination to believe that our feeble efforts might somehow contribute to the coming Kingdom.[313]

In summary, we have seen how we need the imagination to 'see' past, present, and future of God's story of redemption, to rightly appropriate and consider past, present, and future of our personal lives, and to learn from and take into account past, present, and future of other people that surround us—either closely or at a distance in time or place. As these are major dimensions which can impossibly be consciously overseen and rationally assessed in every single decision, thinking of God's guidance in terms of transformation, especially of our heart, desires, and imagination, enables us to do justice to all interrelated dimensions of human life.

6.5.6 But what about sin?
We have seen in this section how our claim that God guides believers primarily through transforming their hearts is in line with Paul's concise description of discipleship in Romans 12:1-2. Furthermore, we have argued that especially the transformation of our desires and imagination performs a crucial role in this process. All of this leads us to the final question to be answered in this section, one that is especially weighty from a Reformed perspective: Are we not at risk, in focusing on sanctification and transformation in this way, to underestimate the impact of abiding sin in believers?[314]

It is important to understand that transformation does not result in faultless and sinless choices. Quite the opposite: in our investigations of vocation, wisdom, and discernment we have stressed that sin and ambiguity will always remain in the decisions we make. We could even argue that in this model there is more room to honestly acknowledge this painful reality than in the other models, where it might remain hidden under the claim of having received specific guidance from God. In a model of guidance that stresses transformation, there is room to reckon with "fallible yet redeemable choices"[315] that do justice to the 'trial and error' often involved in discernment, to the provisonality of our knowledge, and to the ambivalence of our desires.

---

313 Cf. Kevin J. Vanhoozer, "In Bright Shadow: C.S. Lewis on the Imagination for Theology and Discipleship," in *The Romantic Rationalist: God, Life, and Imagination in the Work of C.S. Lewis*, ed. John Piper and David Mathis (Wheaton: Crossway, 2014), 104: "it takes imagination to see that you are building a Cathedral."
314 Remember that Edwards's account of sanctification and virtue drove us to exactly the same question; see the end of §4.4.6.
315 Preece, *Viability of the Vocation Tradition*, 176.

Hence, we need to stress that most of the key words of this section—formation and transformation, learning and unlearning, recalibration, etc.—are terms that focus on a toilsome and often painful process: sanctification never comes to an end in this life and is never complete. We need to think of ourselves as 'split selves,' experiencing an inner struggle between rival desires for our ultimate allegiance.[316] This was also stressed in our discussion of discernment, where the primary role of self-reflection was the recognition and unmasking of the sinful tendencies and desires in the human heart. Because we remain 'split selves,' affected by sin, following Bonhoeffer we should emphasize that "at the end of the day, I can only pray that God may hold merciful judgment over ... all decisions."[317]

It is exactly because the reality of abiding sin in believers must be taken deeply seriously that we placed our account of guidance in the domain of sanctification. Yet at the same time, in doing so we explicitly resist the tendency to focus so much on the impact of abiding sin that it results in a practical distrust of the work of the Holy Spirit.[318] Although Paul's confidence in the (transformed!) mind to discern the will of God might sound overconfident to the modern ear, faith in the transformative presence of the Spirit in the believer must not be nullified by an overemphasis on the influence of abiding sin.[319]

As an important instrument in both this process of transformation and in personal decision-making we have stressed the importance of the Christian community. Even though the Christian community definitely is not a safety lock against sin either, it is an important God-given instrument when it comes to making responsible decisions.[320] In the next section, we will turn to the role of the Christian community in the process of God's guidance.

---

316 See Smith, *Desiring*, 55n30 for the notion of split selves.
317 DBWE 15:227.
318 Hence, those views on guidance that stress that God most likely calls us to the tasks and places that we least desire should be rejected. Their prominence is reflected in the fact that even Karl Barth found it necessary in his KD to reject the 'pietistic rule' "What we take ill, will be God's will." See Barth, *CD III/4*, 635.
319 In this respect the Reformed tradition, including Q114 of the Heidelberg Catechism, has been rightly criticized for its one-sided emphasis on abiding sin and mortification. See e.g. Van den Brink and Van der Kooi, *Christian Dogmatics*, 691.
320 As made sufficiently clear by Niebuhr, communities are no safety locks against sin. See esp. Reinhold Niebuhr, *Moral Man and Immoral Society: A Study in Ethics and Politics* (New York: Charles Scribner's Sons, 1932).

6.6 Community and Guidance

Thesis 11: Formation and transformation take place on the individual level, but are impossible without the constant support and influence of a Christian community, which can be of great aid in the important tasks of deliberation and discernment.

6.6.1 Introduction
In the eleventh thesis on guidance as introduced in section 5.4, I stated that a conception of guidance that stresses vocation, wisdom, discernment, and transformation presupposes various important roles for the Christian community. In this section we will support that thesis through elaborating a number of venues that we encountered in our earlier reflections on these concepts.[321] By explicating the role of the community, we try to overcome the impression that the search for guidance is a "solitary search," in which the individual is isolated from his or her social networks.[322] The stories of our lives are enfolded in countless other stories, hence our decisions influence other lives and are influenced by them.[323]

In our discussion of the various roles of the Christian community in the process of guidance, we start with a discussion of the Christian community as a place of (trans)formation (§6.6.2). We then move on to an analysis of the Christian community as a site of inspiration and challenge (§6.6.3), and as a place of advice and accountability (§6.6.4). Finally, we will focus briefly on the specific role of friends (§6.6.5). In the various sections, different forms of the Christian community will feature, corresponding with the reality that the Christian community is a layered concept. For example, it can refer to the universal church, a specific denomination, a national church, a local congregation, or a group within the local congregation. Given the nature of our approach, most of the times those forms of community that are closest to the individual in question will be in mind.

---

321 Hence, no 'complete' account of the roles of the Christian community is to be expected, but a succinct analysis of the communal aspects of guidance we encountered in the previous sections.

322 Hahnenberg, *Awakening Vocation*, 159–61.

323 Cf. Michael Horton's critique of a spirituality focused on the extraordinary: "It is all too easy to turn other people in our lives into a supporting cast for our life movie. The problem is that they don't follow the role or the lines we've given them. They are actual people with actual needs that get in the way of our plot, especially if they're as ambitious as we are." Michael Horton, *Ordinary: Sustainable Faith in a Radical, Restless World* (Grand Rapids: Zondervan, 2014), 16.

6.6.2 The Christian community as a place of (trans)formation
Earlier in this chapter we have stressed the importance of formation and transformation for a theology of guidance. We have emphasized how *God* is constantly at work to sanctify believers, thus forming and re-forming them into persons who become wise and whose desires are brought in line with God's desires. Although in various places we mentioned the importance of forms of the Christian community in this process of formation, here we want to unpack how placing people into a community is one of the primary ways in which God influences and changes them.[324]

The most basic means of such formation is the local congregation. In the (local) church, we encounter a remarkable assemblage of people who did not choose each other, but who were brought together through their incorporation into the body of Christ. In this diverse community believers are called to the hard work of learning to love brothers and sisters of different ages, lifestyles, and wealth; people with different preferences, dreams, and desires. Here, believers must learn to humbly count others more significant than themselves (Phil. 2:3), looking for ways in which the other can flourish. In this light, the diversity of the local congregation is crucial and congregations that tend to become too homogeneous must not only be concerned about their theology and practices, but also about their future as a transformed people.[325]

One type of diversity within the Christian community must be stressed as particularly important for thinking about guidance primarily through the lens of transformation: the Christian community cannot be a place of genuine formation if it is not cross-generational.[326] Whereas Hauerwas and Pinches rightly emphasize how a cross-generational community is needed to pass on proven practices from one generation to another, from the perspective of guidance the more basic fact of frequent interaction between generations is important in itself: the seasoned wisdom of older generations, if passed on discerningly, will shape the perspectives of new generations and put their desires and dreams into perspective.[327]

---

324 Cf. Cunningham, *Christian Ethics*, 42: "To use a visual metaphor (…) the communities of which we are a part don't merely tell us where to look and what to look for; they actually shape the lenses through which we see the world, such that whatever is 'out there' will be processed, by our optic nerves, according to the patterns that the community has come to expect."
325 In this light, one could also argue that the socalled 'circulation of the saints' in areas with a major diversity of churches might actually hamper the process of transformation.
326 Cf. Hauerwas and Pinches, *Christians Among The Virtues*, 96: "Practical wisdom cannot be had without a cross-generational community in which a tradition of practices is passed on, sustained, and modified."
327 Remember how Aquinas stressed the importance of 'old folk' for the acquisition of wisdom, *ST* II-II.49.4.

Formation takes place through the *practices* the community engages in.[328] First and foremost, through being a *worshipping* community, believers are taught that the ultimate reason for their existence is to serve God and that their worship is to permeate their entire life. Second, through the reading of *Scripture* and the proclamation, believers are frequently confronted with the stories that shape the life of the church and with the perspective these stories provide.[329] Third, *prayer* is learned and offered in community. In praying, believers come before the face of God and express that their own strength, insight, faith, love, and hope are insufficient in themselves and that they are in constant need of God's love, strength, and wisdom. Fourth, the practice of celebrating the *Eucharist* reminds believers of the importance of communion with Christ, reinforcing the sense of being part of his story by resting in his atoning work, and encouraging them to long for the consummation of his work. Equally important, the Eucharist makes the church as the body of Christ visible and teaches the community to love and care for each member. Fifth, the practice of *baptism* reminds the believers that they have died and risen with Christ and have been given a new life in which they are called to live. Furthermore, baptism, by being equal for everyone, emphasizes that although the community is diverse and people have different roles in it, within the Kingdom of God all are equal and there are no 'special Christians.'[330] Finally, in the practice of *offering* believers are shaped after the self-giving character of God and learn what it means to bring personal sacrifices. Giving reinforces the conviction that what we live for is not personal comfort but the flourishing of others and of the entire creation for the glory of God. All these practices reinforce in the believer a vision of the good life that carries over into their everyday life.[331]

---

328 There has recently been a lot of attention for the formative influence of the liturgy and other practices of the church. See for a more detailed account e.g. Smith, *Desiring*, chap. 5. 'Practicing (for) the Kingdom: An Exegesis of the Social Imagery Embedded in Christian Worship.'

329 Wright, *After You Believe*, 283, shows how Scripture permeates all the practices of the church: "Examples can be misconstrued, communities can take on a life of their own, and practices can come, as we've noted, empty or meaningless ritual. With scripture, all that changes. God works, by the Holy Spirit, through the reading, teaching, and preaching of scripture, to create new frameworks of ideas, to remind us of facets of the story we were in danger of forgetting, to correct imbalances, and above all to stir our hearts and minds with fresh visions of God's love." Although we concur with Wright on the importance of Scripture in the praxis of the church, here he seems overly optimistic in stating that using Scripture precludes all the problems he mentions in the first half of the sentence.

330 Cf. Wright, 281.

331 Our account in this section could be charged with being a form of 'ecclesiological docetism' that forgets about the humanness of the church. Although we did indeed sketch a rather idealistic picture of the formative power of the local congregation, two remarks are in order. First, we described the congregation as it *should* be in light of New Testament

We have seen how God shapes believers and their perspective of life through placing them in a local congregation with its characteristic practices. By becoming a member of the local congregation, however, believers also become members of Christ's body throughout history and dispersed over the entire world. Here, additional models, practices, perspectives, and traditions are encountered that can shape, reinforce, challenge, or criticize what goes on in the local congregation. By placing them in the community of the wider church, God shapes individual believers into persons that are enabled to make wise decisions in light of the coming of God's Kingdom. Beyond this basic formative function of the church, however, the community also plays roles more directly related to making important decisions. In the next section we turn to the question how the community provides sources of inspiration, and after that we will focus on the community as the place of concrete accountability.

6.6.3 Community as place of inspiration and challenge
In the Christian community we encounter other people, past and present, who are improvising the Christian faith in their lives.[332] Through observing, asking questions to, and walking alongside each other, members of the community shape each other's perspectives on life in profound ways.[333]

In the context of guidance and decision-making, fellow believers that function as such sources of inspiration perform several important functions. In this connection, we should not only think of the living believers surrounding us, but also of those who preceded us. A particularly important function can be ascribed to the saints and martyrs of church history, although (writing from a Reformed perspective) several caveats must be made in this respect. When we write about gaining inspiration from the lives of other believers, we do not intend to suggest that saints or martyrs

---

exhortations, but often fails to be fully in practice. Second, especially in our description of the local congregation as a community of different people that did not choose each other, we included the challenge of living with and loving each other. In terms of guidance, such a congregation does also offer examples of how we would *not* want our lives to develop.

332 In this context, inspiration can take both a constructive and a critical form: constructive, by showing us how the values we hold as important can be lived out in our concrete lives, and critical, by confronting us with values and ideals that we do not already have and questioning values that we do have.

333 From the perspective of virtue ethics it is commonly acknowledged that role models play a crucial role in the process of becoming virtuous; see e.g. Cunningham, *Christian Ethics*, 178; Christian B. Miller and Angela Knobel, "Some Foundational Questions in Philosophy about Character," in *Character: New Directions from Philosophy, Psychology, and Theology*, ed. Christian B. Miller et al. (Oxford: Oxford University Press, 2015), 36; Jennifer A. Herdt, *Putting On Virtue: The Legacy of the Splendid Vices* (Chicago: University Of Chicago Press, 2008), passim.

must be copied in their exact choices and deeds. Nor should we put them on a pedestal, since in that case we would easily resort to the two-tiered structure of the church we earlier rejected.[334] With these caveats in mind we can, however, ask how the object lessons we encounter in other believers do help us in making personal decisions. In order to answer that question, we need to learn to look beyond the specific actions of those models to what drives or drove them: their dreams, desires, perspective on life, and motives. When seen in that light, models provide inspiration in at least three interrelated ways.[335]

First, models enlarge our vision by reminding us of latent ideals. By their lives and the choices they make, they alert us to ideals that are held in high regard as important Christian values but that had little impact on our own lives as long as they remained abstract ideals. All Christians agree on the importance of love and wisdom, but it is not until we see them fleshed out in the people around us that they start to impact our concrete everyday decisions. Second, role models not only exemplify abstract ideals we already had, but also confront us with concrete possibilities that we did not consider before. By showing us ways of life, dreams, values, and desires different from our own, they question things we consider self-evident. The vision of a life better than ours shapes our conscience and challenges us to grow as believers. Third, exemplary believers that share important aspects of our lives provide examples of how to live the Christian life in specific contexts. For example, a mature Christian who is banker can function as a role model for other Christian bankers, and a rich Christian can show to others how to faithfully deal with the challenge and responsibility of being rich.[336]

These sources of inspiration as encountered in the lives of Christians around us are intensified with regard to saints and martyrs from church history. Due to historical distance, the contrasts often are more intense.

---

334 We are, however, not convinced that pointing at the existence of role models at all is already making such a distinction. In practice, different people, because of differing interests, character, age, etc. will be drawn to different role models.
335 Cf. Packer and Nystrom, *Guard Us, Guide Us*, 166–69.
336 Cf. Matt Bloom, "Middle Adulthood: The Joys and Paradoxes of Vocation," in *Calling All Years Good: Christian Vocation throughout Life's Seasons*, ed. Kathleen A. Cahalan and Bonnie J. Miller-McLemore (Grand Rapids: Eerdmans, 2017), 137: "Most people seem to find a calling by observing several, often many, exemplars and then comparing themselves to those examples. When they found an exemplar that seemed to be a lot like them ... they had taken an important step toward finding their calling. ... We found that people compared their talents, personality, and passions against those possessed by a variety of exemplars. When they found a good match—that is, when they discovered they were very much like a particular exemplar—they sensed that they had likely found their potential calling."

Through sharing stories about the lives of believers from other times,[337] we are all the more confronted with different customs, thoughts, and commitments. As such, models from different times tend to drive us out of our comfort zone by functioning as question marks placed by God in our lives, asking what we love, live for, strive after, and put our trust in.[338]

6.6.4 Community as a place of advice and accountability
Besides being a site of formation and transformation, and a place of inspiration and challenge with regard to decisions we take, the Christian community is also the place where one can get advice and where one is held accountable.

In various Christian traditions, there are old practices in which personal dilemma's are not only seen as a personal responsibility, but also as a responsibility of the Christian community. For example, in the Quaker tradition there is the so-called *Clearness Committee,* in which a member of the community asks for a group of advisers to think through a personal issue.[339] The member asking for advice explains the situation and the advisors are only allowed to ask questions to help remove the confusion. This way, one is expected to finally understand one's 'inner teacher.' A more recent phenomenon in which the community engages with personal issues is the so-called 'huddle', popularized by 3D Movements.[340] A 'huddle' is a small group of people, called together by a leader, which meets at least every two weeks over an extended period of time. Under the guidance of the group leader, who should be sensitive to where she or he "feels the Holy Spirit is leading the group," at the end of each session every member of the huddle should be able to answer two questions: 1. What is God saying to me? 2. What am I going to do about it?[341]

---

337 Following Elizabeth Castelli, Herman Paul rightly argues that even in the case of martyrs the focus should be on their lives and devotion, not on their death. It is the life that results in one's death as a martyr that counts, not this death in itself, Herman Paul, *De slag om het hart: Over secularisatie van het verlangen* (Utrecht: Boekencentrum, 2017), 120, with reference to Elisabeth A. Castelli, *Martyrdom and Memory: Early Christian Culture Making* (New York: Columbia University Press, 2004).
338 The idea of martyrs as question marks is taken from Paul, *Slag om het hart,* 120.
339 See for a clear description of the clearness committee Parker J. Palmer, *A Hidden Wholeness: The Journey Toward An Undivided Life* (San Francisco: Jossey-Bass, 2004), chap. 8.
340 3D Movements is a global organization that provides trainings and resources on discipleship and on being a missional church. In the Netherlands, it is closely linked to the movement *Nederland Zoekt.* For a description of the 'huddle' by the founder of the movement, see Mike Breen, *Building a Discipling Culture,* 2nd edition (Pawleys Island: 3DM Publishing, 2011), esp. part 3, "Using Huddles to Disciple People."
341 See Breen, *Building a Discipling Culture.* Breen does not argue but simply assumes that God is always speaking and guiding in ways that are obvious enough for anyone to recognize.

In light of what we have written about guidance before, there are obviously problems with these forms of group guidance, as both the inner light (Quakers) and the assumption that God frequently 'speaks' to believers about very concrete issues (huddle) must be questioned. Yet there is deep wisdom in the idea that meeting regularly with a set group of people enables members of the community to 'bear each other's burdens' when it comes to making important personal decisions. By asking careful questions, inner confusion may be removed. Moreover, in Christian communities in which we live over extended periods of time relationships of trust can be built in which believers can be honest and vulnerable enough to open up their lives to each other and in this way to receive guidance.

The Christian community is, however, not only to be a place of trust where advice can be asked and given, but also a place where believers must hold each other accountable. Given the fact that, as a Christian, one should not only count with inner confusion when it comes to making weighty decisions but also with sinful desires and self-deception, the accountability offered within the Christian community offers helpful resources for self-criticism.[342] In a community where people share the values of the gospel, we may expect to be held to the standards that flow forth from these. We have pointed before at the importance of being able to explain our choices in other terms than with a reference to a directly revealed 'will of God'. It is within the Christian community, where people largely share our language and perspective, that we might best be able to explain our decisions and the rationale behind them.

6.6.5 The special role of the 'friend'

Thus far we focused on the (local) Christian community, but there is one additional figure of interest that needs to be discussed separately, as it occurred in a number of important places throughout this book: the friend.[343] Especially in our discussion of guidance in the personal lives of John Calvin and Jonathan Edwards, we saw how they sometimes invited

---

342 See for the relation between accountability, self-deception, and wisdom Allen, "Primacy of Phronesis," esp. 364.
343 In a time where the word 'friend' may refer to someone who once clicked on a particular icon, it is necessary to explain who we do refer to: friends here are the 'close friends' with whom one shares a relationship of mutual love, interest, and respect; with whom one shares a history through which the friendship is formed; and, through the shared history, a friend is someone who knows the other, but can also have sufficient distance to be critical of and question his or her choices. Whether partners count as 'friends' when it comes to important decisions depends on the type of decision to be taken and the personal involvement of the partner in it.

a number of trusted friends when they had to make weighty decisions and asked them to think the decisions through with them (see sections 3.5 and 4.6).[344] As this was an advice we also encountered in a number of the contemporary contributions, at the end of this section on the Christian community we have to reflect on the specific role a friend can perform.

Given the concreteness of the situations in which practical wisdom is required it would appear that at the deepest level we are all on our own. Yet, as Pieper holds (following Aquinas), there is a way to grasp the complexities of the decision to be made by another person: "through the love of friendship" (or *amor amicitiae*).[345] He elaborates on this situation as follows:

> A friend, and a *prudent* friend, can help to shape a friend's decision. He does so by virtue of that love which makes the friend's problem his own, the friend's ego his own (so that after all it is not entirely 'from outside'). For by virtue of that oneness which love can establish he is able to visualize the concrete situation calling for decision, visualize it from, as it were, the actual center of responsibility. Therefore it is possible for a friend— only for a friend and only for a *prudent* fiend—to help with counsel and direction to shape a friend's decision or, somewhat in the manner of a judge, help to reshape it.[346]

In light of the account of guidance developed over the previous sections, we could unpack this statement as follows. First, a friend is able to make *the friend's problem* her own. Through the closeness of love, the friend is enabled not just to objectively evaluate the relevant factors of the decision, but to understand what factors of the situation are important to the friend and what is their relative priority from the perspective of the friend.

In order to do so, not only does the friend need to place herself in the other's position, but she is also to a certain extent enabled by the friendship to place herself in the other's heart, to make *the friend's ego her own*. As we have argued before, an account of guidance should not focus exclusively on the moments of decision, and it is the friend who, through a

---

344 Recall how there are some differences between Calvin and Edwards at this point. E.g., whereas Edwards invited wise friends to give advice that he was willing to take very seriously, Calvin at times seems to have gone so far as to place the decision in the hands of such friends.
345 Pieper, *Four Cardinal Virtues*, 29.
346 Pieper, 29.

shared history, is particularly prepared to understand the other's position from a broader perspective. Through this shared history, he or she is able to evaluate the situation with the values, priorities, strengths, weaknesses, and desires of the friend in mind, even if these are not necessarily shared.[347]

By making both the friend's *problem and perspective* her own, the wise friend is the person who can give the most helpful counsel and through that counsel share part of the responsibility of her friend. This counsel can, however, also take the form of critique. This might be, in the terms of Pieper, critique that *reshapes* the decision by pointing at factors the friend knows to be important but lost sight of. There can also be, however, a more fundamental form of critique, in particular when one observes a discrepancy between what one knows the other to value and the actual decision the friend is about to make. Once again, the unique position of friends allows them to offer profound critique that is aimed at the well-being of the other.

Whereas Pieper's remark focuses exclusively on moments of decision, from the broader perspective of this chapter the gift of friendship is an instrument of God's guidance beyond moments of explicit choice, because sharing (parts of) one's life with close friends inevitably means sharing one's perspective on life, one's motives, and desires. Friends function not only as mirrors by having different values and priorities, but also as the ones who enquire into our drive and in this way elucidate our priorities in preparation for upcoming moments of decision.

6.7 Guidance and the Holy Spirit

> *Thesis 12: Guidance by the Spirit primarily takes place in and through ordinary human decision-making processes, as daily life is the normal workplace of the Spirit, not exclusively the extraordinary experiences.*
>
> *Thesis 13: Extraordinary instances of divine guidance may put ordinary decision-making processes in perspective; these extraordinary instances are indeed extra-ordinary and rest upon divine initiative. Hence, they cannot be part of a heuristic procedure to 'find' the will of God.*

6.7.1 Introduction

At the end of this chapter we need to return to one crucial question: In the intra-evangelical discussion we analyzed in chapter 2, the most com-

---

347 This does also mean that, although in this section we focused on the Christian community, the friend in question does not necessarily have to be a *Christian* friend.

mon complaint against the 'wisdom view' was that it endorses a Deist approach to divine guidance. In light of the preceding sections, we are now able to ask whether this is a valid objection. In §6.7.2 we will argue how in every aspect of guidance discussed in this chapter the Holy Spirit performs a crucial and decisive role. In §6.7.3 I will then argue that this complaint emerges from a preference for aligning the Spirit with the extraordinary instead of the ordinary. Section 6.7.4 will take up the issue of the indwelling of the Spirit that plays a crucial role in the account we developed, in order to show that often the most invisible influences of the Spirit are most lasting and transformative. In §6.7.5 we will turn to a question that might have arisen from the reading of this section: does it still make sense to speak about *guidance* when the concept is developed in such a nuanced and qualified way? Could we not do without it and simply speak of sanctification? Finally, §6.7.6 will conclude this chapter with a number of characteristics of the Spirit-led life taken from some of the authors whose work we discussed in this chapter.

6.7.2 A deist account of guidance?
The wisdom model, especially in the original form as advocated by Garry Friesen, has regularly been accused of promoting a deist account of God's involvement in human lives.[348] Packer and Nystrom mention Friesen and his wisdom model as an example of what they label as 'subspiritual' approaches to guidance that tend to overlook "the full reality of the Holy Spirit's ministry in guidance."[349] They identify three main problems of such subspiritual approaches: an overvaluation of reason, an undervaluation of the 'grace of faithful waiting,' and a restriction of the work of the Spirit.[350]

Since we have taken the model that is accused of deism as the starting point of our own proposal, we need to face the question: Is the account we developed one in which the active involvement of God, and especially of the Holy Spirit, is marginalized? Although at first sight this might appear to be true, any serious reading of the themes developed in the current chapter must lead us to a denial of the suggestion. Everything we wrote on guidance and transformation does only make sense in light of

---

348 So e.g. Dallas Willard, *In Search of Guidance: Developing a Conversational Relationship with God* (Ventura: Regal Books, 1984), 99, who speaks of "Bible deism"; Klaus Bockmühl, *Listening to the God Who Speaks: Reflections on God's Guidance from Scripture and the Lives of God's People* (Colorado Springs: Helmers & Howard, 1990), 51, speaks of "practical deism"; Smith, *Listening to God*, 101: "I doubt that God is so removed from our life situations." See also the discussion in Kovach, "Toward a Theology of Guidance," 10ff.
349 Packer and Nystrom, *Guard Us, Guide Us*, 219–21.
350 Packer and Nystrom, 221–25.

the ongoing active influence and involvement of the Holy Spirit throughout the Christian live. For the sake of the argument we will be more specific about the role of the Spirit in several of the aspects discussed.

Wisdom and Spirit. In §6.3.4 we discussed the nature of Christian wisdom and explicitly stated that such wisdom is essentially Spirit-cultivated, nurtured in believers by the Spirit in answer to prayer. The theo-dramatic accounts of wisdom as improvisation provided by Wells and Vanhoozer refer to the ongoing influence of the Spirit throughout. Given the nature of Christian wisdom as we have described it, the fear that once such wisdom is acquired believers can do without the Spirit is unwarranted.[351]

Discernment and Spirit. Speaking theologically about discernment without referring to the Spirit is impossible, as it is the Spirit who equips us for discernment.[352] The Spirit enables believers to 'read' the situation, see what are important aspects, and evaluate possible consequences. More importantly, the Spirit teaches believers to see themselves and their situations in light of the story of God.

Transformation and the Spirit. In stressing the importance of transformation for a Reformed approach to guidance we have located guidance under the rubric of sanctification. If anything is a work of the Spirit, sanctification is. No lasting transformation of the mind, no recalibration of desires, and no enlightening of the imagination is possible without the ongoing sanctification wrought by the Spirit.

Community and Spirit. Finally, the Christian community as the body of Christ is the temple in which the Spirit dwells. If this is the community in which believers are formed, inspired, challenged, given advice, and held accountable, how can the Spirit be absent?[353]

Clearly, in the account of guidance developed in the present chapter the Spirit is present throughout. The reason this view is accused of tending to a practical deism might not be that it is defective with regard to the work of the Spirit, but that it proceeds from a view of that work that refuses to be preoccupied with the extraordinary. We will discuss this aspect further in the next section.

---

351 Cf. the statement of the Curé de Torcy in Georges Bernanos, *The Diary of a Country Priest*, trans. Pamela Morris, reprint (Cambridge: Da Capo Press, 2002), 91: "Prudence is the final imprudence when by slow degrees it prepares the mind to do without God."
352 Cf. O'Donovan, *Finding and Seeking*, 10.
353 Cf. Stanley Hauerwas and William H. Willimon, *The Holy Spirit* (Nashville: Abingdon Press, 2015), 58: "People today often speak of the Spirit as individual and personal, when … the Holy Spirit is intensely communal and corporate."

6.7.3 The Spirit, the ordinary, and the extraordinary
The charge of deism raised against the transformation model brings into focus a skewed understanding of the work of the Holy Spirit that tends to focus on extraordinary experiences of the Spirit.[354] In the classic 'blueprint' view, which we discussed as 'guidance through information,' people are encouraged to seek definite forms of guidance, often towards radical new directions. As a result of speaking of guidance in this way people come to expect definite and unmistakable signs of the Spirit's involvement.

In the theses we used to sketch the contours of a Reformed view on guidance, the final thesis stated that there is no need to deny extraordinary instances of divine guidance from a Reformed perspective (see §5.4). Yet at the same time, we stressed that these are indeed *extra*-ordinary, rest upon divine initiative, and hence cannot be part of a method to find the will of God. In this chapter, we have stressed the importance of God's ordinary means of guidance.

In a time where everything is focused on things visible and quantifiable, this does, however, require a change of perspective and a certain amount of imagination. We need to acknowledge that "too often we look for the Spirit in the extraordinary when God has promised to be present in the ordinary."[355] Or perhaps even starker, we must believe that what we consider ordinary is in fact God's extraordinary: "God's greatest signs and wonders are being done every week through the ordinary means of preaching, baptism, and the Lord's Supper."[356] Hence, it should not surprise us that God guides in ways that we often do not notice.[357]

In this respect, Luke's portrayal of the work of the Spirit in *Acts* exercises an undue influence on many evangelical accounts of guidance. Although there are instances in Acts where the Spirit functions almost like the *bat qol* in later Judaism,[358] two remarks need to be made in this respect. First, as Horton reminds us, "[e]ven in the era of the extraordinary ministry of the apostles, the ordinary means of grace are front and

---

354 Already in 1903, B.B. Warfield complained that the phrase 'the leading of the Spirit' from Romans 8:14 beared such a flavor of fanaticism that "many simple-minded people of God" tended to avoid the terminology; see for a recent edition B.B. Warfield, *The Person and Work of the Holy Spirit* (Vestavia Hills: Solid Ground Christian Books, 2010), Ch.4, esp. p. 32.
355 Smith, *You Are What You Love*, 67.
356 Horton, *Ordinary*, 140.
357 Horton, 140: "God works through ordinary means every day in so many ways that we don't even notice his involvement and our complete dependence on him in each and every moment." Cf. p. 14.
358 See E. Haenchen, *The Acts of the Apostles* (Oxford: Blackwell, 1971), 92–93, 95.

center."³⁵⁹ As O'Donovan points out, even at an extraordinary moment like that of Acts 16, Paul's vision does not have the last word but the conclusion that is drawn from it.³⁶⁰ Second, Luke's account must be read together with those of Paul and John. According to Rowan Williams, in Paul "the Spirit is no longer specified by, and thus potentially limited to, the extraordinary and episodic" and in John "the Spirit is nowhere associated with the extraordinary."³⁶¹ For Williams, "it is clear that the association of Spirit exclusively or chiefly with the more dramatic charismata is a misunderstanding."³⁶² Williams is reticent to answer the question 'where, or what, is Holy Spirit' in a precise way, and so is much of the Christian tradition.³⁶³ This same reticence we encountered for example in the three authors we analyzed in our discussion of discernment, all of whom repeatedly warned against assuming that the Spirit communicates mainly immediately. In this light, we must conclude that the Spirit plays an active and decisive role in the account of guidance we provided, but, as stressed in most classic accounts of Reformed pneumatology, does so primarily in mediated ways. Emphasizing the ordinary work of the Spirit can never be equated with endorsing a practical deism.

6.7.4 The indwelling of the Spirit

That the 'ordinary' work of the Spirit should get pride of place in a Reformed account of guidance could perhaps best be illustrated by focusing on the important notion of *indwelling*.³⁶⁴ As we have seen, the indwelling of the Spirit in believers played a crucial role in the theology of Jonathan Edwards (see esp. §4.4.6). According to Edwards, the Spirit "unites himself with the mind of a saint, takes him for his temple, actuates and influences him as a new, supernatural principle of life and action...."³⁶⁵ Hence, the transformation of one's desires, values, and attitudes has everything to do with this dwelling of the Spirit in believers. Ray Yeo recently showed that for Edwards, the indwelling of the Spirit as "an influence of

---

359 Horton, *Ordinary*, 79.
360 O'Donovan, *Finding and Seeking*, 221: "The verb 'concluding' is all-important; the call was not the dream as such, but what the dream, taken with all the other circumstances, permitted them to recognize."
361 Rowan Williams, "Word and Spirit," in *The Holy Spirit: Classic and Contemporary Readings*, ed. Eugene F. Rogers, Jr. (Malden: Wiley-Blackwell, 2009), 59.
362 Williams, 60.
363 Williams, 62.
364 Calling indwelling an 'ordinary' work of the Spirit highlights the awkwardness of distinguishing between ordinary and extraordinary works of the Spirit. For what could be more extraordinary than the Spirit of God dwelling in human beings? Perhaps distinguishing between the fundamental and the auxiliary work of the Spirit would be more helpful in times where everything normal is at least boring.
365 WJE 17:411.

the Spirit that is internal and inherent within the subject's nature and heart" is crucial,[366] but that his account raises several important questions, and remains underdeveloped especially with regard to the *how* of the Spirit's work in the believer.[367]

Yeo points to William Alston's article 'The Indwelling of the Holy Spirit' for a more helpful understanding of indwelling. According to Alston, the indwelling of the Spirit is transformative in nature and denotes "the ways in which the Spirit modifies the character of the person, her values, tendencies, attitudes, priorities, and so on."[368] As such, sanctification and the indwelling of the Spirit influence one's "motivational structure."[369] For Alston, neither a 'fiat model,' where God transforms by divine fiat, nor an 'interpersonal model,' where God influences believers in the way human persons try to influence each other, only with more 'instruments' at his disposal,[370] do sufficient justice to the internality of God in

---

366 Ray S. Yeo, "Christian Character Formation and the Infusion of Grace," in *Character: New Directions from Philosophy, Psychology, and Theology*, ed. Christian B. Miller et al. (Oxford: Oxford University Press, 2015), 539.
367 Yeo, 542-3: "In particular, how are we to understand the union of the Holy Spirit with one's psychological faculties? More precisely, in what way can a divine person, as opposed to merely the effect of his action or influence, be said to be so united with the faculties within the soul of man so as to form a new nature and intrinsic vital principle?"
368 William P. Alston, "The Indwelling of the Holy Spirit," in *Divine Nature and Human Language: Essays in Philosophical Theology* (New York: Cornell University Press, 1989), 225. Note how this view of indwelling is in line with what we wrote on transformation in §6.5. Alston's article was originally published in Thomas V. Morris, ed., *Philosophy and the Christian Faith* (Notre Dame: University of Notre Dame Press, 1988), 121–50. See also Gijsbert van den Brink's discussion of Alston's article, Gijsbert van den Brink, "De geestelijke groei van de nieuwe mens: Op het snijvlak van theologie en psychologie," in *Onrustig is ons hart: Mens-zijn in christelijk perspectief*, ed. Henri Veldhuis (Zoetermeer: Boekencentrum, 1994), 88–109, where Van den Brink develops a relationship between transformation, character, desire, and heart similar to the one presented in this chapter.
369 Alston, "Indwelling," 229: "tendencies, desires, values, attitudes, emotional proclivities, and the like."
370 Although he rejects the model as a sufficient explanation of indwelling, in his description of how it could work Alston gives a beautiful description of 'subtle' ways in which God could influence people to perform certain actions that is in line with what we developed in this chapter: "God could affect the ideational processes of the individual in more subtle fashion. He could bring it about that facets of the person's present life appear to him in an unfavorable light and that the life of agape appears to him highly attractive, without this being taken by the individual as a communication from God. Again, God could present Himself to the individual as a role model, giving the person more of a sense of things divine, thereby increasing the desire for holiness and communion with God. God could make His love and providence for the individual more obvious, more salient in the person's mind, thereby evoking responses of gratitude and yearning for closer communion. Finally, God could make new resources available to the individual, new resources of strength of will, of energy for perseverance in the face of discouragement, of inner strength that enables one to avoid dependence on the approval of one's associates." (Alston, "Indwelling," 236.)

the process of transformation, as in both models God remains relatively external.[371]

In line with Edwards's remark that the Spirit 'unites himself with the mind of a saint,' Alston suggests a third model, the "partial life sharing" model. Through the indwelling of the Spirit, believers share not substantially in the divine live,[372] but partially "in various psychological elements of the Holy Spirit."[373] Through breaking down the "barriers that normally separate one life from another,"[374] the Spirit shares with believers, in ways they are not aware of, certain feelings, attitudes, tendencies, values, and beliefs. This sharing is not just cognitive in nature, but also *conative*.[375] That is, the indwelling Spirit does not only share certain 'psychological states' but also introduces into our "conative systems" tendencies toward them, however "weak, isolated, and fragile" these might initially be.[376] Through his indwelling influence, the Spirit can guide believers, often in subtle ways, to actions and decisions that reflect God's own heart.

6.7.5 On speaking about 'guidance'
In the previous sections we have argued that it makes sense to speak about our approach of guidance as guidance *by the Spirit*, and that hence the charge of deism is unfounded. It is clear that the Spirit is actively involved throughout the process. At the end of this chapter, an even more fundamental question needs to be answered: given that we have stressed transformation, wisdom, and discernment, does it make sense to speak of *guidance* at all? Would we lose anything if we simply dropped the concept?

To answer this question we must first understand the possible meanings of the word 'guide'. When used for persons the word guide can have two basic meanings.[377] In the first meaning, a guide is someone who shows the way to others, who gives precise directions. A 'tour guide,' or even a *TomTom* are examples of this type of guide. In the second meaning, a guide is someone who advises others, mentors them with regard to behavior or belief, a 'spiritual guide.' Whereas the first type of guide gives

---

[371] Alston, 239. For Alston, both models work with a figurative interpretation of the biblical notion of indwelling (241-2).
[372] Alston, 245. Alston is well aware that as creatures we can never share fully in the divine life.
[373] Yeo, "Christian Character Formation and the Infusion of Grace," 544.
[374] Alston, "Indwelling," 246.
[375] Once again, we find an interesting parallel with Edwards's interpretation of guidance as consisting of both *instruction* and *inducement* (§4.4.3).
[376] Alston, "Indwelling," 251.
[377] See e.g. the *Oxford Dictionary of English*, 3d edition, s.v. "Guide".

concrete information and direction, the second type of guide provides perspective. The first type of guide focuses primarily on destinations, the second on the journey. In the way we developed guidance in this chapter, the Spirit obviously is a guide in the second sense of the word.[378]

Besides the fact that what we present here moves within the normal semantic domain of guiding, there are additional reasons not to abandon speech about divine guidance, as it expresses something that other theological notions do not. For example, while the doctrine of providence is a crucial background belief when it comes to guidance, its focus is on the divine 'side', and hence it does not speak in a direct way to the common human experience of having to make difficult decisions. Similarly, although we have deliberately developed an account of guidance within the domain of the doctrine of sanctification, in itself it lacks the strong biographical connotations the words guidance brings with it. Choosing to speak of vocation instead of guidance, apart from the fact that vocation has its own difficulties (see §6.2.3), risks focusing on a number of key areas and decisions instead of on the entire journey of life. None of these alternatives captures the intimate involvement of God with individual human lives we encounter again and again in the Bible the way the term guidance does.

6.7.6 Living in the Spirit
At the end of this discussion of the role of the Holy Spirit in guidance, and the end of this chapter on a Reformed approach to such guidance, in this concluding section we will capture the essence of the chapter by a number of characterizations of the Christian life provided by some of this chapter's key conversation partners.

Living out of control. In several places Stanley Hauerwas has characterized the Christian life as an exercise in living out of control. Living under the guidance of the Spirit, living the life of a disciple "is rightly construed as life out of our control."[379] As Christians, there is no need to adhere to the myth of self-control, but we are free to confess that life is not under our control and that life is often lived "among the fragments."[380] As Ariaan

---

378 What we state here is in line with the complaints of several authors about the "deeply ingrained desire for maps" in our present culture (culture. See Dorothy C. Bass etc. 237. Cf. Smith Hauerwas and Pinches, *Christians Among The Virtues*, 15, 18, distinguish between viewing the Christian life as journey or destination. In their opinion, Christian ethics has too often focused on a series of consecutive trips than on the journey of life .
379 Hauerwas and Willimon, *The Holy Spirit*, 46. See for a brief overview Paul, *Slag om het hart*, 65–69.
380 Stanley Hauerwas, *The Peaceable Kingdom: A Primer in Christian Ethics* (Notre Dame: University of Notre Dame Press, 1983), 15–16.

Baan has rightly argued, the central question of Hauerwas' work is "how to live truthfully in a world without certainty."[381] Living out of control means believing that "God will use our faithfulness to make his kingdom a reality in the world,"[382] leading to a life that is characterized by patience, hope, and trust in God's grace.

Living with X-Rho eyes. At the end of his book *Pictures as a Theological Exhibition*, in which he frequently touched upon the importance of the imagination for the Christian life, Kevin Vanhoozer includes a sermon on 2 Kings 6:14-23: 'The man with the X-Rho eyes.'[383] In it, he stresses the importance of being able to perceive "what lies beyond the empirical", of hindsight, insight, and foresight.[384] Living with Chi-Rho eyes means perceiving "the depth-dimension of things, the meaning events have in relation to God"[385] in a world suffering from "secular nearsightedness."[386] Seeing with the eyes of the heart for Vanhoozer means seeing through the 'spectacles of faith,' "the sum total of the Bible stories to which Christ is the key."[387] This provides the perspective needed to see what really matters in the situations we find ourselves in, especially when that is not what is most visible. Ultimately, living with x-rho eyes means "seeing our own situation, particularly in moments when we are tempted to feel overwhelmed, as full of horses and chariots of fire: namely, the gracious power and provision of God in Christ through the Spirit."[388]

Walking backwards into the future. In both his books *Improvisation* and *God's Companions*, Samuel Wells draws a distinction between walking forwards into an unknown future, and walking backwards into it.[389] For the one walking forwards into the future, the experience is one of uncertainty, anxiety, bewilderment; in short: of scarcity. Drawing on Johnstone's work on improvisation, Wells argues that life in the Spirit, a life of improvisation, can better be pictured as walking backwards into the future, with eyes fixed on the abundance God has provided, not necessarily in one's own life, but throughout history.[390]

---

381 Ariaan Baan, *The Necessity of Witness: Stanley Hauerwas's Contribution to Systematic Theology* (Eugene: Pickwick, 2015), 43.
382 Hauerwas, *Peaceable Kingdom*, 108.
383 Vanhoozer, *Pictures*, 297–309. Vanhoozer's sermon theme is a play on the 1963 film *The man with the x-ray eyes.*
384 Vanhoozer, 300.
385 Vanhoozer, 301.
386 Vanhoozer, 303.
387 Vanhoozer, 307. Note how the spectacles-metaphor draws upon Calvin's *Institutes*, I.6.1.
388 Vanhoozer, 308.
389 Wells, *Improvisation*, 148; Samuel Wells, *God's Companions: Reimagining Christian Ethics* (Malden: Wiley-Blackwell, 2006), 45.
390 Wells here draws particularly on Keith Johnstone, *Impro: Improvisation in the Theatre* (London: Methuen, 1981).

Living wisely in the Spirit, never past being surprised. As we have seen before, David Ford has written on the importance of wisdom in several places. For him, Christian wisdom, wisdom in the Spirit, is crucial because "we are in unscripted time"[391] and "in the midst of the messy unpredictability of 'real life.'"[392] Living wisely does not mean that we try to control this unpredictability, but, acknowledging that we need forgiveness for things in the past, we need to risk "improvising on into the future," "recognizing that we are conditioned and constrained with so much *beyond control.*"[393] For those who trust in God, the lack of control is no reason for despair, but an invitation to what Ford calls "faith in the optative mood": It searches the heights and depths of our fragile existence, always learning and discerning, never past being surprised. It is a faith whose source, hope and delight is the God of blessing who loves in wisdom."[394]

---

[391] David F. Ford, *The Drama of Living: Becoming Wise in the Spirit* (Grand Rapids: Brazos Press, 2014), 4.
[392] Ford, 79.
[393] Ford, 79 (emphasis in original).
[394] Ford, *Christian Wisdom*, 391. For his idea of the different 'moods' of faith, see pp. 45ff.

Conclusion

I

In this dissertation, I set out to answer the following research question:

How can the contemporary evangelical focus on the notion of divine guidance be incorporated in a Reformed theological account of the Christian life as informed by the writings of John Calvin and Jonathan Edwards?

In order to answer that question, several steps had to be taken. First, we offered an analysis of the views on guidance in contemporary evangelicalism; next, we examined the thought of John Calvin and Jonathan Edwards on aspects related to guidance; third, we developed a proposal for a coherent and theologically robust account of divine guidance. In the intermediate conclusion (Chapter 5) we have already reflected on the results of the first four chapters. Based upon that provisional conclusion, in the final two chapters we have defended and developed the thesis that a contemporary Reformed account of divine guidance can best be developed in interaction with the model that conceives of guidance in terms of wisdom and transformation.

In order to do so in a coherent way, on the one hand we had to argue what misconceptions must be avoided in speaking about divine guidance, while on the other hand a number of concepts had to be developed beyond their treatments in either popular evangelical literature (chapter 2) or the accounts of Calvin and Edwards (chapters 3 and 4).

II

One fundamental decision underlying our approach has to be highlighted once again to clarify the way we proceeded. Most accounts of guidance tend to focus on the so-called extraordinary work of the Spirit, and at times even integrate such extraordinary revelation of the Spirit into their proposed list of 'steps' to find the will of God. Even in the theological project most directly related to our project, Kovach's *Toward a Theology of Guidance* (discussed in §1.2.2), the entire theological framework proposed is aimed at discerning direct forms of guidance by the Spirit. In the literature, this approach leads to two different problems. 1) A superficial distinction must be made between two types of decisions, one in which no special guidance of God is necessary, and one in which a direct form of guidance is always needed; or 2) direct and special communication from the Spirit is (often implicitly) presupposed as something to happen on a regular, sometimes even daily basis.

In the account developed in this book, we consciously took the reverse approach: a coherent theological account of divine guidance that is in line with central Reformed concerns must conceive of God's guidance in terms of the 'ordinary' work of the Spirit, without denying the possibility that at times God may override ordinary human decision-making processes through the direct involvement of the Spirit. In this way, no distinction between different types of decisions is necessary, nor is the misconception reinforced that special communication of the Spirit is a regular phenomenon, while at the same time the connection between human decision-making and God's guidance can be maintained.

III

Flowing forth from this fundamental theological decision and the analysis presented in chapters 2-4, in the proposed theology of guidance presented in chapter 6, I explicitly tried to avoid the following problems that hamper many evangelical accounts of guidance.

A. Moments of choice are not unconnected episodes that can be detached from their context and approached as discrete entities. That is, a robust account of guidance must avoid an 'atomistic approach' to human life (MacIntyre).
B. The narrative dimensions of human life must be stressed in order to ensure that transformation (conversion) can be placed at the heart of our account of guidance.
C. Although discussions of guidance often focus on personal decisions, we must resist the tendency to isolate individuals from their social context. Our theology of guidance must account for the fact that each individual is always involved in a myriad of social networks with their particular influences on the decisions to be made.
D. A realistic account of guidance must not incite people to focus on future possibilities at the neglect of the immediate needs of today.
E. Our theology of guidance must evade the impression that divine guidance always leads to movement and change. In many evangelical accounts guidance is presented as leading (almost) inevitably towards something new.

IV

Based on the one hand upon the fundamental decision taken and the particular caveats to be avoided, and on the other hand on our reading of Calvin and Edwards, we proposed a Reformed approach to divine guidance circumscribed by the following central dogmatic theses (§5.4):

1. The doctrine of divine providence is an expression of God's care for his creation that finds its culmination in the history of salvation and its most intense focus in the church.
2. The conviction that "for those who love God all things work together for good" (Rom. 8:28) means, among other things, that God guides the lives of individual believers, often in mysterious ways.
3. The classic distinction between the hidden and revealed aspects of the divine will is crucial and must be maintained.
4. Providence is a doctrine of faith, and should not be solidified into a worldview (the danger of providentialism).
5. Qualifying one's own plans, priorities, and decisions by use of the Jacobean condition is more pertinent than searching for the will of God or executing a purportedly 'found' will of God.
6. The concept of vocation is still one of the most promising means for Reformed theology to express a belief in concrete divine guidance.
7. A contemporary account of vocation must take into account the highly complex and dynamic nature of (post)modern societies and can in no way reduce its scope to paid professions.
8. A Reformed approach to divine guidance requires robust notions of Christian wisdom and discernment that on the one hand indicate the particularity of Christian decision-making and on the other hand leave the full freedom and responsibility for the chosen path with the individual.
9. Hence, referring to divine guidance behind one's own choices in no way reduces the personal responsibility for those choices.
10. Ultimately, sanctification is the field or *locus* within which guidance is to be discussed.
11. Formation and transformation take place on the individual level, but are impossible without the constant support and influence of a Christian community, which can be of great aid in the important tasks of deliberation and discernment.
12. Guidance by the Spirit primarily takes place in and through ordinary human decision-making processes, as daily life is the normal workplace of the Spirit, not exclusively the extraordinary experiences.

13. Extraordinary instances of divine guidance may put ordinary decision-making processes in perspective; these extraordinary instances are indeed *extra*-ordinary and rest upon divine initiative. Hence, they cannot be part of a heuristic procedure to 'find' the will of God.

V

Because theses 1-4 are common ground between the various models of guidance and thesis 5 formulates the basic insight of the transformation model, in the final chapter we developed the key concepts of the remaining theses in conversation with recent developments in systematic theology and theological ethics.

Although it has been severely criticized from various directions, I argued that there are several good reasons to maintain the concept of *vocation*. It must, however, be developed in a dynamic way. Using O'Donovan's approach of vocation as "the ensemble of worldly relations and functions through which we are given, in particular, to serve God and realize our agency," we were able to broaden the focus of vocation beyond professions and to stress that the focus must be on the content of the vocation, not on the event. This way, we can also stress that, although as Western autonomous people we often do not like the idea, many aspects of our life are given. Such a dynamic concept of vocation is simultaneously a source of comfort and of challenge.

In order to embody such a complex notion of vocation, we need *wisdom*. As a practical kind of wisdom is needed, we developed our account in line with the classic virtue of *phronesis:* practical wisdom in situations where several good options exist. Christian wisdom, however, works from within a distinct framework, characterized first and foremost by God's revelation in Christ. Hence, Christian wisdom comes with a specific combination of values and priorities: the *salus* of the individual, the *shalom* of the community, and the glory of the *shema*. With Wells and Vanhoozer, we contend that living a life characterized by such wisdom can be aptly captured by the metaphor of improvising.

In such improvisation, decisions will have to be taken at 'dangerous moments of opportunity.' For these decisions, *discernment* is required. This discernment is neither based upon forms of immediacy nor on a method, but requires a sober 'reading' of the situation which involves the entire apparatus of human capacities: heart, intellect, observation, and experience. As such, discernment also requires a deep knowledge of oneself, both as a guard against following our habitual inclinations too easily and to take our persisting (good) desires seriously enough. At the end of the process of discernment, even if we detect a sense of purpose, we never have *a priori* verification that the purpose we seem to detect is God's purpose. Even in discernment we depend upon God's grace and must surrender the judgment of our actions to God.

VI

In order to embody our accounts of vocation, wisdom, and discernment in the concreteness of real life stories, in the constructive chapter we discussed three aspects of guidance that reach beyond the actual decision-making and stress the narrative and social dimensions of human life.

First, I argued that wisdom and discernment presuppose transformation. In a discussion of Romans 12:1-2, a text that reoccured throughout the book, it was argued that divine guidance must be based upon a complete surrender to God and a thorough transformation of character, enabling us to become attuned to the 'good, acceptable, and perfect' that characterize the divine will. It is at the deepest level, our 'heart', that we are invited, beckoned, drawn out to become the kind of person that discerns the will of God. Two aspects of our character are crucial: our desires and our imagination. Following Smith, we argued that our desires form our "most basic attunement" to the world and hence prime us to a certain way of living in the world, to aim for particular goals and to pursue specific dreams. A purified imagination is crucial to 'see', with the eyes of faith, how our small lives, dreams, and desires might fit into what God is doing in the world.

Second, I explored the various ways guidance (through transformation) is not a solitary quest but a communal issue. Our character, loves, desires, and priorities are all recalibrated through our involvement in a particular Christian community, where we find both inspiration and challenge. More concretely, in the Christian community we can get advice from those who share our basic perspective on life, while at the same time we are held accountable by them for our decisions. As I argued (in line with the practice of both Calvin and Edwards), friends may have a special role to play in this regard, as, through *amor amicitiae* and a shared history, no one is better equipped to combine insider and outsider perspectives and shed light on complex decisions.

Finally, I returned to the most pervasive critique of the wisdom model of guidance, namely, that it is a form of practical deism. As I argued, this accusation underemphasizes the ongoing active influence and involvement of the Holy Spirit throughout all aspects of guidance described, because it tends to look especially for the work of the Spirit in the extraordinary. By focusing on the concept of indwelling, I showed how the least noticeable involvement of the Spirit might often be the most influential and transformative form of divine presence.

VII

Given the above, we conclude with confidence that it is possible to develop a contemporary account of divine guidance that is consistent with typical Reformed emphases and concerns. Such an account focuses on the ordinary human decision-making processes by taking its point of departure in the model of guidance that is based upon the notions of transformation and wisdom. As I have shown, especially in the final chapter, by taking this approach the question of guidance is no longer an isolated topic and discussion (as it is often in evangelical literature), but is related in many and often insightful ways to contemporary discussions and developments in systematic theology and theological ethics. As such, our approach has resulted in a 'thick description' of divine guidance.

VIII

Although this conclusion can be presented 'with confidence', a brief note on the status of the conclusion is in order. Because of the relative scarcity of academic discussions that specifically focus on the issue of divine guidance, I deliberately chose to formulate this account of a theology of guidance as a *proposal*. That is, my aim was to show that it is possible to formulate a theologically robust and coherent account of guidance that develops it beyond the popular-level treatments and bring it in fruitful interaction with fundamental academic discussions. But also the other way around: that there are interesting and important discussions among believers that academic theology tends to overlook but that can bring to the fore new insights or drives one to draw fresh connections between theological loci.

This means, however, that at times we had to be tentative and leave promising venues for further discussion behind. In particular, we think of the following areas in which further research would be necessary to further support, refine, or extend our argument:

A. In the chapter on guidance in evangelicalism, for practical purposes we decided to focus on English literature. It would, however, be very insightful to know whether the topic of guidance is also a prominent theme in other parts of World Christianity, and whether radically different approaches exist in other contexts. Furthermore, it would be interesting to investigate how developments in charismatic and Pentecostal theology over the last decades have influenced thinking about God's guidance, both in these particular traditions and in mainstream churches.

B. With regard to the historical part of this book, we focused on two main figures, Calvin and Edwards. The same type of research could easily be applied to other major theologians, but it would also be worthwhile to look into slightly different traditions. Given our findings, especially treatments of guidance in puritanism, in German pietism, and in the Further Reformation would seem to harvest interesting new material.

C. Further historical research must be done on the notions of vocation and discernment, as historical treatments of those key notions are often only partial or focus on specific geographic areas. Especially with regard to vocation, promising new interpretations are being developed, but from an academic perspective a thorough historical treatment is sorely missed.

D. Finally, in this book we did not provide a sustained biblical-theological treatment of guidance, whereas biblical material is crucial in the argumentation of most evangelical contributions. In order to be of service in moving the discussion forward, such a treatment must be hermeneutically sensitive and stress forms of exegesis in which Old Testament narratives are taken seriously without being directly applicable to contemporary decision-making processes.

Bibliography

A. Primary Sources

A.1 Evangelical literature on guidance
In this section, I list all books analyzed in chapter 2.

Adams, Jay E. *The Christian's Guide to Guidance: How to Make Biblical Decisions in Everyday Life*. Woodruff: Timeless Texts, 1998.

Ashcraft, Morris. *The Will of God*. Nashville: Broadman Press, 1980.

Benner, David G. *Desiring God's Will: Aligning Our Hearts with the Heart of God*. Downers Grove: InterVarsity Press, 2005.

Blackaby, Henry T., and Claude V. King. *Experiencing God: Knowing and Doing the Will of God*. Nashville: LifeWay Press, 1990.

Bockmühl, Klaus. *Listening to the God Who Speaks: Reflections on God's Guidance from Scripture and the Lives of God's People*. Colorado Springs: Helmers & Howard, 1990.

Carter, Mack King, and Jean Alicia Elster. *Interpreting the Will of God: Principles for Unlocking the Mystery*. Valley Forge: Judson Press, 2002.

Cleave, Derek. *How to Know God's Will*. Phillipsburg: P&R Publishing, 1985.

DeYoung, Kevin. *Just Do Something: A Liberating Approach to Finding God's Will, or, How to Make a Decision Without Dreams, Visions, Fleeces, Impressions, Open Doors, Random Bible Verses, Casting Lots, Liver Shivers, Writing in the Sky, Etc.* Chicago: Moody Publishers, 2009.

Elliff, Jim. *Led by the Spirit: How the Holy Spirit Guides the Believer*. Dundas: Joshua Press, 1999.

Ferguson, Sinclair B. *Discovering God's Will*. Carlisle: Banner of Truth, 1982.

Friesen, Garry, and J. Robin Maxson. *Decision Making and the Will of God*. Colorado Springs: Multnomah Publishers, 1980.

Hayford, Jack W. *Pursuing the Will of God: Reflections and Meditations on the Life of Abraham*. Sisters: Multnomah, 1997.

Hosier, Helen K. *How to Know When God Speaks*. Irvine: Harvest House Publishers, 1980.

Huffman, Douglas S., ed. *How Then Should We Choose? Three Views on God's Will and Decision Making*. Grand Rapids: Kregel Publications, 2009.

Jeffress, Robert. *Hearing the Master's Voice: The Comfort and Confidence of Knowing God's Will*. Colorado Springs: WaterBrook Press, 2001.

Jensen, Phillip D., and Tony Payne. *The Last Word on Guidance*. London: Matthias Press, 1991.

Kincaid, Ron. *Praying for Guidance: How to Discover God's Will*. Downers Grove: InterVarsity Press, 1996.

LaHaye, Tim F. *Finding the Will of God in a Crazy, Mixed-up World*. Grand Rapids: Zondervan, 1989.

Lake, Kyle. *Understanding God's Will: How to Hack the Equation Without Formulas*. Lake Mary: Relevant Books, 2005.

Masters, Peter. *Steps for Guidance in the Journey of Life*. London: Wakeman Trust, 1995.

McDowell, Josh, and Kevin Johnson. *God's Will, God's Best for Your Life*. Minneapolis: Bethany House, 2000.

Meadors, Gary T. *Decision Making God's Way: A New Model for Knowing God's Will*. Grand Rapids: Baker Books, 2003.

Morris, Danny E. *Yearning to Know God's Will: A Workbook for Discerning God's Guidance for Your Life*. Grand Rapids: Zondervan, 1991.

Ogilvie, Lloyd John. *Discovering God's Will in Your Life*. Eugene: Harvest House Publishers, 1982.

Packer, James I., and Carolyn Nystrom. *Guard Us, Guide Us: Divine Leading in Life's Decisions*. Grand Rapids: Baker Books, 2008.

Petty, James C. *Step by Step: Divine Guidance for Ordinary Christians*. Phillipsburg: P&R Publishing, 1999.

Pritchard, Ray. *The Road Best Traveled: Knowing God's Will for Your Life*. Wheaton: Crossway Books, 1995.

Rasnake, Eddie. *Living God's Will: Reading and Applying God's Signs for Your Life*. Chattanooga: AMG Publishers, 2001.

Robinson, Haddon W. *Decision-Making by the Book: How to Choose Wisely in an Age of Options*. Grand Rapids: Discovery House, 1991.

Sanders, J. Oswald. *Every Life Is a Plan of God: Discovering His Will for Your Life*. Grand Rapids: Discovery House, 1992.

Shepson, Charles W. *How to Know God's Will: Divine Direction for the Road Map of Life*. Beaverlodge: Horizon House, 1981.

Sittser, Gerald Lawson. *Discovering God's Will: How to Make Every Decision with Peace and Confidence*. Grand Rapids: Zondervan, 2000.

Smith, Gordon T. *Listening to God in Times of Choice: The Art of Discerning God's Will*. Downers Grove: InterVarsity Press, 1997.

Sproul, R. C. *God's Will and the Christian*. Lake Mary: Reformation Trust, 1984.

Stanley, Charles F. *How to Listen to God*. Nashville: Oliver Nelson Books, 1985.
Swavely, David. *Decisions, Decisions: How (and How Not) to Make Them*. Phillipsburg: P&R Publishing, 2003.
Swindoll, Charles R. *The Mystery of God's Will: What Does He Want for Me?* Nashville: Word Pub. Group, 1999.
Waltke, Bruce K. *Finding the Will of God: A Pagan Notion?* Grand Rapids: Eerdmans, 1995.
Willard, Dallas. *In Search of Guidance: Developing a Conversational Relationship with God*. Ventura: Regal Books, 1984.

A.2 Primary sources John Calvin

For an overview of the writings of Calvin and their original years of publication, see Wulfert de Greef, *The Writings of John Calvin, Expanded Edition: An Introductory Guide* (Louisville 2008), 233-237.

The abbreviations COR, OS and CO refer to the editions of the various writings of Calvin used in this book. I list the translations I used under the relevant titles. For all commentaries, I used the translations of the Calvin Translation Society.

Jacobi Sadoleti epistola. Ioannis Calvini responsio (1539) (CO 5)
Contre la secte phantastique des Libertins qui se nomment spirituelz (1545) (COR IV/1)
Calvin, John. *Treatises against the Anabaptists and against the Libertines*. Translated by Benjamin Wirt Farley. Grand Rapids: Baker Book House, 1982.
Interim adultero-germanum (1549) (CO 7)
Commentarii in Isaiam prophetam (1551) (CO 36-37)
De aeterna Dei praedestinatione (1552) (COR III/1)
Calvin, John. *Concerning the Eternal Predestination of God*. Translated by J.K.S. Reid. Cambridge: James Clarke & Co., 1961.
Commentariorum in Acta apostolorum, Liber I (1552) (COR II/12-1)
In evangelium secundum Iohannem, commentarius (1553) (CO 47)
In primum Mosis librum, qui genesis vulgo dicitur, commentarius (1554) (CO 23)
Commentariorum in Acta apostolorum. Liber posterior (1554) (COR II/12-2)
Harmonia ex tribus evangelistis composita (1555) (CO 45)
In librum Psalmorum commentarius (1557) (CO 31-32)

Calumniae nebulonis cuiusdam, quibus odio et invidia gravare conatus est doctinam Ioh. Calvini de occulta Dei providentia. Ioannis Calvini ad easdem responsio (1558) (CO 9)
Calvin, John. *The Secret Providence of God*. Edited by Paul Helm. Translated by Keith Goad. Wheaton: Crossway Books, 2010.
Institutio christianae religionis (1559) (OS III-V)
Calvin, John. *Institutes of the Christian Religion*. Edited by John T. McNeill. Translated by Henry Beveridge. Vol. I & II. Louisville: Westminster John Knox Press, 2006.
Praelectiones in duodecim prophetas minores (1559) (CO 42-44)
Praelectiones in librum prophetiarum Danielis (1561) (CO 40-41)
Praelectiones in librum prophetiarum Jeremiae et Lamentationes (1563) (COR II/6)
Mosis libri quinque cum commentariis. Genesis seorsum, reliqui quatuor in formam harmoniae digesti (1563) (CO 24-25)
In librum Iosue commentarius (1564) (CO 25)
In viginti prima Ezechielis prophetae capita praelectiones (1565) (CO 40)
Thesauri Epistolici (COR VI/1, CO 10-20)
Letters of John Calvin. Compiled from the original manuscripts and edited with historical notes by Jules Bonnet. Translated by D. Constable and M.R. Gilchrist (Vol. 1-2 Edinburgh 1855-57; vol. 3-4 Philadelphia 1858).
Correspondence Française de Calvin Avec Louis Du Tillet, Chanoine d'Angoulême et Curé de Claix Sur Les Questions de l'église et Du Ministère Évangélique: 1537-1538. Edited by A. Crottet. Geneva: Cherbuliez, 1850.
Lettres à Monsieur et Madame de Falais. Edited by Francoise Bonali-Fiquet. Geneva: Droz, 1991.

A.3 Primary sources Jonathan Edwards

The abbreviation WJE refers to the *Works of Jonathan Edwards*, ed. Perry Miller, John E. Smith and Harry S. Stout (New Haven: Yale University Press, 1957-2008. WJEO refers to the online version of the works of Edwards, which contains additional manuscripts. See http://edwards.yale.edu/research/browse.

A Faithful Narrative of the Surprising Work of God in the Conversion of many hundred soulds in Northampton, and the neighbouring towns and villages of New-Hampshire in New-England (1737) (WJE 4).
Some Thoughts Concerning the present Revival of Religion in New-England, and the way in which it ought to be acknowledged and promoted (1743) (WJE 4)

A Treatise Concerning Religious Affections (1746) (WJE 2)
An Humble Attempt to promote Explicit Agreement and Visible Union of God's people in Extraordinary Prater for the Revival of Religion and the Advancement of Christ's Kingdom on Earth, pursuant to Scripture-Promises and Prophecies concerning the last time (1747) (WJE 5).
An Account of the Life of the late Reverend Mr. David Brainerd (1749) (WJE 7)
An Humble Inquiry into the Rules of the Word of God, Concerning the qualifications requisite to a complete standing and full communion in the visible christian church (1749) (WJE 12).
A Careful and Strict Enquiry into the modern prevailing Notions of that Freedom of Will which is supposed to be essential to moral agency, virtue and vice, reward and punishment, praise and blame (1754) (WJE 1)
The Great Christian Doctrine of Original Sin defended; evidences of it's Truth produced, and arguments to the Contrary answered (1758) (WJE 3).
Dissertation Concerning the End for which God Created the World (1765) (WJE 8)
A Dissertation concerning the nature of true virtue (1765) (WJE 8)
A History of the Work of Redemption (1774) (WJE 9)
Charity and its Fruits (1852) (WJE 8)
Scientific and Philosophical Writings (WJE 6)
Images of Divine Things (WJE 11)
The 'Miscellanies' (Entry nos. A-z, aa-zz, 1-500) (WJE 13)
Sermons and discourses, 1723-1729 (WJE 14)
Notes on Scripture (WJE 15)
Letters and Personal Writings (WJE 16)
Sermons and Discourses, 1730-1733 (WJE 17)
The 'Miscellanies' (Entry nos. 501-832) (WJE 18)
Sermons and Discourses, 1734-1738 (WJE 19).
Writings on the Trinity, Grace, and Faith (WJE 21).
The 'Miscellanies' (Entry nos. 1153-1360) (WJE 23).
Sermons and Discourses, 1743-1758 (WJE 25)
Sermons, Series II, 1744 (WJEO 62)

B. Secondary Sources

Aalders, W.J. *Roeping en beroep bij Calvijn*. Mededeelingen der Nederlandsche Akademie van Wetenschappen, Afdeling Letterkunde, 6(4). Amsterdam: N.V. Noord-Hollandsche Uitgevers Maatschappij, 1943.

Allen, Charles W. "The Primacy of 'Phronesis': A Proposal for Avoiding Frustrating Tendencies in Our Conceptions of Rationality." *The Journal of Religion* 69, no. 3 (1989): 359–74.

———. "The Recovery of Phronesis: Its Implications for the Role of Practical Reason in Theology." University of Chicago, 1987. http://www.therevdrcharleswallen.com/page2.html.

Allen, R. Michael. *Reformed Theology*. London: T&T Clark, 2010.

Almen, Louis T. "Vocation in a Post-Vocational Age." *Word and World* 4, no. 2 (Spring 1984): 131–40.

Alschuler, A.S. "Inner Teachers and Transcendent Education." In *Cultivating Consciousness: Enhancing Human Potential, Wellness, and Healing*, 181–93. Westport: Praeger Publishers, 1993.

Alston, William P. *Perceiving God: The Epistemology of Religious Experience*. Ithaca: Cornell University Press, 1991.

———. "The Indwelling of the Holy Spirit." In *Divine Nature and Human Language: Essays in Philosophical Theology*, 223–52. New York: Cornell University Press, 1989.

Alten, H.H. van. "The Beginning of a Spirit-Filled Church: A Study of the Implications of the Pneumatology for the Ecclesiology in John Calvin's Commentary on the Acts of the Apostles." PhD diss., Theological University Kampen, 2017.

Althaus, Paul. *Die Ethik Martin Luthers*. Gütersloh: Gütersloher Verlagshaus Gerd Mohn, 1965.

Anderson, Wallace E. "Editor's Introduction to 'Images of Divine Things' and 'Types.'" In *Typological Writings*, 1–48. WJE 11. New Haven: Yale University Press, 1993.

Aristotle. *The Nicomachean Ethics*. Translated by David Ross, J.L. Ackrill, and J.O. Urmson. Oxford World's Classics. Oxford: Oxford University Press, 1998.

Baan, Ariaan. *The Necessity of Witness: Stanley Hauerwas's Contribution to Systematic Theology*. Eugene: Pickwick, 2015.

Badcock, Gary D. *The Way of Life: A Theology of Christian Vocation*. Grand Rapids: Eerdmans, 1998.

Baker, Donald. *Decisions, Seeking God's Guidance: 10 Studies for Individuals or Groups*. Downers Grove: InterVarsity Press, 2001.

Barclay, Oliver R. *Guidance: What the Bible Says about Knowing God's Will*. Downers Grove: Inter-Varsity Press, 1978.

Barshinger, David P. *Jonathan Edwards and the Psalms: A Redemptive-Historical Vision of Scripture*. Oxford University Press, 2014.

Bartel, Michelle J. "The Rationality of Discernment in Christian Ethics." Princeton Theological Seminary, 1998.

Barth, Karl. *Kirchliche Dogmatik III/4*. Zürich: EVZ Verlag, 1951.

Bartholomew, Craig G., and Michael W. Goheen. *The Drama of Scripture: Finding Our Place in the Biblical Story*. Grand Rapids: Baker Academic, 2004.

Bass, Dorothy C. "Imagining: Biblical Imagination as a Dimension of Christian Practical Wisdom." In *Christian Practical Wisdom: What It Is, Why It Matters*, edited by Dorothy C. Bass, Kathleen A. Cahalan, Bonnie J. Miller-McLemore, James R. Nieman, and Christian B. Scharen, 232–74. Grand Rapids: Eerdmans, 2016.

Bass, Dorothy C., Kathleen A. Cahalan, Bonnie J. Miller-McLemore, Christian B. Scharen, and James R. Nieman. *Christian Practical Wisdom: What It Is, Why It Matters*. Grand Rapids: Eerdmans, 2016.

Battles, Ford Lewis. *Interpreting John Calvin*. Edited by Robert Benedetto. Grand Rapids: Baker Books, 1996.

Baxter, J. Sidlow. *Does God Still Guide? Or, More Fully, What Are the Essentials of Guidance and Growth in the Christian Life?* London: Marshall, Morgan & Scott, 1968.

Bayer, Oswald. *Freiheit als Antwort: Zur theologischen Ethik*. Tübingen: Mohr Siebeck, 1995.

———. *Martin Luthers Theologie: Eine Vergegenwärtigung*. Tübingen: Mohr Siebeck, 2003.

Bayly, Joseph. *Essays on Guidance*. Chicago: Inter-Varsity Press, 1968.

David W. Bebbington. *Evangelicalism in Modern Britain: A History from the 1730s to the 1980s*. London: Unwin Hyman, 1989.

Beck, Ulrich. *Risk Society: Towards a New Modernity*. Translated by Mark Ritter. London: Sage, 1992.

Benner, David G., and Peter C. Hill, eds. *Baker Encyclopedia of Psychology and Counseling*. 2nd edition. Grand Rapids: Baker Academic, 1999.

Benson, Louis F. *Studies Of Familiar Hymns: Second Series*. Philadelphia: The Westminster Press, 1923.

Berg, Michiel A. van den. *Friends of Calvin*. Translated by Reinder Bruinsma. Grand Rapids: Eerdmans, 2009.

Berkhof, Hendrikus. *Christian Faith: An Introduction to the Study of the Faith (Revised)*. Translated by Sierd Woudstra. Grand Rapids: Eerdmans, 1986.

Berkouwer, G.C. *De Voorzienigheid Gods*. Dogmatische Studiën. Kampen: J.H. Kok, 1950.

———. *The Providence of God*. Translated by Lewis B. Smedes. Studies in Dogmatics. Grand Rapids: Eerdmans, 1952.

Bernanos, Georges. *The Diary of a Country Priest*. Translated by Pamela Morris. Reprint. Cambridge: Da Capo Press, 2002.

Bethge, Eberhard. *Dietrich Bonhoeffer: Theologian - Christian - Man for His Times*. Edited by Victoria J. Barnett. Revised. Minneapolis: Fortress Press, 2000.

Bjerkelund, C.J. *Parakalô: Form, Funktion und Sinn der parakalo-Sätze in den Paulinischen Briefen*. Oslo: Universitetsforlaget, 1967.

Bloom, Matt. "Middle Adulthood: The Joys and Paradoxes of Vocation." In *Calling All Years Good: Christian Vocation throughout Life's Seasons*, edited by Kathleen A. Cahalan and Bonnie J. Miller-McLemore, 123–47. Grand Rapids: Eerdmans, 2017.

Bockmühl, Klaus. *Gesetz und Geist: Eine kritische Würdigung des Erbes protestantischer Ethik*. Giessen: Brunnen Verlag, 1987.

Bohatec, Josef. "Calvins Vorsehungslehre." In *Calvinstudien: Festschrift zum 400. Geburtstage Johann Calvins*, 339–441. Leipzig: Rudolf Haupt, 1909.

Bondi, Richard. "The Elements of Character." *The Journal of Religious Ethics* 12 (1984): 201–18.

Bonhoeffer, Dietrich. *Nachfolge*. Edited by Martin Kuske and Ilse Tödt. Dietrich Bonhoeffer Werke 4. Gütersloh: Gütersloher Verlagshaus, 1989.

———. *Ethik*. Edited by Ernst Feil, Clifford J. Green, H. Eduard Tödt, and Ilse Tödt. Dietrich Bonhoeffer Werke 6. Gütersloh: Gütersloher Verlagshaus, 1992.

———. *Widerstand und Ergebung*. Edited by Christian Gremmels, Eberhard Bethge, Renate Bethge, and Ilse Tödt. Dietrich Bonhoeffer Werke 8. Gütersloh: Gütersloher Verlagshaus, 1998.

———. *Illegale Theologen-ausbildung: Sammelvikariate 1937-1940*. Edited by Dirk Schulz. Dietrich Bonhoeffer Werke 15. Gütersloh: Gütersloher Verlagshaus, 1998.

———. *Konspiration und Haft 1940-1945*. Edited by Jørgen Glenthøj, Ulrich Kabitz and Wolf Krötke. Dietrich Bonhoeffer Werke 16. Gütersloh: Gütersloher Verlagshaus, 1996.

Bouwsma, William J. *John Calvin: A Sixteenth-Century Portrait*. Oxford: Oxford University Press, 1988.

Boyles, Helen. *Romanticism and Methodism: The Problem of Religious Enthusiasm*. London: Routledge, 2017.

Breen, Mike. *Building a Discipling Culture*. 2nd edition. Pawleys Island: 3DM Publishing, 2011.

Brink, Gijsbert van den. "De geestelijke groei van de nieuwe mens: Op het snijvlak van theologie en psychologie." In *Onrustig is ons hart: Mens-zijn in christelijk perspectief*, edited by Henri Veldhuis, 88–109. Zoetermeer: Boekencentrum, 1994.

———. "'Scripture with Reason': Een gereformeerde triniteitsleer bij Jonathan Edwards?" In *Triniteit en kerk: Bundel ter gelegenheid van het afscheid van prof. dr. A. Baars*, edited by G. C. Den Hertog, H.R. Keurhorst, and H.G.L. Peels, 115–27. Heerenveen: Groen, 2014.

Brink, Gijsbert van den, and Cornelis van der Kooi. *Christian Dogmatics: An Introduction*. Grand Rapids: Eerdmans, 2017.

Brink, Gijsbert van den, and Johan Smits. "The Reformed Stance." *Journal of Reformed Theology* 9, no. 4 (2015): 325–47.

Brinkman, Martien E. "De toekomst van de Gereformeerde theologie." *Theologia Reformata* 41, no. 3 (1998): 139–56.

Brooks, A.E.C. *Answers to Prayer from George Müller's Narratives*. Chicago: Moody Press, 1897.

Brunner, Emil. *Dogmatics, Vol. III: The Christian Doctrine of the Church, Faith, and the Consummation*. Translated by David Cairns and T.H.L. Parker. Cambridge: The Lutterworth Press, 1962.

Buechner, Frederick. *Listening to Your Life: Daily Meditations with Frederick Buechner*. New York: Harper Collins, 1992.

Busch, Eberhard. "Reformed Strength in Its Denominational Weakness." In *Reformed Theology: Identity and Ecumenicity*, edited by Wallace M. Alston Jr. and Michael Welker, 20–33. Grand Rapids: Eerdmans, 2003.

———. *Reformiert: Profil einer Konfession*. Zürich: TVZ, 2007.

Cahalan, Kathleen A., and Bonnie J. Miller-McLemore, eds. *Calling All Years Good: Christian Vocation throughout Life's Seasons*. Grand Rapids: Eerdmans, 2017.

Caldwell III, Robert W. *Communion in the Spirit: The Holy Spirit as the Bond of Union in the Theology of Jonathan Edwards*. Eugene: Wipf & Stock, 2007.

Campbell, Archibald. *A Discourse Proving That the Apostles Were No Enthusiasts: Wherein the Nature and Influence of Religious Enthusiasm Are Impartially Explain'd*. London: A. Millar, 1730.

Campbell Morgan, G. *God's Perfect Will*. London: Morgan and Scott, 1901.

Castelli, Elisabeth A. *Martyrdom and Memory: Early Christian Culture Making*. New York: Columbia University Press, 2004.

Claghorn, George S. "Editor's Introduction." In *Letters and Personal Writings*. WJE 16. New Haven: Yale University Press, 1998.

Cochran, Elizabeth A. *Receptive Human Virtues: A New Reading of Jonathan Edwards's Ethics*. University Park: Penn State University Press, 2010.

Cochrane, Arthur C. *Reformed Confessions of the Sixteenth Century*. London: SCM Press, 1966.

Coder, S. Maxwell. *God's Will for Your Life*. Chicago: Moody Press, 1946.

Coleman, Charles G. *Divine Guidance: That Voice Behind You*. Neptune: Loizeaux Brothers, 1977.

Cottret, Bernard. *Calvin: A Biography*. Translated by M. Wallace McDonald. Grand Rapids: Eerdmans, 2000.

Crisp, Oliver D. "Calvin on Creation and Providence." In *John Calvin and Evangelical Theology: Legacy and Prospect*, edited by Sung Wook Chung, 43–65. Louisville: Westminster John Knox Press, 2009.

———. "How 'Occasional' Was Edwards's Occasionalism?" In *Jonathan Edwards: Philosophical Theologian*, edited by Oliver D. Crisp and Paul Helm, 61–77. Aldershot: Ashgate, 2003.

———. *Jonathan Edwards among the Theologians*. Grand Rapids: Eerdmans, 2015.

———. "Jonathan Edwards and Occasionalism." In *Abraham's Dice: Chance and Providence in the Monotheistic Traditions*, edited by Karl W. Giberson, 195–212. Oxford: Oxford University Press, 2016.

Cunningham, David S. *Christian Ethics: The End of the Law*. Abingdon: Routledge, 2008.

Dahill, Lisa E. "Probing the Will of God: Bonhoeffer and Discernment." *Dialog: A Journal of Theology* 41, no. 1 (Spring 2002): 42–49.

———. *Reading from the Underside of Selfhood: Bonhoeffer and Spiritual Formation*. Eugene: Pickwick Publications, 2009.

Danaher Jr., William J. *The Trinitarian Ethics of Jonathan Edwards*. Louisville: Westminster John Knox Press, 2004.

Deere, Jack. *Surprised by the Voice of God: How God Speaks Today through Prophecies, Dreams, and Visions*. Grand Rapids: Zondervan, 1996.

Delattre, Roland. *Beauty and Sensibility in the Thought of Jonathan Edwards: An Essay in Aesthetics and Theological Ethics*. New Haven: Yale University Press, 1968.

Denis, Philippe. "Jacques de Bourgogne, Seigneur de Falais." In *Bibliotheca dissidentium, vol. 4*, edited by André Séguenny, 9–52. Baden-Baden: Koerner, 1984.

Dewey, John. *Human Nature and Conduct*. New York: Modern Library, 1957.

———. *Theory of the Moral Life*. New York: Holt, Rinehart and Winston, 1966.

Dobson, James C. *Life on the Edge: The Next Generation's Guide to a Meaningful Future*. Carol Stream: Tyndale, 1995.

Dodd, C.H. *The Epistle of Paul to the Romans*. London: Hodder and Stoughton, 1932.

Donagan, Barbara. "Godly Choice: Puritan Decision-Making in Seventeenth-Century England." *The Harvard Theological Review* 76, no. 3 (1983): 307–34.

Douma, J. *Responsible Conduct: Principles of Christian Ethics*. Translated by Nelson D. Kloosterman. Phillipsburg: P&R Publishing, 2003.

Dubay, Thomas. *Authenticity: A Biblical Theology of Discernment*. San Francisco: Ignatius Press, 1977.

Dunn, James D.G. *Romans 9-16*. Waco: Word Books, 1988.

Elert, Werner. *Morphologie des Luthertums II*. München: Beck, 1953.

Elliot, Elisabeth. *God's Guidance: Finding His Will for Your Life*. Grand Rapids: Revell, 1973.

Elliott, Mark W. *Providence Perceived: Divine Action from a Human Point of View*. Berlin: De Gruyter, 2015.

Ellul, Jacques. *The Ethics of Freedom*. Grand Rapids: Eerdmans, 1976.

———. "Work and Calling." *Katallagete* 4, no. 2-3 (Fall-Winter) (1972): 8–16.

Elwood, Douglas J. *The Philosophical Theology of Jonathan Edwards*. New York: Columbia University Press, 1960.

English, John J. *Spiritual Freedom: From an Experience of the Ignatian Exercises to the Art of Spiritual Guidance*. Chicago: Loyola University Press, 1995.

Erdt, Terrence. *Jonathan Edwards: Art and the Sense of the Heart*. Amherst: University of Massachussets Press, 1980.

Erickson, Millard J. *Christian Theology*. Third Edition. Grand Rapids: Baker Academic, 2013.

Fitzmyer, Joseph A. *Romans: A New Translation with Introduction and Commentary*. New York: Doubleday, 1993.

Fleeson, William, R. Michael Furr, Eranda Jayawickreme, Erik G. Helzer, Anselma G. Hartley, and Peter Meindl. "Personality Science and the Foundations of Character." In *Character: New Directions from Philosophy, Psychology, and Theology*, edited by Christian B. Miller, R. Michael Furr, Angela Knobel, and William Fleeson, 41–71. Oxford: Oxford University Press, 2015.

Fleeson, William, R. Michael Furr, Eranda Jayawickreme, Peter Meindl, and Erik G. Helzer. "Character: The Prospects for a Personality-Based Perspective on Morality." *Social and Personality Psychology Compass* 8, no. 4 (2014): 178–91.

Ford, David F. *Christian Wisdom: Desiring God and Learning in Love*. Cambridge: Cambridge University Press, 2007.

———. *The Drama of Living: Becoming Wise in the Spirit*. Grand Rapids: Brazos Press, 2014.

Forrester, W. R. *Christian Vocation*. London: Lutterworth Press, 1951.
Forstman, H. Jackson. *Word and Spirit: Calvin's Doctrine of Biblical Authority*. Stanford: Stanford University Press, 1962.
Fraassen, Bas C. van. *The Empirical Stance*. New Haven: Yale University Press, 2002.
Frame, John M. *Systematic Theology: An Introduction to Christian Belief*. Phillipsburg: P&R Publishing, 2013.
Friesen, Garry. "God's Will as It Relates to Decision Making." PhD diss., Dallas Theological Seminary, 1978.
Froehlich, Karlfried. "Luther on Vocation." *Lutheran Quarterly* XIII, no. 2 (1999): 195–207.
Gerrish, Brian A. "Tradition in the Modern World: The Reformed Habit of Mind." In *Toward the Future of Reformed Theology: Tasks, Topics, Traditions*, edited by David Willis and Michael Welker, 3–20. Grand Rapids: Eerdmans, 1999.
Gerstner, John H. *The Rational Biblical Theology of Jonathan Edwards*. Vol. 2. Powhatan: Berea Publications, 1992.
Glaw, Annette M. *The Holy Spirit and Christian Ethics in the Theology of Klaus Bockmuehl*. Eugene: Pickwick Publications, 2014.
Gordon, Bruce F. *Calvin*. New Haven: Yale University Press, 2009.
Grandia, J.J. *Levensleiding: hoe God het leven leidt*. Kampen: De Groot Goudriaan, 1998.
Grudem, Wayne. *Systematic Theology: An Introduction to Biblical Doctrine*. Nottingham: Inter-Varsity Press, 1994.
Guinness, Os. *The Call: Finding and Fulfilling the Central Purpose of Your Life*. Nashville: W Publishing Group, 1998.
Gustafson, James M. "Moral Discernment in the Christian Life." In *Norm and Context in Christian Ethics*, edited by Gene H. Outka and Paul Ramsey, 17–36. London: SCM Press, 1969.
———. *Moral Discernment in the Christian Life: Essays in Theological Ethics*. Edited by Theo A. Boer and Paul A. Capetz. Library of Theological Ethics. Louisville: Westminster John Knox Press, 2007.
Haenchen, E. *The Acts of the Apostles*. Oxford: Blackwell, 1971.
Hagen, Kenneth. "A Critique of Wingren on Luther on Vocation." *Lutheran Quarterly* XVI, no. 3 (2002): 249–73.
Hagin, Kenneth E. *How You Can Know the Will of God*. Tulsa: Kenneth Hagin Evangelistic Association, 1974.
Hahnenberg, Edward P. *Awakening Vocation: A Theology of Christian Call*. Collegeville: Liturgical Press, 2010.
Hardy, Lee. *The Fabric of This World: Inquiries into Calling, Career Choice, and the Design of Human Work*. Grand Rapids: Eerdmans, 1990.

Harmon-Jones, Eddie, and Cindy Harmon-Jones. "Testing the Action-Based Model of Cognitive Dissonance: The Effect of Action Orientation on Postdecisional Attitudes." *Personality and Social Psychology Bulletin* 28, no. 6 (2002): 711-23.

Hartelius, Glenn, Mariana Caplan, and Mary Anne Rardin. "Transpersonal Psychology: Defining the Past, Divining the Future." *The Humanistic Psychologist* 35, no. 2 (2007): 135-60.

Hastings, A. *With the Tongues of Man and Angels: A Study of Channeling*. San Francisco: Holt, Rinehart and Winston, 1990.

Hastings, W. Ross. *Jonathan Edwards and the Life of God: Toward an Evangelical Theology of Participation*. Minneapolis: Fortress Press, 2015.

Hauerwas, Stanley. *Character and the Christian Life: A Study in Theological Ethics*. 3d ed. San Antonio: Trinity University Press, 1985.

———. *The Peaceable Kingdom: A Primer in Christian Ethics*. Notre Dame: University of Notre Dame Press, 1983.

———. "Work as Co-Creation: A Critique of a Remarkably Bad Idea." In *Co-Creation and Capitalism: John Paul II's Laborem Exercens*, edited by J.W. Houck and O.F. Williams, 42-58. Lanham: University Press of America, 1983.

Hauerwas, Stanley, and Charles R. Pinches. *Christians Among The Virtues: Theological Conversations with Ancient and Modern Ethics*. Notre Dame: University of Notre Dame Press, 2015.

Hauerwas, Stanley, and William H. Willimon. *The Holy Spirit*. Nashville: Abingdon Press, 2015.

Hays, Richard B. *The Conversion of the Imagination: Paul as Interpreter of Israel's Scripture*. Grand Rapids: Eerdmans, 2005.

Heimert, Alan. *Religion and the American Mind: From the Great Awakening to the Revolution*. Cambridge: Harvard University Press, 1966.

Helm, Paul. "Calvin (and Zwingli) on Divine Providence." *Calvin Theological Journal* 29 (1994): 388-405.

———. "Calvin, the 'Two Issues,' and the Structure of the Institutes." *Calvin Theological Journal* 42, no. 2 (2007): 341-48.

———. *John Calvin's Ideas*. Oxford: Oxford University Press, 2004.

———. *The Providence of God*. Contours of Christian Theology. Downers Grove: Inter-Varsity Press, 1993.

Henry, Caleb. "Locke, John (1632-1704)." In *The Jonathan Edwards Encyclopedia*, edited by Harry S. Stout, Kenneth P. Minkema, and Adriaan C. Neele, 353-54. Grand Rapids: Eerdmans, 2017.

Heppe, Heinrich. *Reformed Dogmatics: Set Out and Illustrated from the Sources*. Edited by Ernst Bizer. Translated by G.T. Thomson. Grand Rapids: Baker Book House, 1950.

Herdt, Jennifer A. *Putting On Virtue: The Legacy of the Splendid Vices.* Chicago: University Of Chicago Press, 2008.

Herms, Eilert. "Leben in der Welt." In *Luther Handbuch*, edited by Albrecht Beutel, 423–35. Tübingen: Mohr Siebeck, 2005.

Hesselink, I. John. "Governed and Guided by the Spirit: A Key Issue in Calvin's Doctrine of the Holy Spirit." In *Reformiertes Erbe: Festschrift Für Gottfried W. Locher Zu Seinem 80. Geburtstag (Band 2)*, 161–72. Zürich: Theologischer Verlag Zürich, 1993.

———. *On Being Reformed: Distinctive Characteristics and Common Misunderstandings.* Ann Arbor: Servant Books, 1983.

Hewitson, James. "'As Ordered and Governed by Divine Providence': Jonathan Edwards' Use of the Machine as Master Metaphor." *Interdisciplinary Humanities* 24, no. 1 (2007): 6–20.

Heyd, Michael. *Be Sober and Reasonable: The Critique of Enthusiasm in the Seventeenth and Early Eighteenth Centuries.* Leiden: Brill, 2000.

Hof, Eleonora D. *Reimagining Mission in the Postcolonial Condition: A Theology of Vulnerability and Vocation at the Margins.* Zoetermeer: Boekencentrum Academic, 2016.

Hofheinz, Marco, and Matthias Zeindler. *Reformierte Theologie weltweit: zwölf Profile aus dem 20. Jahrhundert.* Zürich: Theologischer Verlag Zürich, 2013.

Holbrook, Clyde A. "Editor's Introduction." In *Original Sin*, 1–101. WJE 3. New Haven: Yale University Press, 1970.

Holl, Karl. "Die Geschichte Des Worts Beruf (1924)." In *Gesammelte Aufsätze Zur Kirchengeschichte, Bd. 3*, 189–219. Tübingen: Mohr, 1928.

———. "The History of the Word Vocation (Beruf)." Translated by Heber F. Peacock. *Review & Expositor* 55, no. 2 (1958): 126–54.

Homiak, Marcia. "Moral Character." Edited by Edward N. Zalta. *The Stanford Encyclopedia of Philosophy.* Metaphysics Research Lab, Stanford University, 2016. https://plato.stanford.edu/archives/fall2016/entries/moral-character/.

Hopkins, Samuel. "The Life and Character of the Late Reverend Mr. Jonathan Edwards." In *Jonathan Edwards: A Profile*, edited by David Levin. New York: Hill and Wang, 1969.

Horst, P.W. van der. *Sortes: het gebruik van heilige boeken als lotsorakels in de oudheid.* Mededelingen van de Afdeling Letterkunde, Nieuwe Reeks, 62 (3). Amsterdam: Koninklijke Nederlandse Akademie van Wetenschappen, 1999.

Horton, Michael. *Calvin on the Christian Life: Glorifying and Enjoying God Forever.* Wheaton: Crossway Books, 2014.

———. *Ordinary: Sustainable Faith in a Radical, Restless World.* Grand Rapids: Zondervan, 2014.

———. *The Christian Faith: A Systematic Theology for Pilgrims on the Way.* Grand Rapids: Zondervan, 2011.

Howard, J. Grant. *Knowing God's Will-and Doing It.* Grand Rapids: Zondervan, 1976.

Hursthouse, Rosalind, and Glen Pettigrove. "Virtue Ethics." Edited by Edward N. Zalta. *The Stanford Encyclopedia of Philosophy.* Metaphysics Research Lab, Stanford University, Winter 2016. https://plato.stanford.edu/archives/win2016/entries/ethics-virtue/.

Jewett, Robert. *Romans: A Commentary.* Minneapolis: Fortress Press, 2007.

Johnson, Ben Campbell. *Discerning God's Will.* Louisville: Westminster John Knox Press, 1990.

———. *To Pray God's Will: Continuing the Journey.* Louisville: Westminster John Knox Press, 1987.

———. *To Will God's Will: Beginning the Journey.* Louisville: Westminster John Knox Press, 1987.

Johnstone, Keith. *Impro: Improvisation in the Theatre.* London: Methuen, 1981.

Kaiser, Joshua A. *Becoming Simple and Wise: Moral Discernment in Dietrich Bonhoeffer's Vision of Christian Ethics.* Eugene: Pickwick Publications, 2015.

Kampen, Pieter van. *Door Zijn hand: Gods leiding in ons leven.* Kampen: Kok Voorhoeve, 1993.

Kaplan, Mark Allan. *The Experience of Divine Guidance: A Qualitative Study of the Human Endeavor to Seek, Receive, and Follow Guidance from a Perceived Divine Source.* Pacific Grove: Original Gravity, 2007.

Keener, Craig S. *The Mind of the Spirit: Paul's Approach to Transformed Thinking.* Grand Rapids: Baker Publishing Group, 2016.

Kelly, Douglas F. *John Calvin's Sermons on 2 Samuel: Chapters 1-13.* Edinburgh: Banner of Truth Trust, 1992.

———. "John Calvin's Teaching on Guidance as Expressed in His Sermons on II Samuel." *Reformed Theological Review* 46, no. 2 (1987): 33–42.

Kim, Sung-Sup. *Deus Providebit: Calvin, Schleiermacher, and Barth on the Providence of God.* Minneapolis: Fortress Press, 2014.

Kirby, W.J. Torrance. "Stoic and Epicurean? Calvin's Dialectical Account of Providence in the Institute." *International Journal of Systematic Theology* 5, no. 3 (2003): 309–22.

Kise, Jane A.G. *Finding and Following God's Will.* Minneapolis: Bethany House, 2005.

Klimo, J. *Channeling: Investigantions on Receiving Information from Paranormal Sources.* Berkeley: North Atlantic Books, 1998.

Klooster, Fred H. "The Uniqueness of Reformed Theology: A Preliminary Attempt at Description." *Calvin Theological Journal* 14 (1979): 32–54.

Knijff, Cornelis van der. "'Guide Me, O Thou Great Jehovah': A Typology of Divine Guidance in Contemporary Evangelicalism." *European Journal of Theology* 25, no. 2 (2016): 179–88.

Knox, Ronald A. *Enthusiasm: A Chapter in the History of Religion, with Special Reference to the XVII and XVIII Centuries.* Oxford: Oxford University Press, 1950.

Kovach, Stephen D. "Toward a Theology of Guidance: A Multi-Faceted Approach Emphasizing Scripture as Both Foundation and Pattern in Discerning the Will of God." PhD diss., Trinity Evangelical Divinity School, 1999.

Kronenburg, Hans. "'De dagteksten zijn mijn dagelijkse vreugde.' Over een vergeten aspect van Bonhoeffers praxis pietatis." *Kerk en Theologie* 66 (2015): 274–85.

Krusche, Werner. *Das Wirken des Heiligen Geistes nach Calvin.* Göttingen: Vandenhoeck & Ruprecht, 1957.

Kuzmič, Rhys. "Beruf Und Berufung in Karl Barth's Church Dogmatics: Towards a Subversive Klesiology." *International Journal of Systematic Theology* 7, no. 3 (2005): 262–78.

Laborie, Lionel. *Enlightening Enthusiasm: Prophecy and Religious Experience in Early Eighteenth-Century England.* Manchester: Manchester University Press, 2015.

Lang, G. H. *Divine Guidance: Its Reality, Methods, Conditions.* Rushden: Stanley Hunt, 1947.

Lange, Frits de. "Becoming One Self: A Critical Retrieval of 'Choice Biography.'" *Journal of Reformed Theology* 1, no. 3 (2007): 272–93.

Larsen, Timothy. "Defining and Locating Evangelicalism." In *The Cambridge Companion to Evangelical Theology*, edited by Timothy Larsen and Daniel J. Treier, 1–14. Cambridge: Cambridge University Press, 2007.

Lee, Sang Hyun. *The Philosophical Theology of Jonathan Edwards.* Princeton: Princeton University Press, 1988.

Leith, John H. *An Introduction to the Reformed Tradition: A Way of Being the Christian Community.* Atlanta: John Knox Press, 1977.

Lesser, M.X. *Reading Jonathan Edwards: An Annotated Bibliography in Three Parts, 1729-2005.* Grand Rapids: Eerdmans, 2008.

Lieburg, Fred van. "De bijbel als orakelboek: Bibliomantie in de protestantse traditie." In *Materieel Christendom: Religie en materiële cultuur in West-Europa*, edited by Arie L. Molendijk, 81–105. Hilversum: Uitgeverij Verloren, 2003.

———. "Dynamics of Dutch Calvinism: Early Modern Programs for Further Reformation." In *Calvinism and the Making of the European Mind*, edited by Gijsbert Van den Brink and Harro Höpfl, 43–66. Leiden: Brill, 2014.

Liester, M.B. "Inner Voices: Distinguishing Transcendent and Pathological Characteristics." *Journal of Transpersonal Psychology* 28, no. 1 (1996): 1–30.

Linde, Simon van der. *De leer van den Heiligen Geest bij Calvijn: bijdrage tot de kennis der reformatorische theologie*. Wageningen: H. Veenman & Zonen, 1943.

Longenecker, Richard N. *The Epistle to the Romans: A Commentary on the Greek Text*. Grand Rapids: Eerdmans, 2016.

MacArthur, John. *Found: God's Will. Find the Direction and Purpose God Wants for Your Life*. Colorado Springs: David C. Cook, 1977.

MacIntyre, Alasdair. *After Virtue: A Study in Moral Theory*. 3d edition. London: Bloomsbury Academic, 2013.

Mahlmann, Theodor. "'Ecclesia semper reformanda': Eine historische Aufarbeitung. Neue Bearbeitung." In *Hermeneutica Sacra: Studien zur Auslegung der Heiligen Schrift im 16. und 17. Jahrhundert*, edited by Torbjörn Johansson, Robert Kolb, and Johann Anselm Steiger, 381–442. Berlin: De Gruyter, 2010.

Markus, Wim. *Multiple Choice? Over Gods leiding en jouw leven*. Zoetermeer: Jes! / Boekencentrum, 2014.

Marsden, George M. *Jonathan Edwards: A Life*. New Haven: Yale University Press, 2004.

Marshall, Paul A. *A Kind of Life Imposed on Man: Vocation and Social Order from Tyndale to Locke*. Toronto: University of Toronto Press, 1996.

Maston, T. B. *God's Will and Your Life*. Nashville: Broadman Press, 1964.

Mather, Cotton. *Ratio Disciplinae Fratrum Nov Angelorum: A Faithful Account of the Discipline Professed and Practiced in the Churches of New England*. Boston, 1726.

McClymond, Michael J., and Gerald R. McDermott. *The Theology of Jonathan Edwards*. New York: Oxford University Press, 2012.

———. *The Theology of Jonathan Edwards*. Oxford: Oxford University Press, 2012.

McCormack, Bruce L. "The End of Reformed Theology? The Voice of Karl Barth in the Doctrinal Chaos of the Present." In *Reformed Theology: Identity and Ecumenicity*, edited by Wallace M. Alston Jr. and Michael Welker, 46–64. Grand Rapids: Eerdmans, 2003.

McLarry, Newman R. *His Good and Perfect Will*. Nashville: Broadman Press, 1965.

Meyer, F.B. *The Secret of Guidance*. Chicago: Fleming H. Revell, 1896.

Miller, Christian B. *Character & Moral Psychology*. Oxford: Oxford University Press, 2014.

———. *Moral Character: An Empirical Theory*. Oxford: Oxford University Press, 2013.

Miller, Christian B., R. Michael Furr, Angela Knobel, and William Fleeson, eds. *Character: New Directions from Philosophy, Psychology, and Theology*. Oxford: Oxford University Press, 2015.

Miller, Christian B., and Angela Knobel. "Some Foundational Questions in Philosophy about Character." In *Character: New Directions from Philosophy, Psychology, and Theology*, edited by Christian B. Miller, Angela Knobel, R. Michael Furr, and William Fleeson, 19–40. Oxford: Oxford University Press, 2015.

Milner, Jr., Benjamin Charles. *Calvin's Doctrine of the Church*. Studies in the History of Christian Thought, V. Leiden: E.J. Brill, 1970.

Minkema, Kenneth P. "A 'Dordtian Philosophe': Jonathan Edwards, Calvin, and Reformed Orthodoxy." *Church History and Religious Culture* 91, no. 1–2 (2011): 241–53.

———. "Preface to the Period." In *Sermons and Discourses: 1723-1729*, 3–47. WJE 14. New Haven: Yale University Press, 1997.

Mitchell, Louis. *Jonathan Edwards on the Experience of Beauty*. Princeton: Princeton Theological Seminary, 2003.

Moehn, Wilhelmus H.Th. *"God Calls Us to His Service": The Relation between God and His Audience in Calvin's Sermons on Acts*. Geneva: Librairie Droz, 2001.

Moltmann, Jürgen. *On Human Dignity: Political Theology and Ethics*. Translated by M. Douglas Meeks. London: SCM Press, 1984.

Moo, Douglas J. *The Epistle to the Romans*. Grand Rapids: Eerdmans, 1996.

Morimoto, Anri. *Jonathan Edwards and the Catholic Vision of Salvation*. University Park: Pennsylvania State University Press, 1995.

Morris, Danny E., and Charles M. Olsen. *Discerning God's Will Together: A Spiritual Practice for the Church*. Nashville: Upper Room Books, 1997.

Morris, Thomas V., ed. *Philosophy and the Christian Faith*. Notre Dame: University of Notre Dame Press, 1988.

Muers, Rachel. *Keeping God's Silence: Towards a Theological Ethics of Communication*. Malden: Wiley-Blackwell, 2004.

Mühlan, Eberhard. *Führung durch den Heiligen Geist: Warum wir sie brauchen; Wie wir sie erleben*. Erzhausen: Leuchter Edition GmbH, 2004.

Müller, George F. *Autobiography of George Müller: A Million and a Half in Answer to Prayer*. Reprint Edition. Denton: Westminster Literature Resources, 2003.

———. *Autobiography of George Müller, or, A Million and a Half in Answer to Prayer*. London: Pickering & Inglis, 1905.

Muller, Richard A. *Dictionary of Latin and Greek Theological Terms: Drawn Primarily from Protestant Scholastic Theology*. Grand Rapids: Baker Book House, 1985.

———. *Post-Reformation Reformed Dogmatics, Vol. 3: The Divine Essence and Attributes*. 2nd edition. Grand Rapids: Baker Academic, 2003.

———. *The Unaccommodated Calvin: Studies in the Foundation of a Theological Tradition*. Oxford: Oxford University Press, 2000.

Munzinger, André. *Discerning the Spirits: Theological and Ethical Hermeneutics in Paul*. Cambridge: Cambridge University Press, 2007.

Murray, Andrew. *Thy Will Be Done*. Chicago: Fleming H. Revell, 1900.

Myers, Warren, and Ruth Myers. *Discovering God's Will: A Study and Meditation on How to Experience God's Good Plan for You*. Colorado Springs: NavPress, 1980.

Nelson, Marion H. *How to Know God's Will*. Chicago: Moody Press, 1963.

Niebuhr, H. Richard. *The Kingdom of God in America*. New York: Harper, 1959.

Niebuhr, Reinhold. *Moral Man and Immoral Society: A Study in Ethics and Politics*. New York: Charles Scribner's Sons, 1932.

Noll, Mark A. *American Evangelical Christianity: An Introduction*. Oxford: Blackwell, 2001.

Oberman, Heiko A. *De erfenis van Calvijn: Grootheid en grenzen*. Kampen: Kok, 1988.

———. "Europa Afflicta: The Reformation of the Refugees." In *John Calvin and the Reformation of the Refugees*, edited by Peter A. Dykema, 177–94. Geneva: Librairie Droz, 2009.

———. "Initia Calvini: The Matrix of Calvin's Reformation." In *John Calvin and the Reformation of the Refugees*, edited by Peter A. Dykema, 89–130. Geneva: Librairie Droz, 2009.

———. *The Two Reformations: The Journey from the Last Days to the New World*. Edited by Donald Weinstein. New Haven: Yale University Press, 2003.

O'Donovan, Oliver. *Entering into Rest*. Ethics as Theology 3. Grand Rapids: Eerdmans, 2017.

———. *Finding and Seeking*. Ethics as Theology 2. Grand Rapids: Eerdmans, 2014.

Ong, Meng-Chai. "John Calvin on Providence: The Locus Classicus in Context." PhD diss., King's College, 2003.

Ortlund, Dane C. *Edwards on the Christian Life: Alive to the Beauty of God*. Wheaton: Crossway, 2014.

Osterhaven, M. Eugene. *The Spirit of the Reformed Tradition*. Grand Rapids: Eerdmans, 1971.

Packer, James I. *Decisions: Finding God's Will. Six Studies for Individuals or Groups*. Downers Grove: InterVarsity Press, 1996.

———. *God's Plans for You*. Wheaton: Crossway Books, 2001.

———. *Knowing and Doing the Will of God: Daily Devotions for Every Day of the Year*. Edited by LaVonne Neff. Ann Arbor: Servant Books, 1995.

———. *Knowing God*. London: Hodder and Stoughton, 1973.

Palmer, Parker J. *A Hidden Wholeness: The Journey Toward An Undivided Life*. San Francisco: Jossey-Bass, 2004.

Parker, Stephen E. *Led by the Spirit: Toward a Practical Theology of Pentecostal Discernment and Decision Making*. Sheffield: Sheffield Academic Press, 1996.

Partee, Charles. *Calvin and Classical Philosophy*. Leiden: Brill, 1977.

———. *The Theology of John Calvin*. Louisville: Westminster John Knox Press, 2008.

Paul, Herman. *De slag om het hart: Over secularisatie van het verlangen*. Utrecht: Boekencentrum, 2017.

Perkins, Pheme. "Paul and Ethics." *Interpretation* 38, no. 3 (1984): 268–80.

Perkins, William. *A Treatise of the Vocations, or, Callings of Men, with the Sorts and Kindes of Them, and the Right Use Thereof*. Cambridge: John Legat, 1605.

Pieper, Josef. *The Four Cardinal Virtues: Prudence, Justice, Fortitude, Temperance*. New York: Pantheon Books, 1954.

Pierson, Arthur T. *George Müller of Bristol and His Witness to a Prayer-Hearing God*. Grand Rapids: Kregel Publications, 1999.

Pipa Jr., Joseph A. "Creation and Providence (I.14, 16-18)." In *Theological Guide to Calvin's Institutes: Essays and Analysis*, edited by David W. Hall and Peter A. Lillback, 123-50. Phillipsburg: P&R Publishing, 2008.

Plantinga Pauw, Amy. "The Future of Reformed Theology: Some Lessons from Jonathan Edwards." In *Towards the Future of Reformed Theology: Tasks, Topics, Traditions*, edited by David Willis and Michael Welker, 456-69. Grand Rapids: Eerdmans, 1999.

———. *"The Supreme Harmony of All": The Trinitarian Theology of Jonathan Edwards*. Grand Rapids: Eerdmans, 2002.

Potgieter, Pieter C. "Providence in Calvin: Calvin's View of God's Use of Means (Media) in His Acts of Providence." In *Calvinus Evangelii Propugnator: Calvin, Champion of the Gospel. Papers from the International Congress on Calvin Research, Seoul, 1998*, edited by David F. Wright, Anthony N.S. Lane, and Jon Balserak, 175-90. Grand Rapids: Calvin Studies Society, CRC Product Services, 2006.

Preece, Gordon R. *The Viability of the Vocation Tradition in Trinitarian, Credal, and Reformed Perspective: The Threefold Call*. Lewiston: Edwin Mellen, 1998.

Quistorp, H.J.J.Th. "Calvins Lehre vom Heiligen Geist." In *De Spiritu Sancto: Bijdragen tot de leer van de Heilige Geest bij gelegenheid van het 2e eeuwfeest van het Stipendium Bernardinum*, 109-50. Utrecht: Kemink en Zoon N.V., 1964.

Rahner, Karl. *Das Dynamische in der Kirche*. Freiburg: Herder, 1958.

Ramsey, Paul. "Editor's Introduction." In *Freedom of the Will*, 1-128. WJE 1. New Haven: Yale University Press, 1957.

Redpath, Alan. *Getting to Know the Will of God*. Downers Grove: InterVarsity Press, 1954.

Ruether, Rosemary R. *Sexism and God Talk: Toward a Feminist Theology*. Boston: Beacon Press, 1983.

Sanders, John E. *The God Who Risks: A Theology of Divine Providence*. Downers Grove: InterVarsity Press, 1998.

Sartre, Jean-Paul. *Being and Nothingness: A Phenomenological Essay on Ontology*. Translated by Hazel E. Barnes. New York: Washington Square Press, 1992.

Schafer, Thomas A. "Editor's Introduction." In *The "Miscellanies": (Entry Nos. a-z, Aa-Zz, 1-500)*, 1-109. WJE 13. New Haven: Yale University Press, 1994.

Schirrmacher, Thomas. *Wie erkenne ich den Willen Gottes: Führungsmystik auf dem Prüfstand*. Hamburg: Reformatorischer Verlag Beese, 2001.

Schreiner, Susan E. *The Theater of His Glory: Nature and the Natural Order in the Thought of John Calvin.* Grand Rapids: Baker Academic, 1995.

Schuurman, Douglas J. "To Follow Christ, to Live in the World: Calling in a Protestant Key." In *Calling in Today's World: Voices from Eight Faith Perspectives*, edited by Kathleen A. Cahalan and Douglas J. Schuurman, 52–81. Grand Rapids: Eerdmans, 2016.

———. *Vocation: Discerning Our Callings in Life.* Grand Rapids: Eerdmans, 2004.

Schwartz, Barry. *The Paradox of Choice: Why More Is Less.* New York: Harper Collins, 2004.

Schweitzer, William M. *God Is a Communicative Being: Divine Communicativeness and Harmony in the Theology of Jonathan Edwards.* London: Bloomsbury T&T Clark, 2012.

Selderhuis, Herman J. *Calvin's Theology of the Psalms.* Grand Rapids: Baker Academic, 2007.

———. *John Calvin: A Pilgrim's Life.* Nottingham: Inter-Varsity Press, 2009.

Sine, Christine, and Tom Sine. *Living on Purpose: Finding God's Best for Your Life.* Grand Rapids: Baker Books, 2002.

Smith, Gordon T. *Courage & Calling: Embracing Your God-given Potential.* Downers Grove: InterVarsity Press, 1999.

———. *The Voice of Jesus: Discernment, Prayer, and the Witness of the Spirit.* Downers Grove: InterVarsity Press, 2003.

Smith, James K.A. *Desiring the Kingdom: Worship, Worldview, and Cultural Formation.* Grand Rapids: Baker Academic, 2009.

———. *You Are What You Love: The Spiritual Power of Habit.* Grand Rapids: Brazos Press, 2016.

Smith, John E. "Religious Affections and the 'Sense of the Heart.'" In *The Princeton Companion to Jonathan Edwards*, edited by Sang Hyun Lee, 103–14. Princeton: Princeton University Press, 2005.

Soelle, Dorothee. *To Work and to Love: A Theology of Creation.* Philadelphia: Fortress Press, 1984.

Spiegel, James S. "Wisdom." In *Being Good: Christian Virtues for Everyday Life*, edited by Michael W. Austin and R. Douglas Geivett, 53–71. Grand Rapids: Eerdmans, 2012.

Stein, Stephen J. "Providence and the Apocalypse in the Early Writings of Jonathan Edwards." *Early American Literature* 13 (1978): 250–67.

Stephens, W.P. *The Holy Spirit in the Theology of Martin Bucer.* Cambridge: Cambridge University Press, 1970.

Strobel, Kyle C. "Jonathan Edwards's Reformed Doctrine of *Theosis*." *Harvard Theological Review* 109, no. 3 (2016): 371–99.

———. *Jonathan Edwards's Theology: A Reinterpretation*. London: Bloomsbury T&T Clark, 2014.

Stroup, George W. "Reformed Identity in an Ecumenical World." In *Reformed Theology: Identity and Ecumenicity*, edited by Wallace M. Alston Jr. and Michael Welker, 257–70. Grand Rapids: Eerdmans, 2003.

Sweeting, George. *How to Discover the Will of God*. Chicago: Moody Press, 1975.

Swindoll, Charles R. *God's Will: Biblical Direction for Living*. Portland: Multnomah Press, 1981.

Tan, Seng-Kong. *Fullness Received and Returned: Trinity and Participation in Jonathan Edwards*. Minneapolis: Fortress Press, 2014.

Taylor, Charles. *Sources of the Self: The Making of the Modern Identity*. 10th ed. Cambridge: Harvard University Press, 2001.

Thielicke, Helmuth. *Theologische Ethik II. Band: Entfaltung. 1. Teil: Mensch und Welt*. 4. unveränderte Auflage. Tübingen: Mohr Siebeck, 1973.

———. *Theologische Ethik, III. Band: Entfaltung, 3. Teil: Ethik der Gesellschaft, des Rechtes, der Sexualität und der Kunst*. 2. verbesserte Auflage. Tübingen: Mohr Siebeck, 1968.

Thomas, Keith. *Religion and the Decline of Magic: Studies in Popular Beliefs in Sixteenth and Seventeenth Century England*. London: Weidenfeld and Nicolson, 1971.

Tidball, Derek. *Who Are the Evangelicals? Tracing the Roots of the Modern Movements*. London: Marshall Pickering, 1994.

Tillich, Paul. *Systematic Theology, Vol. I*. Chicago: University of Chicago Press, 1951.

Tolstoy, Leo. *On Life and Essays on Religion*. Translated by Aylmer Maude. The World's Classics. London: Oxford University Press, 1934.

Tongeren, Paul van. *Leven is een kunst: Over morele ervaring, deugdethiek en levenskunst*. 5th ed. Zoetermeer: Klement Pelckmans, 2013.

Torrey, R.A. *How to Succeed in the Christian Life*. New York: Fleming H. Revell, 1906.

Treier, Daniel J. *Virtue and the Voice of God: Toward Theology as Wisdom*. Grand Rapids: Eerdmans, 2006.

Troeltsch, Ernst. *The Social Teachings of the Christian Churches*. New York: Harper & Row, 1956.

Tyrpak, Joseph K. "Brainerd, David (1718-1747)." In *The Jonathan Edwards Encyclopedia*, edited by Harry S. Stout, Kenneth P. Minkema, and Adriaan C. Neele, 75. Grand Rapids: Eerdmans, 2017.

Vanhoozer, Kevin J. *Faith Speaking Understanding: Performing the Drama of Doctrine*. Louisville: Westminster John Knox Press, 2014.

———. "In Bright Shadow: C.S. Lewis on the Imagination for Theology and Discipleship." In *The Romantic Rationalist: God, Life, and Imagination in the Work of C.S. Lewis*, edited by John Piper and David Mathis, 81–104. Wheaton: Crossway, 2014.

———. *Pictures at a Theological Exhibition: Scenes of the Church's Worship, Witness and Wisdom*. London: Inter-Varsity Press, 2016.

———. *The Drama of Doctrine: A Canonical Linguistic Approach to Christian Doctrine*. Louisville: Westminster John Knox Press, 2005.

Veen, Mirjam G.K. van. "'In excelso honoris gradu': Johannes Calvin und Jacques de Falais." *Zwingliana*, no. 32 (2005): 5–22.

———. "'Supporters of the Devil': Calvin's Image of the Libertines." *Calvin Theological Journal* 40 (2005): 21–32.

Veen, Wilken. "'Verantwoordelijkheid' als omslagpunt in Bonhoeffers ethiek: Het verschil tussen de eerste en tweede versie van 'Die Geschichte und das Gute.'" In *Schuld en vrijheid: Opstellen aangeboden aan prof.dr. G.C. den Hertog*, 284–93. Zoetermeer: Boekencentrum, 2017.

Vlastuin, Wim van. "Calvin, Weber, and the Soul of Europe: Weber's Thesis Tested and Reapplied." In *Protestant Traditions and the Soul of Europe*, edited by Gijsbert Van den Brink and G.C. Den Hertog, 203–15. Leipzig: Evangelische Verlagsanstalt, 2017.

Volf, Miroslav. *Work in the Spirit: Toward a Theology of Work*. Eugene: Wipf and Stock, 2001.

Vollmer, Matthias. *Fortuna Diagrammatica: Der Rad der Fortuna als bildhafte Verschlüsselung der Schrift* De consolatione Philosophiae *des Boethius*. Apeliotes: Studien zur Kulturgeschichte und Theologie 3. Bern: Peter Lang, 2009.

Vroom, Hendrik M. "On Being 'Reformed.'" In *Reformed and Ecumenical: On Being Reformed in Ecumenical Encounters*, edited by Christine Lineman-Perrin, Hendrik M. Vroom, and Michael Weinrich. Amsterdam: Rodopi, 2000.

Wainwright, William J. "Jonathan Edwards and the Sense of the Heart." *Faith and Philosophy* 7 (1990): 43–62.

Walsham, Alexandra. *Providence in Early Modern England*. Oxford: Oxford University Press, 1999.

Warfield, B.B. *Calvin and Calvinism*. The Works of Benjamin B. Warfield 5. New York: Oxford University Press, 1927.

———. *The Person and Work of the Holy Spirit*. Vestavia Hills: Solid Ground Christian Books, 2010.

Wassenaar, Michael R. "Four Types of Calling: The Ethics of Vocation in Kierkegaard, Brunner, Scheler and Barth." PhD diss., Yale University, 2009.

Water, Mark. *Knowing God's Will Made Easier*. Peabody: Hendrickson, 1998.

Weatherhead, Leslie D. *The Will of God*. Nashville: Abingdon Press, 1944.

Weiss, Christian G. *The Perfect Will of God*. Lincoln: Good News Broadcasting Association, 1950.

Wells, Samuel. *God's Companions: Reimagining Christian Ethics*. Malden: Wiley-Blackwell, 2006.

———. *Improvisation: The Drama of Christian Ethics*. Grand Rapids: Brazos Press, 2004.

Wendel, François. *Calvin: The Origins and Development of His Religious Thought*. Translated by Philip Mairet. New York: Harper & Row, 1963.

Westra, Helen. *The Minister's Task and Calling in the Sermons of Jonathan Edwards*. Lewiston: Edwin Mellen, 1986.

Whitefield, George. *George Whitefield's Journals*. Edinburgh: Banner of Truth, 1960.

Wight, Fred H. *The Secret of Divine Guidance*. Los Angeles: Cowman, 1960.

Wilckens, Ulrich. *Der Brief and die Römer: 3. Teilband, Röm 12-16*. 3d ed. Zürich / Neukirchen: Benziger Verlag / Neukirchener Verlag, 2003.

Willard, Dallas. *The Divine Conspiracy: Rediscovering Our Hidden Life in God*. San Francisco: Harper & Row, 1998.

———. *The Spirit of the Disciplines: Understanding How God Changes Lives*. San Francisco: Harper & Row, 1988.

Williams, Rowan. "Word and Spirit." In *The Holy Spirit: Classic and Contemporary Readings*, edited by Eugene F. Rogers, Jr., 53–67. Malden: Wiley-Blackwell, 2009.

Willis, David, and Michael Welker. *Toward the Future of Reformed Theology: Tasks, Topics, Traditions*. Grand Rapids: Eerdmans, 1999.

Wilson, Stephen A. *Virtue Reformed: Rereading Jonathan Edwards's Ethics*. Leiden: Brill, 2005.

Wingren, Gustaf. *Luther on Vocation*. Translated by Carl C. Rasmussen. Eugene: Wipf & Stock, 2004.

———. *Luthers Lehre vom Beruf*. Translated by Egon Franz. München: Chr. Kaiser Verlag, 1952.

Winship, Michael P. *Seers of God: Puritan Providentialism in the Restoration and Early Enlightenment*. Baltimore: Johns Hopkins University Press, 2000.

Wisse, Maarten. *Zo zou je kunnen geloven*. Franeker: Van Wijnen, 2013.

Wolff, Pierre. *Discernment: The Art of Choosing Well. Based on Ignatian Spirituality*. Liguori: Liguori Publications, 2003.
Wolterstorff, Nicholas. *Until Justice and Peace Embrace*. Grand Rapids: Eerdmans, 1983.
Woodman, Dan. "The Mysterious Case of the Pervasive Choice Biography: Ulrich Beck, Structure/Agency, and the Middling State of Theory in the Sociology of Youth." *Journal of Youth Studies* 12, no. 3 (2009): 243–56.
Wright, Henry B. *The Will of God and a Man's Life Work*. New York: Association Press, 1909.
Wright, N. T. *After You Believe: Why Christian Character Matters*. New York: HarperOne, 2010.
———. "How Can the Bible Be Authoritative?" *Vox Evangelica* 21 (1991): 7–32.
———. *Scripture and the Authority of God*. Rev. and exp. edition. London: SPCK, 2013.
———. *The New Testament and the People of God*. 4th ed. London: SPCK, 1997.
Wuthnow, Robert. *After Heaven: Spirituality in America since the 1950s*. Berkeley: University of California Press, 1998.
Yeo, Ray S. "Christian Character Formation and the Infusion of Grace." In *Character: New Directions from Philosophy, Psychology, and Theology*, edited by Christian B. Miller, R. Michael Furr, Angela Knobel, and William Fleeson, 538–54. Oxford: Oxford University Press, 2015.
Yoder, John H. *The Priestly Kingdom: Social Ethics as Gospel*. Notre Dame: University of Notre Dame Press, 1984.
Zachman, Randall C. *Image and Word in the Theology of John Calvin*. Notre Dame: University of Notre Dame Press, 2007.
Zagzebski, Linda Trinkaus. *Virtues of the Mind: An Inquiry into the Nature of Virtue and the Ethical Foundations of Knowledge*. New York: Cambridge University Press, 1996.
Zimmerling, Peter. *Die Losungen: Eine Erfolgsgeschichte durch die Jahrhunderte*. Göttingen: Vandenhoeck & Ruprecht, 2014.
Zwingli, Ulrich. *On Providence and Other Essays*. Edited by William J. Hinke. Eugene: Wipf & Stock, 1999.

Name Index

Aalders, W.J.	153-55
Adams, Jay E.	38, 88-89, 95, 123-24
Allen, Charles W.	274-76, 285, 324
Allen, R. Michael	29
Almen, Louis T.	260
Alschuler, A.S.	26
Alston, William P.	13, 331-32
Alten, Herman H. van	167, 171
Althaus, Paul	17, 150
Anderson, Wallace E.	208
Aquinas	236, 273-79, 319, 325
Aristotle	231, 234, 236, 273-77, 280
Ashcraft, Morris	38, 52-54, 67-68
Augustine	50, 53, 60, 71, 233
Baan, Ariaan	334
Badcock, Gary D.	258, 260-61, 268-69
Baker, Donald	40
Balthasar, Hans Urs von	280
Barclay, Oliver R.	44
Barshinger, David P.	202
Bartel, Michelle J.	287, 292
Barth, Karl	15, 17, 20-22, 262-267, 270-71, 297, 317
Bartolomew, Craig G.	281
Bass, Dorothy C.	279, 333
Battles, Ford L.	137
Bavinck, Herman	14
Baxter, J. Sidlow	44
Bayer, Oswald	150
Bayly, Joseph	37-38, 44
Bebbington, David	32
Beck, Ulrich	10, 47
Benner, David G.	109-10, 116, 122
Benson, Louis F.	6
Berg, Michiel A. van den	190
Berkhof, Hendrikus	16-17, 20
Berkhof, Louis	14

Berkouwer, Gerrit C.	15-16, 20
Bernanos, Georges	328
Bethge, Eberhard	288-89
Beza, Theodore	181-83
Bjerkelund, C.J.	303
Blackaby, Henry T.	13, 39, 68-69, 93, 95, 115, 121
Blackaby, Richard	39, 68-69, 115, 121
Bloom, Matt	322
Bockmühl, Klaus	5, 13, 70-72, 95, 122, 127, 149, 153, 156-163, 181, 190, 327
Bohatec, Josef	139
Bonar, Horatius	6-7
Bondi, Richard	308-314
Bonhoeffer, Dietrich	267, 287-301, 312, 317
Bouwsma, William J.	156, 180, 183, 184, 189
Boyles, Helen	22
Brainerd, David	210-11, 237, 239-40
Breen, Mike	323
Brink, Gijsbert van den	14, 28, 30, 31, 140, 152, 198, 254, 268, 317, 331
Brinkman, Martien E.	32
Brooks, A.E.C.	42
Brunner, Emil	14, 20-21
Buechner, Frederick	269
Bullinger, Henry	184-85
Burr, Aaron	242
Busch, Eberhard	27-28
Cahalan, Kathleen A.	8, 266, 322
Caldwell III, Robert W.	223, 224, 227-229
Calvin, John	13-14, 34-36, 53, 57, 81, 86, 131-195, 203-4, 207-8, 211, 217, 228, 244-45, 247-55, 257-59, 271, 302-3, 314, 324-25, 334, 337, 339, 341-42
Campbell, Archibald	22-23
Campbell Morgan, G.	44
Caplan, Mariana	26
Carter, Mack King	102-4, 116
Castelli, Elisabeth A.	323
Chauncy, Israel	241
Claghorn, George S.	239-40
Cleave, Derek	62-64, 68, 121

Cochran, Elizabeth A.	205, 227, 231-36
Cochrane, Arthur C.	27
Coder, S. Maxwell	44
Coleman, Charles G.	44
Cottret, Bernard	183-84, 193
Crisp, Oliver D.	136-37, 198, 204, 215
Cunningham, David S.	253, 308, 319, 321, 333
Dahill, Lisa E.	287-88, 290, 292, 294
Danaher Jr., William J.	231-37
Deere, Jack	39
Delattre, Roland	225
Denis, Philippe	190
Dewey, John	314
DeYoung, Kevin	113-16, 123, 124, 126
Dobson, James C.	40
Dodd, C.H.	306
Donagan, Barbara	24
Douma, Jochem	24-25
Dubay, Thomas	39
Dunn, James D.G.	303-6
Edwards, Jonathan	33-36, 60, 138, 195, 197-245, 247-54, 257, 271, 295, 302-3, 311-12, 316, 324-25, 330, 332, 337, 339, 341-42
Edwards, Sarah	210
Elert, Werner	150
Elliff, Jim	38, 93-95
Elliot, Elisabeth	44, 126
Elliott, Mark W.	135
Ellul, Jacques	260-61, 268
Elster, Jean Alicia	102
Elwood, Douglas J.	225
English, John J.	39
Erdt, Terrence	222
Erickson, Millard J.	19-20
Erskine, John	197, 240, 242
Falais, Jacques de	182, 190-92
Falais, Yolande de	182, 190-92
Farel, Guillaume	183-89
Ferguson, Sinclair B.	55-57, 68

Fitzmyer, Joseph A.	304
Fleeson, William	308-9
Ford, David F.	274, 277-80, 311, 313, 335
Forrester, W.R.	260, 263
Forstman, H. Jackson	134, 144
Fraassen, Bas C. van	30
Frame, John M.	18, 20
Friesen, Garry	12-13, 20, 39, 43, 45, 47, 50-52, 62, 66-68, 70, 81, 83, 84, 102, 115, 117-19, 123, 124, 127, 164, 271-73, 285, 327
Froehlich, Karlfried	151
Gadamer, Hans-Georg	284-85
Geisler, Norman	14
Gerrish, Brian A.	29-30
Gerstner, John H.	199, 203
Glaw, Annette M.	162
Goheen, Michael W.	281
Gordon, Bruce F.	182, 189, 193
Grandia, J.J.	39
Grudem, Wayne	19-20
Guinness, Os	44
Gustafson, James M.	277, 287, 295-98, 300-1
Haenchen, E.	329
Hagen, Kenneth	151
Hagin, Kenneth E.	44
Hahnenberg, Edward P.	8, 10, 14, 21-22, 251-52, 258-69, 318
Hardy, Lee	150-54, 258, 261
Harmon-Jones, Eddie	25
Harmon-Jones, Cindy	25
Hartelius, Glenn	26
Hastings, A.	26
Hastings, W. Ross	226, 232
Hauerwas, Stanley	261, 272, 275, 307-8, 319, 328, 333-34
Hayford, Jack W.	38, 86-88, 95, 121
Hays, Richard B.	315
Heimert, Alan	225
Helm, Paul	19-20, 135, 136, 138, 141, 143, 145, 205
Henry, Caleb	222
Heppe, Heinrich	149, 204
Herdt, Jennifer A.	321

Herms, Eilert	150
Hesselink, I. John	27-28, 32, 160-61, 163-67, 179, 181
Hewitson, James	199-200
Heyd, Michael	22
Hill, Peter C.	109
Hof, Eleonora D.	264, 266-67, 269
Hofheinz, Marco	27
Holbrook, Clyde A.	204
Holl, Karl	150
Homiak, Marcia	309
Hopkins, Samuel	243
Horst, P.W. van der	23
Horton, Michael	18, 20, 134, 142, 318, 329-30
Hosier, Helen K.	49-50, 67-68, 126
Howard, J. Grant	44
Huffman, Douglas S.	38-39, 42, 115-16
Hursthouse, Rosalind	276
Ignatius of Loyola	22, 86, 99, 110
Jeffress, Robert J.	43, 100-2, 116
Jensen, Phillip D.	38, 76-78, 95, 114
Jewett, Robert	303-7
Johnson, Ben Campbell	40, 118
Johnson, Kevin	96-97, 116
Johnstone, Keith	334-35
Kaiser, Joshua A.	287-92, 298
Kampen, Pieter van	39
Kaplan, Mark A.	26
Keener, Craig S.	303-6
Kelly, Douglas F.	163-67, 181
Kim, Sung-Sup	134-35, 137, 139
Kincaid, Ron	83-84
King, Claude V.	68-69, 121
Kirby, W.J. Torrance	135
Kise, Jane A.G.	126
Klimo, J.	26
Klooster, Fred H.	28
Knijff, Cornelis van der	117
Knobel, Angela	321
Knox, Ronald A.	22

Kooi, Cornelis van der	14, 140, 254, 268, 317
Kovach, Stephen D.	12-14, 39, 118, 327, 337
Kronenburg, Hans	289
Krusche, Werner	159-61, 163, 166-67, 181
Kuzmič, Rhys	266
Laborie, Lionel	22
LaHaye, Tim F.	65-68, 120-21, 126
Lake, Kyle	107-9, 116, 126
Lang, G.H.	44
Lange, Frits de	10
Larsen, Timothy	32-33
Lee, Sang Hyun	205, 236
Leith, John H.	27-28
Lesser, M.X.	198, 212
Lieburg, Fred van	23, 30
Liester, M.B.	26
Linde, Simon van der	160
Longenecker, Richard N.	303-5
Luther, Martin	20, 53, 63, 150-51, 153-54, 253, 258-68
MacArthur, John	44
MacIntyre, Alisdair	251, 264, 267, 338
Mahlmann, Theodor	30
Markus, Wim	39
Marsden, George M.	202, 238-43
Marshall, Paul A.	154-55, 259, 261, 265
Masters, Peter	38, 81-83, 95, 121, 126
Maston, T.B.	44
Mather, Cotton	242
Maxson, J. Robin	39, 50, 81, 118, 123, 272-73
McClymond, Michael J.	197-98, 201-2, 205-6, 208, 223, 225
McCormack, Bruce L.	29-30
McDermott, Gerald R.	197-98, 201-2, 205-6, 208, 223, 225
McDowell, Josh	96-97, 116
McLarry, Newman R.	44
Meadors, Gary T.	106-7, 116
Meyer, Frederick B.	43-44, 100
Miller, Christian B.	307-9, 321, 331
Miller-McLemore, Bonnie J.	8, 266, 322
Milner Jr., Benjamin C.	160, 163-64, 166-67, 178-79
Minkema, Kenneth P.	197, 208, 213, 223

Mitchell, Louis	225
Moehn, Wilhelmus H.Th.	167
Moltmann, Jürgen	20, 262-63
Moo, Douglas J.	303-6
Morimoto, Anri	228
Morris, Danny E.	72-73
Muers, Rachel	287
Mühlan, Eberhard	39
Müller, George F.	42-44, 49, 94-95, 100
Muller, Richard A.	133, 141, 149
Munzinger, André	24
Murray, Andrew	43-44
Myers, Ruth	40, 126
Myers, Warren	40, 126
Nelson, Marion H.	44
Newman, Henry	6
Niebuhr, H. Richard	124-25, 229
Niebuhr, Reinhold	283, 288, 317
Noll, Mark A.	32
Nystrom, Carolyn	44-45, 111-13, 116, 123, 322, 327
Oberman, Heiko A.	134, 137, 154, 172
O'Donovan, Oliver	7-8, 24, 252, 258, 266, 287, 295, 298-301, 328, 330
Ogilvie, Lloyd John	43, 57-58, 68
Olsen, Charles M.	82
Ong, Meng-Chai	133, 137
Ortlund, Dane C.	225
Osterhaven, M. Eugene	28
Packer, James I.	38, 44-45, 11-13, 116, 123, 273, 322, 327
Palmer, Parker J.	323
Pannenberg, Wolfhart	14
Parker, Stephen E.	12-13, 39
Partee, Charles	134-35
Paul, Herman	323, 333
Payne, Tony	38, 76-78, 95, 114
Perkins, Pheme	304
Perkins, William	12
Pettigrove, Glen	276
Petty, James C.	39, 45-46, 89-91, 95, 118, 123-24

Pieper, Josef	275, 277-79, 325-26
Pierson, Arthur T.	42
Pipa Jr., Joseph A.	141
Pinches, Charles R.	272, 275, 319, 333
Plantinga Pauw, Amy	197, 202, 206
Potgieter, Pieter C.	142
Preece, Gordon R.	20-21, 155, 260-70, 316
Pritchard, Ray	78-79, 95
Quistorp, H.J.J.Th.	160
Rahner, Karl	17-18, 20, 22
Ramsey, Paul	202
Rardin, Mary A.	26
Rasnake, Eddie	99-100, 116
Redpath, Alan	44
Robinson, Haddon W.	38, 73-75, 95, 123
Ruether, Rosemary R.	262
Sanders, John E.	20
Sanders, J. Oswald	38, 75-76
Sartre, Jean-Paul	46
Schafer, Thomas A.	205, 210
Schirrmacher, Thomas	39
Schreiner, Susan E.	133-34, 140, 142, 144-45
Schuurman, Douglas J.	21, 250, 253, 258-69, 288
Schwartz, Barry	9, 46
Schweitzer, William M.	227
Selderhuis, Herman J.	133, 182
Shepson, Charles W.	38, 54-55, 68
Sittser, Gerald L.	97-99, 114, 116
Sine, Christine	40, 126
Sine, Tom	40, 126
Smith, Gordon T.	13, 85-86, 110, 115, 118-119, 122, 127, 327
Smith, James K.A.	311-13, 317, 320, 329, 333, 341
Smith, John E.	222
Smits, Johan	28-31
Soelle, Dorothee	262
Spiegel, James S.	274, 279
Sproul, Robert C.	58-60, 68
Stanley, Charles F.	64-65, 68, 121
Stein, Stephen J.	198, 202, 207

Stephens, W.P.	160
Stoddard, Solomon	251
Strobel, Kyle C.	227-29, 232
Stroup, George	27-30
Swavely, David	104-6, 116
Sweeting, George	44
Swindoll, Charles R.	91-93
Tan, Seng-Kong	227-32
Taylor, Charles	254
Tennent, Gilbert	239
Thielicke, Helmut	25
Thomas, Keith	23
Tidball, Derek	32
Tillet, Louis du	183-87
Tillich, Paul	12-15, 20
Tolstoy, Leo	262
Tongeren, Paul van	9
Torrey, R.A.	44
Tozer, A.W.	283
Treier, Daniel J.	278-80
Troeltsch, Ernst	155
Tyrpak, Joseph K.	210
Vanhoozer, Kevin J.	274, 278, 280-86, 300, 313-16, 328, 334, 340
Veen, Mirjam G.K. van	158, 190, 192
Veen, Wilken	293
Viret, Pierre	183, 185, 189
Vlastuin, Willem van	152
Volf, Miroslav	20, 260, 262-64
Vollmer, Matthias	199
Vroom, Hendrik M.	27, 31
Wainwright, William J.	222
Waltke, Bruce K.	13, 38, 80-81, 95, 124
Walsham, Alexandra	11, 23-24, 45
Warfield, B.B.	159, 329
Wassenaar, Michael R.	21
Water, Mark	40
Weatherhead, Leslie D.	103-4
Weiss, Christian G.	44
Welker, Michael	28

Wells, Samuel	271, 280-86, 314, 328, 334-35, 340
Wendel, François	137-39
Westra, Helen	212
Whitefield, George	33, 239
Wight, Fred H.	44
Wilckens, Ulrich	305
Willard, Dallas	13, 38, 44, 60-62, 68, 118, 122, 327
Williams, Rowan	330
Williams, William	6
Willimon, William H.	328, 337
Willis, David	28
Wilson, Stephen A.	204, 227, 232-37
Wingren, Gustaf	20, 151, 252, 259
Winship, Michael P.	208
Wisse, Maarten	38
Wolff, Pierre	39
Wolterstorff, Nicholas	5
Woodman, Dan	10
Wright, Henry B.	44
Wright, Nicholas T.	280-81, 284, 305-6, 308, 313, 320
Wuthnow, Robert	265
Yeo, Ray S.	330-32
Yoder, John H.	262
Zachman, Randall C.	139, 142, 144-45
Zagzebski, Linda T.	273-76
Zeindler, Matthias	27
Zimmerling, Peter	289
Zwingli, Ulrich	136, 143

CPSIA information can be obtained
at www.ICGtesting.com
Printed in the USA
BVHW040524030820
585257BV00008B/16